THE SIRIUS MYSTERY

ROBERT K. G. TEMPLE

The
SIRIUS MYSTERY

Illustrated with plates and diagrams

SIDGWICK & JACKSON
LONDON

I.S.B.N. 0.283.98136.9

Printed in Great Britain by
Billing & Sons Limited,
Guildford and London
for Sidgwick and Jackson Limited

TO MY MOTHER

who has persevered

ACKNOWLEDGEMENTS

My first thanks must go to my wife, Olivia, who has been an excellent proof-reader and collater and who made the greatest number of helpful suggestions concerning the manuscript.

Two friends who read the book at an early stage and took extreme pains to be helpful, and devoted much of their time to writing out or explaining to me at length their lists of specific suggestions, are Adrian Berry of the London *Telegraph*, and Michael Scott of Tangier. The latter gave meticulous attention to details which few people would trouble to do with another's work.

This book would never have been written without the material concerning the Dogon having been brought to my attention by Arthur M. Young of Philadelphia. He has helped and encouraged my efforts to get to the bottom of the mystery for years, and supplied me with invaluable materials, including the typescript of an English translation of *Le Renard pâle* by the anthropologists Griaule and Dieterlen, which enabled me to bring my survey up to date.

Without the stimulus and early encouragement of Arthur C. Clarke of Ceylon, this book might not have found the motive force to carry it through many dreary years of research.

My agent, Miss Anne McDermid, has been a model critic and adviser at all stages. Her enthusiasm and energy are matched only by her penetrating intuition and her skill at negotiation.

Others who have read all or part of this book and who made helpful suggestions of some kind are Professor W. H. McCrea of the Department of Astronomy, University of Sussex, John Moore of Robinson & Watkins, Brendan O'Regan of the Stanford Research Institute, Edward Bakewell of St Louis, and Anthony Michaelis of the Weizmann Institute Foundation.

I am indebted to Adrian and Marina Berry for bringing me into touch with A. Costa, and to A. Costa for generously supplying his splendid photographs of the Dogon, some of which appear in this book, and also for his introduction to Mme Germaine Dieterlen. I am indebted to Mme Dieterlen for giving her permission and the permission of the Société des Africainistes of Paris (of which she is Secretary-General) to publish in English the entire article 'Un Système Soudanais de Sirius', which Mme Dieterlen wrote in collaboration with the late Marcel Griaule.

Among those whom I have consulted on specific points in my research and who have been extremely helpful are Geoffrey Watkins, Brigadier R. G. S. Bidwell, O.B.E., the Hon. Robin Baring, James Serpell, Seton Gordon, and Herbert Brown. I am also indebted for help or encouragement of varying kinds to Fred Clarke, Professor Cyrus Gordon, Robert Graves, Kathleen Raine, William Gunston, Professor D. M. Lang, Professor Charles Burney, Professor O. R. Gurney, Dr Irving Lindenblad, Dr Paul Murdin, Hilton Ambler, Gillian Hughes, Carol MacArthur, Roy Markham, Richard Robinson, Dr Michael Barraclough, and Angela Earll.

In production of this book my British editor, Mrs Jan Widdows, and my American editor, Thomas Dunne, have been cooperative, helpful, and sympathetic. The cartographer Daniel Kitts has cheerfully prepared maps and diagrams to requirements which were often exasperating. Miss Mary Walsh showed ingenuity in picture research. Stephen du Sautoy has also been helpful and shown a great deal of imagination in connection with production of the British dust-jacket design, allowing the author a considerable say in a matter which is often barred to him.

I would like to acknowledge indirect debts to the African priests Manda, Innekouzou, Yébéné, and Ongnonlou, without whom the subject for this book could not honestly be said to exist, since it probably could never have been formulated. Two early pioneers deserve especial mention: the late Sir Norman Lockyer, who found ways to consider together the previously separate fields of astronomy and archaeology, and the late Thomas Taylor of London, who devoted his life to the translation and exposition of texts which have survived the centuries of malignity, abuse, book burnings, and slaughter which for two millennia have been the fate of those who adhered to 'the Great Tradition' – nor did Taylor himself escape the consequences of his position in pain and suffering. Thanks are also due to the philosopher Proclus for making public certain specific allusions to secret traditions which he might have concealed.

R. K. G. T.

CONTENTS

		page
Acknowledgements		vii
Author's Note		xi

TO THE READER

What is the Mystery? — I

PART ONE

The Sirius Question is posed

1	The Knowledge of the Dogon	11
	A Sudanese Sirius System by M. Griaule and G. Dieterlen	35

PART TWO

The Sirius Question is rephrased

2	A Fairytale	55
3	The Sacred Fifty	82
4	The Hounds of Hell	101
5	The Oracle Centres	121
6	Origins of the Dogon	153
7	The Rising of 'Serpent's Tooth'	175

PART THREE

Beyond the Mystery

8	A Fable	203

APPENDICES

I	The Moons of the Planets, the Planets around Stars, and Revolutions and Rotations of Bodies in Space – Described by the Neoplatonic Philosopher Proclus	228
II	The Surviving Fragments of Berossus, in English Translation	248
III	Why Sixty Years?	258
IV	The Meaning of the E at Delphi	265
V	Why the Hittites were at Hebron in Palestine	268
VI	The Dogon Stages of Initiation	273
	Bibliography	274
	Index	283

AUTHOR'S NOTE

Summaries follow each chapter in Part Two. The sheer amount of the material dealt with makes it advisable for the reader to put it into a smooth perspective by reading over these summaries which have been prepared so that the reader may refresh his memory if he wishes. The author can offer no apology for the complexity of the material, but he can present these slight aids for its comprehension.

Every effort has been made to trace the ownership of all illustrative material reproduced in this book. Should any error or omission in acknowledgement have been made the author offers his apologies and will make the necessary correction in future editions.

THE SIRIUS MYSTERY

What is the Mystery?

The question which this book poses is: Has Earth in the past been visited by intelligent beings from the region of the star Sirius?

When I began writing this book in earnest in 1967, the entire question was framed in terms of an African tribe named the Dogon, who live in Mali in the former French Sudan. The Dogon were in possession of information concerning the system of the star Sirius which was so incredible that I felt impelled to research the material. The results, in 1974, seven years later, are that I have been able to show that the information which the Dogon possess is really more than five thousand years old and was possessed by the ancient Egyptians in the pre-dynastic times before 3200 B.C., from which people I show that the Dogon are partially descended culturally, and probably physically as well.

What I have done, therefore, is to push back by over five thousand years the terms of reference of the original question, so that it now becomes more tantalizing than ever. But now that I have done that, it becomes less easy to answer. The Dogon preserve a tradition of what seems to have been an extra-terrestrial contact. It is more satisfactory not to have to presume the preposterous notion that intelligent beings from outer space landed in Africa, imparted specific information to a West African tribe, then returned to space and left the rest of the world alone. Such a theory never really struck me as possible. But in the beginning it did have to serve as a working hypothesis. After all, I had no idea that the Dogon could have preserved ancient Egyptian religious mysteries in their culture. I also had no idea that the ancient Egyptians knew anything about Sirius. I was in that state of ignorance so common among people who know nothing more about ancient Egypt than that the Egyptians built pyramids, left mummies, had a Pharaoh named Tutankhamen, and wrote in hieroglyphs. My own academic background concerned oriental studies, but I never touched on Egypt except regarding the Islamic period after A.D. 600. I knew almost nothing whatsoever about ancient Egypt. If I had, perhaps I might have saved myself a lot of time.

It took many, many months for two or three small clues to work themselves around in my head long enough to force me to study ancient Egypt and a whole range of subjects which I had never previously tackled. I doubt if, even then, I could have been persuaded to spend considerable sums of money such as the necessary fifty pounds for the essential and out-of-print Wallis Budge *Egyptian Hieroglyphic Dictionary*, which consists of 1,356 pages and cannot even be lifted off the table by a ten-year-old child. But as fate would have it, I was actually given one of these huge dictionaries, along with many other essential books on the subjects with which I needed to become concerned. This helped overcome my natural disinclination to erect a camp bed in some scholarly library and move in for a couple of years. I must therefore note my debt to my dear friend the late Miss Mary Brenda Hotham-Francklyn for giving me in the ninety-fourth year of her life what amounted to a sizeable library of books, which were so interesting that I found it impossible to neglect them, and the result is now before us.

This entire matter of the Sirius mystery first came to my attention around 1965. I was working on some philosophical and scientific problems with Arthur M. Young of Philadelphia, the inventor of the Bell helicopter and more recently (1972) co-editor of and contributor to the book *Consciousness and Reality*. Arthur single-handedly taught me more science concurrently with my official university studies from 1961–7 than an entire university faculty might have done. For while I was ploughing my way through the Sanskrit language and other onerous subjects at the official university level, I imbibed a considerable scientific education from Arthur in company with a few friends from the university, with whom I participated for years in a series of extremely stimulating seminars and research projects supervised by Arthur Young and occasionally linked to a philanthropic foundation which he had established, entitled the Foundation for the Study of Consciousness.

Arthur Young had a particular passion for reading about mythologies from all over the world, including those of obscure tribes. One day he showed me a book entitled *African Worlds*, which contained several chapters, each dealing with a different tribe, with its views of life and its customs and mythology. There was a chapter about the Dogon translated into English from the French of Marcel Griaule and Germaine Dieterlen, the eminent anthropologists.[1]

Arthur pointed out to me a passage he had just read in this chapter, in which these anthropologists were describing the cosmological theories of the Dogon. I shall quote the paragraph which I read then, which first brought to my attention this whole extraordinary question, so that the reader will begin this subject just as I did, with this brief reference:

'The starting-point of creation is the star which revolves round Sirius and is actually named the "*Digitaria* star"; it is regarded by the Dogon as the smallest and heaviest of all the stars; it contains the germs of all things. Its movement on its own axis and around Sirius upholds all creation in space. We shall see that its orbit determines the calendar.'

That was all. There was no mention by the anthropologists of the actual existence of such a star which revolves around Sirius. Now Arthur Young and I both knew of the existence of the white dwarf star Sirius B which actually does orbit around Sirius. We knew that it was 'the smallest and heaviest' type of star then known. (Neutron stars and 'black holes' were not much discussed and pulsars had not yet even been discovered.) We both naturally agreed that this was a most curious allusion from a supposedly primitive tribe. How could it be explained? I had to let the matter drop, due to other activities and concerns at that time.

Approximately two years later in London, I suddenly was struck by the irresistible urge to investigate this question. I was prompted to do so by reading the rousing futuristic essays of Arthur C. Clarke, whom I had come to know by then. By this time I could not even remember the name of the African tribe, so I wrote to Arthur Young for it. He replied and kindly sent me a photostat of the entire chapter I had seen in *African Worlds*. So, armed with the knowledge that it was a tribe called the Dogon that I was after, I bravely made my way to the Royal Anthropological Institute to see what I could find out about this peculiar tribe.

The librarian went over the catalogue listings with me and I ran into a problem: everything was in French, and I did not know French. However, I persevered and found an article listed which included the word 'Sirius' in its title. That looked promising (for nothing else did). I asked for a photostat. When I picked this up a week or two later (in early November 1967) I was unable to make any sense of it, of course. So I eventually found someone to translate it for me in return for a fee. Finally I was presented with the material in English – and it was quite as rewarding as I could have wished.[2] For this article dealt exclusively with the most secret of all the traditions of the Dogon which, after years of living with them, the anthropologists Griaule and Dieterlen had managed to extract from four of their head priests,[3] after a special priestly conference among the tribe and a 'policy decision' to make their secrets known to Marcel Griaule, the first outsider in their history to inspire their confidence.

The most secret traditions of the Dogon all concern the star which the Dogon call after the tiniest seed known to them, the botanical name for which is *Digitaria*, and which is thus used in the article as the name of the star instead of the actual Dogon name, *po*. However, even in this article which deals exclusively with this subject, Griaule and Dieterlen only mention the actual existence of a star which really exists and does what the Dogon say Digitaria does, in a passing footnote and in this brief remark: 'The question has not been solved, nor even asked, of how men with no instruments at their disposal could know the movements and certain characteristics of stars which are scarcely visible.' But even in saying this, the anthropologists were indicating their own lack of astronomical expertise, for the star, Sirius B which revolves around Sirius, is by no means 'scarcely visible'. It is *totally invisible* and was only discovered in the last century with the use of the telescope. As Arthur Clarke put it to me in a letter of 17 July 1968, after he had suggested he would check the facts: 'By the way, Sirius B is about magnitude 8 – quite invisible even if Sirius A didn't completely obliterate it.' Only in 1970 was a photograph of Sirius B successfully taken by Irving Lindenblad of the U.S. Naval Observatory; this photograph is reproduced in Plate 1.

In the article which I had obtained from the Royal Anthropological Institute, Griaule and Dieterlen recorded that the Dogon said the star Digitaria revolved around Sirius every fifty years. It didn't take me long to research Sirius B and discover that its orbital period around Sirius was indeed fifty years. I now knew that I was really on to something. And from that moment I have been immersed in trying to get to the bottom of the mystery.

Arthur C. Clarke was extremely helpful during the next few months. He wrote from Ceylon and was fairly often in London, so he and I also discussed at great length many of the mysterious facts from around the world which have since been given such public prominence by the Swiss-German author Erich von Däniken in his best-selling book *Chariots of the Gods* and its sequels. At first I found myself preparing a book on all these exciting mysteries. (No one had at that time heard of von Däniken.) Arthur Clarke introduced me to one interesting professor after another – each with a pet mystery all his own. Derek Price, Avalon Professor of the History of Science at Yale University, had discovered the true nature of the now famous mechanical computer of approximately 100 B.C. found in the Anti-Kythera shipwreck at the turn of the century and unappreciated until it was dropped on the floor in Athens, cracked open and they saw what it was. He also had found traces of Babylonian mathematics in New Guinea and talked a lot about 'the Raffles shipwreck'.

Then there was Dr Alan McKay, a crystallographer of Birkbeck College at the University of London, who was interested in the Phaistos Disc of Crete, in a mysterious metal alloy found in a Chinese tomb, and in the wilder stretches of the Oxus River. I found that, with people like this around every corner, I was rapidly becoming distracted from my true quest by so many glittering riddles.

I therefore abandoned all those mysteries and determined to concentrate in depth on cracking the one really hard and concrete puzzle that I had been initially confronted with: how did the Dogon know such extraordinary things and did it mean that the Earth had been visited by extraterrestrials?

The trouble with trying to undertake a serious investigation about the possibility of extraterrestrial contact with Earth, is that a lot of sensible people will ⁚⁚ put off by the very idea. Then again, a lot of the people who will enthu iastically receive my researches with open arms are the sort of people one least wants to be classed with. I have therefore undertaken all the work on this subject with a certain degree of reluctance, and if anyone pressed me during several years to say what I was doing and they extricated from me the confession that I was working on a book, I did not say what it was about, but merely mumbled it was 'about the ancient Egyptians' or, before that stage, 'about the mythology of some tribe in Africa – not very interesting, really'. This book will inevitably, I suppose, put me in that most unenviable category of 'those people who write about little green men from outer space'. However, this is meant to be a serious inquiry. I am tempted to apologize for the subject, but that would be pointless.

It is important that this strange material be placed before the public at large. Since learning was freed from the tyranny of the few and opened to the general public, through first the invention of printing and now the modern communications media and the mass proliferation of books and periodicals and more recently the 'paperback revolution', any idea can go forth and plant the necessary seeds in intellects around the world without the mediation of any panel of approval or the filtering of a climate of opinion based on the currently accepted views of a set of obsolescent individual minds.

How difficult it is to keep in mind that this was not always the case. No wonder, then, that before such things were possible, there were secret traditions of priests which were handed down orally for centuries in unbroken chains and carefully guarded lest some censorship overtake them and the message be lost. In the modern age, for the first time secret traditions can be revealed without the danger that they will be extinguished in the process. Can it be that the Dogon came to realize something of this when, through some powerful instinct and after mutual consultations among the highest priests, they decided to take the unprecedented step of making public their highest mysteries? They knew they could trust the French anthropologists, and when Marcel Griaule died in 1956, approximately a quarter of a million tribesmen massed for his funeral in Mali, in tribute to a man whom they revered as a great sage – equivalent to one of their own high priests. Such reverence must indicate an extraordinary man in whom the Dogon could believe implicitly. There is no question but that we are indebted to Marcel Griaule's personal qualities for laying open to us the sacred Dogon traditions. I have now been able to trace these back to ancient Egypt, and they seem to reveal a contact in the distant past between our planet Earth and an advanced race of intelligent beings from another planetary system several light years away in space. If there is another answer to the Sirius mystery it may be even more surprising rather than less so. It certainly will not be trivial.

It should not surprise us that there must be other civilizations in our galaxy and throughout the entire universe. Even if the explanation of the Sirius mystery is found to be something entirely different in the years to come (though I cannot imagine what), we should bear in mind that, as we are definitely not alone in the universe, the Sirius mystery will have served to help us speculate along proper and necessary lines, and opened our innately lazy minds that much further to the important question of extraterrestrial civilizations which must certainly exist.

At the moment, we are all like fish in a bowl, with only the occasional leap out of the water when our astronauts go aloft. The public is becoming bored with space exploration before it has even really begun properly. We even find that Congressmen need continual injections of 'space rescues' and 'satellite gaps' in their tired bloodstreams, like a heroin fix, in order to stimulate them in their horrible state of lethargy to vote funds for the space programmes which so many of them consider a bore and lacking in excitement and suspense.

The psychological impact of photographs of the Earth from space, a giant and beautiful orb resting on nothing, pearled with clouds and sparkling with sea, has begun to send resonances down the long and sleepy corridors of our largely drugged psyches. Mankind is imperceptibly struggling to the new and undeniable realization that we are all in this game together. We are all perched on a globe suspended in what appears to be emptiness, we are made up of atoms which are mostly themselves emptiness, and above all, we are the only really intelligent creatures directly known to us. In short, we are alone with each other, with all the fratricidal implications of such a tense situation.

But at the same time as we are all slowly realizing these things, the inevitable conclusion which follows upon all this is beginning to make some headway with us as well. It has begun to occur to more than a handful of exceptional people (exceptionally intelligent or exceptionally insane) that if we are sitting here on this planet fighting among ourselves for lack of any better distraction, then perhaps there are lots of planets all over the universe where intelligent beings are either sitting and stewing in their own juice as we are, or where those beings have broken out of the shell and established contact with other intelligent beings on other planets. And if this is really going on all over the universe, then perhaps it will not be all that long before we find ourselves linked up with our fellows elsewhere – creatures living beside another star out in that vast emptiness which spawns planets, suns, and minds.

For years I have thought that those organizations which spend millions of dollars on 'peace' and attempts to find out what is wrong with human nature that it should indulge in so perverse a thing as conflict, would be better advised to donate their entire treasuries to the space programmes, and to astronomical research. Instead of seminars for 'peace research' we should build more telescopes. The answer to the question: 'Is mankind perverse?' will be known when we can compare ourselves with other intelligent species and evaluate ourselves according to some scale other than one which we fabricate out of the air. At the moment we are shadow-boxing, chasing phantoms. . . . The answers lie out there somewhere with other stars and other races of beings. We can only compound our neuroses by becoming even more introspective and narcissistic. We must look outward. At the same time, of course, we must look back relentlessly into our own past. To go forward with no conception of where we have been makes no sense whatsoever. There is also the probability that we may discover mysteries about our own origins. For instance, one result of my research, which began harmlessly with an African tribe, has been to demonstrate the possibility that civilization as we know it was an importation from another star in the first place. The linked cultures of Egypt and Sumer in the Mediterranean area simply came out of nowhere. That is not to say that there were no people alive before that. We know there were lots of people, but we have found no traces of civilization. And people and civilization are vastly different things. Take for instance these words by the late Professor W. B. Emery from his book *Archaic Egypt*:

> At a period approximately 3400 years before Christ, a great change took place in Egypt, and the country passed rapidly from a state of advanced neolithic culture with a complex tribal character to two well-organized monarchies, one comprising the Delta area and the other the Nile valley proper. At the same time the art of writing appears, monumental architecture and the arts and crafts developed to an astonishing degree, and all the evidence points to the existence of a well-organized and even luxurious civilization. All this was achieved within a comparatively short period of time, for there appears to be little or no background to these fundamental developments in writing and architecture.

Now, whether or not one supposes that there was an invasion of advanced people into Egypt who brought their culture with them, the fact remains that when we get back to that period of history we are faced with so many imponderables that we can hardly say anything for certain. What we do know is that primitive people suddenly found themselves living in thriving and opulent civilizations and it all happened rather abruptly. In the light of the evidence connected with the Sirius question, as well as other evidence which has either been dealt with by other authors or remains to be tackled in the future, it must be entertained as a serious possibility that civilization on this planet owes something to a visit by advanced extraterrestrial beings. It is not necessary to postulate flying saucers, or even gods in space suits. My own feeling is that this matter has not been dealt with in a sophisticated enough manner so far. But rather than enter into mere speculation as to what extraterrestrials landed in, etc., let us move on to the evidence that at least indicates that they might have been here. In Part Three we shall consider some details and clues that the extraterrestrial visitors from Sirius, whom I postulate, may have been amphibious creatures with the need to live in a watery environment. But all this gets into the speculative areas which are such treacherous ground. It has always been my policy, as well as my temperamental inclination, to stick to solid facts. We shall see as we proceed just how solid the facts are, and that is a strange enough tale for the moment. As usual, truth has proved itself stranger than fiction. The reader is advised to read Part III of this book for some 'wild speculation'.

The book which now follows poses a question. It does not present, but merely suggests, an answer. In Part One the question is posed in its original form, and in Part Two it is rephrased. But nowhere is it answered with any certainty. The best questions are the ones which often remain unanswered for a long time and lead us down new avenues of thought and experience. Who knows where the Sirius mystery will lead us in the end? But let us follow it for a while. At the very least it will be an adventure. . . .

Notes

1. *African Worlds*, ed. by Daryll Forde, Oxford University Press, 1954, pp. 83–110. I wish to point out to the reader that in the article in *African Worlds*, the French word *arche* is mistranslated 'arch' and should instead be rendered 'ark'.
2. The translation was, it turned out, extremely inept. The article has been entirely retranslated by a professional translator for inclusion in this book. It has also been vetted by Mme Germaine Dieterlen herself, who has kindly given permission for the publication in English of the entire article written by herself and Marcel Griaule. It is to be found just after Chapter One.
3. Photographs of these four tribal priests are reproduced in Plate 2. I thought it particularly important that these original native informants be seen by the reader. Apart from the fact that their faces are extremely interesting, we owe these four people a great deal. Without them the public at large might never have known anything about the Sirius mystery, and the entire tradition might, after its thousands of years on earth, actually have sunk without trace.

PART ONE

The Sirius Question is Posed

CHAPTER ONE

The Knowledge of the Dogon

If you look up at the sky, the brightest star you can see is Sirius. Venus and Jupiter are often brighter but they are not stars; they are planets going round our own sun, which is a star itself. Now no astronomer will tell you there is any particular reason for intelligent life to be in the area of Sirius. The reason Sirius is so bright is that it is large and close, bigger than the sun and bigger than the handful of other nearby stars. But an intelligent astronomer will tell you that perhaps the stars Tau Ceti or Epsilon Eridani, which are rather similar to our sun, have planets with intelligent life. It would be a good guess. But among the stars most frequently discussed as possibly harbouring intelligent life, Sirius is not included. It is not a particularly 'obvious' choice.

Project Ozma in the spring of 1960, and, in more recent years, other radio searches for intelligent life in space, listened for meaningful signals from the stars Tau Ceti and Epsilon Eridani. But none were detected. Not that that proves anything but that these two nearby stars were thought by some sensible astronomers to be possible locations of intelligent life in our neighbourhood of space.[1] Project Ozma only listened to these two stars to see if any signals were coming from them on a certain wavelength at a certain time with a lot of energy behind them. Nothing happened. Later such attempts have more realistically widened their scope somewhat, but the astronomers are fully aware that they are waltzing in the dark, and their efforts really take on the nature of a gesture which can only be described as bravado in the face of enormous odds. They cannot be certain that they are going about the task in the right way, but are doing what they hope is their best. Since Project Ozma, the giant radio telescope at Arecibo in Puerto Rico, which is the largest in the world, has listened selectively to several stars – but not to Sirius. It is the author's hope that the evidence presented in this book will be sufficient to stimulate an astronomical investigation of the Sirius system more thorough than all those to date, and build on the recent studies by Irving Lindenblad.[2] I also believe that a programme should be instituted at a major radio telescope to listen to the Sirius system for indications of any possible intelligent signals.

Now the basis of speculations about intelligent life in space is always going to include the possibility that contact with life on our planet has already been made by some more highly evolved society from elsewhere in the universe.[3] It is the possibility that our planet has had contact with a culture apparently from the area of Sirius that this book will discuss. There seems to be substantial evidence that at some relatively recent time in the past – possibly between seven and ten thousand years ago – this may have happened, and any other interpretation of the evidence would not seem to make enough sense.

Before we come to the evidence, I should say a little more about Sirius. About the middle of the last century an astronomer was looking rather hard at Sirius over a period of time and got annoyed because it wasn't sitting still.[4] It was wobbling. He had a difficult time figuring this out, but he finally concluded that an extremely heavy and massive star going around Sirius could make it wobble that way. The only trouble was that there wasn't any large star going around Sirius! Instead there turned out to be a tiny little thing going around it every fifty years, and so Sirius came to be called Sirius A and the little thing became Sirius B.

Sirius B was at that time unique in the universe as far as anyone knew. Over a hundred of these things have now been actually seen scattered around the sky and there are many thousands more which we cannot see even through our modern telescopes because they are so tiny and their light so feeble. They are called white dwarfs.[5]

White dwarfs are strange because although they are feeble they are strong. They do not give out much light, but they are fantastically powerful gravitationally. On a white dwarf we would not even be a fraction of an inch high. We would be flat, pulled in by the gravity.* You see, the 'big' star that was necessary to make Sirius A wobble turned out to be a little thing, but it still had to be as massive and heavy as an ordinary star of much more enormous size. It is, in short, a star so dense and closely packed that it is not even made out of regular matter. It is made out of what is called 'degenerate' matter or 'super-dense' matter, where the atoms are pressed together and the electrons squashed. This matter is so heavy that it cannot be thought of in any familiar terms. There is nothing in our solar system, to our knowledge, comparable to this stuff. But physicists have considered it theoretically, and in this century we are making some progress towards understanding it.

It is even claimed by some astronomers that the Sirius system has a Sirius C, or a third star. Fox claimed to see it in 1920, and in 1926, 1928, and 1929 it was supposedly seen by van den Bos, Finsen, and others at the Union Observatory. But then for several years when it should have been seen, it was not. Zagar and Volet said it was there because there were wobbles that pointed to it. So perhaps it's there and perhaps it isn't.[6]

The most recent full study of the Sirius system by an astronomer has been carried out by Irving W. Lindenblad of the U.S. Naval Observatory in Washington, D.C. He and I have corresponded, and he has sent me his publications (the latest appeared in 1973) and also the photograph in Plate 1, which was taken by him in 1970 after several years' preparation and is the first photograph ever taken of the star Sirius B, which in the photograph is a tiny spot of light near the main star Sirius A, which is 10,000 times brighter.

Lindenblad's accomplishment in getting a successful photograph is described in 'Notes to the Plates'. He has studied the Sirius system for seven years and has

---

* A cubic foot of the matter of Sirius B would weigh 2,000 tons. A match-box full of matter from the star would weigh a ton and a quarter. But a match-box full taken from the star's core would weigh approximately 50 tons. The star is 65,000 times denser than water, whereas our own Sun has a density about equal to that of water.

found no evidence of a third star, Sirius C. He says:[7] 'There is no astrometric evidence, therefore, of a close companion to either Sirius A or Sirius B'. At the moment, as this book goes to press, a study of Sirius B is being carried out by Dr Paul G. Murdin of the Royal Greenwich Observatory, who is trying to measure the light from the tiny star. He had still had no success by early 1974 when he and I entered into correspondence. Murdin has informed me that another astronomer, D. Lauterborn, believes there is a third star in the Sirius system.[8] Murdin adds: 'Whether the unseen companion of A is the same star C in Aitken[9] I cannot say' (from a letter to me of 12 February 1974). Lindenblad's evidence is conclusive as far as it goes, but it is not at all clear that no Sirius C exists. This is an interesting point for further study, and may require observations of longer than Lindenblad's seven years (which were taking place during the seven years I was preparing this book). As Lindenblad has written to me: 'Like Jacob's service for Rachel, the mysteries of Sirius appear to require seven years of labour; then we hope not to have received Leah!' But also like Jacob, the seven years may be just a prelude.

Now we see that the Sirius system is rather interesting and complicated. Only in this century have we advanced towards knowing about degenerate matter and understanding white dwarfs through our researches into nuclear physics. So we would be surprised, would we not, if someone without our modern science had known as much about the Sirius system as we do?

At this point I want to quote from an interesting book entitled *Intelligent Life in the Universe* by two eminent astronomers, Carl Sagan, of Cornell and formerly of the Smithsonian Astrophysical Observatory, and I. S. Shklovskii of the Soviet Academy of Science. (Sagan saw a book by Shklovskii and extensively rewrote it in English, and this is the book referred to.) In a very sensible chapter called 'Possible Consequences of Direct Contact' Sagan says:[10]

[Matters of human evolution], while difficult for us to reconstruct from a distance of millions of years, would have been much clearer to a technical civilization greatly in advance of the present one on Earth, which visited us every hundred thousand years or so to see if anything of interest was happening lately. Some 25 million years ago, a Galactic survey ship on a routine visit to the third planet of a relatively common G dwarf star [our Sun] may have noted an interesting and promising evolutionary development: Proconsul [the ancestor of *homo sapiens*, or modern man]. The information would have filtered at the speed of light slowly through the Galaxy, and a notation would have been made in some central information repository, perhaps at the Galactic center. If the emergence of intelligent life on a planet is of general scientific or other interest to the Galactic civilizations, it is reasonable that with the emergence of Proconsul, the rate of sampling of our planet should have increased, perhaps to once every ten thousand years. At the beginning of the most recent post-glacial epoch, the development of social structure, art, religion, and elementary technical skills should have increased the contact still further. But if the interval between sampling is only several thousand years, there is then a possibility that contact with an extraterrestrial civilization has occurred within historical times.

This is a very interesting prelude to our own story, and I believe Sagan and Shklovskii's attitude is broadly true of the entire astronomical profession. I have certainly never met an astronomer of today who seriously doubted that there must be countless numbers of intelligent civilizations scattered throughout the universe on other planets which are orbiting around other stars.[11] Any people who still believe human beings are unique as intelligent life in the universe are seriously out of touch with reliable and informed estimates by scientists and astronomers. An attitude which asserts that man is the only intelligent life form in the universe is intolerably arrogant today, though as little as twenty years ago it was probably common belief. But anyone who holds such an opinion today is, fortunately for those who like to see some progress in human conceptions, something of an intellectual freak equivalent to a believer in the Flat Earth Theory. I mention that theory because I once met a woman who appeared quite sane and yet who was a member of a cult who believe the Earth is flat. This was one of the more startling experiences anyone can have, and a salutary education to me. It taught me never to underestimate the power of the human mind to believe what it wants to believe despite any amount of evidence.

Dr Melvin Calvin, of the Department of Chemistry, University of California at Berkeley, has said: 'There are at least 100,000,000 planets in the visible universe which were, or are, very much like the earth. . . . this would mean certainly that we are not alone in the universe. Since man's existence on the earth occupies but an instant of cosmic time, surely intelligent life has progressed far beyond our level on some of these 100,000,000 planets.'[12]

Dr Su-Shu Huang of the Goddard Space Flight Center, Maryland, has written: '. . . planets are formed around the main-sequence stars of spectral types later than F5. Thus, planets are formed just where life has the highest chance to flourish. Based on this view we can predict that nearly all single stars of the main sequence below F5 and perhaps above K5 have a fair chance of supporting life on their planets. Since they compose a few per cent of all stars, life should indeed be a common phenomenon in the universe.'[13]

Dr A. G. W. Cameron, Professor of Astronomy at Yeshiva University, has discussed the stars Tau Ceti and Epsilon Eridani, which are considered the two likeliest localities for intelligent life within our immediate neighbourhood of space (within five 'parsecs' of us, a parsec being an astronomical unit of distance). He has then said, however: 'But there are about 26 other single stars of smaller mass within this distance, each of which should have a comparable probability of having a life-supporting planet according to the present analysis'.[14]

Dr R. N. Bracewell of the Radio Astronomy Institute, Stanford University, has said:[15]

As there are about one billion stars in our galaxy, the number of planets would be about 10 billion. . . . Now not all of these would be habitable, some would be too hot and some too cold, depending on their distance from their central star; so that on the whole we need only pay attention to planets situated as our earth is with respect to the sun. Let's describe such a situation as being within the habitable zone.

This is not to imply that no life would be found outside the habitable zone. There may very well be living things existing under most arduous physical conditions. . . . After elimination of frozen planets and planets sterilized by heat, we estimate that there are about 10^{10} [ten thousand million] likely planets in the galaxy [for life]. . . . Of the 10^{10} likely planets, we frankly do not know how many of them support intelligent life. Therefore, we explore all possibilities, beginning with the possibility that intelligent life is abundant and in fact occurs on practically every planet. In this case, the average distance from one intelligent community to the next is 10 light-years. For comparison, the nearest star, of any kind, is about 1 light-year away.

Ten light-years is a very large distance. A radio signal would take 10 years to cover the distance. . . . Consequently, communicating with someone 10 light-years away would not be like a telephone conversation . . . are we sure that we can send a radio signal as far as 10 light-years? A definite answer can be given to this question.

There is no need for me to continue marshalling quotations from distinguished scientists and astronomers in support of the possibility of intelligent life in space, as the situation is by now obvious. The odds against intelligent life occurring fairly frequently within our galaxy are impossible ones. Since this is established, we are faced with yet another factor: in our own history, technological development has been rapid within a short space of time. When civilizations all over the universe reach 'take-off point', they have a technological explosion. It is familiar to older members of our species today that when they were young there were no airplanes, automobiles, rockets, satellites, electricity, radio, or atom bombs. People were dying of diseases which today we do not take seriously, no one with a toothache could obtain modern dental treatment, the concept of elementary hygiene was a novelty. I am not reciting all these wonders merely as a ritual incantation to our new god of progress. The point to be grasped is the sudden combustible nature of progress of this kind. In the lifetime of a single person all this can come about.

'Take-off point' is probably a universal phenomenon. Intelligent societies all over the universe will probably have experienced it, or are due to. Now the lifetime of a single person is of no consequence on the great universal time scale for the development of civilizations, not to mention the formation of planets. Therefore any society in advance of our own is certain to be very much in advance of ours. Once intelligent societies reach take-off point, they rush so quickly upward in technological competence that a comparison between them and non-technological societies is almost absurd. It would be foolish for us to suppose that any society more advanced than ours would be just a few years ahead of us. It would more likely be just a few tens of thousands of years ahead of us. And the technology and nature of such a society are beyond our abilities to imagine. The intelligent societies existing in the universe, then, are going to be of two kinds: less advanced than ourselves, 'primitive'; and fantastically more advanced than ourselves, 'magical'. To be at the point where we are now, at the watershed between 'primitive' and 'magical', is such a rare event in the universal history, that we may be the only intelligent society in the entire galaxy which is at this moment experiencing such a stage in our evolution. We therefore should feel privileged to be witnesses of it. Of course, the nature

of time comes in again with the impossibility of talking sensibly about simul-
taneity in the galaxy at all. But that is another subject, and one which we may
ignore here.

A further thought follows upon the above observations. Granted that
there are two forms of society in the universe aside from our own bizarre
transition stage, the 'primitive' societies are obviously only of interest to
those more advanced than themselves, for they are incapable of communicating
with anybody else. They are like we were as little as a hundred years ago:
provincial, quiet, probably quite murderous, and smug, with the occasional
visionary who is burned at the stake or crucified causing a moral ripple. But they
cannot send or receive messages between the stars. In our transition stage,
aptly enough, we can receive such messages with existing equipment, but could
not send any unless we constructed expensive and special means to do so.
Now that means that the only societies carrying on an interstellar dialogue of
any kind are the 'magical' societies. These societies will be so advanced that
they probably have emerging primitives like ourselves 'taped'. They certainly
have standard sets of procedures for dealing with the likes of us, and may
already have commenced their operations with the long-range intent of bringing us into their club. But just as no London gentlemen's club wishes to have a
savage in a g-string waving his spear and poisoned arrows about in the members' lounge, so the interstellar club is unlikely to plug us straight into the circuits as a fully-fledged member.

But what I am getting at is not merely to impress upon the reader that a
pecking order is likely to exist in the interstellar club of any galaxy, at least to
the extent of having restrictions on novices, but to make the point which
emerges from this. And the point is, that such highly advanced societies have
possibly developed to such a pitch of technological expertise that interstellar travel has become possible for them, whereby they can physically
transport themselves over at least modest interstellar distances of a few light-
years to their near neighbours. And if that is the case, then our own planet,
which any half-witted extraterrestrial astronomer in the neighbourhood could
assume as a likely place for life to exist, has almost certainly been physically
visited by extraterrestrials in their travels. This could have happened at any
time in our lengthy history as a planet. No doubt, at the very least, our distant
ancestors the cave-men would have been observed by extraterrestrial probes,
who would have made a note that something was happening on this planet –
slowly happening, but nevertheless actually happening. And as Sagan and
Shklovskii said in the quotation from their book: 'It is reasonable that . . .
the rate of sampling of our planet should have increased, perhaps to once every
ten thousand years. . . . But if the interval between sampling is only several
thousand years, there is then a possibility that contact with an extra-terrestrial
civilization has occurred within historical times.'[16]

If this were so, it would certainly have left some impact upon man and
been incorporated somehow into his traditions. But if several thousand years
had elapsed between that time and the present, the traces of the impact
on man's culture would have been mostly dissipated and, it would seem,
nearly impossible to elucidate. Unless some specific and unmistakable survival
were found to exist, in circumstances which would probably be unusual, it

seems that the hope of reconstructing scattered clues and fragments of the original tradition would be futile. That there would be something there if you could find the key seems certain. Let us return to a continuation of that passage from Sagan and Shklovskii for suggestions as to how a memory of an extraterrestrial contact might have been preserved from prehistoric or early historic times on Earth, through comparison with a verifiable story of French contact made with certain American Indians in 1786, as it was told to a modern anthropologist in the form of a tribal myth:[17]

There are no reliable reports of direct contact with an extraterrestrial civilization during the last few centuries, when critical scholarship and non-superstitious reasoning have been fairly widespread. Any earlier contact story must be encumbered with some degree of fanciful embellishment, due simply to the views prevailing at the time of the contact. The extent to which subsequent variation and embellishment alters the basic fabric of the account varies with time and circumstance. [An example] relevant to the topic at hand is the native account of the first contact with the Tlingit people of the northeast coast of North America with European civilization – an expedition led by the French navigator, La Perouse, in 1786. The Tlingit kept no written records; one century after the contact, the verbal narrative of the encounter was related to the American anthropologist G. T. Emmons by a principal Tlingit chief. The story was overlaid with the mythological framework in which the French sailing vessels were initially interpreted. But what is very striking is that the true nature of the encounter had been faithfully preserved. One blind old warrior had mastered his fears at the time of the encounter, had boarded one of the French ships, and exchanged goods with the Europeans. Despite his blindness, he reasoned that the occupants of the vessels were men. His interpretation led to active trade between the expedition of La Perouse and the Tlingit. The oral rendition contained sufficient information for later reconstruction of the true nature of the encounter, although many of the incidents were disguised in a mythological framework – for example, the ships were described as immense black birds with white wings.

As another example, the people of sub-Saharan Africa, who had no written language until the colonial period, preserved their history primarily through folklore. Such legends and myths, handed down by illiterate people from generation to generation, are in general of great historical value.

I don't know why the people of sub-Saharan Africa – with whom our initial evidence deals – are mentioned at this point in the Sagan book, for they do not crop up again in this chapter and it is something of a coincidence that they are mentioned out of the blue like this. Sagan goes on to discuss some fascinating creatures credited with founding the Sumerian civilization (which sprang up out of nowhere, as many Sumerian archaeologists will unhappily admit). They are described in a classical account by Alexander Polyhistor as amphibious. He says they were happier if they could go back to the sea at night and return to dry land in the daytime. All the accounts describe them as being semi-demons, personages, or animals endowed with reason, but they are never called gods. They were 'superhuman' in knowledge and length of life and they eventually returned in a ship 'to the gods' carrying with them representatives of the fauna of the earth. I discuss these traditions particularly in Chapter Eight, and the surviving accounts of them are to be found in Appendix II, reprinted here in their entirety for the first time since 1876.

The Sumerian culture is very important. We shall be discussing it later in this book. It formed the original basis of that Mesopotamian civilization which is better known to most people through the much later Babylonians and Assyrians who inherited much of the Sumerian culture. The actual language of the Sumerians was superseded rather early by the Akkadian language (which is Semitic; Sumerian is non-Semitic and seems to have no linguistic affinities at all). The Akkadians and the Sumerians intermingled and eventually formed a meld like that which now exists between what once were the separate Normans and Anglo-Saxons in Britain, except that the Akkadians were Semitic and the Sumerians were not, and with considerable physical differences between them. Then the city of Babylon with its Babylonians and the region of Assyria with its Assyrian warriors to the north – and later the distant region of Fars with its Persians to the east – commanded the Mesopotamian area. From the Sumerian–Akkadian milieu also evolved those Semites known as Hebrews or Jews.

It should be more widely realized that when those famous Biblical figures Noah and Abraham 'lived' there was no such thing as a Hebrew yet in existence. Indeed, Noah is merely a Hebrew name for a much more ancient flood hero discussed in ancient texts which we have now recovered from early Sumer.[18] It is these Sumerians to whom Sagan has just referred, with their legend of an amphibious creature who founded their civilization. But all this does not concern us quite yet. I will just add that the Jews and the Arabs are both traditionally said to be descendants of Abraham, and Abraham was neither a Jew nor an Arab.

Now the peoples of sub-Saharan Africa are the source of our first arresting information. The particular people are called the Dogon, and they live in the present state of Mali. The nearest cities to them are Timbuctoo, Bamako, and Ouagadougou in Upper Volta. Initial research by me on the Dogon turned up an article in an anthropological journal by the French anthropologists Marcel Griaule and Germaine Dieterlen.[19] The article was written in French and an English translation of it is published, for the first time, as sequel to Part One of this book. I decided to publish the article in full because of the difficulty most interested readers would find in locating the French journal in which the original article appeared. And, of course, the original article could only be read by those who know French. The complete article, with its footnotes and all its illustrations, and in English, is therefore available for anyone who wishes to read it for himself. It is thus not necessary for me to summarize its contents.

When I first read the article, which is entitled 'A Sudanese Sirius System' (and refers to the French Sudan area, not the Republic of Sudan over a thousand miles to the east below Egypt), I could hardly believe what I saw. For here was an anthropological report of four tribes, the Dogon and three related ones, who held as their most secret religious tradition a body of knowledge concerning

LOCATION OF
THE DOGON TRIBE
OF MALI

THE DOGON'

Figure I

the system of the star Sirius, including specific information about that star system which it should be impossible for any primitive tribe to know.

The Dogon consider that the most important star in the sky is Sirius B, which cannot be seen. They admit that it is invisible. How, then, do they know it exists? Griaule and Dieterlen say: 'The problem of knowing how, with no instruments at their disposal, men could know the movements and certain characteristics of virtually invisible stars has not been settled, nor even posed.' But even in saying this, Griaule and Dieterlen imply that Sirius B is only 'vir-

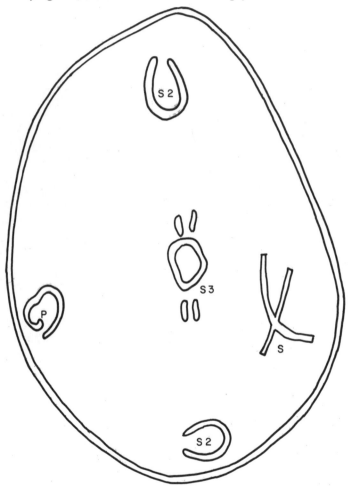

KEY : S =   SIRIUS

S2 =   POSITIONS OF SIRIUS B

S3 =   ANOTHER   STAR

P =   A PLANET

Figure 2

tually invisible', whereas we know it is totally invisible except through a power-ful telescope. What, then, is the answer?

Griaule and Dieterlen make clear that the large and bright star of Sirius is not as important to the Dogon as the tiny Sirius B, which the Dogon call *po tolo* (*tolo* meaning 'star'). *Po* is a cereal grain commonly called 'fonio' in West Africa, and whose official botanical name is *Digitaria exilis*. In speaking of the *po* star, Griaule and Dieterlen call it 'the star Digitaria', or just simply 'Digitaria'. What is significant about the *po* grain is that it is the smallest grain known to the Dogon, being extremely minute, and unknown as food in Europe or America. To the Dogon, this tiny grain represents the tiny star, and that is why the star is called *po*, after the grain.

In the article we read: 'Sirius, however, is not the basis of the system: it is one of the foci of the orbit of a tiny star called Digitaria, *po tolo* . . . which . . . hogs the attention of male initiates.' Now, this is a most unsettling statement. The casual reader may not notice just how unusual it is for an African tribe to put it quite this way. But the orbit of Digitaria, which the Dogon elsewhere describe as egg-shaped or elliptical (see also Figures 6 and 7, as well as the illustrations to the article), is specifically described as having the main star Sirius as 'one of the foci of [its] orbit'. Of course, the technical term 'focus' has here been supplied by the anthropologists. But they were faithfully render-ing the meaning of what the Dogon said in their own language. And what the Dogon were saying, and which they also make quite clear graphically in their drawings (see Figures 2 and 6), is that the orbit of Sirius B around Sirius A is of a kind which obeys one of Kepler's laws of planetary motion, extended to other orbiting bodies. It was Johannes Kepler (1571–1630) who first proposed that heavenly bodies do not move in perfect circular paths. He hit upon the brilliant insight that the planets in their motions around the sun were moving in elliptically shaped orbits, with the sun at one of the two foci of each ellipse. Most people I speak to have no idea that the planets don't go in circles around the sun. Even if they were taught the truth at school, they have long since for-gotten about things like that. And many people honestly don't know what an ellipse is unless you show them one.

An ellipse is a kind of 'stretched' circle. You can conceive of grabbing the centre of a circle and ripping the centre into two pieces, and then pulling those two portions away from each other. This would naturally make the circle flatten at the top and the bottom and bulge at the two sides, and the two pieces of the centre would fall along a straight line joining the two most distant points. These two fragments of centre each then have the name of *focus*, and the two

AN ELLIPSE
Figure 3

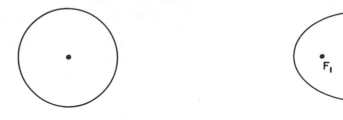

CIRCLE,ONE CENTRE   ELLIPSE,TWO FOCI

Figure 4

together are 'the foci of the ellipse.' If you could get your hands on that ellipse
and push at the bulging ends, you might force it back together again and make
it a proper circle.

But what I ask all readers to take note of is this: How did the Dogon tribe,
who had no access to the theories of Kepler or his successors, know about matters like this? How did they even get the idea in the first place that elliptical
orbits existed, rather than circular – much less apply this idea to some invisible
star way out in space? And also to get it right by saying that Sirius A was at
one of the foci, rather than just somewhere in the ellipse? And not at the centre?
Wouldn't the natural primitive idea seem to be, even if you wanted to say the
orbit was elliptical, still to have Sirius itself at the centre? But no. They knew
too much to make a mistake like that. For the whole point about Kepler's Law
is that not only are the orbits ellipses, but the sun must always be at one of the
foci; otherwise nothing will work. Now, in order to know about all this, you
need not have had Kepler. Elliptical orbits are a universal truth, as true here
as they are on the other side of the galaxy, or even in some other galaxy. Kepler
merely discovered a natural principle. He didn't invent it. So there was no need
for the Dogon to know about Kepler personally. All that is required is an explanation of how they could have learned the universal principle from any other
source, considering that they exist on this planet, and we don't know of anyone
else on this planet, living in Africa, say, who has discovered any of these things.

In Fig. 6, I compare the Dogon drawings of the orbit of Sirius B around

Figure 5

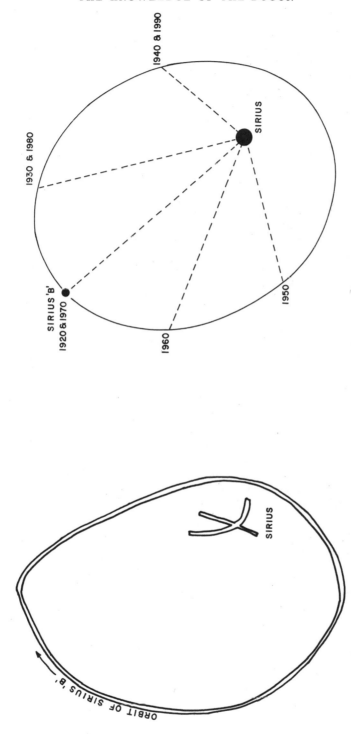

Figure 6. On left: the orbit of Digitaria (Sirius B) around Sirius as portrayed by the Dogon in their sand drawings. On right: A modern astronomical diagram of the orbit of Sirius, the years indicated being the positions of Sirius B in its orbit on those dates. Note that the Dogon do not place Sirius at the centre of their drawing but seem to place it near one focus of their approximate ellipse – which constitutes one of the most extraordinary features of their information, and matches the diagram on the right to an uncanny degree

Sirius with the modern astronomical diagrams of the same (which have just been confirmed as accurate at this scale by Lindenblad's latest work); also there is a comparison of the same information, tribal and modern, as seen in a linear perspective, stretched through time. I do not need to claim any perfect scientific accuracy for the Dogon drawings. The similarity is so striking that the most untrained eye can immediately see that the general picture is identical, in each instance. There is no need for perfectionists to get out their slide rules or measuring tapes. The fact is demonstrated, and it is that the Dogon have an accurate general knowledge of the most unobvious and subtle principles of the orbiting of Sirius B around Sirius A.

The Dogon also know the actual orbital period of this invisible star, which is fifty years. Referring to the sacred Sigui ceremony of the tribe, Dieterlen and Griaule tell us: 'The period of the orbit is counted double, that is, one hundred years, because the Siguis are convened in pairs of "twins", so as to insist on the principle of twin-ness'.

The Dogon also say that Sirius B rotates on its axis, demonstrating that they know a star can do such a thing. In reality, all stars really do rotate on their axes. How do the Dogon know such an extraordinary fact? In the article, the Dogon are recorded as saying: 'As well as its movement in space, Digitaria also revolves upon itself over the period of one year and this revolution is honoured during the celebration of the *bado* rite'. It is not known to modern astronomy what the period of rotation of Sirius B is; the star is so small we think we are doing well to see it at all. I asked one astronomer, G. Wegner, of Oxford's Department of Astrophysics and the University Observatory, whether one year might be a sensible estimate of the rotation period of Sirius B. He naturally replied that we had no way of determining it, but that a year could be right; in other words, it cannot be ruled out, which was all I was seeking to establish.

The Dogon describe Sirius B as 'the infinitely tiny'. As we know, Sirius B is a white dwarf and the tiniest form of visible star in the universe. But what is really the most amazing of all the Dogon statements is this: 'The star which is considered to be the smallest thing in the sky is also the heaviest: "Digitaria is the smallest thing there is. It is the heaviest star." It consists of a metal called *sagala* which is a little brighter than iron and so heavy "that all earthly beings combined cannot lift it". In effect the star weighs the equivalent of . . . .all the seeds, or of all the iron on the earth . . .' (all this from the following article by Griaule and Dieterlen).

So we see the Dogon presenting a theory of Sirius B which fits all known scientific facts, and even some which are not known it presents as well. They know that the star is invisible, but they know it is there nevertheless. They know that the star's orbital period is fifty years, which it really is. They know that Sirius A is not at the centre of its orbit, which it is not. They know that Sirius A is at one of the foci of Sirius B's elliptical orbit, which it is. They know that Sirius B is the smallest kind of star, which it is (barring totally invisible collapsing neutron stars). They know that Sirius B is composed of a special kind of material which is called *sagala*, from a root meaning 'strong', and that this material does not exist on the earth. They know that this material is heavier than all the iron on earth, etc., all of which is perfectly true. For

Figure 7. The linear extension on the right is scientifically reliable, based on measurements of the rate of revolution of Sirius B around Sirius A. The linear extension on the left is *not* scientifically reliable. It is a presumed correlation, for there is no way in which the *rate* of revolution of Digitaria can be known certainly from the Dogon information. These linear extensions cannot, therefore, be considered to constitute hard evidence of a correlation. It is likely, though, that they do correlate because Digitaria is presumed to move at a rate which makes astronomical sense (for if the shape of the orbit and the distance match, the period should match)

Sirius B is in reality made of super-dense matter of a kind which exists nowhere on earth.

All this forms the most sacred and most secret tradition known to the Dogon, the basis of their religion and of their lives. Connected with all this are statements they make about the existence of a third star in the Sirius system, which they call the *emme ya* star which, in comparing it to Digitaria, they say is 'four times as light (in weight), and travels along a greater trajectory in the same direction and in the same time as it (fifty years). Their respective positions are such that the angle of their radii is at right angles.' This last star has a satellite, indicating that the Dogon appreciate that bodies other than stars are satellites of stars. Of *emme ya* itself, they say: 'It is the "the sun of women" . . . "a little sun" . . . In fact it is accompanied by a satellite which is called the "star of women" . . . or Goatherd . . . as the guide of (*emme ya*).'

Figure 8. Dogon drawing of a planet going round Sirius C-*Emme ya*

Around the astronomical facts of this extraordinary system, the Dogon have a complicated system of mythology. Sirius B they see as 'relentlessly revolving around Sirius . . . and never capable of reaching it'. All these facts have mythological tales and personages connected with them. I have tried to extract the bare facts from the article and present them here for the reader. But the reader will by now see quite clearly why I have included the entire article in this book, for the information is so incredible that I thought the reader would simply think I had made it all up unless I presented the source for him to read through himself.

But let us move beyond the Griaule and Dieterlen article 'A Sudanese Sirius System'. Let us now consider a later and fuller publication of book length, which is obviously too bulky to include within this book as an appendix. I refer to the book *Le Renard pâle* (The Pale Fox) published in 1965. This book, by Griaule and Dieterlen, was produced ten years after the death of Marcel Griaule himself. It contains Mme Dieterlen's latest reflections on the Sirius system of the Dogon. In this definitive compendium[20] of much of the joint findings of herself and Marcel Griaule (it is only the first such volume of theirs to appear in a planned series summing up their work), Mme Dieterlen has actually added a brief appendix on pages 529–31 which gives information about Sirius and its companion star in the form of an extract from an article by Dr P. Baize which appeared in the September 1931 issue of *Astronomie*. She says: 'The excerpts concern the discovery, orbit, period and density of the Companion of Sirius'.[21] Her curiosity has obviously developed since 1950 and the publication of 'A Sudanese Sirius System'. But like a true professional, Mme Dieterlen merely cites the astronomical facts in this way in a short appendix at the back of her book[22] without drawing any conclusions or even indicating the connection of this subject with the Dogon's traditions. In fact, lest the reader assume otherwise, I must make clear that neither Marcel Griaule nor Mme Dieterlen has at any time (to my knowledge) made any claim of extraterrestrial contact to do with the Dogon. They have not even made any direct comments on the extraordinary impossibility of the Dogon knowing all the things which they know. I could never have made discoveries such as those of Griaule and Dieterlen and merely said (as in the article): 'The problem of knowing how . . . has not been settled, nor even posed.' I do believe such restraint calls for a medal; it is so phenomenal that it is the greatest factor in favour of Griaule and Dieterlen's discoveries. If they had trumpeted their findings, I suppose I would never have taken them seriously. I would have thought them unreliable. Such are the ironies by which information can be revealed – by almost disappearing through diffidence.

I sat down and rewrote this book in the light of *Le Renard pâle* (I have not been able to discover whether this has been published in English; I read the translation in manuscript), with its more complete information. Much of this will be found in the context of a more advanced discussion in Chapter Eight.

In *Le Renard pâle* it is possible to learn much more of the Dogon beliefs and knowledge relating to astronomy and the Sirius system. Of the moon, they say it 'is dry and dead like dry dead blood'.[23] Their drawing of the planet Saturn has a ring around it, and is reproduced as Figure 10 in this book. They know that the planets revolve around the sun. Planets are called *tolo tanaze*, 'stars that turn (around something)'.[24] But this does not mean turning around the Earth. The Dogon specifically say, for instance: 'Jupiter follows Venus by turning slowly around the sun.'[25] The various positions of Venus are recalled on a very large geographical space by a series of altars, raised stones, or arrangements in caves or shelters.[26] The positions of Venus determine a Venus calendar.[27] In fact, the Dogon have four different kinds of calendar. Three of them are liturgical calendars: a solar calendar, a Venus calendar, and a Sirius calendar. Their fourth is an agrarian one, and is lunar.[28]

The Dogon know of the existence of four other invisible heavenly bodies

Figure 9. Dogon drawing of Jupiter with its four main moons

besides Sirius B and its possible companions in the Sirius system. These other four bodies are in our own solar system. For the Dogon know of the four major 'Galilean' moons of Jupiter. These four moons are called 'Galilean' because Galileo discovered them when he began to use the telescope. The other moons of Jupiter are small and insignificant, having formerly been asteroids which were captured by Jupiter's gravitation at some unknown time in the past. (They are thought to have come from the asteroid belt between Mars and Jupiter which some astronomers think once constituted a planet which exploded.) The Dogon say: 'The mutilation (the Fox) suffered was still bloody. The blood of his genitals fell on the ground, but Amma made it ascend to heaven as four satellites that turn around *dana tolo,* Jupiter, . . . "The four little stars are Jupiter wedges" . . . When Jupiter is represented by a rock, it is wedged in with four stones.'[29] A Dogon drawing of Jupiter with its four moons is reproduced in Figure 9 in this book. Griaule and Dieterlen describe this drawing as follows:[30]

> This figure represents the planet – the circle – surrounded by its four satellites in the collateral directions and called *dana tolo unum* 'children of *dana tolo* (Jupiter)'. The four satellites, associated to the four varieties of *sene* (acacia), sprang from the drops of blood from the Fox's mutilated genitals. 'The four small stars are Jupiter's hulls' . . . . The sectors between the satellites represent the seasons. They turn around Jupiter and their movements will favour the growth of the *sene* leaves, for the *sene* moves on the ground at night like the stars in the sky; they turn on their own axes (in a year) like the satellites.

> They add in a footnote that 'the trunks of certain varieties of *sene* are spiralled. A house is not built with *sene* wood, which would make the house "turn". The "movements" of the *sene* at night are supposed to attract the souls of the dead who "change place".'

> As for Saturn, drawn in Figure 10, the Dogon specifically describe its famous halo, which is only visible through a telescope. According to Griaule and Dieterlen:[31] '. . . the Dogon affirm there is a permanent halo around the star, different from the one sometimes seen around the moon . . . the star is always associated to the Milky Way.'

Figure 10. Saturn with its ring. Dogon drawing

Saturn is known as[32] 'the star of limiting the place' in association somehow with the Milky Way. The meaning is unclear, and the anthropologists say the subject must be pursued further,[33] but it would seem they may be trying to convey the idea that Saturn 'limits the place' of the solar system, separating it from and acting as link with, the Milky Way itself, in which the solar system is situated. Saturn being the outermost planet which the Dogon mention, this may be their intended meaning. The Dogon realize that the Milky Way contains the earth:[34] '. . . the Milky Way . . . is in itself the image of the spiralling stars inside the "world of spiralling stars" in which the Earth is found. In this "world of stars", the axis ("Amma's fork") around which they move, links the Polar Star . . . ' and so on. The Milky Way is described as the 'more distant stars' – that is, than the planets.

We are told that[35] 'For the Dogon an infinite number of stars and spiralling worlds exist'. They carefully differentiate the three kinds of *tolo* or 'stars': 'The fixed stars are a part of the "family of stars that doesn't turn" (around another star) . . . the planets belong to the "family of stars that turns" (around another star) . . . the satellites are called *tolo gonoze* "stars that make the circle".'[36] The heavenly motions are likened to the circulation of the blood. The planets and satellites and companions are 'circulating blood'.[37] And this brings us to the extraordinary point that the Dogon do know about the circulation of the blood in the body from their own tradition. In our own culture, the Englishman William Harvey (1578–1657) discovered the circulation of the blood. Strange as it may seem to us now, before his time the notion seems not to have occurred to anyone. John Aubrey, author of *Brief Lives*, knew Harvey well, and tells us:[38] 'I have heard him say, that after his Booke of the *Circulation of the Blood* came out, that . . . 'twas beleeved by the vulgar that he was crack-brained . . . '. However, the same theory does not seem to arouse among the Dogon notions that their wise men are crack-brained. Here is an account of the theory by the Dogon themselves and recorded in their own words:[39]

> The movement of the blood in the body which circulates inside the organs in the belly, on the one hand 'clear' blood, and on the other the oil, keeps them both united (the words in man): that is the progress of the word. The blood-water – or clear – goes through the heart, then the lungs, the liver and the

spleen; the oily blood goes through the pancreas, the kidneys, the intestines and the genitals.

The Dogon say: '. . . the food you eat, the beverage you drink, that Amma changes into red blood; white blood is a bad thing'.[40] They also say: 'The essence of nourishment passes into the blood'.[41] They know that the blood passes into the internal organs 'starting with the heart'.[42] The Dogon even seem to understand the role of oxygen – or at least, air – entering the bloodstream. For they equate air with 'the word' which they say enters the bloodstream bringing 'nourishment of the interior' by 'the impulse raised by the heart'. The 'integration of the "word" (air) into the body also has to do with the food nourishing the blood. All the organs of respiration and digestion are associated with this integration.'[43]

The Milky Way, likened as I said to a circulation of the blood, is described further: '. . . the term *yalu ulo* designates the Milky Way of our galaxy, which sums up the stellar world of which the Earth is a part, and which spins in a spiral. . . . . (it encompasses) the multiplication and the development, almost infinite, of the spitaloid stellar worlds that Amma created . . . (there are) spiralling worlds that fill the universe – infinite and yet measurable.'[44] Amma is the chief god, the creator, of the universe, to the Dogon. There is an interesting account of Amma and the creation: 'The active role of fermentation at the time of the creation is recalled in the present brewing of beer. . . . the fermentation of the liquid constitutes a "resurrection" of the cereals destroyed in the brewing. . . . Life . . . is comparable to a fermentation. "Many things were fermenting inside Amma" ' at the creation.[45] And 'Spinning and dancing, Amma created all the spiralling worlds of the stars of the universe.'[46] '. . . Amma's work realized the universe progressively, it was made up of several stellar worlds spiralling around.'[47]

The Dogon have no difficulty in conceiving of intelligent life all over the universe. They say:[48]

> The worlds of spiralling stars were populated universes; for as he created things, Amma gave the world its shape and its movement and created living creatures. There are creatures living on other 'Earths' as well as on our own; this proliferation of life is illustrated by an explanation of the myth, in which it is said: man is on the 4th earth, but on the 3rd there are 'men with horns' *inneu gammurugu*, on the 5th, 'men with tails' *inneu dullogu*, on the 6th, 'men with wings' *inneu bummo*, etc. This emphasizes the ignorance of what life is on the other worlds but also the certainty that it exists.

The Dogon know that the Earth turns on its own axis. When the fox walks over the tables of divination which have been drawn in the sand, 'the planet begins to turn under the action of (the fox's) paws'.[49] 'When the only traces that are visible are made by the tail, the image is likened to the movement of the Earth turning on its own axis; it is said: "The Fox turned with his tail; the Earth turned on its own axis".'[50] 'So the divination table represents the Earth "which turns because of the action of the Fox's paws" as he moves along the registers; while the instruction table represents the space in which the

Earth moves, as well as the sun and the moon, which were placed by Amma out of his reach.'[51] The instruction table here referred to has twelve registers and constitutes a lunar calendar, with each register representing a month. It is Figure 96 in *Le Renard pâle*. These twelve months, then, are 'the space in which the Earth moves' – that is, one year's orbit around the sun. And within this orbit, the Earth's rotations on its own axis every day take place. The orbit around the sun is 'the Earth's space'.

The Dogon know perfectly well that it is the turning of the Earth on its axis which makes the sky seem to turn round. They speak of '. . . the apparent movement of the stars from east to west, as men see them'.[52] The Dogon are thus free from the illusions of our European ancestors, who thought the sky and stars wheeled round the Earth (though there was an exception to such primitive notions in Europe which no historian of science has ever reported, at least as far as I have been able to discover after a great deal of searching. I have summarized this 'secret' tradition in Appendix 1, and pointed out its connection with the Sirius mystery).

The placenta is used by the Dogon as a symbol of a 'system' of a group of stars or planets. Our own solar system seems to be referred to as 'Ogo's placenta',[53] whereas the system of the star Sirius and its companion star and satellites, etc., is referred to as 'Nommo's placenta'.[54] Nommo is the collective name for the great culture-hero and founder of civilization who came from the Sirius system to set up society on the Earth. Nommo – or, to be more precise, the Nommos – were amphibious creatures, and are to be seen in the two tribal drawings in Figure 32 and Figure 34 in this book. These Nommos are more or less equivalent with the Sumerian and Babylonian tradition of Oannes. All of this subject is discussed in Chapter Eight, where it is necessary to consider details of what kind of creatures may live on a planet in the Sirius system. For the moment we are really more concerned with the Dogon astronomical and other scientific knowledge. Their descriptions of 'spacemen' and landings of 'spaceships' – or at least what seem to be such – are left to Chapter Eight.

Here is the way in which Griaule and Dieterlen record the Dogon beliefs about the two cosmic placentas I have just mentioned:[55]

> Two systems, that are sometimes linked together, intervene, and are at the origin of various calendars, giving a rhythm to the life and activities of man. . . . One of them, nearest to the Earth, will have the sun as an axis, the sun is the testament to the rest of Ogo's placenta, and another, further away, Sirius, testament to the placenta of the Nommo, monitor of the Universe.

The movements of the bodies within these 'placentas' are likened to the circulation of blood in the actual placenta, and the bodies in space are likened to coagulations of blood into lumps. This principle is also applied to larger systems: 'In the formation of the stars, we recall that the "path of the blood" is represented by the Milky Way . . .',[56] '. . . the planets and satellites (and companions) are associated to the circulating blood and to the "seeds" . . . that flow with the blood.'[57] The system of Sirius, which is known as 'land of the fish',[58] and is the placenta of Nommo, is specifically called the 'double placenta in the sky',[59] referring to the fact that it is a binary star system. The 'earth' which is in the Sirius system is 'pure earth', whereas the 'earth' which is in our solar system is 'impure earth'.[60]

The landing of Nommo on our Earth is called 'the day of the fish',[61] and the planet he came from in the Sirius system is known as the '(pure) earth of the day of the fish . . . not (our) impure earth . . .'[62] In our own solar system all the planets emerged from the placenta of our sun. This is said of the planet Jupiter,[63] which 'emerged from the blood which fell on the placenta'. The planet Venus was also formed from blood which fell on the placenta.[64] (Venus 'was blood red when she was created, her colour fading progressively'.[65]) Mars, too, was created from a coagulation of 'blood'.[66] Our solar system is, as we have noted, called the placenta of Ogo, the Fox, who is impure. Our own planet Earth is, significantly, 'the place where Ogo's umbilical cord was attached to his placenta . . . and recalls his first descent'.[67] In other words, the Earth is where Ogo 'plugged in', as it were, to this system of planets. What Ogo the Fox seems to represent is man himself, an imperfect intelligent species who 'descended' or originated on this planet, which is the planet in our solar system to which the great umbilical cord is attached. Ogo is ourselves, in all our cosmic impurity. It comes as a shock to realize that we are Ogo, the imperfect, the meddler, the outcast. Ogo rebelled at his creation and remained unfinished. He is the equivalent of Lucifer in our own tradition in the Christian West. And in order to atone for our impurity it is said over and over by the Dogon that the Nommo dies and is resurrected, acting as a sacrifice for us, to purify and cleanse the Earth. The parallels with Christ are extraordinary, even extending to Nommo being crucified on a tree, and forming a eucharistic meal for humanity and then being resurrected. But these religious elements are not the subject with which I propose to deal. Let each reader pursue them as he sees fit, on his own initiative. I only raise the subject that, as Ogo, we may be cosmic pariahs, because I only hope that we must not always remain so. The Dogon seem to hold out hope of 'redemption' just as Jesus Christ did in his great message to the world. Redemption can mean what you want it to mean. But perhaps it would be more sensible to view 'sin' less as a sort of infraction of social rules and more as a form of impurity such as Ogo represents. The perversions of Christianity have always seemed to me to incorporate a perversion of the notion of 'sin' and the means by which 'sin' can be exploited as a means of temporal blackmail over other human beings. To rid ourselves of some impurity may be closer to what is needed, and those writers who have speculated that we suffer from a genetic fault may even be correct. If so, are we actually in cosmic quarantine at this moment?

We are told that the Nommo will come again. A certain 'star' in the sky will appear once more[68] and will be the 'testament to the Nommo's resurrection'. When the Nommo originally landed on Earth, he 'crushed the Fox, thus marking his future domination over the Earth which the Fox had made'.[69] So perhaps man's brutish nature has already been sufficiently subdued in our distant past. Perhaps it was those visitors whom the Dogon call the Nommos who really did 'crush the Fox' in us, who all but destroyed Ogo, and have given us all the best elements of civilization which we possess. We remain as a curious mixture of the brute and the civilized, struggling against the Ogo within us.

The Dogon seem to have come to terms with life, amid the bewildering multiplicity of heavenly motions in which they exist. '. . . the Earth turns on its own axis . . . and makes a great circle (around the Sun) . . . The moon turns like a conical spiral around the earth. The Sun distributes light in space and on the earth with its rays.'[70] The sun is 'the remainder of Ogo's placenta'[71] and the centre of our system. For some reason, which they say is the visitation to earth of the amphibious bringers of civilization from there, the Dogon centre their life and religion not on all this glorious panoply of solar and planetary activity of which they know, but on the system of a nearby star and its invisible companions. Why? Can it really be for the reason they say? And if so, will the Nommo come again? We should really investigate the details of the Dogon knowledge as fully as possible, for a start. In *Le Renard pâle*, as opposed to the earlier article reproduced here, it is said, for instance, that the star *emme ya* in the system of Sirius may have an orbital period of thirty-two years instead of the fifty years which others maintain. It is larger than Sirius B and 'four times lighter'. In relation to Sirius B, 'Their positions are straight'. It is watched over by Sirius B and acts as an intermediary, transmitting Sirius B's 'orders'.[72] Does such a body exist? Can we treat Dogon prognostications as evidence to be tested? Dr Lindenblad says he cannot find evidence of a Sirius C of the kind which was presumed earlier by astronomers. But can evidence be found of the kind of Sirius C suggested by the Dogon? And if such a discovery were made, would it conclusively establish the validity of the Dogon claims?

Among the Dogon, an allusion to the great Creator's immortality and stability is expressed in good wishes of greetings or farewell that are addressed to a friend or relative: 'May the immortal Amma keep you seated'.[73] It is just as well that we keep our seats, for we are about to launch into the dark waters of our planet's past, which may bring quite an alteration of our normal conceptions of it. For beyond the fact that a culture contact between ourselves and an alien civilization from outer space may have taken place, of which we may find some evidence from our own ancient cultures, we may discover that the ancient world, the further back one goes in time, tends to develop a more and more odd flavour. The mysteries become denser, the strangeness thicker and more viscous. Just as in tracing the origins of sugar one goes from lighter syrup back to the thick and pungent molasses which develops, it seems, qualities far removed from one's expectations at the beginning, so with the past. Its doors encrusted with almost solid cobwebs give off the stench of air last breathed by ancestors forgotten by us all.

Notes

1. Cameron, A. G. W., ed., *Interstellar Communication*, W. A. Benjamin, Inc., New York, 1963. See p. 75 (Calvin), p. 88 (Huang), p. 110 (Cameron), and particularly p. 176 (Drake).
2. For account see *Sky and Telescope*, June 1973, p. 354. Publications: Lindenblad, Irving, 'Relative Photographic Positions and Magnitude Difference of the Components of Sirius' in *Astronomical Journal*, 75, no. 7 (September 1970), pp. 841–8, and 'Multiplicity of the Sirius System' in *Astronomical Journal*, 78, no. 2 (March 1973), pp. 205–7.
3. Sagan, C. and Shklovskii, I. S., *Intelligent Life in the Universe*, Dell Publishing Co., New York, 1966, pp. 437, 440–64.
4. The astronomer Johann Friedrich Bessel in 1834. Just before his death in 1844 he decided

Sirius must be a binary system. In 1862 the American Alvan Clark looked through the largest telescope then existing and saw a faint point of light where Sirius B should be, confirming its existence. In 1915 Dr W. S. Adams of Mt Wilson Observatory made the necessary observations to learn the temperature of Sirius B, which is 8000°, half as much again as our sun's. It then began to be realized that Sirius B was an intensely hot star which radiated three to four times more heat and light per square foot than our sun. It then became possible to calculate the size of Sirius B, which is only three times the radius of the Earth, yet its mass was just a little less than that of our sun. A theory of white dwarfs then developed to account for Sirius B, and other white dwarfs were later discovered.

5. See previous note.
6. Aitken, R. G., *The Binary Stars*, Dover Publications, New York, 1964, pp. 240–1. The account of Sirius extends from p. 237 to p. 241.
7. 'Multiplicity of the Sirius System,' art. cit. (see above, Note 2).
8. *Mass Loss and Evolution in Close Binaries*, Copenhagen University, 1970, pp. 190–4. (A seminar held in Elsinore Castle, with Lauterborn as a participant.)
9. Op. cit. (Note 6 above).
10. Op. cit. (Note 3 above) Chapter 33.
11. See for instance the book *Interstellar Communication*, op. cit. (Note 1 above), an anthology with contributions from nineteen astronomers and scientists.
12. Ibid., p. 75.
13. Ibid., p. 92.
14. Ibid., p. 110.
15. Ibid., pp. 232–5.
16. Op. cit. (Note 3 above), pp. 440–64.
17. Ibid.
18. See for instance Pritchard, J. B., *Ancient Near Eastern Texts relating to the Old Testament*, Princeton University Press, 1955, p. 42, the introductory remarks to trans. of 'The Deluge' and also pp. 93–5, account of the Flood.
19. Griaule, M., and Dieterlen, G., 'Un Système Soudanais de Sirius', *Journal de la Société des Africainistes*, Tome XX, Fascicule 1, 1950, pp. 273–94. An English translation of this article follows Chapter One in this book.
20. Griaule, Marcel, and Dieterlen, Germaine. *Le Renard pâle* (Tome I, Fascicule 1), Institut d'Ethnologie, Musée de l'Homme, Palais de Chaillot, Place du Trocadéro, Paris 16° (75016 Paris), 1965. 544 pp.
21. Ibid., p. 529.
22. Nine references are given to Baize's publications, extending to 1938, and one given to Schatzman in *L'Astronomie*, 1956, pp. 364–9
23. *Le Renard pâle*, p. 478.
24. Ibid., pp. 480–1.   25. Ibid., pp. 480–1.   26. Ibid., p. 486.
27. Ibid., p. 481.   28. Ibid., p. 226.   29. Ibid., p. 264.
30. Ibid., p. 329.   31. Ibid., p. 292.   32. Ibid., p. 291.
33. Ibid., p. 292.   34. Ibid., p. 321.   35. Ibid., p. 321.
36. Ibid., p. 323.   37. Ibid., p. 323.
38. Aubrey, J., *Brief Lives*, Penguin, London, 1972. See entry for Harvey, William, pp. 290–1.
39. *Le Renard pâle*, p. 348.
40. Ibid., p. 287 n. 1.   41. Ibid., p. 141.   42. Ibid., p. 141.
43. Ibid., p. 141.   44. Ibid., pp. 102–4.   45. Ibid., p. 128.
46. Ibid., p. 163.   47. Ibid., p. 168.   48. Ibid., p. 170 n. 2.
49. Ibid., p. 276.   50. Ibid., p. 279, inc. n. 4.   51. Ibid., p. 280.
52. Ibid., p. 335.   53. Ibid., p. 470.   54. Ibid., p. 470.
55. Ibid., p. 470.   56. Ibid., p. 489.   57. Ibid., p. 323.
58. Ibid., p. 384.   59. Ibid., p. 384.   60. Ibid., p. 381.
61. Ibid., p. 381.   62. Ibid., p. 381.   63. Ibid., p. 287.
64. Ibid., p. 248.   65. Ibid., pp. 248–9.   66. Ibid., p. 249.
67. Ibid., p. 219.   68. Ibid., p. 440.   69. Ibid., p. 440.
70. Ibid., p. 477.   71. Ibid., p. 477.   72. Ibid., p. 475.
73. Ibid., p. 499 n. 2.

A Sudanese Sirius System

by

M. GRIAULE and G. DIETERLEN

Note: The following article is translated and published in its entirety. It is written for professional anthropologists and ethnographers, and is presented here for the reader who is sufficiently interested in the subject to wish to pursue the source material. It is, therefore, supplementary information, and is not essential for the reader who merely wishes to follow the argument.

FOREWORD

The indigenous knowledge about the Sirius system which is set forth in this chapter has been gathered from four Sudanese peoples: the Dogon in Bandiagara, the Bambara and the Bozo in Segou[1] and the Minianka in Koutiala.

The main investigation was carried out among the Dogon between 1946 and 1950, where the four major informants were:

Innekouzou Dolo, a woman aged between sixty-five and seventy, *ammayana* 'priestess of Amma', and soothsayer, living in the Dozyou-Orey quarter of Ogol-du-Bas (Lower Ogol Sanga-du-Haut (Upper Sanga). Tribe: Arou. Language: Sanga.

Ongnonlou Dolo, between sixty and sixty-five years old, patriarch of the village of Go, recently established by a group of Arou in the south-west of Lower Ogol. Language: Sanga.

Yébéné, fifty years old, priest of the Binou Yébéné of Upper Ogol, living in Bara (Upper Sanga). Tribe: Dyon. Language: Sanga.

Manda, forty-five years old, priest of the Binou Manda, living in Orosongo in Wazouba. Tribe: Dyon. Language: Wazouba.

The system as a whole was expounded by Ongnonlou, its various details by the other informants. Although he was not responsible for drawing up the Sigui calendar, Ongnonlou was acquainted with the principles behind it and, during the periods when the investigators were there, was able to obtain further information from the Arou at Yougo Dogorou on the one hand and, on the other, from the permanent steward of the supreme chieftain of the Arou at Arou-by-Ibi.[2] Ongnonlou is in fact patriarch of the family from which the next holder of the title will be designated when the next holiday comes around.

Ongnonlou's learning, within an extremely secret body of knowledge, thus represents an initial acquaintance or, to use a Bambara expression, a 'slight acquaintance', and this point should be kept in mind. Just as, for the layman, the star Sirius is the brightest star in the sky, attracts his gaze, and plays the major role in the computation of the Sigui, so the rules of the Sirius system as revealed to the initiated in the first instance are at once simplified in some parts and complicated in others, so as to divert the attention from calculations which are more secret by far.

It must therefore be understood, once and for all, that the system described here represents one phase of the revelations permitted to initiates who are top-ranking but not specifically responsible for the calculations to do with this part of the sky.

For our part, the documents gathered together have not given rise to any original hypothesis or research. They have been simply pieced together in such a way that the accounts of the four principal informants are merged into one and the same statement. The problem of knowing how, with no instruments at their disposal, men could know the movements and certain characteristics of virtually invisible stars has not been settled, nor even posed. It has seemed more to the point, under these special circumstances, to present the documents in the raw.

THE CALCULATION OF THE TIME OF THE SIGUI

Every sixty years[3] the Dogon hold a ceremony called the Sigui (ceremony). Its purpose is the renovation of the world, and it has been described at length by them in 1931.[4] Since the beginning of this investigation, we were faced with the question of determining the method used to calculate the period separating two Sigui ceremonies. The common notion, which dates back to the myth of creation, is that a fault in the Yougo rock, situated at the centre of the village of Yougo Dogorou,[5] lights up with a red glow in the year preceding the ceremony. This fault contains various altars, in particular busts of Andoumboulou (the name given to the people of small stature who formerly lived in the rocks), and a rock painting called *amma bara*, 'god helps', to which we shall refer later. Furthermore, and before this red glow appears, a spot situated outside the village becomes covered with elongated gourds of a type which no one would have sown.

When these signs are observed, an apparently simple procedure of calculation is carried out, solely by the people of Yougo Dogorou who belong to the Arou tribe:[6] the council of elders assesses the interval by means of thirty two-yearly drinking-bouts when beer made from millet is drunk; and the eldest elder marks up each bout with a cowrie shell.

These bouts are held about one month before the first rains, sometimes in May or June, in a tent or shelter pitched to the north of the village centre.[7] But this rule is only theoretical: between the last Sigui, celebrated at the beginning of the century, and 1931[8] there has been only one bout, halfway through the period; but the two-yearly cowries were set down and gathered into a pile representing the first thirty years. From 1931 onwards, the drinking bouts took place every two years. When the second pile consisting of fifteen cowries has been collected, the second Sigui of the twentieth century will be celebrated.[9]

According to Manda, the priest, the calculation of the Sigui is recorded above the door of the sanctuary of Binou by two figures made of millet pulp representing the god Amma and his son, Nommo, Instructor of the new world.[10] The first consists of a vertical oval – the egg of the world – and its major axis, Amma in the original darkness. In the right-hand half, each year is marked with a dot, starting from the bottom. When the seventh year comes round, a kind of trident is drawn on the outside, as an extension to the line of dots. The same thing is done on the left-hand side, in the order top-to-bottom. Fourteen years are counted in this way: the seven twin years during which the world was created, and to which a unit, symbolizing the whole, is added.[11] Diagrammatically speaking, the figure shows the god's last gesture, raising one hand and lowering the other, thereby showing that sky and earth are made.

This drawing is repeated four times, making it possible to reckon a period of sixty years; it is accompanied by the figure of the Instructor,[12] composed of two vertical legs supporting a head atop a long neck. During the first thirty years which are recorded by two ovals, the figure features only the right leg. During the second thirty-year period, the left leg is made a little longer each year in such a way that when the Sigui actually occurs it is the same length as the right leg. It is by allusion to this figure that people talk about the Sigui 'getting to its feet' during this latter period.

THE CALCULATION OF THE SIGUI CEREMONIES

When it is time for the Sigui, the elders gathered in the *täna tono* shelter at Yougo draw a symbol on the rock with red ochre (fig. i), which represents a *kanaga* mask;[13] this, in turn, represents the god Amma; a hole is made in the ground below it symbolizing the Sigui, and thus Amma in the egg of the world. In effect these two signs should be 'read' in the opposite order: Amma, in the shadow of the egg (the hole) reveals himself to men (the red design) in his creative posture (the mask depicts the god's final gesture, showing the universe.)[14]

Figure i. The *Kanaga* sign, connoting the sixty-year ceremonies, at Yougo Dogorou (indigenous painting)

The hole is also interpreted as the hole which must be dug to put seeds in. From this viewpoint the holes are arranged in series of three, connoting three Siguis, placed respectively beneath the sign of three seeds, after which they are named. Thus the Sigui at the beginning of this century was called *emme sigi*, the 'sorghum Sigui'; the next one will be called *yu sigi*, the 'millet Sigui'; and the one after *nu sigi*, the 'haricot Sigui'.

In theory, then, it would seem possible to record the Siguis using this simple method. In practice, the holes become obliterated and the painting, more often than not, is touched up instead of being reproduced and thus forming part of a countable series. But there is another figure painted on the façade of the sanctuaries which reveals rather more specific data; it is called *sigi lugu*, 'calculation of the Sigui', and consists of a line of vertical chevrons, the notches of which are painted alternately black, red, and white; each colour corresponds to a seed, the first to millet, the second to the haricot and the third to sorghum (fig. ii). This line can be read in two ways: Either by using just one counting system (for example the left-hand one), whereby each notch is the equivalent of twenty years; here, the notch upon which a Sigui actually falls is carried over to the following series: or, by taking the whole figure and counting twenty years for each notch, regardless of its positioning (the right column in fig. ii); here, the notch upon which a Sigui falls is recounted.

More consistent evidence of the celebration of the Sigui is provided by the large wooden mask, whose carving is one of the major concrete purposes of the ceremony. This mask – usually of considerable size[15] – is seldom used, and is kept in some shelter or hideaway in the rocks, along with those which have been carved at previous ceremonies. The care with which these masks are treated – for in some ways they are the village archives – means that it is not uncommon to come across series of three or four of them, the oldest of which date back, respectively, to 1780 and 1720,[16] give or take a year or two. In exceptional cases, when the shelter has been well selected and under constant surveillance, the series may be longer still; thus at Ibi, in 1931, nine poles were counted, and

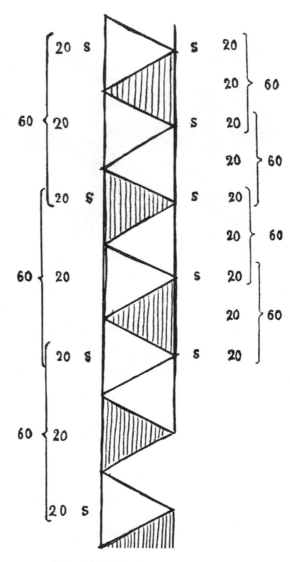

Figure ii. The calculation of the Sigui

these must have succeeded three more which had been reduced to a few fragments and piles of dust and were still visible; as were the special places earmarked for them at the back of the shelter, all perfectly protected from the damp, vermin and animals. The oldest in the series of nine, which showed a continuous progression of ageing in the course of time,[17] thus date from the beginning of the fifteenth century; and if the three others are taken into account, the remnants of the earliest would date back to the first half of the thirteenth century.[18]

It is not easy to come across material evidence dating back further than the traces of these poles at Ibi. But there is another object, existing in a single edition, which is fashioned during these Sigui ceremonies and which might also, be a significant milestone in the calculation process. With the festival in mind, each regional Hogon, as well as the supreme Hogon of Arou, has a fermentation stand woven out of baobab fibres; this stand is used during the preparation of the first ritual beer. This beer is distributed in small quantities to each family; it is then added to everybody's cup, and thus ensures the homogeneousness of the beer drunk by the community. In addition to this, all the other fermentation stands are associated, by contact, with the principal one, which is exceptionally large: the lid measures 40 cm. (16 in.) in diameter, and the four 'pompoms' are the size of the normal object. As a result, it can only enter the large jars.

These objects are kept in the Hogon's house where they are hung from the main beam, and thus form a permanent sequence. Ongnonlou saw six or seven of them in the official residence of the Hogon of Sanga; the latter, one of the oldest men in Dogon country, has it that his great-great-grandfather had seen eight others which preceded the oldest in the present series.[19] Assuming a total of fourteen objects for the Sanga chieftainry, the first – which almost certainly does not denote the first ceremony held in this region – would have been woven in the twelfth century, if one reckons on the period separating two Siguis being sixty years.

Again, Ongnonlou counted a series of eight in the house of the supreme Hogon of the Arou, at Arou-by-Ibi. But he adds that the number 'should' be twenty-four, although he cannot explain if there is an ideal series which a complete sequence would aim for, or which, conversely, would correspond to reality if the fibres had not turned to dust.[20]

The methods described above for both keeping track of the ceremonies and for calculating the intervals between Siguis are simple and tend to be mnemotechnic. For the initiate they simply act as understudies for other more complex practices and knowledge to do with the Sirius system. The Dogon names for this star – sigi tolo, star of the Sigui;[21] or yasigi tolo, star of Yasigui[22] – sufficiently indicate its relation with the ceremony of the renovation of the world which takes place every sixty years.

Sirius, however, is not the basis of the system: it is one of the foci of the orbit of a tiny star called Digitaria, po tolo,[23] or star of the Yourougou,[24] yurugu tolo, which plays a crucial role, and which, unaided as it were, hogs the attention of male initiates.

This system is so important that, unlike the systems of other parts of the sky, it has not been assigned to any particular group. In effect the Ono and Dommo tribes govern the stars, the former including Venus rising among its attributes, the latter Orion's belt. The sun should be assigned to the most powerful tribe, the Arou; but so as not to be guilty of excess, the Arou handed the sun over to the Dyon, who are less noble, and hung on to the moon. As far as the star Digitaria and the system to which it belongs are concerned, these are common to all men.

THE ORBIT OF DIGITARIA

The orbit described by Digitaria around Sirius is perpendicular to the horizon, and this position is alluded to in one of the most common ceremonies in which masks play a part:

laba ozu pǫ
ozugo pǫ ya
(the path of the mask (is) straight (vertical)
this path runs straight)

But if one takes the pun into account – familiar to the initiated – between *po*:[25] 'straight' and *pŏ* : Digitaria, the translation becomes:

the path of the mask (is the star) Digitaria
the path runs (like) Digitaria.

A figure made out of millet pulp (fig. iii) in the room with the daïs in the house of the Hogon of Arou gives an idea of this trajectory, which is drawn horizontally: the oval (lengthwise diameter about 100 cm. = 40 in.) contains to the left a small circle, Sirius (S), above which another circle (DP) with its centre shows Digitaria in its closest position. At the other end of the oval a small cluster of dots (DL) represent the star when it is farthest from Sirius. When Digitaria is close to Sirius, the latter becomes brighter; when it is at its most distant from Sirius, Digitaria gives off a twinkling effect, suggesting several stars to the observer.[26]

Figure iii. The trajectory of the star Digitaria around Sirius

This trajectory symbolizes excision and circumcision, an operation which is represented by the closest and furthest passage of Digitaria to Sirius. The left part of the oval is the foreskin (or clitoris), the right part is the knife (fig. iv).

This symbolism is also expressed by a figure used for other performances[27] (fig. v). A horizontal figure rests on a vertical axis which connects two circles: S (Sirius) and D (Digitaria); the centre of the figure is a circle T, which represents the trajectory of D. The line E is the penis, the hook B' the foreskin. Two horns hinge on the circle and reproduce once again the two parts of the trajectory (cf. fig. iv): A, the knife; B, the foreskin. Thus the Sirius system is associated with the practices of renovating people, and, consequently – in accordance with the Black mentality – with the ceremonies which celebrate the renovation of the world.

Figure iv. The symbolism of the trajectory of Digitaria. S: Sirius, A: knife, B: foreskin

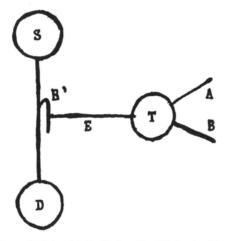

Figure v. The symbolism of Digitaria. S: Sirius, D: Digitaria, T: trajectory of Digitaria, A: knife, E: penis, B and B': foreskin

The period of the orbit is counted double, that is, one hundred years,[28] because the Siguis are convened in pairs of 'twins', so as to insist on the basic principle of twin-ness.[29] It is for this reason that the trajectory is called *munu*, from the root *monye* 'to reunite', from which the word *muno* is derived, which is the title given to the dignitary who has celebrated (reunited) two Siguis.

According to Dogon mythology, before the discovery of Digitaria the supreme chief was sacrificed at the end of the seventh year of his reign (the seventh harvest). This was the only computation known about; the year-unit had not then been established. The spiritual and material principles of the victim were conveyed to Digitaria – to regenerate the victim – whose existence was known but whose features had not been revealed to man, because the star was invisible.

This was the rule for forty-nine years for the first seven chiefs who thus nourished the star, and enabled it to renovate the world periodically. But, having discovered the star, the eighth chief resolved to avoid the fate of his predecessors: with his son's complicity, he feigned death, lay dormant for a few months and reappeared before the chief who had succeeded him; he announced that he had been to Digitaria, knew its secrets, and that, from then onwards, every Hogon would reign for sixty years – the period which would later separate one Sigui from the next.[30] Restored to office, he raised the level of the sky which, hitherto, had been so close to the earth that it could be touched,[31] and he completely revised the method of calculating time, and the method of reckoning.

Until that time the ceremonies celebrating the renovation of the world had in fact taken place every seventh harvest;[32] the Hogon made his calculations on the basis of five-day periods, a unit which established the week as it still is today, and five harvest cycles. And as he was eighth in line, he counted eight cycles, in other words forty years, and the number forty became the basis for computation: the month had forty days, the year forty weeks (of five days each). But the Hogon lived sixty years, a number which was interpreted as the sum of forty (basis of calculation) and twenty (the twenty fingers and toes, symbolizing the person and thus, in the highest sense of the word, the chief). Thus sixty became the basis for calculations[33] and it was first applied to establish the period of time separating two Siguis. Although the orbit of Digitaria takes approximately fifty years and although it corresponds to the first seven reigns of seven years respectively, it none the less computes the sixty years which separate two ceremonies.[34]

As well as its movement in space, Digitaria also revolves (rotates) upon itself over the period of one year and this revolution is honoured during the celebration of the *bado* rite. On this occasion it ejects from its three spirals the beings and the things which it contains. This day is called *badyu*, 'surly father', because it is marked by a general movement of the world which upsets people and places them in an unsure relationship with themselves and with each other.

THE ORIGINS AND FEATURES OF DIGITARIA

The eighth Hogon instructed his people in the features of the star, and, more generally, of the Sirius system.

Sirius appears red to the eye, Digitaria white. The latter lies at the origin of things. 'God created *Digitaria* before any other star'.[35] It is the 'egg of the world', *aduno tal*, the infinitely tiny and, as it developed, it gave birth to everything that exists, visible or invisible.[36] It is made up of three of the four basic elements: air, fire and water. The element earth is replaced by metal.[37] To start with, it was just a seed of *Digitaria exilis*,[38] *põ*, called euphemistically *kize uzi*, 'the little thing',[39] consisting of a central nucleus which ejected ever larger seeds or shoots in a conical spiral motion (fig. vi). The first seven seeds or shoots are represented graphically by seven lines, increasing in length, within the sac formed in turn by an oval symbolizing the egg of the world.

The entire work of Digitaria is summarized in a drawing whose various parts are carried out in the following order:[40] a vertical line issues from the oval – the first shoot to emerge from the sac; another segment, the second shoot, takes up a crosswise position, and thus supplies the four cardinal points: the stage of the world. The straightness of these two segments symbolizes the continuity of things, their perseverance in one state. Last, a third shoot, taking the place of the first, gives it the form of an oval which is open in its lower section, and surrounds the base of the vertical segment. The curved form, as opposed to the straight, suggests the transformation and progress of things. The personage thus obtained, called the 'life of the world', is the created being, the agent, the microcosm summarizing the universe.

In its capacity as the heavy embryo of a world issued each year, Digitaria is repres-

Figure vi. The origin of the spiral of creation (indigenous drawing: actual size)

ented in Wazouba either by a dot or by a sac enveloping a concentric circle of ten dots (the eight ancestral Nommos and the initial couple of Nommo). Its continual movement produces beings whose souls emerge at intervals from the dots and are guided towards the star Sorghum[41] which sends them on to Nommo. This movement is copied by the rhombus which disperses the creation of the Yourougou in space. Six figures are arranged around the circle, as if ejected from it (fig. vii):[42]

 a two-pronged fork: trees;
 a stem with four diagonal lines: small millet;
 four dots arranged as a trapezium: cow with its head marked by a short line;[43]
 four diverging lines starting from the base of a bent stem: domestic animals;
 four dots and a line: wild animals;
 an axis flanked by four dots: plants and their foliage.[44]

The original work is likewise symbolized by a filter-basket made of straw called *nun goro*, 'bean cap'. This utensil consists of a sheath in the form of a continuous helical spiral, the centre of which starts at the bottom.[45] The spiral supports a network of double radii.[46] The spiral and the helix are the initial vortical motion of the world; the radii represent the inner vibration of things.

Originally, then, Digitaria is a materialized, productive motion. Its first product was an extremely heavy substance which was deposited outside the cage of movement represented by the filter-basket.[47] The mass thus formed brought to mind a mortar twice as big as the ordinary utensil used by women.[48] According to the version told to the men, this mortar has three compartments: the first contains the aquatic beings, the second, terrestrial beings, and the third, the creatures of the air. In reality the star is conceived of as a thick oval forming a backcloth from which issues a spiral with three whorls (the three compartments).

According to the version instructed to the women, the compartments are four in number and contain grain, metal, vegetables and water. Each compartment is in turn made up of twenty compartments; the whole contains the eighty fundamental elements.

The star is the reservoir and the source of everything: 'It is the granary for everything in the world.'[49] The contents of the star-receptacle are ejected by centrifugal force, in the form of infinitesimals comparable to the seeds of *Digitaria exilis* which undergo rapid development: 'The thing which goes (which) emerges outside (the star) becomes as

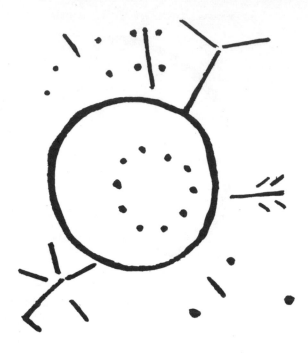

Figure vii. The star Digitaria (indigenous drawing: actual size[50])

large as it every day.'[51] In other words, what issues from the star increases each day by a volume equal to itself.

Because of this role, the star which is considered to be the smallest thing in the sky is also the heaviest: 'Digitaria is the smallest thing there is. It is the heaviest star.'[52] It consists of a metal called *sagala*,[53] which is a little brighter than iron and so heavy 'that all earthly beings combined cannot lift it'. In effect the star weighs the equivalent of 480 donkey-loads[54] (about 38,000 kg. = 85,000 lb.), the equivalent of all seeds, or of all the iron on earth,[55] although, in theory, it is the size of a stretched ox-skin or a mortar.

THE POSITION OF DIGITARIA

The orbit of Digitaria is situated at the centre of the world, 'Digitaria is the axis of the whole world,'[56] and without its movement no other star could hold its course. This means that it is the master of ceremonies of the celestial positions; in particular it governs the position of Sirius, the most unruly star; it separates it from the other stars by encompassing it with its trajectory.

OTHER STARS IN THE SIRIUS SYSTEM

But Digitaria is not Sirius's only companion: the star *emme ya*, Sorghum-Female, is larger than it, four times as light (in weight), and travels along a greater trajectory in the same direction and in the same time as it (fifty years). Their respective positions are such that the angle of the radii is at right angles. The positions of this star determine various rites at Yougo Dogorou. Sorghum-Female is the seat of the female souls of all living or future beings.[57] It is euphemism that describes them as being in the waters of family pools: the star throws out two pairs of radii (beams) (a female figure) which, on reaching the surface of the waters, catch the souls.

It is the only star which emits these beams which have the quality of solar rays because it is the 'sun of women', *nyān nay*, 'a little sun', *nay dagi*. In fact it is accompanied by a satellite which is called the 'star of Women', *nyān tolo*, or Goatherd, *enegirin* (literally: goat-guide), a term which is a pun on *emme girin* (literally: sorghum-guide). Nominally then it would be more important as the guide of Sorghum-Female. Furthermore, there is some confusion with the major star, the Goatherd, which is familiar to everyone.

The star of women is represented by a cross,[58] a dynamic sign which calls to mind the movement of the whole Sirius system (fig. viii).

Sorghum-Female is outlined by three points, a male symbol of authority, surrounded by seven dots, or four (female) plus three (male) which are the female soul and the male soul (fig. ix).

Taken as a whole, the Sorghum-Female system is represented by a circle containing a cross (the four cardinal directions), whose centre consists of a round spot (the star itself) and whose arms serve as a receptacle for the male and female souls of all beings. This figure, called the 'Sorghum-Female pattern', *emme ya tõnu*, occupies one of the centres of an ellipse called 'the pattern of men', *anam tõnu*, consisting of a full line called the 'goatherd's course', *enegirin ozu*, flanked by two dotted lines, the outside of which is the path of the male souls, and the inside the path of the female souls (fig. x).

Figure viii. The star of women

Figure ix. The star Sorghum-Female

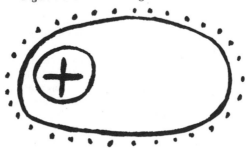

Figure x. The Sorghum-Female system

The Sirius–Digitaria–Sorghum system is represented by a 'pattern of the Sigui', *sigi tõnu*, consisting of an oval (the world) in which one of the centres is Sirius. The two alternate positions of Digitaria at the time of the Sigui are marked and the positions at the same moment of Sorghum-Female are marked on two concentric circles encompassing Sirius.

Figure xi. The course of the stars of the Sirius system

The Sirius system as a whole is drawn at Sanga in different ways, in particular at the *bado* ceremony. On the façade of the residence of the great Hogon of Arou and inside the official houses assigned to the Hogons of Dyon, the course of these stars is represented by 'the pattern of the master of the star of the Shoemaker', *dyãn tolo bãna tõnu* (fig. xi), composed of a vertical axis supporting, two-thirds of the way up, a bulge, Sirius (S), and broken at its base to form an elongated foot jutting to the left at right-angles, the course of the star of the Shoemaker (C). It is topped by a semi-oval whose arms extend quite low down; the meeting-point (D) with this oval symbolizes Digitaria, whose course is traced by the right arm (F). But this arm is also the star of women whilst the left arm is Sorghum-Female (E). The lower part of the axis (SC), longer than the upper part (SD), reminds one that the Shoemaker (C) is farther than Sirius is from the other stars, and revolves in the opposite direction.

Thus it is that during the *bado* ceremony the oldest woman of the family draws, at the entrance to the house, the 'pattern of the world of women', *nyãn aduno tõnu*, [59] or 'pattern of the top and bottom of the world', *aduno dale doñule tõnu* (fig. xii).

It consists of an oval, the egg of the world, containing nine signs:

Da. – Digitaria. The open curve on the right indicates the acceptance of all the substances and matter placed in it by the Creator.

Db. – Digitaria in its second position. The open oval below marks the exit of the matter which spreads across the world; A and B also indicate the extreme positions of Digitaria in relation to Sirius.

Figure xii. The Sirius system

E. – The star Sorghum-Female, counterpart of Digitaria. As it is the 'sun of women', it is placed at the centre of the egg, like the sun at the centre of the solar system. The oval is framed by two times two small vertical lines symbolizing the rays emitted by the star.

S. – Sirius, 'star of the Sigui' or 'star of Yasigui'. The sign, so placed that it materializes the liaison worked by Sirius between the two stars described above, consists of a kind of X with one right arm – the ant, *key* – dividing a curved arm, the lower part of which is Yasigui, and the other part the piece of the organ which is detached during excision. Although female, the ant is here depicted by a straight rod, as if it were a man. This marks its domination of Yasigui's feminity, for Yasigui is maimed.

R. – The Yourougou. A hook, made up of a circular arc and a straight segment indicates that the first movement of the Yourougou describes a curve which goes around the sky; falling short of the goal, it descended directly, as is shown by the right-hand segment which is also the piece of bared placenta[60].

In effect, with Digitaria as the egg of the world (see earlier) this latter was split into two twin placentas which were to give birth respectively to a pair of Nommo Instructors. What happened, however, was that a single male being emerged from one of the placentas; in order to find his twin, this being tore off a piece of this placenta, which became earth. This intervention upset the order of creation: he was transformed into an animal, the pale fox, *yuruga*,[61] and communicated his own impurity to the earth, which rendered it dry and barren. But the remedy to this situation was the sacrifice, to the sky, of one of the Nommo Instructors which had issued from the other placenta, and the descent of his twin to earth with life-giving, purifying rain.[62] The destiny of Yourougou is to pursue his twin to the end of time – the twin being his female soul at the same time. On the mythical level, Digitaria is thus considered to be the Yourougou held in space by Nommo, relentlessly revolving around Sirius, or Yasigui in other words, and never capable of reaching it.

N. – The figure of the Nommo consists of a vertical segment, Nommo in person, upon which, and slightly below the upper edge, rests a line broken into three unequal parts; the first is the seat of future female souls; the second the seat of the souls of the dead; and the third the seat of living souls.

Fa. – The star of Women, *nyăn tolo*. An embryonic spiral calls to mind that it is the satellite of Sorghum-Female.

Fb. – The 'sign of women', *nyăn tŏnu*, consists of a diagonal line, man, cut by a line which ends in a convex curve, woman. This shows the contact between the sexes.[63] The rod is upright with astonishment at the sight of creation, which started with the system of women. Woman is a heavy-bellied profile, ready to give birth.

Fc. – The sex of women is depicted by an oval which is open in the lower part, womb-world, ready for procreation, gaping downwards to spread the seeds.

THE SIRIUS SYSTEM AMONG THE BAMBARA

The Bambara call Sirius 'the star of the foundation', *sigi dolo*, which is the same term used by the Dogon, and like them they call the star Digitaria *fini dolo*.[64] The expression *fă dolo fla*, 'the two stars of knowledge', is generally attributed to it, because 'it represents in the sky the invisible body of Faro', conceived as a pair of twins.[65] This name also implies that the star is the seat of all learning.

The Sirius system is depicted on the chequered blanket called *koso wala*, 'coloured picture', consisting of ten sequences made up of some thirty rectangles coloured alternately indigo and white which symbolize, respectively, darkness and light, earth and sky, and, in Bambara mythology, Pemba and Faro. Scattered throughout there are twenty-three rectangles with different patterns of small stripes placed in the direction of the thread, alternating the indigo, white and red. Twenty of them represent stars or constellations; the other three respectively represent the rainbow, hailstones and rain. The fifth sequence in the centre, in which there is no coloured rectangle, symbolizes the Milky Way. The ninth sequence, at one end, contains five black (not indigo) rectangles which point to the 'fifth creation, in darkness, which will occur with the arrival of the waters to come'.[66]

Sigi dolo is first depicted alone 'in the cold season and in impurity' by the ninth rectangle (third sequence); it is next depicted flanked by *fā dolo fla* (two red lines) in the fifteenth rectangle (eighth sequence).[67]

In Bambara mythology, Sirius represents Mousso Koroni Koundyé, twin of Pemba, maker of the earth, a mythical woman whom he chased through space and was never able to catch. In every respect Mousso Koroni Koundyé is comparable to Yasigui.[68] She inaugurated circumcision and excision and, as a result, Sirius is the star of circumcision, for both Bambara and Dogon alike.

THE SIRIUS SYSTEM AMONG THE BOZO

The system is also known to the Bozo, who call Sirius *sima kayne* (literally: sitting trouser) and its satellite *toñõ ñalema* (literally: eye star).

Notes

1. A member of the Bambara living in Bandiagara also confirmed the most important features of the system.
2. Various pieces of information were supplied direct by the people of Yougo-Dogorou in 1931, 1936, 1948, 1949 and 1950.
3. We ourselves accepted this figure in 1931 and it can safely be retained for the time being.
4. Cf. Griaule, *Masques Dogons*, Travaux et Mémoires de l'Institut d'Ethnologie de l'Université de Paris, vol. xxxiii (1938), chapter 1.
5. Ibid., pp. 167 ff., where this fault in the rock is described in detail.
6. The Dogon are divided into four tribes, each of which had a different role at one time. The four are the Arou (soothsayers), the Dyon (farmers), the Ono (merchants), and the Dommo (who were confused in this respect with the Ono).
7. The spot is called *tǎna tõne*; cf. Griaule, op. cit., p. 171.
8. Or 1933.
9. Probably in 1961 or 1963, if this computation is valid. (The information came from a prominent member of the Yougo aged between fifty-five and sixty.) It is a matter of common knowledge that the next Sigui will not be celebrated for another ten years or so (we were told this in late 1950).
10. These figures are described in M. Griaule and G. Dieterlen, 'Signes graphiques soudanais' *L'Homme*, 3 (Paris: Hermann).
11. The Dogon count a week of five days as six days, just as in French a week of seven days is referred to as 'eight days' and a fortnight as 'fifteen days'.
12. For a discussion of this substitute for God the Creator cf. Griaule, *Dieu d'eau*, Paris, Editions du Chêne, 1948.
13. For a description of the mask cf. *Masques Dogons*, pp. 470 ff.
14. This information came from a prominent member of the Yougo Dogorou. According to all the initiates, the *kanaga* mask represents on the one hand the static gesture of the god, and on the other hand the swastika, through the repetition of the same gestures at an angle of 90° to the first. The second figure represents the god whirling round as he comes down to earth to reorganize the world in chaos.
15. The largest known example is ten metres long. It was brought back by the Dakar–Djibouti Mission and given to the Musée de l'Homme in Paris; cf. M. Griaule, *Masques Dogons*, pp. 234 ff.
16. Thus the Yendoumman Damma niche contains three specimens; the Yendoumman Banama contains four; the Yendoumman Da, three; the Barna, four; and the Ennguel-du-Bas, three. Cf. M. Griaule, *Masques Dogons*, pp. 242 ff.
17. Ibid., pp. 245 ff.

18. For another index that enables us to establish the minimum age of some of the villages, cf. Griaule, 'Le Verger des Ogol (Soudan français)', *Journal de la Société des Africainistes*, xvii, pp. 65–79.

19. The Hogon of Sanga, who was enthroned in 1935, was thus the oldest man in the area at that date (i.e. the oldest of the Dyon). If we agree that he was born in about 1855, his great-grandfather, who, he claims, was very old when he himself was a young goatherd, was probably born between 1770 and 1780.

   Each fermenting-receptacle is evidence of the Sigui for which it was woven and is known as such. This means that these objects form a sequence that is considered by the people to be more than purely numerical.

20. The period indicated by a series of this kind would be 1,440 years by the time the next Sigui came round. It would apparently correspond to the sequence of sixty reigns in which each Hogon appears and which itself covers a period of about 1,500 years. The supreme chiefs of the Arou tribe are in fact chosen when still young, unlike the practice current among the other tribes. The average reign is likely to be twenty-five years.

21. *Sigō dolo* in Bambara.

22. For a discussion of this mythical figure, who corresponds to the Bambaras' Mousso Koroni, see later in this article.

23. The *pŏ*, *Digitaria coilis* is commonly called '*fonio*' in West Africa.

24. For a discussion of this mythical figure see later in text.

25. In the song the vowel becomes slightly nasal.

26. The saying that 'if you look at Digitaria it's as if the world were spinning (*pŏ tolo yeneñe aduno gŏnode ginwo*) was probably coined to convey this impression.

27. Cf. M. Griaule, 'Signes graphiques des Dogon', in M. Griaule and G. Dieterlen, 'Signes graphiques soudanais', *L'Homme*, 3 (Paris, Hermann).

28. In the system of notation based on the figure 80 this number is called '80 and 20'. The period of fifty years is very close to that of Sirius's companion. Cf. P. Baize, 'Le Compagnon de Sirius', *L'Astronomie* (Sept. 1931), p. 385.

29. For a discussion of this principle cf. Griaule, *Dieu d'eau*, pp. 183 ff.

30. After this reform the Hogons' sacrifice was replaced by animal sacrifice.

31. This belief still obtains among the Dogon, and also among many other peoples; cf. Griaule, *Jeux Dogons*, *Travaux et Mémoires de l'Institut d'Ethnologie* de l'Université de Paris, vol. xxxii.

32. For a discussion of the symbolism attached to the number 7 cf. Griaule, *Dieu d'eau*, p. 60.

33. The figure 60 is the old base of the system of notation still used in the Sudan for a number of ritual calculations. In several Sudanese languages 60 is known as the 'Mandé calculation', because the system is believed to have spread from Mandé. Nowadays the various districts use 80 as a base for their calculations. Cf. G. Dieterlen, *Essai sur la religion bambara* (Paris: PUF).

34. There is a contradiction here that has not so far been solved. On the one hand the Dogon accept that Digitaria is in orbit for fifty years and this figure governs the way the Sigui is calculated. On the other hand Siguis are held at sixty-year intervals. Nevertheless, it should be noted that the date of the last Sigui, which was celebrated at the very beginning of the twentieth century, was allegedly brought forward. Does this indicate that the date was regularly brought forward for each ceremony? The uninitiated would thus be kept going with the idea that the official period was sixty years and that, for accidental reasons, it happened to be reduced to a half-century.

   The foregoing myth is given here as an indication of the changes or combinations in the system of computation that occur in the 'history' of the black peoples.

35. *pŏ tolo amma tolo lā woy mānu.*

36. According to Innekouzou, *pŏ tolo*, 'Digitaria star', has a hidden etymological derivation from *polo to*, 'profound beginning'.

37. See below.

38. The *Digitaria* seed is made up of four parts, only one of which, the outer casing, has a name, *kobu*. The other three are known as *yolo*.

39. This expression is always being used by Manda, whose extremely punctilious mind thus avoids even mentioning the name of one of the most basic tabus of the totemic priests.

40. For further details cf. Griaule, 'Signes graphiques des Dogons'. See also Griaule, 'L'image du monde au Soudan', *Journal de la Société des Africainistes*, xix, 2, pp. 81–9.

41. Cf. below.
42. They are counted clockwise, starting from the highest figure on the right-hand side.
43. This cow is an avatar of the Nommo.
44. It should be remembered that the Dogon, like the other black peoples, use several different symbols or even several different sequences of images to express a single idea or object. Conversely, a symbol often represents several different things.
45. The shape of this basket is roughly the same as the outline of a mortar.
46. On the system of symbols represented by this basket.
47. It is understood that Digitaria was the same shape as a basket, but was not a basket.
48. The initiates have a different idea of these dimensions.
49. *aduno kize fŭ guyoy.*
50. This drawing is executed in Wazouba inside the sanctuaries during the festival of *agu.*
51. *kize wogonode para gwăy wokuwogo dega bay tuturu byede.*
52. *pŏ tolu kize woy wo gayle be dedemogo wo sige be.*
53. This has the same root as *sagatara*, 'strong, powerful' (native etymology).
54. The number 480 is the product of the base number 80 times the number of tens in the base number 60, which was formerly in use. It is used here to symbolize the largest number of all.
55. Versions of, respectively, Innekouzou, Manda and Ongnonlou.
56. *pŏ tolo aduno fŭ dudın gowoy.*
57. The men have two twin-souls of different sexes. Cf. Griaule, *Dieu d'eau*, pp. 183 ff. The same idea is current among the Bambara, cf. Dieterlen, *Essai sur la religion Bambara*, chapter 3.
58. The figures reproduced here are used in Wazouba.
59. This figure was taught to Ongnonlou in August 1950, by the Hogon of Sanga.
60. Yourougou, who was born a single being, is fated to pursue the female soul that is his ideal twin to the end of time. In particular he tried to seize it by snatching away from his mother, the Earth, part of the placenta that emerged after he was born, because he thought it was his twin soul.
61. *Vulpes pallida.*
62. Cf. Griaule and Dieterlen, 'Le harpe-luth des Dogon', *Journal de la Société des Africainistes*, xx, 2.
63. A man could just as well call it *anam tŏñu*, 'drawing of men'.
64. *Fini*, from which *fonio*, a word used throughout Sudanese Africa, is derived, is the same word as *pŏ.*
65. The expression may possibly indicate the Sirius and Digitaria grouping, or Digitaria and another companion. For Faro, or Fanro, the Bambara equivalent of the Dogon Nommo, cf. Dieterlen, *Essai sur la religion Bambara*, chapters 1 and 2.
66. Cf. ibid., chapter 1. This refers to a future world that will be heralded by flood-waters.
67. The *koso wata* blanket, which is worn by elderly initiates at the major Bambara institutions (*dyo*), belongs to a series of eight ritual blankets with patterns and colours representing mythology, cosmology and the social structure. They are used at night or worn as clothing, depending on the status, duties and aims of the wearer. Apart from their economic value, they are evidence of the wearer's knowledge. Their ritual use is plain, particularly during marriage ceremonies. The Dogon have similar blankets. The one known as *yanunu* represents a sort of very rough map of the world showing the most important stars.
   For a discussion of the way the Bambara and Dogon set great store by weaving and the various cotton strips, cf. Dieterlen, *Essai*, chapter 5, and Griaule, *Dieu d'eau.*
68. For a discussion of the parallels between Mousso Koroni Koundyé and Yasigui, cf. Dieterlen, *Essai*, chapter 1. For a discussion of Mousso Koroni Koundyé, Pemba and Faro, cf. S. de Ganay, 'Aspect de mythologie et de symbolique bambara', *Journal de psychologie normale et pathologique* (April/June 1949); Dieterlen, *Essai*, chapters 1 and 2.

The Sirius Question is Rephrased

INTRODUCTION

We shall turn now to the star Sirius in history. What was its importance, if any, in ancient religions? Is there evidence from the ancient cultures that the mysterious details of the Sirius system were known to others than the Dogon tribe? And can we discover where the Dogon got their information?

I must warn the reader that Part Two is difficult, by the nature of its subject-matter. I have tried to make it readable, but beg the reader's indulgence if I have not succeeded. It is exciting material and the reader should stick with it. I am certain he will come out at the end of the tunnel with a great deal of amazement. For the ancient cultures are far more bizarre than the ordinary person is generally led to expect.

CHAPTER TWO

A Fairytale

Once there was a beautiful bright star named Sothis, as fine as any goddess. She had long held a dominant position in the sky and been admired by all for her beauty. But of late she had felt unwell; indeed, it distinctly seemed to her that she felt her life ebbing away. Night by night she fell further from her high, proud place in the sky – closer to the skyline and what must surely be her certain death. Failing, failing, she clung to any companion star she could find, only to discover that they too felt this deathly weakness, and were sinking into a kind of sweet sleep. What was she to do? She felt her strength going nightly; she could hardly shine the way she wished. Once she had been as glamorous, as scintillating a queen of the night sky as ever had been seen. And now she felt she was as worthless as any old woman, her position at the centre of things gone, and her beauty fading steadily. . . . Towards the end she wept bitterly and her eyes reddened with the shame of her coming eclipse. She was so ill, her discomfort so acute. She was almost glad to welcome her fate, and that terrible line of earth and hills which she had dreaded, at last devoured her brilliant presence entirely. The night came and she was no more. Beneath the earth she rested in the balm of death.

But because this queen of the sky had been good during her ascendancy and had not been too haughty or vulgar, there were many admirers of her beauty to mourn her passing. Down on the lowly earth moved less brilliant mortals. Many nights they had stood in awe of the beautiful Sothis when she was in her prime. Some, indeed, had watched her birth when, red as a baby from the womb or as the Sun when he rises daily, this bright and beautiful immortal (or so she had seemed) had first flashed the most piercing and glittering rays of her incomparable presence sideways across the earth – seeming almost to scorch the very ground with her flaming beauty. This first appearance had been brief, for immediately behind her had come the all-engrossing grandeur of the great Sun himself. Heedless of Sothis, he soon washed the sky white with his splendour. All the stars dissolved like tiny drops of milk, lost when their bowl is suddenly filled to overflowing. So great was the Sun, so irresistible his presence – he whom some compared to a great wild bull bellowing and lording it over the heavens and the earth alike. But every night the Sun retired to his resting place, and night by night the flaming goddess Sothis entranced and bewitched mortal men, as she rose steadily higher and grew to great perfection. And further and further ahead of the Sun she rose each night.

But with her absence, how barren, how bleak, the sky now seemed. The disappearance of this renowned beauty from the vault of the heavens seemed such an unbearable deprivation. How the goddess was missed! Many mortal men shed bitter tears not to see the beauty who had infatuated them with her glancing eyes, her winsome smile, her slim waist and delicate feet. Were they never again to see her light tread in the celestial round dance of the stars?

Day followed night, and the sorrow of many became soothed by time's healing wings, which slowly fold themselves around the sufferer in invisible layers of sleep, forgetfulness, and the new interests which life must bring. The beautiful Sothis, though mourned, was lost only to the sight. For all remembered her, and that image of her burned into memory was so glorious, that to expect her actual presence came to seem almost too much to ask of many-hued, shifting, and various Fate.

Seventy days had elapsed. Hope had long since been abandoned to acceptance; sorrow had become numb. A shepherd had gone out before sunrise to his lambs now fully six months old. The Sun would not long be delayed, it was approaching the time of daybreak. The shepherd looked towards the skyline in the east. And as he looked, he saw the horizon burn with a refulgent fire, and the shimmering red birth of the goddess. It was she, it must be she! No other star had that aura, such a penetrating persona. The shepherd stood transfixed; his eyes were seared by this fresh star, dripping it seemed, with the waters of life, and aflame also with the fiery resurgence of its renewed existence. As the quick Sun behind her moved up to erase Sothis's tantalizingly brief appearance, the shepherd turned and ran to the nearest settlement. 'Awake! Awake! The goddess has returned! She is reborn, immortal, come back from death!' And all the devotees assembled with excitement and renewed hope. They heard the tale, saw for themselves the next morning, and they instituted a yearly celebration. This celebration exists to this day, and many are the temples, many are the priests, who gather in the month of July throughout all our land of Egypt to witness the much-heralded yearly rebirth of the great Sothis, Mother Isis, bestower of concord and blessings to her people. And in honour of her seventy days spent in the underworld, we have instituted the seventy-day embalming and mummification rites for our own dead, as it is pious and indeed right that we should do.

*　　*　　*

I wrote this fairytale, from the point of view of an ancient Egyptian priest, in order to convey to the reader not only certain facts but also certain equally important and, unfortunately, extinct emotions. For the attitudes and feelings of ancient peoples are just as important as the dry description of what facts they believed.

Sothis was the ancient Egyptian name for Sirius as it was spelt by the Greeks. The Egyptians had a Sothic calendar and the first appearance of Sirius on the eastern horizon just before the sun – after 70 days in the Duat (Underworld) – was what is called the heliacal rising (or 'with-the-sun' rising) of Sirius. This event occurred once a year and gave rise to the Sothic Calendar, whose details we need not go into.

Figure 11. The heliacal rising of Sirius. Dogon drawing of Sirius and the sun joined together at this moment

The heliacal rising of Sirius was so important to the ancient Egyptians (as indeed it is to the Dogon as well[1]) that gigantic temples were constructed with their main aisles oriented precisely towards the spot on the horizon where Sirius would appear on the expected morning. The light of Sirius would be channelled along the corridor (due to the precise orientation) to flood the altar in the inner sanctum as if a pin-pointed spotlight had been switched on. This blast of light focused from a single star was possible because of the orientation being so incredibly precise and because the temple would be otherwise in total darkness within. In a huge, utterly dark temple, the light of one star focused solely on the altar must have made quite an impact on those present. In this way was the presence of the star made manifest within its temple. One such temple to the star Sirius was the temple of Isis at Denderah. An ancient hieroglyphic inscription from that temple informs us:[2]

She shines into her temple on New Year's Day, and she mingles her light
with that of her father Rā on the horizon.

(Rā is an ancient Egyptian name for the sun.)

The heliacal rising of Sirius was also important to other ancient peoples.
Here is a dramatic description by the ancient Greek poet Aratus of Soli of the
rising of Sirius[3] (often known as the Dog Star as it is in the constellation Canis,
or 'Dog'):

> The tip of his [the Dog's] terrible jaw is marked by a star that keenest of
> all blazes with a searing flame and him men call Sirius. When he rises
> with the Sun [his heliacal rising], no longer do the trees deceive him by the
> feeble freshness of their leaves. For easily with his keen glance he pierces
> their ranks, and to some he gives strength but of others he blights the bark
> utterly.

We see that this dramatic description of the rising of the star indicates an
event which was certainly noticed by ancient peoples. Throughout Latin
literature there are many references to 'the Dog Days' which followed the
heliacal rising of Sirius in the summer. These hot, parched days were thought
by that time to derive some of their ferocity and dryness from the 'searing' of
Sirius. Traditions arose of Sirius being 'red' because it was in fact red at its
heliacal rising, just as any other body at the horizon is red. When making
rhetorical allusion to the Dog Days, the Latins would often speak of Sirius
being red at that time, which it was.

We tend to be unaware that stars rise and set at all. This is not entirely
due to our living in cities ablaze with electric lights which reflect back at us
from our fumes, smoke, and artificial haze. When I discussed the stars with a
well-known naturalist, I was surprised to learn that even a man such as he,
who has spent his entire lifetime observing wildlife and nature, was totally
unaware of the movements of the stars. And he is no prisoner of smog-bound
cities. He had no inkling, for instance, that the Little Bear could serve as a
reliable night clock as it revolves in tight circles around the Pole Star (and
acts as a celestial hour-hand at half speed – that is, it takes 24 hours rather
than 12 for a single revolution).

I wondered what could be wrong. Our modern civilization does not ignore
the stars only because most of us can no longer see them. There are definitely
deeper reasons. For even if we leave the sulphurous vapours of our Gomorrahs
to venture into a natural landscape, the stars do not enter into any of our
back-to-nature schemes. They simply have no place in our outlook any more.
We look at them, our heads flung back in awe and wonder that they can exist
in such profusion. But that is as far as it goes, except for the poets. This is
simply a 'gee whiz' reaction. The rise in interest in astrology today does not
result in much actual star-gazing. And as for the space programme's impact
on our view of the sky, many people will attentively follow the motions of a
visible satellite against a backdrop of stars whose positions are absolutely
meaningless to them. The ancient mythological figures sketched in the sky were
taught us as children to be quaint 'shepherds' fantasies' unworthy of the
attention of adult minds. We are interested in the satellite because we made it,

but the stars are alien and untouched by human hands – therefore vapid. To such a level has our technological mania, like a bacterial solution in which we have been stewed from birth, reduced us.

It is only the integral part of the landscape which can relate to the stars. Man has ceased to be that. He inhabits a world which is more and more his own fantasy. Farmers relate to the skies, as well as sailors, camel caravans, and aerial navigators. For theirs are all integral functions involving the fundamental principle – now all but forgotten – of orientation. But in an almost totally secular and artificial world, orientation is thought to be unnecessary. And the numbers of people in insane asylums or living at home doped on tranquilizers testifies to our aimless, drifting metaphysic. And to our having forgotten orientation either to seasons (except to turn on the air-conditioning if we sweat or the heating system if we shiver) or to direction (our one token acceptance of cosmic direction being the wearing of sun-glasses because the sun is 'over there').

We have debased what was once the integral nature of life channelled by cosmic orientations – a wholeness – to the ennervated tepidity of skin sensations and retinal discomfort. Our interior body clocks, known as circadian rhythms, continue to operate inside us, but find no contact with the outside world. They therefore become ingrown and frustrated cycles which never interlock with our environment. We are causing ourselves to become meaningless body machines programmed to what looks, in its isolation, to be an arbitrary set of cycles. But by tearing ourselves from our context, like the still-beating heart ripped out of the body of an Aztec victim, we inevitably do violence to our psyches. I would call the new disease, with its side effect of 'alienation of the young', *dementia temporalis*.

When I tried to remedy my own total ignorance of this subject originally, I found it an extremely difficult process. I discovered that I was reading coherent explanatory matter which I 'understood' but did not comprehend. For comprehension consists of understanding from the inside as well as understanding from the outside. Things that do not really matter to us, or into which we do not imaginatively project our own consciousness, remain strange to us; we understand them outside (like a man feeling the skin of an orange) but we have no inherent relation with the thing, and hence are ultimately divorced from its reality. This increasing isolation and alienation, a cultural blight of which there is almost universal complaint in the 'civilized' world, is yet another consequence of *dementia temporalis*. For how can you get inside anything in the end if you have ceased to be inside your own local universe with its cycles and natural events? To be outside nature is to be an outsider in all things.

With these observations in mind and a child's fairytale to help guide us into the anteroom of the Egyptian psyche, let us prepare to take a plunge over a waterfall in the certainty that there is no chance of drowning. I have been over this particular waterfall before, and I assure you that the thrill is absolutely delicious if you just let yourself go. But there is no question about the fact that you will have to swim pretty hard. We're off . . . and immediately we are in the frothing rapids where names and basic guidelines must be established quickly. Professors Parker and Neugebauer, who are experts in such matters as these, tell us:[4]

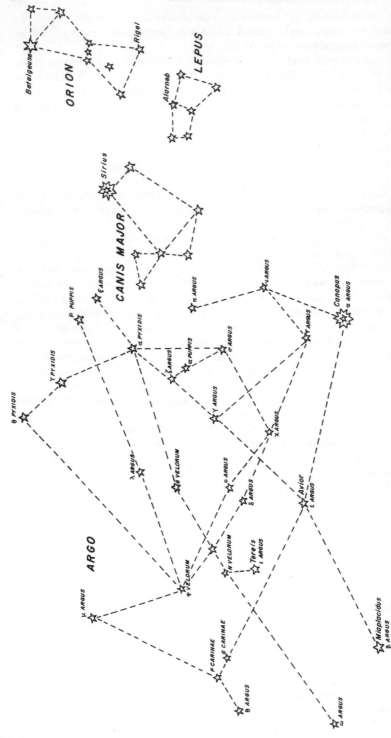

Figure 12. A star map showing the constellations Orion, Lepus (The Hare), Canis Major (the Great Dog, which contains the 'Dog Star' Sirius), and the huge constellation *Argo* (the Ship). The arrangement of the stars in *Argo* has been altered somewhat in this star map by the author and cartographer, which is not unusual, since *Argo* is so large and sprawling that it can rarely if ever be found on a single detailed star map. One can draw a ship almost any way one wants for *Argo* and still be 'within the rules'. Notice that Orion stands on the hare, which is portrayed in the Greek vase painting in Plate 19

The Egyptian calendar-year on which the diagonal star clocks (hitherto called 'diagonal calendars') were constructed is the well-known civil or 'wandering' year which consisted of twelve months of three 10-day weeks, divided into three seasons of four months each, followed by five epagomenal days, called by the Egyptians 'the days upon the year'. The total of 365 days did not vary and as a consequence the Egyptian year moved slowly forward in the natural year by, on the average, one day in four years. As we shall see later . . . this was a continuously vexing complication in keeping the star clocks adjusted.

The basis of these clocks was the risings of the stars (conventionally referred to as 'decans') at twelve 'hour' intervals through the night and in 10-day weeks through the year.

The main star or decan was Sirius. The four decans immediately before it in order comprise the constellation Orion. The last portion of Orion rises above the horizon one 'hour' before Sirius. It was for this reason that Orion took on significance in the Egyptian mythology and religion. The Egyptians were so concerned with Sirius, the star whose rising formed the basis of their entire calendar, that the decan immediately preceding it came to be looked on as Sirius's 'advance man'. Sirius itself was known to the Egyptians as Ŝpd or Ŝpdt (a 't' ending is feminine). This is sometimes spelt Sept and pronounced thus. Orion was known to the Egyptians as S3h which is transliterated as Sah or Sah, and pronounced thus.

Now that we have established a few names and facts, we have to consider the next fundamental point. We must establish, on the professors' word for it, that the star Sirius was actually identified with the famous goddess Isis, the head of the Egyptian pantheon. This will be a major breakthrough in our search for understanding. We must be careful not to be just saying things without evidence. The most common and most offensive characteristic of previous books about 'visiting spacemen' has often been the impossibility of checking any of their statements about ancient cultures (aside from the many obvious errors). Sometimes there are even references to newspaper articles which never existed, or to mysterious professors behind the Iron Curtain who have gone into hiding, taking their unpublished manuscripts with them. There are some such writers who claim that mysterious hierarchies of 'initiates' exist – some of them residing in secret caves deep in the centres of mountains – and some of these 'initiates' are directly in touch with and take their orders from 'flying saucers'!

Now on to the Egyptians: The heliacal rising of Sirius is called in Egyptian *prt Spdt*. Neugebauer and Parker say:[5] 'We offer the suggestion that Ŝpdt was in origin a nisbe of śpd referring to Isis as "the one of śpd". That śpd and śpdt Sothis are both identified with Sirius is one of the rare certainties in Egyptian astronomy.' Sothis is a goddess firmly identified with *Ŝpdt* and residing there. *Sothis* is also identified with the goddess known to us as Isis but whose Egyptian name is 3st which is transliterated as *Ȧst*.

Professor Wallis Budge makes this interesting observation:[6] 'The throne or

seat, ∬ , is the first sign in the name of Ȧs-t, ∬◠ , who is the female counterpart of Osiris, and it is very probable that originally the same conception underlay both names.' Osiris as the husband of Isis was identified with the constellation Orion.

Wallis Budge also said, after giving the following hieroglyphic forms of Osiris:[7]

Osiris,   , Ås-Ȧr, or

From the hieroglyphic texts of all periods of the dynastic history of Egypt we learn that the god of the dead, *par excellence*, was the god, whom the Egyptians called by a name which may be tentatively transcribed Ås-Ȧr, or Us-Ȧr, who is commonly known to us as 'Osiris'. The oldest and simplest

form of the name is   ,
that is to say, it is written by means of two hieroglyphics the first of which represents a 'throne' and the other an 'eye', but the exact meaning attached to the combination of the two pictures by those who first used them to express the name of the god, and the signification of the name in the minds of those who invented it cannot be said.

There is a great elaboration of what Ås-Ȧr does *not* mean, referring to the use of puns which particularly delighted Egyptian priests, etc. Two pages later he winds up by saying: 'The truth of the matter seems to be that the ancient Egyptians knew just as little about the original meaning of the name Ås-Ȧr as we do, and that they had no better means of obtaining information about it than we have.'

The Bozo tribe in Mali, cousins to the Dogon, describe Sirius B as 'the eye star', and here we see the Egyptians designating Osiris by an eye for reasons which are not clear. And Osiris is the 'companion' of the star Sirius. A coincidence? The Bozo also describe Sirius A as 'seated' – and a seat is the sign for Isis.

A little later Budge adds: '. . . in some passages (Ås-Ȧr or "Osiris") is referred to simply as "god",

without the addition of any name. No other god of the Egyptians was ever mentioned or alluded to in this manner, and no other god at any time in Egypt ever occupied exactly the same exalted position in their minds, or was thought to possess his peculiar attributes.' He adds:[8] 'The plaque of Ḥemaka proves that a centre of the Osiris cult existed at Abydos under the Ist Dynasty, but we are not justified in assuming that the god was first worshipped there, and . . . it is difficult not to think that even under the 1st Dynasty shrines had been built in honour of Osiris at several places in Egypt.'*

* Emery estimates the First Dynasty as commencing around 3200 B.C.

Thus we see the immense antiquity of the recognition of Ast and Asar (Isis and Osiris), going back well before the dynastic period in Egypt.

Wallis Budge says:[9] 'The symbol of Isis in the heavens was the star Sept,

which was greatly beloved because its appearance marked not only the beginning of a new year, but also announced the advance of the Inundation of the Nile, which betokened renewed wealth and prosperity of the country. As such Isis was regarded as the companion of Osiris, whose soul dwelt in the star Sah,

i.e. Orion . . .'

Wallis Budge also says:[10]

ÅST, ⌡, or ⌡◠ , or ⌡◯◺ , ISIS

Notwithstanding the fact that Ås, or Åst, i.e. Isis, is one of the goddesses most frequently mentioned in the hieroglyphic texts, nothing is known with certainty about the attributes which were ascribed to her in the earliest times. . . . The name Åst has, like Åsår, up to the present defied all explanation, and it is clear from the punning derivations to which the Egyptians themselves had recourse, that they knew no more about the meaning of her name than we do. . . . The symbol of the name of Isis in Egyptian is a seat, or throne, ⌡ , but we have no means of connecting it with the attributes of the goddess in such a way as to give a rational explanation of her name, and all the derivations hitherto proposed must be regarded as mere guesses. . . . An examination of the texts of all periods proves that Isis always held in the minds of the Egyptians a position which was entirely different from that of every other goddess, and although it is certain that their views concerning her varied from time to time, and that certain aspects or phases of the goddess were worshipped more generally at one period than at another, it is correct to say that from the earliest to the latest dynasties Isis was the greatest goddess of Egypt. Long before the copies of the Pyramid Texts which we possess* were written the attributes of Isis were well defined, and even when the priests of Heliopolis assigned her the position which she held in the cycle of their gods between B.C. 4000 and B.C. 3000 the duties which she was thought to perform in connexion with the dead were clearly defined, and were identical with those which belonged to her in the Graeco-Roman period.

I had begun to suspect that the sister-goddess of Isis, who is called Nephthys, represented a possible description of Sirius B, the dark companion star that described a circle around Sirius. (For we have just seen that Isis was identified with Sirius quite precisely by the Egyptians, a fact which no Egyptologist would ever dream of disputing, as it is quite undeniably established as we have

---

* Wallis Budge believes those of the Vth and VIth Dynasties to be copies of earlier writings including those of the Ist Dynasty; see p. 117 of his book.

seen.) But I must confess that I was not prepared to discover this following passage:[11]

On the subject of Anubis Plutarch reports (44;61) some interesting beliefs. After referring to the view that Anubis was born of Nephthys, although Isis was his reputed mother, he goes on to say, 'By Anubis they understand the horizontal circle, which divides the invisible part of the world, which they call Nephthys, from the visible, to which they give the name of Isis; and as this circle equally touches upon the confines of both light and darkness, it may be looked upon as common to them both – and from this circumstance arose that resemblance, which they imagine between Anubis and the Dog, it being observed of this animal, that he is equally watchful as well by day as night.

This description could be taken to be one of the Sirius system. It clearly describes Isis (whom we know to have been identified with Sirius) as 'the confines of light' and 'the visible', and her sister Nephthys is described as being 'the confines of darkness' and 'the invisible', and common to both is the horizontal circle which divides them – the horizontal circle described, perhaps, by the orbit of the dark companion about the bright star? And here, too, is an explanation of the symbolism of the dog which has always been associated with Sirius, which has borne throughout the ages the name of the 'Dog Star'.

Anubis is variously represented as jackal-headed and dog-headed in Egyptian art. Wallis Budge adds:[12] 'Thus much, however, is certain, that in ancient times the Egyptians paid the greatest reverence and honour to the Dog. . . .'

Anubis was also variously represented as the son of Nephthys by Osiris and as being really identical with Osiris himself. A famous tale has him embalm the corpse of Osiris. Osiris was known as Anubis, though, at Oxyrhynchus and Cynopolis.[13]

A name similar to Anubis (which is really Anpu in Egyptian) and which is also associated with Isis-Sothis (Sirius), is Anukis, a fellow-goddess of Sothis who, along with the goddess Satis, sails in the same celestial boat with Sothis in the Egyptian paintings. There are thus the three goddesses together, possibly a description of Sirius A, Sirius B, and Sirius C, and emphasizing that the Sirius system is really thought to be a three-star system. Just to underline the point, Neugebauer specifically states:[14] 'The goddess Satis, who like her companion Anukis is hardly to be taken as a separate constellation but rather as an associate of Sothis.'

The goddess Anukis holds two jars from which she pours water, possibly indicating two watery planets around her star? All the references to the Sothic heavens are to a watery, reed-growing paradise. Many archaeologists have surmised that this refers to some specifically Egyptian locale. But no one is sure. What is known is that heaven is almost invariably associated with the Sirius system and is described as being prolific of vegetation and watery.

In Plutarch's famous and lengthy treatise (from his immense work the *Moralia*, which is even longer than his *Lives*), 'Isis and Osiris' (356) we read: '. . . Isis was born in the regions that are ever moist.' In the Loeb Library edition of this, the translator F. C. Babbitt adds a footnote at this point saying: 'The meaning is doubtful. . . .' In other words, no one is really sure what is meant by all these references to Isis-Sothis and the 'moist regions', which are supposed by most scholars quite sensibly to be projections of local Egyptian conditions around the Nile into an ideal celestial region. But most scholars admit that this is mere conjecture. The 'moist regions' could just as well be an attempt to describe some watery planets.

It is worth pointing out that in the event of planets in the Sirius system being watery, we must seriously consider the possibility of intelligent beings from there being amphibious. This ties in with the legend of Oannes which I mentioned in Part One. He was the amphibious being mentioned by the astronomer Carl Sagan from the Sumerian tradition, and was the bringer of civilization to man. In other words, beings of this type would be a bit like mermaids and mermen – and might in some way resemble our intelligent friends the dolphins. I discuss this subject further in Part Three of this book.

Perhaps 'the sirens' are, figuratively, a chorus of mermaids recalled from earlier times. By coincidence, in zoology a siren is 'one of a genus (Siren) of eel-shaped amphibians having small forelimbs, but destitute of hind legs and pelvis, and having permanent external gills as well as lungs'. It would be interesting to see how far back in time these creatures were called by their name. As for the singing sirens who lure sailors to the rocks, they are called in Greek *Seirēn* (singular), *Seirēnes* (plural) and are first mentioned in Homer's *Odyssey*. Homer knew of two sirens, but later there was a third, and some added a fourth. (Plato decided there were eight because of that number matching the number of musical notes in the octave.) It is interesting that in Greek Sirius is *Seirios*. Liddell and Scott in their definitive Greek lexicon give a meaning of the previous *Seirēn* as 'a constellation, like Seirios, Eust. 1709. 54'.

Another similar word *Seistron* became in Latin *sistrum* and Liddell and Scott define it as '*A rattle* used in the worship of Isis. . . .'

Let us now turn our attention to a remarkable book, *Star Names, Their Lore and Meaning* by Richard Hinckley Allen. In this book, under a discussion of the constellation Canis Major (The Dog), which contains Sirius,[15] on p. 130, is a description of the star of the constellation represented by the Greek letter δ (delta):

It is the 'modern Wezen, from (the Arabic) Al Wazn, Weight, "as the star seems to rise with difficulty from the horizon," but Ideler calls this an astonishing star-name.'

Yes, concerning what we know, it is astonishing!

Before leaving the star, it is worth noting that Allen says the Chinese knew it as well as some stars in Argo as 'Hoo She, the Bow and Arrow', and that the bow and arrow is a variation motif associated with the Sirius system by the Egyptians. In Neugebauer we read:[16] 'The goddess Satis, who like her companion Anukis is hardly to be taken as a separate constellation but rather as an associate of Sothis. In Dendera B, the goddess holds a drawn bow and arrow.'

More information regarding Al Wazn, 'Weight', is found in Dr Christian Ludwig Ideler's *Untersuchungen ueber den Ursprung und die Bedeutung der Sternnamen*, Berlin, 1809, which Allen describes as 'the main critical compendium of information on stellar names – Arabic, Greek, and Latin especially. It is to him that we owe the translation of the original Arabic text of Kazwini's *Description of the Constellations*, written in the 13th century, which forms the basis of the *Sternnamen*, with Ideler's additions and annotations from classical and other sources. From this much information in my book is derived.'

Ideler might well comment that Al Wazn is 'an astonishing star-name'. To call a star in the same constellation as Sirius 'too heavy to rise over the horizon with ease' looks suspiciously like an attempt to describe a 'heavy star' such as Sirius B.

Could this reference to a 'heavy star' be a reference to Sirius B by people who have inherited a slightly garbled version of the tradition of its being a super-dense star invisible to the unaided eye – resulting in their seizing on one of Sirius's apparent companions (as seen from the Earth) and giving it a description properly applying to its actual companion? The Arabs do not mention '480 ass loads' to describe its weight in the quaint fashion of the Dogon, but the substance of the idea seems to be present. It is well known that ancient Arabic astronomical lore derives from Egypt and is found in Arabic traditions in a degenerate form. Obviously the search must now be on for this concept of a super-heavy star in Egyptian traditions! I had always suspected that this most secret tradition of the Dogon reached them from Egypt, just as the lore of stars reached the Arabs from Egypt. It will not be easy for us to discover, as it must have been an extremely esoteric and secret teaching of the Egyptians, just as it was the most secret teaching of the Dogon.

A further use of the name Wazn is its loose application to the star Canopus in the constellation Argo.[17] Allen, in describing the Argo, quotes the ancient Greek poet Aratos, in a passage showing us something of the relation Argo bears to Canis Major, the Great Dog:

> Sternforward Argo by the Great Dog's tail
> Is drawn . . .

Argo is the constellation representing both Jason's ship with its fifty Argonauts and Noah's ark.

Jason's *Argo* 'carried Danaos with his fifty daughters from Egypt to Rhodes', as Allen puts it. He adds: 'The Egyptian story said that it was the ark that bore Isis and Osiris over the deluge; while the Hindus thought that it performed the same office for their equivalent Isi and Iswara.'

Allen's old-fashioned spelling 'Iswara' is a reference to the word 'Ishvara'. There are some interesting facts to be gleaned from perusing the meanings of the Sanskrit word *ishu*, which basically means 'an arrow'. Recall the connection of the bow and arrow with Sirius among both the Egyptians and the Chinese. (Further examples are given in the book *Hamlet's Mill*, along with interesting illustrations.) Now note from Monier-Williams's definitive Sanskrit dictionary that *ishu* means not only 'arrow' but 'ray of light'. *Ishvasa* means 'a bow' or 'an archer'. Remember the three goddesses and note this: that *Ishustrikanda*, which literally means 'the threefold arrow', is specifically meant to be the name of a constellation! Monier-Williams says it is 'perhaps the girdle of Orion' (which has three prominent stars). The interested reader must refer to *Hamlet's Mill* by Santillana and von Dechend for a great deal of discussion of Sirius the Bow Star.

But to return to the celestial *Argo*-boat (or ark); we have previously encountered this Egyptian idea of the celestial boats in which their gods sailed through the waters of the heavens. The three Sirius-goddesses: Sothis, Anukis, and Satis, were all in the same boat. So it is interesting to see that *Argo* was a boat connected with Isis and Osiris, for a concept which seems to be peculiarly stubborn in attaching itself to *Argo* is the number fifty. It is my suspicion that this is a remnant of the concept of Sirius B taking fifty years to complete an orbit around Sirius A. This suggestion is not as far-fetched as it may seem at first sight. Indeed, the reader will discover as he proceeds that the suggestion will become more and more obvious. We must realize that in Egyptian terms the orbit of Sirius B around Sirius A could have been expressed in terms of a celestial boat. Now since *Argo* is the boat of Isis and Osiris, what better way to express the fifty-year orbit than by giving the boat fifty oarsmen? And that is what *Argo* has – in the tradition there are fifty rowers, or Argonauts.

In order to fortify my argument I shall quote Allen's precise way of describing this:[18] 'Mythology insisted that it was built by Glaucus, or by Argos, for Jason, leader of the fifty Argonauts, *whose number equalled that of the oars of the ship* . . .' In other words, it is not the men but the *number of oars* laid out in line round the ship that is important. A ship (an orbit) with fifty oars (fifty 'markers' or yearly stages)! And just so that we don't miss the importance of the figure fifty, we are told there were fifty daughters of Danaus transported from Egypt on the *Argo*! (Readers who wonder what other connection there may be between the *Argo* of the Greeks and ancient Egypt must be patient.) *Argo* is therefore totally involved in the picture, as we now see. There are many further ramifications of this, not only of *Argo*, but of the number fifty.

But before moving on to what that entails, it is worth giving an illustration of the concept of 'the rower' in the celestial barque from an ancient Egyptian coffin text 'The Field of Paradise'.[19] It is quite likely that from concepts such as these the idea of a rower and his oar developed and became incorporated in the *Argo* myth and came to be symbolic: '. . . in the place where Re (the Sun) sails with rowing. I am the keeper of the halyard in the boat of the god; I am the oarsman who does not weary in the barque of Re.' (Re is another form of the more familiar Ra.)

The first person in this text refers to the deceased Pharaoh. This is one of the examples of the common Egyptian conception that when a Pharaoh died he became a celestial rower. It should be obvious, then, how the concept of 'fifty rowers' by fifty positions, or oars, came to be important as symbols. It harks back to this Egyptian motif.

Now we must turn to the Sumerian civilization (which later developed into the Babylonian civilization). We shall be back in Egypt soon enough, with more *Argo* material. But we must go east. Sumer-Akkad was roughly contemporaneous with ancient Egypt, and the lands are known to have been in contact. In a major source we read[20] of the Sumerian word Magan: 'The land Magan is usually identified either with Arabia or with Egypt.'

But whatever contact the two civilizations may have had, we must first investigate the Sumerian religion and mythology. For this we rely primarily on the excellent work of Samuel Noah Kramer of the University of Pennsylvania.

The Sumerian heaven-god is called Anu. (In Sanskrit *anupa* means 'a watery county'.) I had a considerable shock when I discovered that Alexander Heidel says in *The Babylonian Genesis*: '. . . just as the departed spirits of

Enlil and Anu were pictured as the wild ass and the jackal, respectively'.[21] Anu is represented by the jackal. Well, of course, the jackal is the symbol (interchangeable with the dog) of the Egyptian Anpu (Anubis)!

I shall explain later why I consider Anu to be related to the Sirius question, apart from this obvious parallel. At the moment I shall deal with further related parallels which I consider amazing. Anu is the king of some attendant deities called the Anunnaki. We shall shortly see why they are so involved in the Sirius question. But note the recurrence in Sumer of 'Anu' in both Anu and the Anunnaki, and in Egypt with both Anpu (Anubis) and Anukis. In all these cases Sirius is involved. Even the jackal or dog is common as a symbol to the 'Anu' in both countries. There are other parallels, but we shall come to them in due course.

In Sumerian the word *an* means 'heaven' and Anu is the god of heaven.

Wallis Budge says[22] that the Egyptian god Nu was often identified with Nut, which is 'heaven'.

Significantly, he expressly states:[23]

> It is surprising therefore to find so much similarity existing between the primeval gods of Sumer and those of Egypt, especially as the resemblance cannot be the result of borrowing. It is out of the question to assume that Ashur-banipal's editors borrowed the system from Egypt, or that the literary men of the time of Seti I borrowed their ideas from the *literati* of Babylonia or Assyria, and we are therefore driven to the conclusion that both the Sumerians and the early Egyptians derived their primeval gods from some common but exceedingly ancient source. The similarity between the two companies of gods seems to be too close to be accidental . . . it is certain that the company of primeval gods . . . was quite different from . . . those which formed in Babylonia and Assyria when these countries were inhabited by Semitic populations.

I had come to all these conclusions myself before seeing this passage by Wallis Budge.

But to return to Anu. Osiris is sometimes known as An.[24] In a hymn to Osiris[25] he is called the 'god An of millions of years . . .' and also 'An in An-tes, Great One, Ḥeru-khuti, thou stridest over heaven with long strides'. Therefore this designation as An is specifically connected with heaven and the long strides mean heavenly motion.

In considering An and Anu we must look again at Anubis. But as we do so we shall take a glance at the Sanskrit. Recall that Anubis in Plutarch's account seemed to refer specifically to the *orbit* of Sirius B. In Sanskrit the word *anda* means 'ellipse', and the word *anu* means 'minute, atomic, "the subtle one", an atom of matter' and *animan* means 'minuteness, atomic nature, the smallest particle, the superhuman power of becoming as small as an atom'. The first word could describe an orbit. Since Kepler, we have known that our planets move in elliptical orbits rather than circular ones, and the orbit of Sirius B is that of an ellipse. As for the next two forms *anu* and *animan*, they seem to have meanings perilously peripheral to an account of that level of matter (the atomic) where the nature of Sirius B is manifested. We shall see much later in the book that other similarities exist between certain Sanskrit terms relevant to the Sirius question and like terms in Egypt and the Near East. But we shall leave those philological matters until later, when they will be shown to have considerable importance.

Back to Anubis. Wallis Budge says of him:[26] 'His worship is very ancient, and there is no doubt that even in the earliest times his cult was general in Egypt; it is probable that it is older than that of Osiris.' Also he points out here, as elsewhere, that the face of the deceased human becomes identified with Anubis, and it is just the head of Anubis which is symbolically represented by the jackal or dog. I have already pointed out that he is described as the circle or orbit separating the dark Nephthys from the light Isis or Sirius. In other words, I take Anubis to represent the orbit of Sirius B around Sirius A. We also find him described as 'time',[27] a particularly intelligent way of looking at an orbit as progressive and sequential in time. 'Time the devourer', a motif common to us all, is no stranger to the Egyptians. It should not surprise us that Anubis is also represented as a devourer! More specifically, he is accused of devouring the Apis bull. The Apis bull is the animal into which the dead Osiris was sewn and transported, according to a late legend which is widely known. But more basically, the 'Apis Bull' (the deity known under the Ptolemies as Serapis) is Āsar-Ḥāpi. It is Osiris himself! In *The Gods of the Egyptians*, we read 'Apis is called "the life of Osiris, the lord of heaven" ' and 'Apis was, in fact, believed to be animated by the soul of Osiris, and to be Osiris incarnate'.[28] So, consequently, when Anubis devoured Apis, he was eating the husband of Isis! It is very colourfully represented in these dramatic mythological terms, but the meaning is clear. We read later:[29]

> 'Others again are of the opinion that by Anubis is meant Time, and that his denomination of *Kuon* [the Greek word for 'dog'] does not so much allude to any likeness which he has to the dog, though this be the general rendering of the word, as to that other significance of the term taken from *breeding*; because Time begets all things out of itself, bearing them within itself, as it were in a womb. But this is one of those secret doctrines which are more fully made known to those who are initiated into the worship of Anubis.'

Exactly. A secret doctrine! What one would give for a fuller account! This is the trouble with most of our sources; they give away little except by inference. Secret doctrines are not scribbled down too frequently and left for posterity. The most secret doctrine of the Dogon was only revealed with great reluctance after many, many years, and following upon a conference by the initiates. The Egyptians were no fools, and we can hardly expect them to have left papyri or texts specifically revealing in so many words what they were not supposed to reveal. We can only try to piece together clues. But we will see our clues eventually turn into a veritable avalanche.

The last passage from Wallis Budge was a quotation by him from Plutarch's 'Isis and Osiris'. Many Egyptologists have remarked on the irony that we have nowhere in Egyptian sources a full, coherent account of Isis and Osiris – not even in all the sources put together! And we are forced to rely on Plutarch, who did preserve a long account which he wrote in his native Greek. Plutarch is thought to have been a priest himself, and was certainly a Delphic initiate.

He had a talent for befriending priests and priestesses. One of his best friends was the priestess Clea of the oracle at Delphi. His treatise 'Isis and Osiris' is dedicated to Clea and addressed to her. It begins with these words: 'All good things, my dear Clea, sensible men must ask from the gods; and especially do we pray that from those mighty gods we may, in our quest, gain a knowledge of themselves, so far as such a thing is attainable by men.' This gives some indication of what Plutarch was like as a man.

The Introduction to the Loeb edition of Isis and Osiris by F. C. Babbitt says: '[Plutarch] once visited Egypt, but how long he stayed and how much he learned we have no means of knowing. It is most likely that his treatise represents the knowledge current in his day, derived, no doubt, from two sources: books and priests.' It is certain that Plutarch's friend Clea, who was so important at Delphi, would have seen to it that Plutarch had ample introductions to leading priests of Egypt. This sort of thing was standard practice – as with the study of Egyptian religion and astronomy undertaken centuries earlier by the Greek scholar Eudoxus (colleague of Plato and Aristotle), who was given a letter of introduction to the last of the native Pharaohs, Nectanebo, by the Spartan general Agesilaus, and who in turn sent him off to associate with his priests. The fact that Plutarch's treatise is addressed to Clea may indicate a debt to her for its preparation as well as common religious enthusiasms. So, no doubt Plutarch did with the Egyptian priests what Griaule and Dieterlen did with the Dogon – drew some secret traditions out of them. It is thus not surprising that Plutarch's essay is more respected by Egyptologists than by classicists.

Plutarch says: 'Some are of the opinion that Anubis is Cronos.'[30] Chronos, of course, was the Greek 'time the devourer', spelt with an h. Cronos in Latin is Saturn. There is a considerable debate among scholars whether Cronos (Saturn), the former chief god prior to Zeus (Jupiter), has any definite relation to the word *chronos* spelt with the h and sometimes used as a proper name for Time. From this latter word we derive *chronology, chronicle*, etc. The Sumerian god Anu is quite similar to the Greek Cronos because both Cronos and Anu were 'old' gods who were displaced by younger blood – by Zeus and Enlil respectively. Thus another possible link between Anu and Anubis, if one be willing to grant that Cronos and Chronos are not entirely separate words and concepts in ancient pre-classical Greece.

Wallis Budge continues with reference to Plutarch:

> Referring to Osiris as the 'common Reason which pervades both the superior and inferior regions of the universe', he [Plutarch] says that it is, moreover, called 'Anubis, and sometimes likewise Hermanubis (i.e. Ḥeru-em-Ȧnpu); the first of these names expressing the relation it has to the superior, as the latter, to the inferior world. And for this reason it is, they sacrifice to him two Cocks, the one white, as a proper emblem of the purity and brightness of things above, the other of a saffron colour, expressive of that mixture and variety which is to be found on those lower regions.'

Here is what I take to be a possible reference to the white Sirius A and the 'darker' Sirius B. But also, the 'lower regions' are the horizons, where white heavenly bodies at their 'births' and 'deaths' become saffron-coloured.

There is a clearer translation by Babbitt in the precise description of Anubis as 'the combined relation of the things'[31] rather than as 'the common Reason which pervades' the light world and the dark world. A circular orbit is just that – 'a combined relation' between the star revolving and the star revolved around. In order to make this more firmly established less as fancy than as fact, I shall cite Plutarch's words from his next paragraph (Babbitt's translation):

'Moreover, they (the Egyptians) record that in the so-called books of Hermes (the Trismegistic literature?) it is written in regard to the sacred names that they call the power which is assigned to direct the revolution of the Sun Horus . . .'

This is important because we see here that they specifically call the orbit of the sun by a god's name. If they can call the revolution of the sun by a god's name, they can call the revolution of Sirius B (assuming they really knew about it) by a god's name. We are dealing with a precedent. Now we resume this quotation because it is interesting for other reasons: '. . . but the Greeks call it Apollo; and the power assigned to the wind some call Osiris and others Serapis; and Sothis in Egyptian signifies "pregnancy" (cyesis) or "to be pregnant" (cyein): therefore in Greek, with a change of accent, the star is called the Dog-star (Cyon), which they regard as the special star of Isis.'

A further piece of information from Plutarch about Anubis is:[32] 'And when the child (Anubis, child of Nephthys by Osiris) had been found, after great toil and trouble, with the help of dogs which led Isis to it, it was brought up and became her guardian and attendant, receiving the name Anubis, and it is said to protect the gods just as dogs protect men.'

If Anubis is conceived of as an orbit around Sirius, then he would indeed be attendant upon Isis! He would go round and round her like a guard dog.

Plutarch has an interesting tale: 'Moreover, Eudoxus says that the Egyptians have a mythical tradition in regard to Zeus that, because his legs were grown together, he was not able to walk . . .'[33] This sounds very like the amphibious Oannes of the Sumerians who had a tail for swimming instead of legs for walking.

Plutarch provides us with an important and crucial clue linking Isis with the *Argo* and the Argonauts and demonstrating a probable derivation of an idea that has puzzled classicists enormously (and later on we shall see the links between Isis and the *Argo* considerably elaborated): 'Like these also are the Egyptian beliefs; for they oftentimes call Isis by the name of Athena, expressive of some such idea as this, "I came of myself," which is indicative of self-impelled motion.'[34]

It must be remembered that the Greek goddess Athena, the goddess of the mind and of wisdom, was reputed to have sprung full-fledged from the brow of Zeus. She was not born. She came of herself. However, the quotation must be continued to make the point:

Typhon, as has been said, is named Seth and Bebon and Smu, and these names would indicate some forcible and preventive check or opposition or reversal.

Moreover, they call the lodestone the bone of Horus, and iron the bone of Typhon, as Manetho records. For, as the iron oftentimes acts as if it were being attracted and drawn toward the stone, and oftentimes is rejected and repelled in the opposite direction, in the same way the salutary and good and rational movement of the world at one time, by persuasion, attracts and draws towards itself and renders more gentle that harsh and Typhonian movement, and then again it gathers itself together and reverses it and plunges it into difficulties.

The identification of Isis with Athena here in connection with lodestones and 'self-impelled motion' brings to mind the placing by Athena of a cybernetic* oak timber from the holy sanctuary of Dodona (supposedly founded by Deukalion, the Greek Noah, after his ark landed) in the keel of the *Argo*. H. W. Parke in his books *Greek Oracles* and *The Oracles of Zeus* refers to this: 'Athena when the *Argo* was built took a timber from the oak tree of Dodona (the oracular centre of Zeus) and fitted it into the keel. This had the result that the *Argo* itself could speak and guide or warn the Argonauts at critical moments, as it actually is represented as doing in our extant epics on the subject. The original epic is lost, but there is no reason to doubt that this miraculous feature went back to it, and, if so, was at least as old as the *Odyssey* in which the *Argo* and its story are mentioned.' Parke then emphasizes most strongly that it is the timber itself that acts as guide. It is self-sufficient and not merely an oracular medium. Thus we see that the *Argo* had a unique capacity for 'self-impelled motion' which was built into it by Athena (whom Plutarch identifies with Isis).[35]

Now is a suitable stage to return to the Sumerians, as in their culture we shall find many significant references to 'fifty heroes', 'fifty great gods', etc. But first we shall leave the fifty Argonauts and their magical ship to turn our attention to what appears to be a rather precise Egyptian description of the Sirius system preserved in an unusual source. The source is G. R. S. Mead (who was a friend of the poet Yeats and is mentioned by his nickname 'Old Crore' in Ezra Pound's *Cantos*), whose three-volume *Thrice Greatest Hermes*[36] contains a translation of, with extensive prolegomena and notes to, the obscure and generally ignored ancient 'Trismegistic literature' of the Hermetic tradition. These writings are largely scorned by classical scholars who consider them Neoplatonic forgeries. Of course, ever since the wild Neoplatonic boom in the Italian Renaissance period when Marsilio Ficino translated and thereby preserved for posterity (one must grant the Medicis the credit for finding and purchasing the manuscripts!) such Neoplatonists as Iamblichus, as well as these Trismegistic writings, the Neoplatonists have been in the doghouse. The Loeb Classical Library still has not published all of Plotinus even now.

But most readers will not be familiar either with the term 'trismegistic' or with the Neoplatonists. So I had better explain. The Neoplatonists are Greek philosophers who lived long enough after Plato to have lost the name of Platonists as far as modern scholars are concerned (though they were intellectual disciples of Plato and considered themselves Platonists). Modern scholars have added the prefix 'Neo-' to 'Platonist' for their own convenience, in order to

---

* Norbert Wiener in *Cybernetics*, the pioneer textbook of computer theory, said: 'We have decided to call the entire field of control and communication theory, whether in the machine or in the animal, by the name *Cybernetics* . . . (from the Greek for) *steersman*.'

distinguish them from their earlier predecessors, those Platonists who lived within 150 years of Plato himself. The Platonic Academy existed for over nine centuries at Athens. In actuality, scholars talk about 'Middle Platonists', 'Syrian Platonists', 'Christian Platonists', 'Alexandrian Platonists', and so on. I suggest the reader look at my Appendix I, which will tell him a lot about the Neoplatonists and their connection with the Sirius mystery, and which deals primarily with Proclus.

G. R. S. Mead, at the beginning of his work *Thrice Greatest Hermes*, explains fully what 'the Trismegistic Literature' is. He calls it 'Trismegistic' instead of by its earlier designation 'Hermetic' (from the name of the Greek god Hermes) in order to distinguish it from other less interesting writings such as the Egyptian Hermes prayers and also the 'Hermetic Alchemical Literature'. The Trismegistic writings are now fragmentary and consist of a large amount of exceedingly strange sermons, dialogues, excerpts by Stobaeus and the Fathers of the Church from lost writings, etc. I hesitate to give a brief summary of them and suggest that the interested reader actually look into this subject himself. There are some matters which defy summary, and I consider this to be one of them. The writings contain some 'mystical' elements and certainly some sublime elements. Old Cosimo de Medici was told by Ficino that he could translate for him either the Hermetic Literature or the dialogues of Plato, but not both at once. Cosimo knew he was dying. He said something like: 'If only I could read the Books of Hermes, I would die happy. Plato would be nice but not as important. Do the Hermes, Ficino.' And Ficino did.

As I explain fully in Appendix I, the Neoplatonists are so thoroughly despised through the bias of the moment, however one cares to define that bias, that the Trismegistic literature suffers with Neoplatonism under the onus of being considered too far removed from reality and logic and being inclined towards the mystical. This does not fit well with the hard rationalism of an age still bound by the (albeit decaying) fetters of nineteenth-century scientific deterministic prejudice. The sublime irony is, of course, that proven and authentic Egyptian texts are obviously mystical, but that is considered all right. However, as long as there is a belief that the Trismegistic literature is Neoplatonic it will be despised because it is mystical.

The Trismegistic literature may be Neoplatonic. But that does not make what it has to say about Egyptian religion any less valid *per se* than the 'Isis and Osiris' by the Greek Plutarch, who was only slightly earlier in time than the Neoplatonist Greeks. It is time for scholars to pay some attention to this sadly neglected material. Much of the Trismegistic literature probably goes back to genuine sources or compilations such as Manetho's lost *Sothis*. Or the literature may be quite ancient, in which case some of it cannot, in its present form, be earlier than the Ptolemaic period when the Zodiac as we know it was introduced into Egypt by the Greeks who in turn had it from Babylon. (I cannot here discuss the matter of earlier forms of zodiac, such as at Denderah.)

Mead quotes an Egyptian magic papyrus, this being an uncontested Egyptian document which he compares to a passage in the Trismegistic literature: 'I invoke thee, Lady Isis, with whom the Good Daimon doth unite, He who is Lord in the perfect black.'[37]

We know that Isis is identified with Sirius A, and here we may have a description of her star-companion 'who is Lord in the perfect black', namely the invisible companion with whom she is united, Sirius B.

Mead, of course, had no inkling of the Sirius question. But he cited this magic papyrus in order to shed comparative light on some extraordinary passages in a Trismegistic treatise he translated which has the title 'The Virgin of the World'. In his comments on the magic papyrus Mead says: 'It is natural to make the Agathodaimon ("the Good Daimon") of the Papyrus refer to Osiris; for indeed it is one of his most frequent designations. Moreover, it is precisely Osiris who is pre-eminently connected with the so-called "underworld", the unseen world, the "mysterious dark". He is lord there . . . and indeed one of the ancient mystery-sayings was precisely, "Osiris is a dark God." '

'The Virgin of the World' is an extraordinary Trismegistic treatise in the form of a dialogue between the hierophant (high priest) as spokesman for Isis and the neophyte who represents Horus. Thus the priest instructing the initiate is portrayed as Isis instructing her son Horus.

The treatise begins by claiming it is 'her holiest discourse' which 'so speaking Isis doth pour forth'. There is, throughout, a strong emphasis on the hierarchical principle of lower and higher beings in the universe – that earthly mortals are presided over at intervals by other, higher, beings who interfere in Earth's affairs when things here become hopeless, etc. Isis says in the treatise: 'It needs must, therefore, be the less should give place to the greater mysteries.' What she is to disclose to Horus is a *great* mystery. Mead describes it as the mystery practised by the arch-hierophant. It was the degree (here 'degree' is in the sense of 'degree' in the Masonic 'mysteries', which are hopelessly garbled and watered-down versions of genuine mysteries of earlier times) 'called the "Dark Mystery" or "Black Rite". It was a rite performed only for those who were judged worthy of it after long probation in lower degrees, something of a far more sacred character, apparently, than the instruction in the mysteries enacted in the light.'

Mead adds: 'I would suggest, therefore, that we have here a reference to the most esoteric institution of the Isiac tradition . . .', Isiac meaning of course 'Isis-tradition', and not to be confused with the Book of Isaiah in the Bible (so that perhaps it is best for us not to use the word-form 'Isiac').

It is in attempting to explain the mysterious 'Black Rite' of Isis at the highest degree of the Egyptian mysteries that Mead cited the magic papyrus which I have already quoted. He explains the 'Black Rite' as being connected with Osiris being a 'dark god' who is 'Lord of the perfect black' which is 'the unseen world, the mysterious black'.

This treatise 'The Virgin of the World' describes a personage called Hermes who seems to represent a race of beings who taught earthly mankind the arts of civilization after which: 'And thus, with charge unto his kinsmen of the Gods to keep sure watch, he mounted to the Stars'.

According to this treatise mankind have been a troublesome lot requiring scrutiny and, at rare intervals of crisis, intervention.

After Hermes left Earth to return to the stars there was or were in Egypt someone or some people designated as 'Tat' (Thoth) who were initiates into the celestial mysteries. I take this to refer to the Egyptian priests. However, one of the most significant passages in the treatise follows immediately upon this statement, and indicates to me that this treatise must have some genuine Egyptian source, for no late Greek should have been capable of incorporating this. But in order to recognize this one must know about the extraordinary Imhotep, a brilliant genius, philosopher, doctor, and Prime Minister (to use our terms) during the Third Dynasty in Egypt circa 2600 B.C. under King Zoser, whose tomb and temple he constructed and designed himself. (This is the famous step-pyramid at Sakkara, the first pyramid ever built and the world's earliest stone building according to some.) Imhotep was over the centuries gradually transformed into a god and 'a son of Ptah'. One reason why the process of his deification may have been retarded for some thousands of years is that writings by him survived, rather like the survival of the *Gathas* by Zarathustra (Zoroaster), making it impossible to claim that a man who left writings could in fact have been a god. Just like Mohammed and Zoroaster, Imhotep remained a sort of 'prophet' through his surviving writings.

For the significant passage, now, here is the entire paragraph: 'To him (Hermes) succeeded Tat, who was at once his son and heir unto these knowledges [this almost certainly implies a priesthood]; and not long afterwards Asclepius-Imuth, according to the will of Ptah who is Hephaestus, and all the rest who were to make enquiry of the faithful certitude of heavenly contemplation, as Foreknowledge (or Providence) willed, Foreknowledge queen of all.'

Now this is a really striking passage. We have the mysterious 'Hermes' succeeded by an Egyptian priesthood of Thoth. Then 'not long afterwards' we have someone called Asclepius-Imuth 'according to the will of Ptah'. This is Imhotep! Ptah, known to the Greeks as Hephaestus, was considered the father of Imhotep in late Egyptian times. In fact, it is interesting that this text avoids the late form 'son of Ptah' to describe Imhotep. Imhotep was known to the Greeks and provided the basis for their god Asclepius (the Greek god of medicine, corresponding to Imhotep's late form as Egyptian god of medicine). Imhotep is also spelled Imouthes, Imothes, Imutep, etc. Hence the form in this treatise 'Asclepius-Imuth'.

There is absolutely no question that Imhotep is being referred to here. And in the light of that, certain other statements in this passage become quite interesting.

It has already been mentioned that in a treatise like 'The Virgin of the World', where gods' names are thrown round like birdseed, the authors were exceedingly restrained to have avoided labelling Asclepius-Imhotep as 'a son of Ptah-Hephaestus'. This may, indeed, point to a genuine early source from the time before that when the Egyptians ceased to regard Imhotep as a mortal.

Hurry says:[38]

For many years Egyptologists have been puzzled to explain why Imhotep, who lived in the days of King Zoser, *ca.* 2900 B.C., was not ranked among the full gods of Egypt until the Persian period, dating from 525 B.C. The apotheosis of a man, however distinguished, so many centuries after his life on earth seems mysterious. The explanation appears to be that first suggested by Erman, viz. that Imhotep, at any rate during a large part of the interval was regarded as a sort of hero or demigod and received semi-divine worship. Erman suggested that this rank of demigod was bestowed on him at the time of the New Kingdom, i.e. about 1580 B.C., but more recent evidence seems to indicate that this demigod stage was reached at a much earlier period.

Here a bit of chronology helps. 'The Virgin of the World' correctly described Imhotep as 'not long afterwards', following upon the creation of the Egyptian priesthood, presumably in the First Dynasty after Menes, in the form in which it would be known after the unification of Egypt. Imhotep lived in the Third Dynasty, at the beginning of the Old Kingdom. I. E. S. Edwards[39] estimates this as commencing about 2686 B.C. He puts the start of the First Dynasty about 3100 B.C. Imhotep is thus literally 'not long afterwards'. Whoever wrote 'The Virgin of the World' knew his Egyptian chronology and also did not call Imhotep 'son of Ptah'.

There is another point. Looking at this statement from 'The Virgin of the World': '. . . and all the rest (i.e. after Imhotep) who were to make enquiry of the faithful certitude of heavenly contemplation . . .', we find that we have a reference to successors of Imhotep who 'enquired' into the riddles of the universe and also a description of Imhotep's own activities as an 'enquirer'. This also is accurate and reflects considerable knowledge of the subject. For Imhotep is often described as the first genuine philosopher known by name. And on p. 30 of his book, Hurry refers to apparent successors mentioned in an Oxyrhyncus papyrus (in Greek, edited by Grenfell and Hunt) which relates that 'Imhotep was worshipped as early as the IVth Dynasty, and his temple was resorted to by sick and afflicted persons'. Hurry further says: 'The other persons are Horus son of Hermes, and Kaleoibis son of Apollo (Imhotep being a son of Ptah); it is not known who these were.' Could they have been successors of Imhotep at 'enquiring'? It seems likely that we shall be learning more of these people as excavations in Egypt proceed. In 1971–2 there came to light at Sakkara a remarkable group of texts written by a man named Hor (from Horus), describing his life at an Egyptian temple in the Ptolemaic period, recounting his dreams and his political encounters. These texts should have been published by 1976 by the Egypt Exploration Society.

Hurry refers to the Trismegistic (Hermetic) literature as follows: 'If the references to Imhotep in Hermetic literature can be trusted, he was also interested in astronomy and astrology, although no special observations are associated with his name. Sethe gives various references to that literature, showing that Imhotep was reputed to have been associated with the god Thoth (Hermes) in astronomical observations.'[40] Obviously Imhotep, as chief priest under King Zoser (for he held that office as well), was associated with Thoth (Tat) in the form of the priesthood previously mentioned who had the 'Dark Rite' as their highest mystery. Here is actual confirmation, then, that it was astronomical matters with which they dealt. In other words, my astronomical interpretation receives some confirmation from this source as well. It is nice when loose ends tie up.

Inscriptions in a temple at Edfu built by Ptolemy III Euergetes I (237 B.C.) describe Imhotep as 'the great priest Imhotep the son of Ptah, who speaks or lectures'. Hurry says 'Imhotep enjoyed the reputation of being "one of the greatest of Egyptian sages";[41] his fame for wisdom made so deep an impression on his countrymen that it endured as a national tradition for many centuries.

'As regards his literary activities, he is said to have produced works on medicine and architecture, as well as on more general subjects, and some of his works were extant at the dawn of the Christian era. . . . his eminence as a man of letters led him to be recognized as the "patron of scribes." '

In other words, he was the first great philosopher. And he obviously 'spoke and lectured' in his lifetime. Perhaps he was the first classical Greek in prototype. We also have something to look forward to – his tomb has yet to be discovered. It is thought to be at Sakkara, and the late Professor Emery more than once thought he had come close to discovering it in his excavations there, which are now being carried on by Professor Smith, who is a man with a strange enough aura about him to convince anyone that he is capable of making a discovery which would be the most important in archaeological history and beside which the minor and later tomb of a boy Pharaoh named Tutankhamen would entirely pale by comparison. But perhaps the most interesting thing about the possible forthcoming discovery of Imhotep's tomb is that it will almost certainly be full of books. Would a man like Imhotep be buried without them?

Bearing these books in mind (and I am sure they are there waiting underground like a time bomb for us), it is interesting to read this passage in 'The Virgin of the World' following shortly upon that previously quoted:

> The sacred symbols of the cosmic elements were hid away hard by the secrets of Osiris. Hermes, ere he returned to Heaven, invoked a spell on them, and spake these words: . . . 'O holy books, who have been made by my immortal hands, by incorruption's magic spells . . . (at this point there is a lacuna as the text is hopeless) . . . free from decay throughout eternity remain and incorrupt from time! Become unseeable, unfindable, for every one whose foot shall tread the plains of this land, until old Heaven doth bring forth meet instruments for you, whom the Creator shall call souls.'
>
> Thus spake he; and, laying spells on them by means of his own works, he shut them safe away in their own zones. And long enough the time has been since they were hid away.

In the treatise the highest objective of ignorant men searching for the truth is described as: '(Men) will seek out . . . the inner nature of the holy spaces which no foot may tread, and will chase after them into the height, desiring to observe the nature of the motion of the Heaven.

'These are as yet moderate things. For nothing more remains than Earth's remotest realms; nay, in their daring they will track out Night, the farthest Night of all.'

We 'will chase out into the height' of space to 'observe the nature of the motions of the Heavens', says this old (indeterminately old) treatise. How correct it was. We have now landed on the moon, which is 'chasing out into the height' with a vengeance. And we are indeed 'observing the nature of the motion of the Heavens'. And the treatise is also right in saying that 'these are yet moderate things'. For, as everyone knows, the people in the space programme feel as if they have only just begun. Man will only pause properly again when he has made the entire solar system his familiar and his own. Then we shall be faced with the limitations of our solar system and the barrier that separates it from the stars. What then? Yes, what we have done to date certainly deserves the description of 'yet moderate things'. Vasco da Gama may have congratulated himself on his brilliant navigational accomplishments, but as we can clearly see in his case, a beginning is only a beginning. It is 'yet moderate things'.

According to the treatise, after these moderate things we shall 'in our daring' even learn the greatest secret . . . we shall discover 'Night'. And the meaning of the 'Dark Rite' will become clear. And as this rite and this mystery concern Isis and the star Sirius and by the context of this prophecy clearly concerns the heavens, can we be accused of sensationalism in making the suggestion that nothing would shake up the human race more than having the discovery of intelligent life elsewhere in the universe proven for the first time? And what if the dark companion of Sirius really does hold the answer to this mystery? What if the nearest centre of civilization really is based at the Sirius system and keeps a watchful eye on us from time to time? What if this is proven by our detecting on our radio telescopes actual traces of local radio communications echoing down those nine light years of space in the vast spreading ripple of disintegrating signals that any culture remotely near to us in development would be bound to dribble forth into the surrounding universe? What if this happens? It will be like the sky falling in, won't it?

Notes

1. *Le Renard pâle*, p. 325. Figure 109 in that book shows it, drawn as 'the meeting of Sirius with the Sun'.
2. Mariette, *Denderah*, Vol. I, p. 206.
3. Aratus, *Phaenomena* 331–6. English translation in Loeb Library series, in volume with Callimachus and Lycophron. See bibliography.
4. Vol. I, p. 1, of *Egyptian Astronomical Texts*, Otto Neugebauer and Richard Parker, Brown University Press, 1960–7.
5. Ibid., Vol. I, p. 25.
6. *The Gods of the Egyptians*, London, 1904, Vol. II, p. 114.
7. Ibid., Vol. II, p. 113.
8. Ibid., Vol. II, p. 117.
9. Ibid., Vol. II, p. 215.
10. Ibid., Vol. II, pp. 202–3.
11. Ibid., Vol. II, p. 264.
12. Ibid., Vol. II, p. 265.
13. Ibid., Vol. II, p. 139.
14. Neugebauer and Parker, op. cit.
15. *Star Names, Their Lore and Meaning*, R. H. Allen, Dover Publications, New York, 1963, p. 130.
16. Neugebauer and Parker, op. cit.
17. *Star Names, Their Lore and Meaning*, p. 68.
18. Ibid., p. 65.
19. *Ancient Near Eastern Texts relating to the Old Testament*, ed. by James B. Pritchard, Princeton University Press, 1955, p. 33.
20. Ibid., p. 41.
21. Alexander Heidel, *The Babylonian Genesis*, University of Chicago Press, 1965, p. 86.
22. Wallis Budge, op. cit., Vol. I, p. 284.
23. Ibid., Vol. I, p. 290.
24. Ibid., Vol. II, p. 154, and Vol. I, p. 446.
25. Ibid., Vol. I, p. 154.

26. Ibid., Vol. II, p. 261.
27. Ibid., Vol. II, pp. 264–5.
28. Ibid., Vol. II, pp. 195–200.
29. Ibid., Vol. II, pp. 264–5.
30. 'Isis and Osiris', Loeb edition, p. 107.
31. Ibid., p. 145.
32. Ibid., p. 39.
33. Ibid., p. 149.
34. Ibid., p. 147.
35. *The Oracles of Zeus*, H. W. Parke, p. 13.
36. *Thrice Greatest Hermes*, G. R. S. Mead, John Watkins, London, 1964.
37. Ibid, Vol. III, p. 95. He quotes from Wessley, *Denkschr d. k. Akad.* (1893), p. 37, l. 500.
38. See *Imhotep, the Vizier and Physician of King Zoser and afterwards the Egyptian God of Medicine*, by Jamieson B. Hurry, Oxford University Press, 1926.
39. I. E. S. Edwards, *The Pyramids of Egypt*, Penguin, 1970.
40. Hurry, op. cit., p. 20.
41. Ibid., p. 40.

SUMMARY

Sirius was the most important star in the sky to the ancient Egyptians. The ancient Egyptian calendar was based on the rising of Sirius. It is established for certain that Sirius was sometimes identified by the ancient Egyptians with their chief goddess Isis.

The companion of Isis was Osiris, the chief Egyptian god. The 'companion' of the constellation of the Great Dog (which includes Sirius) was the constellation of Orion. Since Isis is equated with Sirius, the companion of Isis must be equated, equally, with the companion of Sirius. Osiris is thus equated on occasion with the constellation Orion.

We know that the 'companion of Sirius' is in reality Sirius B. It is conceivable that Osiris-as-Orion, 'the companion of Sirius', is a stand-in for the invisible true companion Sirius B.

'The oldest and simplest form of the name' of Osiris, we are told, is a hieroglyph of a throne and an eye. The 'eye' aspect of Osiris is thus fundamental. The Bozo tribe of Mali, related to the Dogon, call Sirius B 'the eye star'. Since Osiris is represented by an eye and is sometimes considered 'the companion of Sirius', this is equivalent to saying that Osiris is 'the eye star', provided only that one grants the premises that the existence of Sirius B really was known to the ancient Egyptians and that 'the companion of Sirius' therefore could ultimately refer to it.

The meanings of the Egyptian hieroglyphs and names for Isis and Osiris were unknown to the earliest dynastic Egyptians themselves, and the names and signs appear to have a pre-dynastic origin – which means around or before 3200 B.C., in other words 5,000 years ago at least. There has been no living traditional explanation for the meanings of the names and signs for Isis and Osiris since at least 2800 B.C. at the very latest.

'The Dog Star' is a common designation of Sirius throughout known history. The ancient god Anubis was a 'dog god', that is, he had a man's body and a dog's head.

In discussing Egyptian beliefs, Plutarch says that Anubis was really the son of Nephthys, sister to Isis, although he was said to be the son of Isis. Nephthys was 'invisible'. Isis was 'visible'. (In other words, the visible mother was the stand-in for the invisible mother, who was the true mother, for the simple reason that the invisible mother could not be perceived.)

Plutarch said that Anubis was a 'horizontal circle, which divides the invisible part . . . which they call Nephthys, from the visible, to which they give the name Isis; and as this circle equally touches upon the confines of both light and darkness, it may be looked upon as common to them both.'

This is as clear an ancient description as one could expect of a circular orbit (called 'Anubis') of a dark and invisible star (called 'Nephthys') around its 'sister', a light and visible star (called 'Isis') – and we know Isis to have been equated with Sirius. What is missing here are the following specific points which must be at this stage still our assumptions: (a) The circle is actually an orbit. (b) The divine characters are actually stars, specifically in this context.

Actually, Anubis and Osiris were sometimes identified with one another. Osiris, the companion of Isis who is sometimes 'the companion of Sirius' is also sometimes identified with the orbit of the companion of Sirius, and this is reasonable and to be expected.

Isis-as-Sirius was customarily portrayed by the ancient Egyptians in their paintings as travelling with two companions in the same celestial boat. And as we know, Sirius does, according to some astronomers, have two companions, Sirius B and Sirius C.

To the Arabs, a companion-star to Sirius (in the same constellation of the Great Dog) was named 'Weight' and was supposed to be extremely heavy – almost too heavy to rise over the horizon. 'Ideler calls this an astonishing star-name,' we are told, not surprisingly.

The true companion-star of Sirius, Sirius B, is made of super-dense matter which is heavier than any normal matter in the universe and the weight of this tiny star is the same as that of a gigantic normal star.

The Dogon also, as we know, say that Sirius B is 'heavy' and they speak of its 'weight'.

The Arabs also applied the name 'Weight' to the star Canopus in the constellation Argo. The *Argo* was a ship in mythology which carried Danaos and his fifty daughters to Rhodes. The *Argo* had fifty oarsmen under Jason, called Argonauts. There were fifty oars to the *Argo*, each with its oarsman-Argonaut. The divine oarsman was an ancient Mediterranean motif with sacred meanings.

The orbit of Sirius B around Sirius A takes fifty years, which may be related to the use of the number fifty to describe aspects of the *Argo*.

There are many divine names and other points in common between ancient Egypt and ancient Sumer (Babylonia). The Sumerians seem to have called Egypt by the name of 'Magan' and to have been in contact with it.

The chief god of Sumer, named Anu, was pictured as a jackal, which is a variation of the dog motif and was used also in Egypt for Anubis, the dog and the jackal apparently being interchangeable as symbols. The Egyptian form of the name Anubis is 'Anpu' and and is similar to the Sumerian 'Anu', and both are jackal-gods.

The famous Egyptologist Wallis Budge was convinced that Sumer and Egypt both derived their own cultures from a common source which was 'exceedingly ancient'.

Anu is also called An (a variation) by the Sumerians. In Egypt Osiris is called An also.

Remembering that Plutarch said that Anubis (Anpu in Egyptian) was a circle, it is interesting to note that in Sanskrit the word Aṇḍa means 'ellipse'. This may be a co-incidence.

Wallis Budge says that Anubis represents time. The combined meanings of 'time' and 'circle' for Anubis hint strongly at 'circular motion'.

The worship of Anubis was a secret mystery religion restricted to initiates (and we thus do not know its content). Plutarch, who writes of Anubis, was an initiate of several mystery religions, and there is reason to believe his information was from well-informed sources. (Plutarch himself was a Greek living under the Roman Empire.) A variant translation of Plutarch's description of Anubis is that Anubis was 'a combined relation' between Isis and Nephthys. This has overtones which help in thinking of 'the circle' as an orbit – a 'combined relation' between the star orbiting and the star orbited.

The Egyptians used the name Horus to describe 'the power which is assigned to direct the revolution of the sun', according to Plutarch. Thus the Egyptians conceived of and named such specific dynamics – an essential point.

Plutarch says Anubis guarded like a dog and attended on Isis. This fact, plus Anubis being 'time', and 'a circle' suggests even more an orbital concept – the ideal form of attendance of the prowling guard dog.

Aristotle's friend Eudoxus (who visited Egypt) said that the Egyptians had a tradition that Zeus (chief god of the Greeks whose name is used by Eudoxus to refer to his Egyptian equivalent, which leaves us wondering which Egyptian god is meant – presumably Osiris) could not walk because 'his legs were grown together'. This sounds like an amphibious creature with a tail for swimming instead of legs for walking. It is like the semi-divine creature Oannes, reputed to have brought civilization to the Sumerians, who was amphibious, had a tail instead of legs, and retired to the sea at night.

Plutarch relates Isis to the Greek goddess Athena (daughter of Zeus) and says of them they were both described as 'coming from themselves', and as 'self-impelled motion'. Athena supervised the *Argo* and placed in its prow the guiding oak timber from Dodona (which is where the Greek ark landed, with the Greek version of the Biblical Noah, Deukalion, and his wife Pyrrha). The *Argo* thus obtained a distinctive 'self-impelled motion' from Athena, whom Plutarch specifically relates to Isis in this capacity.

The earliest versions of the *Argo* epic which were written before the time of Homer are unfortunately lost. The surviving version of the epic is good reading but relatively recent (third century B.C.)

The Sumerians had 'fifty heroes', 'fifty great gods', etc., just as the later Greeks with their *Argo* had 'fifty heroes' and the *Argo* carried 'fifty daughters of Danaos.'

An Egyptian papyrus says the companion of Isis is 'Lord in the perfect black'. This sounds like the invisible Sirius B. Isis's companion Osiris 'is a dark god'.

The Trismegistic treatise 'The Virgin of the World' from Egypt refers to 'the Black Rite', connected with the 'black' Osiris, as the highest degree of secret initiation possible in the ancient Egyptian religion – it is the ultimate secret of the mysteries of Isis.

This treatise says Hermes came to earth to teach men civilization and then again 'mounted to the stars', going back to his home and leaving behind the mystery religion of Egypt with its celestial secrets which were some day to be decoded.

There is evidence that 'the Black Rite' did deal with astronomical matters. Hence the Black Rite concerned astronomical matters, the black Osiris, and Isis. The evidence mounts that it may thus have concerned the existence of Sirius B.

A prophecy in the treatise 'The Virgin of the World' maintains that only when men concern themselves with the heavenly bodies and 'chase after them into the height' can men hope to understand the subject-matter of the Black Rite. The understanding of astronomy of today's space age now qualifies us to comprehend the true subject of the Black Rite, if that subject is what we suspect it may be. This was impossible earlier in the history of our planet. It must be remembered that without our present knowledge of white dwarf stars which are invisible except with modern telescopes, our knowledge of super-dense matter from atomic physics with all its complicated technology, etc., none of our discussion of the Sirius system would be possible; it would not be possible to propose such an explanation of the Black Rite at all – we could not propound the Sirius question. Much material about the Sumerians and Babylonians has only been circulated since the late 1950s and during the 1960s, and our knowledge of pulsars is even more recent than that. It is doubtful that this book could have been written much earlier than the present. The author began work in earnest in 1967 and finished the book in 1974. Even so, he feels the lack of much needed information: sites remain unexcavated, texts untranslated from various ancient languages, astronomical investigations are perpetually incomplete. The author has also found it difficult to master material from so many different fields and wishes he were much better qualified. The Sirius question could not realistically have been posed much earlier, and future discoveries in many fields will be essential to its full consideration.

CHAPTER THREE

The Sacred Fifty

We must return to the treatise 'The Virgin of the World'. This treatise is quite explicit in saying that Isis and Osiris were sent to help the Earth by giving primitive mankind the arts of civilization:

And Horus thereon said:
'How was it, mother, then, that Earth received God's Efflux?'
And Isis said:
'I may not tell the story of (this) birth; for it is not permitted to describe the origin of thy descent, O Horus (son) of mighty power, lest afterwards the way-of-birth of the immortal gods should be known unto men – except so far that God the Monarch, the universal Orderer and Architect, sent for a little while thy mighty sire Osiris, and the mightiest goddess Isis, that they might help the world, for all things needed them.
' 'Tis they who filled life full of life. 'Tis they who caused the savagery of mutual slaughtering of men to cease. 'Tis they who hallowed precincts to the Gods their ancestors and spots for holy rites. 'Tis they who gave to men laws, food and shelter.' Etc.

They are also described as teaching men how to care for the dead in a specifically Egyptian way, which inclines one to wonder how a Greek could conceivably have written this unless during the Ptolemaic period: "Tis they who taught men how to wrap up those who ceased to live, as they should be.'
Now anyone knows this is Egyptian and not Greek practice. What Neoplatonist would include such a statement unless it were actually taken from an early source which he used, and which had been written by someone actually living in Egypt?
The treatise ends this long section with:

' 'Tis they alone who, taught by Hermes in God's hidden codes, became the authors of the arts, and sciences, and all pursuits which men do practise, and givers of their laws.
' 'Tis they who, taught by Hermes that the things below have been disposed by God to be in sympathy with things above, established on the earth the sacred rites over which the mysteries in Heaven preside. [The absence here of a blatant propaganda for astrology argues a pre-Ptolemaic date for this treatise; after the Greek and Babylonian influx a mild statement like this would have been almost impossible to make without the author dragging in all the paraphernalia of the astrology-craze of late Egypt.]

' 'Tis they who, knowing the destructibility of (mortal) frames, devised the grade of prophets, in all things perfected, in order that no prophet who stretched forth his hands unto the Gods, should be in ignorance of anything, that magic and philosophy should feed the soul, and medicine preserve the body when it suffered pain.

'And having done all this, my son, Osiris and myself perceiving that the world was (now) quite full, were thereupon demanded back by those who dwell in Heaven . . .'

And in the treatise Isis claims that the 'Black Rite' honours her and 'gives perfection'. It is also concerned with the mysterious thing called 'Night' – 'who weaves her web with rapid light though it be less than Sun's'. It is made plain that 'Night' is not the night sky because it moves in the Heaven along with 'the other mysteries in turn that move in Heaven, with ordered motions and with periods of times, with certain hidden influences bestowing order on the things below and co-increasing them'.

We must scrutinize the description of what is labelled 'Night' in this treatise. This description makes it perfectly clear that 'Night' is not 'night', but a code word. For it is said to have 'light though it be less than Sun's'. The dark companion of Sirius is a star and has light, though less than the sun. Also 'Night' is said 'to weave her web with rapid light' which specifically describes the object as being in motion. Since Sirius B orbits Sirius A in fifty years, it moves more rapidly even than three of our sun's planets in our own solar system – Pluto, Neptune, and Uranus. Of these three, Uranus is the most rapid, and its orbit about the sun takes eighty-four years. So here is a star orbiting more rapidly than a planet! That may indeed be said to constitute 'weaving a web with rapid light'!

Now to turn to the Sumerian culture, or, more properly, the Sumero-Akkadian culture. It was roughly contemporaneous with ancient Egypt and I had already suspected its basic religious concepts to be so similar to those of Egypt that I imagined them to have a common origin. Then I discovered that Wallis Budge thought the same thing from his point of view as a distinguished Egyptologist. I am not aware of any Sumerologists having dealt with this particular problem. Far more attention has been given to the known trading links which existed between Sumer and the Indus valley civilization, and also to the problem of deciding where Dilmun was located. Kramer thinks Dilmun was the Indus valley; Bibby follows Peter B. Cornwall and thinks it was the island of Bahrein in the Persian Gulf. But to the Sumerians this land, which lay in a direction seemingly other than that of Egypt, had immense importance. Consequently, it has tended to monopolize the attention of modern scholars investigating Sumerian geographical references. Kramer thinks that the land 'Magan' was probably Egypt and that Sargon even sent his armies there.

The basic Egyptian astronomy and the basic Sumero-Akkadian astronomy (this assumes a continuity of some sort, as there is no overtly astronomical treatise from the early period of Sumer) are identical. For the multitude of variations at a less basic level, one may consult Professor Otto Neugebauer's *The Exact Sciences in Antiquity*. But Neugebauer's interests lie with late material, as he admits, and he does less than justice to the earlier material, skimming over it quickly and making little of some things which are important. Here is an example of his attitude expressed in his own words near the beginning of Chapter V: 'Our description of Babylonian astronomy will be rather incomplete. The historical development will be given in bare outline. As in the case of Egypt, a detailed discussion of the few preserved early texts would require not only too much room but would also unduly exaggerate their historical importance. For the late period, however, the opposite situation prevails.' Well, at least Professor Neugebauer is honest about his preferences.

Having nodded in the direction of an authority who has voluntarily abdicated, we proceed. For our evidence we turn to E. A. Speiser's translation[1] of the Akkadian creation epic know as the *Enuma elish* from the first two words of the text which mean 'When on high . . . '. At the very beginning of this text we read:

> He constructed stations for the great gods,
> Fixing their astral likenesses as constellations.
> He determined the year by designating the zones:
> He set up three constellations for each of the twelve months.
> After defining the days of the year [by means] of (heavenly) figures,
> He founded . . ., etc.

In other words, the text gives a system identical with that recorded in the Egyptian star clocks. Twelve months composed of three ten-day weeks each, resulting in thirty-six constellations or 'decans' designating astral likenesses of gods. The text specifically states that there are twelve months consisting of three periods each (unless one strains the point enormously and maintains on no grounds whatsoever that these three periods are unequal, they must be of ten days each – hence 'ten-day weeks' as in Egypt), and that a constellation or 'zone' of the sky applies to each of these 'weeks'. Since three times twelve equals thirty-six, we have thirty-six decans, each of which is 'designated' by a constellation. And also as in Egypt, each decan is an 'astral likeness' of a great god. It is surprising that no scholar has seen that this passage in the *Enuma elish* describes the Egyptian star-clock system down to the last detail.

No doubt also the five 'epagomenal' days left over in order to fill out this resulting 360-day year to a 365-day year are referred to in the line: 'After defining the days of the year of (heavenly) figures,' which is again identical with the Egyptian tradition where the five left-over days are each assigned to five different gods or heavenly figures and thus defined. In Egypt these five left-over days are called 'the days upon the year'. These five days are also extremely important in Maya astronomy. But if we get into a discussion of Maya astronomy, we shall be stirring up a hornets' nest. It is not relevant to the purposes of this book.

We can see that the astronomical systems in Egypt and Sumer were absolutely identical in their fundamentals. Now these similarities between Egypt and Sumer are a far different matter from similarities of names of gods and religious concepts. One can always maintain that people in different parts of the globe spontaneously produce identical sounds when awe-struck by divine concepts. 'Everybody around the world says "Ma!" to Mother,' as we have all heard many times. But an astronomical system of this kind is a complex set of specific data. The fact that this Akkadian text tentatively dated by Speiser at the Old Babylonian period (i.e. the early part of the second millennium B.C.) records an astronomical system of this complexity which is identical with that of the Egyptian star clocks can be said to prove either contact between these two civilizations or a common derivation for the system. And it suggests a date which could serve as an upper limit. Culture contact during which this information was shared could not have been any later. Let any latest date accepted for the writing of the *Enuma elish* serve as an upper limit. If this be done, we find the first millennium B.C. as the upper limit, even for those who require incontrovertible physical proof. The contact between Egypt and Sumer must have been considerably earlier if direct, or it may not have been a contact, but rather a common derivation (which was Wallis Budge's favoured idea).

The Egyptian star clocks date from at least the reigns of Seti I (1303 – 1290 B.C.) and Ramses IV (1158 – 1152 B.C.) of the XIXth and XXth Dynasties respectively, on the walls of whose tombs they are found. Therefore these star clocks are at least as old as 1300 B.C. and seem to go back to the very origins of Egyptian culture. By the first millennium B.C. they had been changed and a fifteen-day week substituted for the ten-day week. Other innovations took place as well at later dates, and the system fell into a considerable decay and became, it seems, a relic. I should imagine that a rise in the popularity of the sun god Ra made stars and especially Sirius seem less important. In any case, the innate integrity of the Sirius system in Egypt began to rot away and be ignored by the first millennium B.C., as it was superseded by ideas more obvious and less eso-teric to impatient priests. Perhaps when this began to happen some purists may have gone off to other places where they hoped to retain the traditions without interference from decadent Pharaohs. We shall return much later to this idea, with some surprising information.

But let us return to Sumer and continue in hot pursuit. In Tablet VI of the *Enuma elish* we find an interesting passage. In it are mentioned the Anunnaki, who were the sons of An (An means 'heaven'), also known as Anu the great god. These Anunnaki were fifty in number and were called 'the fifty great gods'. Nearly always these Anunnaki were anonymous, the emphasis being on their number and their greatness and their control over fate. No certain identifica-tion of any important Sumerian god with any one of the Anunnaki exists except peripherally (as I shall describe later). In fact, all Sumerologists have been puzzled by the Anunnaki. They have not been 'identified' and no one knows exactly what is meant by them. They recur often throughout the texts, which makes it all the more annoying that nowhere are they explicitly explained. But their apparent importance to the Sumerians cannot be questioned.

In an early Sumerian fragment (from a time long before the civilization of the Babylonians) of the material concerning the epic hero Gilgamesh, entitled 'Gilgamesh and the Land of the Living', we find an antecedent to the tradition of the Argonauts of the Greeks. This fragment appears in a translation by Kramer.[2] In fact, I feel it is safe to say that this Sumerian fragment is the earliest known form of the story of that hero who was later to be named Jason. In the story from this fragment, the hero, Gilgamesh, wishes to go to the 'land of the living', which is described as being in the charge of the sun god Utu. In the story of Jason and the Argonauts, the hero, Jason, wishes to search for the golden fleece, which is known to be a solar symbol. In the Sumerian fragment we also find the surprising line: 'The hero, his teeth are the teeth of a dragon.' In the Jason story, the hero, Jason, sows the dragon's teeth! (So does Cadmus in another Greek tale which we shall examine later.)

In the Jason story, Jason is accompanied on his quest by the fifty Argonauts. In the Sumerian fragment, Gilgamesh is accompanied by fifty companions also! Here is the relevant passage (in which Gilgamesh is speaking):

'Who has a house, to his house! Who has a mother, to his mother!
'Let single males who would do as I (do), fifty, stand by my side.'
Who had a house, to his house; who had a mother, to his mother,
Single males who would do as he (did), fifty, stood at his side.
To the house of the smiths he directed his step,
The . . . , the . . . -axe, his 'Might of Heroism' he caused to be cast there.
To the . . . garden of the plain he [directed] his step,
The . . . -tree, the willow, the apple tree, the box tree, the . . . [-tree] he
     [felled] there.
The 'sons' of his city who accompanied him [placed them] in their hands.

The fifty companions are mentioned several times. The fragmentary text is extremely broken and confused. Further light on the motif of sowing the dragon's teeth seems to come from a passage where Gilgamesh, who has for some unknown reason been asleep, was awakened, girded himself, stood like a bull on the 'great earth' and: 'He put (his) mouth to the ground, (his) teeth shook.' Note that it is at least open to question that the mouth and the teeth are actually his, and the word 'his' is both times in parentheses, put thus by the translator. But here is the entire passage:

He put (his) mouth to the ground, (his) teeth shook.
'By the life of Ninsun, my mother who gave birth to me, of pure Lugulbanda,
     my father,
'May I become as one who sits to be wondered at on the knee of Ninsun,
     my mother who gave birth to me.'

Apart from the fact that Gilgamesh's desire to sit on the knee of his mother, the goddess Ninsun, is similar to Horus sitting on the knee of his mother, the goddess Isis, as a constant motif in Egyptian art, there seems to be here an obscure but significant reference to the fact that if the hero puts his mouth to the ground and his teeth shake, he can invoke a kind of rebirth in strength. I suspect that the translation needs to be worked on further, but it is difficult, as there are so many words in Sumerian whose meanings are not precisely understood. Whether or not it is Gilgamesh's own mouth and teeth that are being discussed here, the fact is that Gilgamesh seeks strength by putting some teeth to the ground – either his or someone else's. As previously in the same tale, there has been the clear statement: 'The hero, his teeth are the teeth of a dragon', we may assume that Gilgamesh's own teeth are probably being referred to – *his own teeth which have previously been described as being dragon's teeth!*

Now in the lines following the putting of the teeth to the ground, we learn that Gilgamesh needs to summon strength by putting his teeth to the ground because he needs to fight. In the story of the *Argo*, Jason sows the dragon's teeth in the ground, and from them spring up armed soldiers who begin to fight – as is also the case in the story of Cadmus. So we see that in the two Greek myths, as also in this Sumerian fragment, the dragon's teeth go to the ground and a fight ensues where the hero has acquired superhuman strength. Later in this book we shall see the precise explanation of where this curious jumble originated, that it is specifically derived from an Egyptian sacred pun, and what it all means.

Meanwhile we must stay at our present level of enquiry. This book is an anabasis, or journey upward.

Let us look a little closer at the story of Jason and the golden fleece. The golden fleece was given to Phrixus and Helle by the god Hermes. The Egyptian god Anubis became known to the Greeks as their own Hermes. Furthermore, Diodorus Siculus (IV, 47) and Tacitus (*Ann.* VI, 34) explain the golden fleece's origin by saying that Phrixus and Helle (who flew away on the golden ram's back to Colchis, Helle falling in the Hellespont on the way and giving that body of water its name) really sailed in a ship with a ram's head on the prow, rather than having ridden the magical ram of the story. The fact that the more widespread myth which had an actual ram in the story maintained specifically that they *flew* on the golden ram, could refer to the idea of a celestial boat. Thus everyone is correct.

In any case, this boat would definitely have been a boat of Egypt, which to the Sumerians would have been called a 'Magan-boat', if we accept what Kramer and others believe, namely, that Magan is Egypt. And the boat was a 'gift from Hermes' – in other words from Anubis. No wonder, then, that the Sirius-related fifty is connected with the golden fleece as well as Anubis. It is worth mentioning also that the fifty Argonauts were also called the Minyae, as they were all related to each other and of the same family, descended all of them from Minyas, who had been the king of the Minyan city of Orchomenus in Boeotia, in Greece. So Jason and the Argonauts, fifty in number, all shared a kind of shadowy anonymity somewhat reminiscent of the fifty Anunnaki of Sumer, as they were often referred to simply as 'the Minyae' – a group of fifty related oarsmen in a celestial boat.

Later on we shall look extremely closely at the *Argo* story and also at the connections between the land Colchis, the object of its quest, and ancient Egypt, as attested for us by the historian Herodotus. But we must complete our look at the story of Gilgamesh and the Land of the Living. For even a boat is mentioned in that fragment, corresponding to the *Argo*. My equating a moment ago of the *Argo* with an Egyptian celestial barque must now be seen in conjunction with the following passage in which Gilgamesh's boat is specifically referred to as the 'Magan-boat'! I might add that the trees which Gilgamesh cut down and which his fifty companions 'placed in their hands' according to the text were probably their oars! (The text is too broken for anything at all to be certain, even punctuation, among the fourteen lines which follow that particular passage.) Here, then, is the passage about the boat:

'For me another will not die, the loaded boat will not sink,
The three-ply cloth will not be cut,
The . . . will not be overwhelmed,

House (and) hut, fire will not destroy.
Do thou help me (and) I will help thee, what can happen to us?
After it had sunk, after it had sunk,
After the Magan-boat had sunk,
After the boat, "the might of Magilum", had sunk,
In the . . . , the boat of the living creatures, are seated those who come out
    of the womb;
Come, let us go forward, we will cast eyes upon him,
If we go forward,
(And) there be fear, there be fear, turn it back,
There be terror, there be terror, turn it back,
In thy . . . , come, let us go forward.'

I must emphasize that there is confusion here, In a footnote Kramer emphasizes that from the line 'After it had sunk' it is no longer certain that Gilgamesh is still speaking. It is not clear whether the Magan-boat has really
sunk or whether this is a statement injected by Gilgamesh's 'faithful servant'
who immediately before the passage just quoted had told Gilgamesh:

'O my master, journey thou to the "land", I will journey to the city,
I will tell thy mother of thy glory, let her shout,
I will tell her of thy ensuing death, [let her] shed bitter tears.'

What seems to happen is that Gilgamesh here tells his frightened servant
(who just previously in the text is described as 'terror-stricken') that no other
will die for him and that 'the loaded boat will not sink'. Then the servant would
seem to break in again in his terror with his hypothetical tale to Gilgamesh's
mother with 'After it had sunk . . .' Then Gilgamesh again speaks, beginning
with, 'Come, let us go forward . . .'

The phrase 'those who come out of the womb' to describe those who are
seated in the Magan-boat may be meant to refer to those who are children of
the goddess Nintu (also known as Ninmah, Ninhursag, and Ki – 'earth').
This, combined with the strange reference to teeth, seems to refer to the children
of the earth-goddess springing from the womb of the earth – for Ki, the earth-
goddess (*ki* means 'earth' in Sumerian) is also Nintu or 'the goddess who gives
birth'. (Ninmah means 'the great goddess' and Ninhursag means 'the goddess
of the hill', a *hursag* or hill having been erected by her son – and she was named
after it by him in commemoration of a significant mythical event; in Egypt
Anubis is also called 'Anubis of the Hill', about which I shall have much to say
later on, but suffice it here to note that if the Sumerians were to speak of 'Anubis
of the Hill' they would call him Anpu-hursag.)

Basically in the goddess who gives birth, and also in the earth-goddess,
we thus find antecedents to the soldiers springing up from the dragon's teeth
sown in the earth, and also the throwing over his shoulder of the 'earth's bones'
(stones) by Deukalion, the Greek Noah, with the stones becoming men much as
the teeth did in the other stories. (And teeth are bones!)

In fact there are several points of contact other than this one between the
Deukalion and Jason stories. For the ark of Noah is a concept which is identical
with that of the ark of Deukalion, and both are magical ships in which sit 'those

who come out of the womb', in the sense that they repopulate the world after
the deluge. And both arks, but particularly that of Deukalion, are concepts
related to the *Argo*. (As anyone who has read the full *Epic of Gilgamesh* will
know, the ark of Noah in the Middle East before either the Hebrews or the
name Noah even existed, was the ark of Ziusudra or the ark of Utnapishtim,
and it occurs as an established element of the mythical background brought
into the *Epic*.) For the ark of Deukalion rested on the mountain by the sacred
oracle grove of Dodona, from which the *Argo* received its cybernetic guiding
timber. Also, of course, the origin of the story of the flood and the ark (containing as it does 'archetypes' of all living creatures in pairs, and the word *arche*
in Greek being definitely related to *ark*, as we shall see all too well much later
in this book) is Sumerian at least, if not even before that something else (which
we shall see in due course). But it was from this early source that the Greeks
obtained their Deukalion and the Hebrews their Noah – both of which are extremely late forms of an exceedingly ancient story, which existed thousands of
years before there were such things as either Greeks or Hebrews in existence.
(Anyone really interested in the origins of Greek and Hebrew civilizations should
read Professor Cyrus Gordon's brilliant book *The Common Background of Greek
and Hebrew Civilizations*.[3])

Now the point of going into all this is really to show that the Argonaut
motif of fifty heroes in a boat on a heroic quest exists in Sumer and forms a
complement to the 'fifty great gods'. For if the Magan-boat's fifty heroes are
seated, as the Anunnaki usually are, and are 'those who come forth out of the
womb', and thus children, so to speak, of Nintu, 'the goddess who gives birth',
then they may be directly equated with the Anunnaki. For the Anunnaki, as the
children of An, would also be the children of An's ancient consort Ki or Nintu.
In other words, the fifty heroes are heroic counterparts of the celestial Anunnaki. The corollary of this is, that the fact that there are fifty Anunnaki is not
so likely to be a coincidence as might have been thought. This brings out all
the more the immense significance of the number fifty.

The number occurs also in 'Gilgamesh, Enkidu, and the Nether World'.
There Gilgamesh dons armour which weighs 'fifty minas'. And in this tale also
Gilgamesh has fifty companions. In the later Babylonian version the fifty
companions are omitted from the story. At that date the true nature of the
symbolism of fifty must have been forgotten.

In his book *The Sumerians*, Kramer points out[4] that cultic and symbolic
weapons, maces with fifty heads, were fashioned by the ruler Gudea.

If we return for a moment to the intriguing *hursag* of the Sumerians, the
strange 'hill', we must recall that Ninhursag the goddess of the hill is identical
with Nintu the goddess who gives birth. Those are two separate names for the
same deity. Now it is interesting to note that in Egyptian the word *tu* means
'hill', so that if we take the word *nin* which means 'goddess' and add the Egyptian *tu* we have 'the goddess of the hill', which in fact is a synonym.

This is by no means the end of this interesting investigation. For if we
note that the Egyptian form of Horus (the son of Isis and Osiris) is Ḥeru
(which is a bit like Hero, isn't it?) and the traditional usage in Egyptian is to
speak continually of Ḥeru-sa-*something* which means Horus-the-son-of-*something*,
then we shall note that the strange and puzzling word *hursag* might really be the

Egyptian Ḥeru-sa-Agga, which means 'Horus the son of Agga'. It so happens
that Agga is an Egyptian synonym for Anubis. And 'Anubis of the Hill' has
already been mentioned. What is more, the word *hursag* in its older Sumerian
form is indeed *hursagga*, as may be seen in *The Babylonian Genesis*, Chapter 2,
by Alexander Heidel, 'A Sumerian Creation Account from Nippur', where we
read of the goddess Ninhursagga.

It also happens that Agga is in fact a reputable Sumerian name. There is in
translation a short 115-line text entitled 'Gilgamesh and Agga' from the
Sumerian period.[5] In line eighty of this text is the mention of a 'magurru-boat',
which is referred to in much the same way as the Magan-boat in 'Gilgamesh and
the Land of the Living'. Just as in that previous text the Magan-boat was being
discussed as to whether or not it would sink, so in this latter text the '*magurru*-
boat' is being discussed as to whether or not it would have its prow cut down.
Curiously, as in the other tale, in this one also the boat is described as having
had the worst fate actually occur, for in line ninety-eight we learn that 'the
prow of the *magurru*-boat was cut down', just as in the previous text we read:
'After the Magan-boat had sunk,/After the boat, "the might of Magilum",
had sunk.'

The connections between Egyptian and Sumerian words in sacred contexts
become so multifold that it is impossible to ignore the continuities between the
two cultures. Let us look, for instance, at the curious phenomenon of the cedar
which Gilgamesh is always being claimed to have cut down. In 'Gilgamesh and
the Land of the Living' Gilgamesh says: 'I would enter the land of the cut-
down cedar' and later he is described as he 'who felled the cedar', etc. That is
an early Sumerian text. In the actual *Epic* proper, as we have it, Gilgamesh
goes to the Cedar Mountain and slays the monster Humbaba (or Huwawa)
in 'the cedar mountain, the abode of the gods'. In Tablet V we read:

> [Gilgamesh] seized [the axe in (his) hand]
> [. . . and] felled [the cedar].
> [*But when Huwawa*] heard the *noise*,
> [He] became angry: 'Who has [come],
> [*Has slighted the trees, which*] had been grown in my mountains,
> And has felled the cedar?'

In Chapter XXII of *Hamlet's Mill*, Santillana and von Dechend identify
Huwawa with the planet Mercury. Now, remembering that Huwawa is also
the god of the cedar forest, it is interesting to note that in Egyptian the word
seb means 'cedar' and also means 'the planet Mercury'! The subject is far more
complicated than that, but I wanted to note the further source of an Egyptian
pun for yet another crucial Sumerian motif. In other words, Huwawa is connected with both Mercury (the planet) and the cedar, because the planet Mercury and the cedar are both called by the same name in Egyptian – namely,
seb.

Let us now put aside the enigmatic monster-god Huwawa and turn to the
Epic of Gilgamesh for another purpose. But in doing so let us note Kramer's
opinion in his essay 'The Epic of Gilgamesh and Its Sumerian Sources',[6]
that 'the poem was current in substantially the form in which we know it, as
early as the first half of the second millennium B.C.'

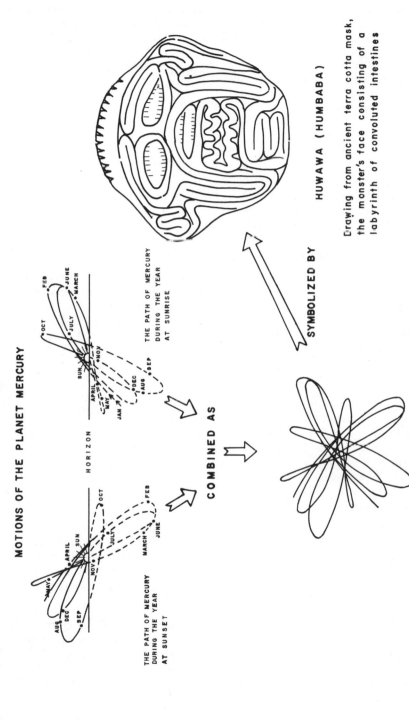

MOTIONS OF THE PLANET MERCURY

THE PATH OF MERCURY
DURING THE YEAR
AT SUNRISE

THE PATH OF MERCURY
DURING THE YEAR
AT SUNSET

COMBINED AS

SYMBOLIZED BY

HUWAWA (HUMBABA)

Drawing from ancient terra cotta mask,
the monster's face consisting of a
labyrinth of convoluted intestines

COMBINED MOTIONS OF MERCURY
THROUGHOUT THE YEAR

Figure 13

Let us recall that, in an early Sumerian fragment, Gilgamesh's mother was the goddess Ninsun 'who is versed in all knowledge', and upon whose knee he wanted to sit (like Horus on the knee of Isis). In the First Tablet we read:

Indeed, Gilgamesh arose to reveal dreams, saying to his mother:
'My mother, last night I saw a dream.
There were stars in the heavens;
As if it were the host of heaven [one] fell down to me.
I tried to lift it, but it was too heavy for me;
I tried to move it away, but I could not remove [it].
The land of Uruk was standing around [it],
[The land was gathered around it];
[The peop]le pressed to [ward it],
[The men th]ronged around it,
[. . .] while my fellows kissed its feet;
I bent over it [as] [over] a woman
[And] put it at [thy] feet,
[And thou thyself didst put] it on a par with me.'

There is another version of this (both as translated by Heidel)[7] at the beginning of Tablet II in the Old Babylonian version which is older than the above Assyrian version and preserves more of the original significance:

Gilgamesh arose to reveal the dream,
Saying to his mother:
'My mother, last night
I felt happy and walked about
Among the heroes.
There appeared stars in the heavens.
[The h]ost of heaven fell down toward me.
I tried to lift it but it was too heavy for me;
I tried to move it, but I could not move it.
The land of Uruk was gathered around it,
While the heroes kissed its feet.
I put my forehead [firmly] against [it],
And they assisted me.
I lifted it up and carried it to thee.'

Kramer translates the two versions somewhat differently.[8] One of the most important changes occurs in his translation of what Heidel before him had rendered as 'the host of heaven'. Kramer renders '*An*' not as 'heaven' but as An (or Anu), the god who was the father of the Anunnaki. And the word which Heidel renders as 'host' he comments on in a footnote at considerable length:

As regards *ki-sir*, there are too many possible meanings. Furthermore, the one adopted for this passage ('the *ki-sir* of Ninurta' earlier than our passage) should also apply to . . . the war-god Ninurta, and the sky-god Anu, Enkidu, and something that fell down from heaven. The common assumption that the author may have used in these passages the same term in more than one sense is unsatisfactory.

In the earlier edition I tried to justify for *kiṣru* the rendering 'liegeman' for the several passages in question. I now withdraw that suggestion. The correct sense, I believe, is indicated by the use of the term in medical contexts as 'concentration, essence', cf. E. Ebeling, *JCS*, IV (1950), 219. 'Essence', or some nuance of this term, could well be applied to deities as well as to missiles from heaven. Our poet had in mind, no doubt, some specific allusion, but the general meaning appears clear enough.

Kramer, then, renders 'the host of heaven' as 'the essence of An'. He says: 'Like the essence of Anu it descends upon me.' He adds another footnote to comment on the word 'it' in this sentence: 'One of the stars?'

Kramer also changes the last lines in the first version:

'[I] was drawn to it as though to a woman.
And I placed it at [thy] feet,
For thou didst make it vie with me.'

The emphasis here on being 'drawn to it' may be important. He continues:

[The wise mother of Gilgamesh, who] is versed in all knowledge,
Says to her lord;
[Wise Ninsun], who is versed in all knowledge,
Says to Gilgamesh:
'Thy rival, – the star of heaven,
Which descended upon thee like [the essence of Anu];
[Thou didst seek to lift it], it was too stout for thee;
[Thou wouldst drive it off], but couldst not remove it;
[Thou didst place] it at my feet,
[For it was I who made] it vie with thee;
Thou wert drawn to it as though to a woman –'

Let us look once again at part of the second version, this time as Kramer gives it:[9]

'My mother, in the time of night
I felt joyful and I walked about
In the midst of the nobles.
The stars appeared in the heavens.
The essence of Anu descended towards me.
I sought to lift it; it was too heavy for me!
I sought to move it; move it I could not!'

All this, which we have examined here in two translations each of two versions, was worth seeing from these several angles. It helps us cover all the possibilities of meaning. It should be obvious that the reference is clearly to a star connected with 'the essence of Anu' which 'draws him towards it' and is in the area of the (fifty) heroes – and is super-heavy.

Thus we see that in Sumer both the concepts of the heavy star (later *al Wazn*) and of the figure 'fifty' associated somehow with that star are present. Does this look familiar to anybody?

In Tablet VI of the *Enuma elish* we read[10] about the Anunnaki and something called 'the Bow Star' which is their brother and is in the midst of them as
they are seated in the celestial regions. This Bow Star is also the daughter of
Anu, who raises it up in their midst. (Remember 'the essence of Anu'.) What is
being referred to seems to be Sirius. Remember the Egyptian goddess Sati (or
Satis) with her bow, who was one of the three goddesses (one was Sothis and
the third was Anukis) riding in the celestial barque of Sothis (Sirius). Also
recall the other connections of the bow with Sirius, even in China. (And here
one must refer to the book *Hamlet's Mill* for many examples.[11]) Now with particular reference to the three goddesses which Neugebauer claims are versions
of Sothis ('The goddess Satis, who like her companion Anukis is hardly to be
taken as a separate constellation but rather as an associate of Sothis'), note the
following emphasis on three names for the star, only one of which is 'Bow
Star':

> The fifty great gods took their seats.
> The seven gods of destiny set up the three hundred [in heaven].
> Enlil raised the bo[w, his wea]pon, and laid (it) before them.
> The gods, his fathers, saw the net he had made.
> When they beheld the bow, how skilful its shape,
> His fathers praised the work he had wrought.
> Raising [it], Anu spoke up in the Assembly of the gods,
> As he kissed the bow: 'This is my daughter!'
> He mentioned the names of the bow as follows:
> 'Longwood is the first, the second is [. . .];
> Its third name is Bow-Star, in heaven I have made it shine.'
> He fixed a place which the gods, its brothers, [. . .].

A footnote says of the word 'its' in the last line: 'Referring to the Bow, as
indicated by the feminine possessive prefix in line 94.' (In Egyptian the word
Sept, which is the name of the star Sirius, also has the meaning 'a kind of wood',
though whether this could be 'longwood' or not is anyone's guess.) We continue:

> After Anu had decreed the fate of the Bow,
> And had placed the exalted royal throne before the gods,
> Anu seated it in the Assembly of the gods.

The phrase 'the Assembly of the gods' invariably refers to the seated assembly of the fifty Anunnaki. So it is clearly stated, we see, that this 'Bow Star'
– the daughter of An – was placed by An on the exalted royal throne in the
midst of the fifty Anunnaki. In Egypt, Isis as Sothis was also pictured as seated
on a white royal throne in the heavens. She too was the daughter of the sky
god. Recall also that the hieroglyph for Ast (or Isis) is a throne. And the
hieroglyph for her husband Asar (or Osiris) is a throne above an eye.

Before proceeding, we had better see who 'the seven gods of destiny'
are. They are often referred to as the seven Anunnaki of the underworld. This,
we shall see, also relates to the Sirius question. But the use of Anunnaki in this
way underscores the total anonymity of the term 'Anunnaki'. Needless to say,
none of these seven Anunnaki is ever identified as an individual god. They are
always 'the seven' underworld gods who determine destiny. The strictly celestial

Anunnaki are also known as the Igigi. No Sumerologist has satisfactorily explained all this. It is terribly imprecise and confusing – unless one had a structure to supply which fits under the cloth and matches the contours and can
thereby be accepted as a tentative basis of explanation.

Now let us try to think of what we know is connected with the celestial
Anunnaki and Sirius which also fits into this idea of there being seven Anun-
naki-gods in the underworld. Remember that in both Sumer and Egypt each
god of significance in astronomical terms has his own ten-day period or 'week'.
If we multiply seven (gods) times ten days we get seventy days. Is there any
basis for this length of time being of significance for the underworld in either
Sumer or Egypt? Yes! In Egypt the underworld is called the Duat (or Tuat)
and the seventy-day period is very significant there and relates intimately to
Sirius, as we have seen in our fairytale.

Parker and Neugebauer say[12]: 'It is here made clear that Sirius (Sothis)
gives the pattern for all the other decanal stars.' Sirius was, astronomically,the
foundation of the entire Egyptian religious system. Its celestial movements
determined the Egyptian calendar, which is even known as the Sothic Calendar.
Its heliacal rising marked the beginning of the Egyptian year and roughly
coincided with the flooding of the Nile. (Plutarch says the Nile itself was sometimes called Sirius.) This heliacal rising was the occasion of an important feast.
One can imagine a kind of New Year-cum-Easter. The heliacal rising was the
occasion when Sirius again rose into visibility in the sky after a period of seventy
days of being out of sight, during which time it was conceived of as being in the
Duat, or underworld. A further connection with Anubis comes in here, as
Anubis was conceived of as embalming Sothis for these seventy days in the Duat.
But as we all know, an embalmed mummy is supposed to come alive again.
And this is what happens to the mummy of Sothis. Sothis is reborn on the
occasion of her heliacal rising. Parker and Neugebauer also say:[13] 'During the
entire time of its purification it (Sothis, the star) was considered dead and it
was only with its rising again out of the Duat that it could once more be considered as living.'

The Egyptians stubbornly clung to the traditional seventy days as the prototype of an underworld experience, despite its inconvenience, and, as we have
already seen, 'Sirius gives the pattern for all the other decanal stars'. In
fact, it was the practice through all of Egyptian history for there to be a period
of precisely seventy days for the embalming of a human mummy – in imitation
of Sirius. Even during the late Ptolemaic period, the embalming process invariably lasted the precise period of seventy days.

Thus we find the explanation of the seven Anunnaki of the underworld!
It is also interesting to note that in ancient Mexico the underworld was thought
to have seven caves.

It is worth noting that in the story *Etana*,[14] about the legendary King Etana
not long after the Great Flood, who had to ascend to heaven in order to have
something done about his inability to have children (and thereby managed to
have a son and heir), mentions 'the divine Seven' and describes them as Igigi,
emphasizing the apparent interchangeability of the terms Igigi and Anunnaki.
Also 'the great Anunnaki' are described as 'They who created the regions, who
set up the establishments'.

In the 'Descent of Ishtar to the Nether World'[15] the Anunnaki are described as being brought forth (they are referred to as if they were stuffed animals being brought out of a closet, dusted off, and displayed in a taxidermists' contest) and seated on thrones of gold. Once more the throne concept appears. It seems all the Anunnaki ever do is sit and be symbolic.

Good little Anunnaki, like poodles, sit and smile at Anu. They are never given personalities, poor fellows. I might mention that in this story the nether world is described as having seven gates leading to seven successive rooms (or caves). It is obvious that the period of seventy days during which Sirius was 'in the underworld' to the Egyptians led to a breaking down of the seventy days into ten-day weeks, each with a god, giving seven gods. But these seven gods of the underworld must not have personalities lest there be the distraction of personal qualities to detract from the purely numerical significance of the concept. And of course the seven rooms of the seven gods are successive, leading from 'week' to 'week' until Sirius again rises. So we see yet another essential link between the early Sumerian concepts and the Egyptian concepts. When will Professor Neugebauer take notice of this and cease ruminating among the late Babylonians and Persians?

In later times the god Marduk usurped the central position of the pantheon from all the other gods in Babylon. The *Enuma elish* is largely a description of this process and is basically written to Marduk, telling of his honours. This was quite an innovation, a real centralization of power. 'The black-headed people', which is how the Sumerians usually referred to themselves in their writings (when the context is sufficiently pious they meekly call themselves 'the be-clouded'; it is also interesting to note that the Egyptians were known as 'the *melampodes*' or 'the black-*footed* people' to the Greeks!) obviously didn't take to the rise of Marduk with unanimous acclaim. In many ways the *Enuma elish* is a blatant propaganda tract for Marduk, alternately trying to convert and to denounce the people. Here we see the author trying to woo them:[16]

> Let his sovereignty be surpassing having no rival.
> May he shepherd the black-headed ones, his creatures.
> To the end of days, without forgetting, let them acclaim his ways.

Here, however, we see a more authoritarian approach, where the sugary smile dissolves:

> May he order the black-headed to re[vere him],

But the next moment, compromise comes again in the form of a mock-tolerance:

> Without fail let them support their gods!
> Their lands let them improve, build their shrines,
> Let the black-headed people wait on their gods.

In other words, the author despairs and goes into a sulk. For his next words indicate the sentiment, 'We don't need them, we'll go it alone':

> As for us, by however many names we pronounce it, he is our god!
> Let us then proclaim his fifty names!

In other words, the supporters of Marduk thought the best way to glorify their god was to give him fifty names. Then, with any luck, he would be omnipotent.

As Marukka, Marduk 'gladdens the heart of the Anunnaki, appeases their [spirits]'. All the fifty names are given, along with short comments following each. In a footnote Speiser says, revealingly, that: 'The text etymologizes the names in a manner made familiar by the Bible; the etymologies, which accompany virtually every name on the long list are meant to be cabalistic and symbolic rather than strictly linguistic, although some of them happen to be linguistically sound.'

The list ends and we read in the text:

With the title 'Fifty' the great gods
Proclaimed him whose names are fifty and made his way supreme.

This final note adds a last flourish of emphasis to the importance to the supreme god of the title 'Fifty' as well as the designation by fifty names.

There is one cluster of names among the fifty given which is of particular interest. They are Asaru, Asarualim, Asarualimnunna, and the group of three centred round the similar name Asaruludu (the other two being Namtillaku and Namru). I suspect these names of being related to the Egyptian Asar (Osiris). We have already seen how the An of Egypt was known in Sumer not only as An but as Anu, picking up a 'u' ending. It is therefore not so senseless to see in Asaru a Sumerian form of Asar, with the same 'u' ending added. But the Egyptians themselves also had an Asaru, or more precisely, an Asar-uu, whom Wallis Budge describes as 'a form of Osiris worshipped in lower Egypt'.

Since Asaru in Sumer corresponds to Asar-uu in Egypt, what about the Sumerian Asaruludu? In Egyptian a vegetative Osiris would be known as Asar-ruṭu but as is well known, the liquid 'r' and 'l' are in Egyptian entirely interchangeable and represented by the same hieroglyph. So Asar-ruṭu could just as well be Asar-luṭu, and the lingual 't' as opposed to a dental 't' is pronounced rather like a 'd', being a softer sound. If we merely transliterate it thus, we have Asar-ludu. It would mean, 'Osiris of the growing plants'. And in fact, in the Sumerian text, we find Asaru described as 'bestower of cultivation . . . creator of grain and herbs, who causes vegetation to sprout'.

Immediately after one of the Asaru-names of Marduk in the *Enuma elish* we find that his thirteenth name is Tutu. It so happens that Tutu is the name of an Egyptian god. Wallis Budge describes him as 'a lion-god, son of Neith'. (Wallis Budge says that Neith was: 'One of the oldest goddesses of Egypt. She was the goddess of hunting and weaving, but was identified with many other goddesses such as Isis, Meḥ-urt, and their attributes were assigned to her.'[17]) There is even an Egyptian precedent for the use of Tutu as one name of a god who has many names. The Egyptian monster of darkness, Apep, 'possessed many names; to destroy him it was necessary to curse him by each and every name by which he was known. To make quite sure that this should be done effectively, the Papyrus of Nesi-Amsu adds a list of such names, and as they are the foundation of many of the magical names met with in later papyri they are here enumerated . . .'[18] And one of these is Tutu. Surely this almost identical preoccupation with the need to enumerate every one of the magical names of a god in both countries must have common origins – especially as the name *Tutu* is in the lists of both countries.

It is important to look even closer at the Egyptian god Tutu. In Heidel's translation of the *Enuma elish* he gives for Asaruludu the early Sumerian epithet *namshub* as opposed to the late Babylonian form *namru* – both meaning 'bright', and in the text further explained as, 'The bright god who brightens our way'. In a footnote Heidel explains: 'The poets are here apparently playing on the Sumerian term *shuba*, which is equated with the Babylonian words *ebbu*, *ellu*, and *namru*, all of which mean "bright".' Now, what is so interesting is that in Egyptian the word *shu* means 'bright' and also describes the sun god – who is indeed a 'bright god who brightens our way'. So we see that *shu* in Egyptian means the same as *shuba* in Sumerian. Furthermore, both are made to apply to a description of the sun. Also the Sumerian *shuba* is made to refer to Asarluhi, and we may now take note of the further surprising fact that the Egyptian god Tutu is, according to Wallis Budge: 'a form of the god Shu, whose symbol was a lion walking'.[19]

So as we examine the material we find an increasingly complex weave of common patterns in Egypt and early Sumer both linguistically and in religion-astronomy. Later in the book we shall see this all reach a meaningful climax.

Notes

1. In Pritchard, *Ancient Near Eastern Texts*.
2. Also in Pritchard, ibid.
3. Pub. by W. W. Norton & Co., New York, 1965. An earlier edition of this book had a different title: *Before the Bible*.
4. *The Sumerians*, University of Chicago Press, 1963, p. 67.
5. Also in Pritchard, op. cit.
6. *Journal of the American Oriental Society*, 64 (1944), p. 11.
7. Heidel, Alexander, *The Gilgamesh Epic and Old Testament Parallels*, University of Chicago Press, 1970.
8. Pritchard, op. cit.
9. Ibid.
10. Ibid. Also see p. 514, Addenda: New Text Fragments, in same vol.
11. de Santillana, Giorgio, and von Dechend, Hertha, *Hamlet's Mill*, Macmillan & Company Ltd., London, 1969.
12. *Egyptian Astronomical Texts*, Vol. I, p. 74.
13. Ibid., p. 73.
14. Pritchard, op. cit., p. 114.
15. Ibid., p. 106.
16. In Pritchard, ibid.
17. *Book of the Dead*, trans. by Wallis Budge, p. 176, n.
18. Wallis Budge, *The Gods of the Egyptians*, Vol. I, p. 326.
19. Wallis Budge, op. cit., Vol. I, pp. 463-4.

SUMMARY

'The Black Rite' concerned something called 'Night' which was apparently an object that moves in heaven along with 'the other mysteries in turn that move in heaven, with ordered motions and periods of times'. It has less light than the sun and it 'weaves a web with rapid light'.

Sirius B moves in heaven with ordered motion and period, has less light than our sun, and distinctly weaves a web with its rapid motion, since it revolves round Sirius A in much less time than the planets Uranus, Neptune, and Pluto revolve around our own sun.

'Night' may thus refer to Sirius B, just as may 'black Osiris' and 'invisible Nephthys'.

In really early times the basic concepts of Egyptian astronomy and Sumerian astronomy were identical. Later many differences appeared. Authorities on ancient astronomy tend to give short shrift to the earlier times, hence the similarities between the two cultures in this particular field have tended to go unremarked.

In Egypt and Sumer (Babylonia) there were identical systems of dividing the calendar year into twelve months each composed of three weeks which lasted ten days apiece. Each week had a constellation of the night sky associated with it (which in modern parlance we might describe as 'being a kind of zodiac'). Thirty-six of these weeks added up only to 360 days, which was less than a year, so the 365-day year was obtained by adding on five extra days at the end.

Identical systems of such complexity in these two cultures mean that the relationship between Egypt and Sumer must be explored further.

In Sumer the 'fifty great gods' called the Anunnaki were anonymous as individuals and only ever spoken of as 'the fifty great gods' with the emphasis on their number. They were literally restricted to the level of being a numerological cipher. They are continually invoked and are of importance – but they never did anything but sit on their thrones and 'be fifty'.

In an early Sumerian tale of their epic hero Gilgamesh, we find him accompanied in his adventures by fifty heroes, reminiscent of the fifty Argonauts who accompanied Jason. 'His teeth are the teeth of a dragon', we are told – reminiscent of Jason sowing the dragon's teeth. And Gilgamesh also puts his teeth to the ground (that much we can gather, but the passage is obscure and he may really be sowing teeth). Each of his fifty heroic companions carries a specially felled tree for the journey – and the only reasonable purpose to go around carrying a tree seems to be that these trees were used as oars, especially as there is an association with a boat. This again is like the Argonauts. We thus seem to have found a Near Eastern tale from which the tale of the Argonauts was derived two thousand years or so later by the Greeks.

Gilgamesh somehow derives strength from putting his teeth to the ground. In the Greek tale, Jason sows the teeth and they spring up as strong soldiers – another parallel.

Anubis, who is now familiar to us from Egypt, was identified by the Greeks with their own god Hermes (known in Latin as Mercury). Hermes turned the Golden Fleece to gold originally, in the Greek myth. It was this same Golden Fleece that Jason and the Argonauts sought in their quest, and which they succeeded in seizing and taking away with them.

In the early Gilgamesh tale of the Sumerians, Gilgamesh and his fifty proto-Argonauts have some connection with a ship (the text is tantalizingly fragmented) called 'the Magan-boat'. It should be remembered that Magan is the Sumerian name for Egypt. Hence the boat is connected with Egypt.

All the Greek Argonauts were related to one another and more or less anonymous as individuals – reminiscent of the earlier Sumerian 'fifty heroes' accompanying Gilgamesh and also the 'fifty great gods' known as Anunnaki.

The Greek ark of Deukalion came to rest after the Flood at Dodona, from where the *Argo* received its guiding timber. The ark and the *Argo* apparently were related in other ways too.

Professor Cyrus Gordon has written an important book on common origins of Greek and Hebrew cultures from the Egyptian–Sumerian milieu of the cosmopolitan world of the ancient Mediterranean (see bibliography).

The 'fifty great gods' of Sumer, the Anunnaki, are invariably seated. Sacred oarsmen or Argonauts are all, of course, invariably seated while they are rowing. 'The fifty who sit' and 'the fifty who sit and row' seem to be a motif.

The other element besides the eye in the Osiris-name hieroglyph is the throne, which is the hieroglyph for Isis as well. The throne is a divine seat. The Sumerians frequently intoned of the Anunnaki that they were 'they who are seated on their thrones'; or sometimes for a bit more drama, 'the fifty great gods took their seats'. (Of course they did nothing even then.)

The Egyptian Anubis (Anpu) was a god 'of the hill'. The Sumerian god Anu's wife was a goddess 'of the hill'.

The older form of the Sumerian word for hill, *hursagga*, may be derived from the Egyptian Ḥeru-sa-agga, where 'agga' refers to Anubis (who was 'of the hill'). There are many other word and name similarities between Egypt and Sumer.

In the *Epic of Gilgamesh* a dream of Gilgamesh is described where he encounters a heavy star that cannot be lifted despite immense effort. This star descends from heaven to him and is described as connected with Anu (who is the god of heaven). Thus we find 'the heavy star' concept in Babylonia long before the Arabs even existed and were to have their star in the Great Dog (and the other in Argo) called 'Weight' and described as 'the heavy star'.

Gilgamesh is drawn to this heavy star irresistibly, in a manner described in a way that seems to hint at a kind of gravitational attraction (to those, that is, who are conscious of a 'heavy star' like Sirius B being gravitationally powerful as well as 'heavy').

The *Epic of Gilgamesh* refers to 'the essence of Anu' possessed by the star. The word rendered as 'essence' is used elsewhere in medical contexts referring to 'concentration, essence' – an intimation of super-dense matter? This 'concentrated star essence of Anu' was too heavy for Gilgamesh to lift in his dream.

It must be recalled that Gilgamesh had his fifty companions in the early versions of the *Epic* (they were discarded later, by Babylonian times). Hence connected with Gilgamesh we find: (a) Fifty anonymous companions seemingly important only as a numerological element in the story and in later times discarded as useless. (b) A super-heavy star connected with An (also an Egyptian name of Osiris, husband of Isis who was identified with Sirius). (c) A description of the star as being composed of a 'concentrated essence' and of having extreme powers of attraction described in a manner reminiscent of gravitational attraction.

These elements comprise almost a complete description of Sirius B: a super-heavy gravitationally powerful star made of concentrated super-dense matter ('essence') with the number fifty associated with it (describing its period?) – and connected with An (Anu), which we know to be linked in Egypt (and Gilgamesh's 'Magan-boat' seems Egyptian) with Sirius.

CHAPTER FOUR

The Hounds of Hell

Since Sirius is the Dog Star, let us turn to the dog-headed Sumerian goddess Bau. According to Thorkild Jacobsen,[1] 'Bau seems originally to have been goddess of the dog and her name, Bau, to have constituted an imitation of the dog's bark, as English "bowwow"'.* Bau was also the daughter of An. So here the dog-goddess is the daughter of An, whereas in Egypt the dog-god was himself An-pu (Anubis). Since An is connected with Sirius, we should thus not be surprised that he has a dog-goddess for a daughter in Sumer. Sirius as the Dog Star was a tradition which was not thought to have existed in Sumer, however, before now.

Since the fifty Anunnaki were children of An, and Bau is a daughter of An, it is not far-fetched to see in Bau a survival (for she is an old goddess who faded into obscurity in later times) of the concept of a dog-star goddess equivalent to Isis as Sothis. And it is interesting that she was dog-*headed*. For Anubis was not entirely a jackal or dog, he was merely jackal- or dog-*headed*.

Bau's husband Ninurta was the son of Enlil. Just as Marduk usurped the position of chief god, at a somewhat earlier time Enlil had usurped this position from An. (The situation is analogous to Greek mythology where Cronos usurped the position of Uranus and was in turn overthrown by Zeus.) There is an interesting 170-line hymn to Enlil[2] which seems to describe a stellar abode for the god. The 'lifted eye' or 'lifted light' scanning and searching the lands sounds reminiscent of the Dogon concept of the ray of Digitaria which once a year sweeps the Earth. In any case, a 'lifted light' which searches and scans is definitely a beam or ray, and is in its own right an interesting concept for the Sumerians to have had as situated in the celestial abode. I must emphasize in advance for the reader that lapis lazuli was considered by the Sumerians to represent the night sky. Here then are significant excerpts from the hymn:

> Enlil, whose command is far-reaching, whose word is holy,
> The lord whose pronouncement is unchangeable, who forever decrees
>   destinies,
> Whose lifted eye scans the lands,
> Whose lifted light searches the heart of all the lands,
> Enlil who sits broadly on the white dais, on the lofty dais . . .

---

* In Egyptian a word for 'dog, jackal', is Àuàu, which probably has the same 'dog's bark' derivation as the Sumerian Bau.

The lofty white dais of Sothis-Sirius is an Egyptian concept. It is Ast (Isis). It is also Asar (Osiris), with the addition of a hieroglyphic eye. Later we find in this hymn from Sumer the city of Nippur's temple in comparison:

Nippur – the shrine, where dwells the father, the 'great mountain',
The dais of plenty, the Ekur which rises . . . ,
The high mountain, the pure place . . . ,
Its prince, the 'great mountain', Father Enlil,
Has established his seat on the dais of the Ekur, lofty shrines;
The temple – its divine laws like heaven cannot be overturned,
Its pure rites, like the earth cannot be shattered,
Its divine laws are like the divine laws of the abyss, none can look upon
    them,
Its 'heart' like a distant shrine, unknown like heaven's zenith. . . .

And:

The Ekur, the lapis-lazuli house, the lofty dwelling place, awe-inspiring,
Its awe and dread are next to heaven,
Its shadow is spread over all the lands
Its loftiness reaches heaven's heart.

These mentions of the lapis lazuli aspect of Enlil's abode and also that it reaches heaven's heart make quite clear that we are not merely dealing with a solar description. It is not the sun but a stellar abode that is being distinctly described. Hence the references to the ray or beam are all the more curious as they do not refer to the sun's light as might have been thought from a superficial reading. We continue:

Heaven – he is its princely one; earth – he is its great one,
The Anunnaki – he is their exalted god;
When in his awesomeness, he decrees the fates,
No god dare look on him.

Here we see Enlil has been called the exalted god over the Anunnaki (in other texts his son Enki, or Ea, boasts that *he* is their 'big brother' and leader). Here Enlil has also himself been given the power of decreeing the fates, which the Anunnaki traditionally do themselves. In the fourth line from the end above, 'heaven' is An and 'earth' is Ki. An and Ki were married. The compound *an-ki* is Sumerian for 'heaven–earth' and is the word meaning 'universe'. Note the similarity between *an-ki* and the name of the Egyptian goddess Anukis who is identified with Sothis-Sirius. Also, of course, the similarity to the name Anunnaki.

So we find the above stellar descriptions of Enlil, the father-in-law of the dog-headed goddess we tentatively identify with Sirius. And we find those fifty irrepressible Anunnaki creeping in again. They manage to turn up everywhere, given half a chance, when the subject of Sirius comes up.

Now the many similarities between Sumer and Egypt which we have so far noted (with more to come), which have led us to consider the possibility of the two nations having been in some way linked, may be referred to in a most interesting passage from Josephus,[3] in which 'the children of Seth' are mentioned. Many ancient writers supposed Seth to have been Hermes Trismegistus.

This fact may suddenly be more important in the light of what we have begun to suspect about a scantily surviving authentic Hermetic tradition (maligned and obscured by a welter of useless, trivial co-survivals from later times). Here is the passage:

'The children of Seth' were the inventors of that peculiar sort of wisdom which is concerned with the heavenly bodies, and their order; and that their inventions might not be lost before they were sufficiently known, upon Adam's prediction, that the world was at one time to be destroyed by the force of fire, and at another time by the violence and quantity of water, they made two pillars, the one of brick, the other of stone. They described their discoveries on them both, that in case the pillar of brick should be destroyed by the flood, the pillar of stone might remain, and exhibit those discoveries to mankind, and also inform them that there was another pillar of brick erected by them. Now this remains in the land of Syria or Seirad to this day.

This passage calls forth many comments. The point which immediately springs to one's notice is that there is a 'pillar of brick' in the land of Syria, or in the land of Sumer-Akkad-Babylonia. Well, this is the very land of brick! It is the land of the brick ziggurat or 'great mountain' – a giant pillar if you like. But where is the land of stone? Why, it is obviously Egypt, the land of the great stone pyramids. Here, then, is a description of two linked cultures, one building brick edifices and the other building stone edifices. In Egypt we have the Great Pyramid, which so many people have believed to contain in its basic construction the proportions and measurements to demonstrate that it was constructed by highly advanced and civilized men. The great ziggurats of Babylon and other cities, too, though in a more ruinous state, seem to embody in their construction much that is profound. Can it be that Josephus has preserved a tradition of the link between Egypt and Sumer and their respective types of building? He says the link was an astronomically-defined one. 'The children of Seth' first possessed 'that peculiar sort of wisdom which is concerned with the heavenly bodies'. Well, we have already discovered for ourselves that the fundamental astronomical and astronomical-religious concepts were common to earliest Egypt and Sumer. And here is Josephus telling us the same thing, and what is more, telling us what the treatise 'The Virgin of the World' would have us know – that it all began with Hermes Trismegistus in the way we have previously discussed.

But now let us pursue other relevant ramifications of Egypt found elsewhere. And let us do so by returning to the subject of the *Argo* and the fifty Argonauts, who were all Minyae (descendants of Minyas), who were led by Jason (also a descendant of Minyas) in the quest for the golden fleece at the mysterious land of Colchis, which actually existed and was just about as strange a locale as one could wish. For if you sail through the Hellespont (named after Helle, who fell from the golden ram) into the Black Sea (called the Euxine Sea by the Greeks), and follow the coast of present-day Turkey until you come to the region of the border with the Soviet Union of today, you will have come to Colchis. It is a pretty strange place for the Greeks to attach so much importance to. It sits at the foot of the formidable Caucasus Mountains and not far away are the Georgian people who live in their mountains to such amazing ages as a hundred and ten, with a culture peculiarly their own. Not far to the south is that strange place, Mount Ararat, where the ark of Noah landed after the Flood. Surely this is a most unusual land, and far removed from the Greek world. Or is it?

Minyas had a great-grandson called Phrixus. Phrixus had four sons who lived in Colchis, to which he had fled on the back of the golden ram and where he gave the golden fleece to the local King of Colchis, and in return was made welcome and married the king's daughter. It is obvious that these four sons were only half-Colchian and would feel some loyalty towards their father's homeland which was in mainland Greece. Sure enough, on his deathbed Phrixus asked his sons to return to Orchomenos, his home in Greece, to reclaim their birthright there. This they agreed to do. For Phrixus's father had been the King of Orchomenos (as had Minyas) and these sons should be able to claim what honour and position (not to mention more material matters) was rightly theirs. However, they knew that setting things straight might be a bit difficult, as their father and his sister Helle (who fell into the Hellespont) had left in rather a hurry on the golden ram with the blessing of Hermes, but not with too many tears being shed in Orchomenos at the time.

So these four sons set out and were shipwrecked but were fortunately picked up and rescued. Who rescued them? None other than our fifty Argonauts who were just passing. In fact, these Argonaut cousins of theirs were at that moment just happening by on their way to Colchis where their mission was to try to get that fleece back. The four young fellows had no objection to such a plan, especially as they were also descended from Minyas. The Argonauts had been losing some of their men (for instance, Hercules and Hylas had vanished; Hylas was dragged down into a stream by a passionate water nymph and Hercules went berserk and wandered off into Turkey calling his name in vain, later founding cities and doing various Herculean things). So these four fellows from Colchis were just the thing to recharge the ranks.

But what about this place Colchis? Perhaps if we examine it we shall find some Egyptian connections. Anything seems to be possible in a magical land like this.

In fact if we look at the *Histories* of Herodotus[4] we read: 'It is undoubtedly a fact that the Colchians are of Egyptian descent. I noticed this myself before I heard anyone else mention it, and when it occurred to me I asked some questions both in Colchis and in Egypt, and found that the Colchians remembered the Egyptians more distinctly than the Egyptians remembered them. The Egyptians did, however, say that they thought the Colchians were men from Sesostris' army.' This Sesostris is identified tentatively by scholars with Ramses II. Herodotus continues:

My own idea on the subject was based first on the fact that they have black skins and woolly hair (not that that amounts to much, as other nations have the same), and secondly, and more especially, on the fact that the Colchians, the Egyptians, and the Ethiopians are the only races which from ancient times have practised circumcision. The Phoenicians and the Syrians of Palestine themselves admit that they adopted the practice from

Egypt, and the Syrians who live near the rivers Thermodon and Parthenius, learnt it only a short time ago from the Colchians. No other nations use circumcision, and all these are without doubt following the Egyptian lead. As between the Egyptians and the Ethiopians, I should not like to say which learned from the other, for the custom is evidently a very ancient one; but I have no doubt that the other nations adopted it as a result of their intercourse with Egypt, and in this belief I am strongly supported by the fact that Phoenicians, when they mix in Greek society, drop the Egyptian usage and allow their children to go uncircumcized.

And now I think of it, there is a further point of resemblance between the Colchians and Egyptians: they share a method of weaving linen different from that of any other people; and there is also a similarity between them in language and way of living.*

So here we see a probable (indeed, almost entirely certain) explanation for the connection of Colchis with the Argonaut story. No wonder the Hermes-given (which is to say, Anubis-given) golden fleece was at Colchis. For Colchis was a thoroughly Egyptian country. But because the heroes of a Greek tale must be Greeks and not Egyptians, the Argonauts are all Minyae from Greece. The familiar anonymity of 'the fifty' witnessed by us with the Anunnaki of Sumer, prevails here among the Argonauts as well. Different epic poets who treated of the tale chucked in various epic heroes. In the main surviving *Argonautica* by Apollonius of Rhodes, Orpheus and Herakles (Hercules) are among the crew, though Hercules is left behind as I have just said. In fact, Hercules was so obviously borrowed for his 'box-office draw' as a 'guest star' in a cameo performance that we can't really take the matter seriously.

On with the story and those Argonauts. I said that Orpheus was included in the cast by that great film producer Apollonius of Rhodes. But another competing film producer, Pherecydes, insisted that Orpheus was not an Argonaut. Diodorus Siculus, a great supporter of women's lib, maintained that Atalanta was an Argonautess. Apollonius says pointedly that super-star Theseus was in Hades at the time and otherwise engaged (with another contract), but Statius (who was obviously with the other studio) later made Theseus an Argonaut anyway. H. W. Parke has pointed out that the Apolline seers were apparently injected into the Argonaut story as a propaganda effort by the rising power of the Delphic Oracle which was trying to squeeze out the premier oracle of Dodona and achieve first place for itself in the eyes of the Greek public.

Parke has shown how the really central oracular elements in the Argo story were all related to Dodona, not Delphi. Delphi was quite an upstart in the centuries immediately preceding the classical period, and initially was not more important than Dodona, though it was to become so and held precedence by the time of Socrates and the classical Greeks. Parke concludes that all the Delphic and Apolline elements in the *Argo* story are late accretions from the time after Delphi had usurped the primacy of Dodona. They would not have been in the *Argo* epic referred to by Homer, who proves the antiquity of the *Argo* saga by his mention in the *Odyssey* (XII, 69–72) of 'the celebrated *Argo*' and of Jason and the Clashing Rocks. Significantly, no other

* Circumcision is absolutely fundamental to Dogon culture for religious reasons.

Argonaut is mentioned by name by Homer. It is obvious, in fact, from what I said above, that the Argonauts were primarily noted for being fifty in number and related (a comfortable kind of anonymity – cousins!). Outstanding Hellenic heroes were thrown into their ranks by the caprices of successive epic poets to provide recognizable colour. With the exception of Jason there is total disagreement among everyone concerned about just who were the Argonauts. And according to Robert Graves in *The Greek Myths*, Jason was originally Hercules. And Hercules was originally Briareus. Of course, the answer is that they were not individuals and were not meant to be.

They were fifty and they were related and usually seated and they sailed in a magic boat. Just like the Anunnaki, and just like the fifty anonymous companions of Gilgamesh! And in the Gilgamesh fragments from the early Sumerian times, the boat mentioned is a 'Magan-boat', or Egyptian boat. It must be remembered also that Sumer is located between Egypt and Colchis.

We are now beginning to get down to the bare bones of the *Argo* story. I don't believe that the earliest levels of this ancient tale have ever previously been reached.

Not only Herodotus, but Pindar as well, describes the Colchians as dark. In his IVth Pythian Ode, which is largely about the Argonauts, Pindar says (212): 'Among the dark-faced Kolchians, in the very presence of Aeetes'. Pindar therefore confirms Herodotus on this point.

It remains to attempt a dating. If Herodotus is correct and the Colchians were Egyptian soldiers dating from the reign of Sesostris (Ramses II), then they would have gone to Colchis at some time during the years 1301–1234 B.C., which is estimated by John A. Wilson[5] as the period of the reign of Ramses II. This dating is only of use as an indicator of the general antiquity of the origins of our material. There does not seem to be any archaeological information of any kind from the undiscovered site of Aea, the capital city of Colchis, which is on the coast of the Black Sea (just by a river known anciently as the Phasis), just across the border of the Soviet Union from Turkey. I would suspect the site of Aea has never even been sought! It would certainly make an interesting site for excavation. It would presumably offer an unusual amount of Egyptian-style material mixed with Armenian-Caucasian styles. It should be extraordinarily interesting from the point of view of ancient art, almost certainly being quite rich in precious metals and beautiful metal-working, particularly gold. We shall see later in this book that it was near a famous ancient metallurgical centre. And, of course, there should be finds which would confirm Herodotus's account.

Here is a description of the site, for those who wish to seek it: 'They reached the broad estuary of the Phasis, where the Black Sea ends . . . and then rowed straight up into the mighty river, which rolled in foam to either bank as it made way for *Argo*'s prow. On their left hand they had the lofty Caucasus and the city of Aea, on their right the plain of Ares and the god's sacred grove, where the snake kept watch and ward over the fleece, spread on the leafy branches of an oak.' (Another hint of Dodona, with the oak and the grove. This similarity will be seen to become extremely relevant later on.)

To return to the question of dates (also bearing in mind Homer's early casual reference to 'the celebrated *Argo*'), we'll recall my mention of dates when I showed the identical nature of the Sumerian and Egyptian astronomical systems in their essential details. I pointed out then that the Babylonian tablets were dated from the second millennium B.C., giving us an upper limit on time in the Sumerian region. The Egyptian star clocks to which they bear such total resemblance calendrically had already altered (such as by the introduction of a fifteen-day week instead of a ten-day one, indicating the advanced degeneration of the traditions) in Egypt in the first millennium B.C.

Hence we see that the Egyptian star clocks no longer existed in the necessary form by the first millennium, giving us an upper limit date in Egypt of the end of the second millennium B.C., identical with the upper limit we have in Sumer. I am tempted now to steal a phrase of the physicists and remind the reader that these dates are of an order of magnitude comparable with the date of Ramses II's reign adopted tentatively for the settlement at Colchis of Egyptian colonists. Surely these three dates cannot coalesce accidentally round the same material! We have no choice but to adopt the approximate date of 1200 B.C. as the upper limit for the spread (and subsequent degeneration) of our Sirius-related material throughout the Mediterranean area, from whichever source it originated.

It may perhaps be of some relevance that this coincides roughly with the end of Minoan domination of the Mediterranean. From the point of view at least of the spread of the Sirius material, I would connect it with what seems to me an obvious fact: that when Minoan sea power, based on Crete, collapsed, the Egyptians and inhabitants of the Near East could and did expand their own maritime activities to fill the vacuum left by the disintegration of the Minoan fleets. (An alternative but unlikely suggestion is that fleeing Minoans dispersed their culture with them as they settled in exile in different areas of the Mediterranean following the collapse of their nation; but I do not believe they alone were the source of the Sirius material.)

I am inclined to believe the increasingly strong and accumulating evidence that the Minoan culture was dealt a death blow by eruptions of the volcano Thera. F. Matz, in 'Minoan Civilization: Maturity and Zenith' in the *Cambridge Ancient History*, says: 'The peaceful transfer of power in Crete from the Minoans to the Mycenaeans is difficult to explain.' But not, surely, if volcanic eruptions had enfeebled the Minoans. The Minoan cities had no walls. On their island the Minoans relied, it seems, on their unchallenged sea power to keep enemies at bay, just as the Spartans in their unwalled city of Sparta in mainland Greece relied on their unchallenged land power to keep enemies at bay in late classical times. For the Cretan island could not be reached by enemies on foot, and as the Minoans had total naval superiority they could not be threatened at home. The latest conclusions about Thera seem to be that the towns on that small volcanic island near Crete were first evacuated due to earthquakes some years before the final volcanic eruption which destroyed Minoan civilization.

Herodotus in Book I of his *Histories* gives us a good illustration of how hopeless it is for a land power to challenge a sea power on the sea, when he shows the landlubber Lydians abandoning their plans to build ships and extend their conquests to the islands because they are aware they just don't know what they're doing. If the Minoan fleets had been sunk in great tidal waves following volcanic eruptions, the Minoans would have had no choice but to come to an understanding with the Mycenaeans. Any other possibility would have meant suicide. Probably they made a graceful and dignified pact or series of pacts which made the inevitable seem voluntary. And if the Mycenaeans were traditionally a good bit in awe of the more sophisticated Minoans, so much the better for the Minoans who 'condescended' to come to terms like gentlemen.

But the 'spheres of influence' of the sea-going Minoans could not be taken over immediately by the Mycenaeans, who lacked the maritime skill (not to mention ships) to complement on the waves their success in overrunning most of the island of Crete, probably leaving certain areas to the native Minoans according to the pacts I have suggested. It is not that the Mycenaeans would have lacked the energy or will, but the Minoan fleets would have been destroyed and even the most willing Minoan sailors could not sail non-existent ships for the Mycenaean invaders. Furthermore, the work of consolidating power on the recently taken island would have been a protracted and distracting matter for the Mycenaeans. So, for all these reasons, the new Cretan rulers could not attain to the full stature of their predecessors and be in complete command of the Mediterranean Sea.

The Mycenaeans had been competing with the Minoans (and raiding them, apparently under Theseus) as best they could for some time before the cataclysm. In fact F. H. Stubbings[6] informs us that the Minoans made a 'disastrous Sicilian expedition' against the Mycenaean trading interests in the central Mediterranean. This is reminiscent, of course, of the famous Athenian expedition to Sicily which was a total disaster and caused Athens to lose the Peloponnesian War. Sicily was thus responsible for two great historical disasters that altered the course of events to an unknown extent elsewhere than in Sicily.

So we see the Minoan power may already have been declining. Stubbings says: 'All that is really certain, however, is that the fall of Crete laid the way clear for a vastly increased Mycenaean activity.' And, we may be sure, for a vastly increased Egyptian maritime activity as well. Egypt, which is known to have traded heavily with Crete under the Minoans, must have found itself without choice: expanded maritime activity on her own account or a severe starvation of imported goods. There may even be a possibility that the name Minyas (and, hence, Minyae for the Argonauts) may have some connection with Minos (which gave us the word Minoan). After all, the Minoans were in considerable contact with the Egyptians and were the best sailors of their day.

It has been worth while to go into all this about the Minoan collapse at about the time of the upper limit dates which we have arrived at in other ways. For with the disappearance of Minoan supremacy at sea, vast numbers of other people were free to ply the sea lanes and no doubt did so, bringing a proliferation of variegated contacts between cultures which the uniform Minoan sea traffic had ironed flat and featureless. Enterprising folk from almost anywhere – ethnics from mainland Greece, sophisticates from riverine Egypt, and clever Semites from Lebanon, Canaan, Palestine, all with their eyes on the main chance, could find something that would float and have a go.

All these folk suddenly let loose on the high seas brought an inevitable cross-fertilization at the cultural level, even if piracy must have increased alarmingly. There must have been a lot more drowned sailors and shipwrecked merchants, but an amazing amount of syncretism, during which our Sirius material must have leaked out into wider currency beyond the confines of Egypt and Sumer. Two millennia earlier, or even before that, the Egyptian and Sumerian cultures had shared many secrets: now these secrets were let out of Pandora's box and entered what was to become the Greek culture through synthesis in the white heat of warlike Mycenaean exploits at Troy and elsewhere. The Heroic Age was beginning, *arete* (the classical Greek ideal of *excellence* in all things) was to be forged by blood and iron in the lost *Thebaid* and the surviving *Iliad*, with the subsidiary sources of the great *Odyssey* and what remains of the *Argo* tales. Deeply imbedded like subtle dragon's teeth sunk in tough battle flesh, the bony outline of our Sirius material was to peer through the membrane of Greek epic tradition, to spring forth now in our century as the armed men of controversy. They have re-entered the field, we must face them. Rather than enter into combat, let us question these strangers about their origins. We are faced with the living fossils of a world almost entirely beyond our modern comprehension. These creatures are shaggy with the cobwebs of the centuries that preceded even classical Greece, and came before even Hesiod and Homer. These ghosts are antique in a sense which we rarely encounter except inside the tombs of Egypt or the burials at Ur.

To continue with elucidations of the Argonaut complex, we turn now to that invaluable compendium of all that is strange and wonderful about the world of the Greeks, Robert Graves's superb work *The Greek Myths*. There we find:[7] 'Aeaea ("wailing") is a typical death island where the familiar Death-goddess sings as she spins. The Argonautic legend places it at the head of the Adriatic Gulf; it may well be Lussin near Pola. Circe means "falcon", and she had a cemetery in Colchis, planted with willows, sacred to Hecate.' In the *Argonautica*, we recall, Jason offers a sacrifice to the goddess Hecate at Colchis at the suggestion of Medea. We shall see later that Hecate is a degenerate form of Sothis, or Sirius. But let us examine the above information from Graves. First we note that Circe, who figures so prominently in the *Argonautica*, has the meaning of 'falcon'. This brings to mind the prominent Egyptian symbolic 'falcon of Horus', which was the symbol of rising from the dead, or resurrection. The hawk or falcon of Horus presided over the Egyptian necropolis at Memphis, so it is quite obvious that it could have presided over the Egyptian necropolis at Colchis.

Naturally, the Greeks would have thought of the falcon in terms of their death-goddess Hecate.* There was no reason for them to preserve the masculine gender of a Horus of whom they knew nothing. But the falcon of Horus could have had a powerful effect on them as a symbol and have been transferred to a feminine figure of Greek myth. In fact, this cemetery of Circe in Colchis is almost undoubtedly an Egyptian cemetery surviving from Herodotus's Egyptian Colchians, and presided over by the falcon of Horus which in Greek was called Circe, and eventually became a female figure. The springing

---

* 'Hesiod's account of Hecate shows her to have been the original Triple-goddess, supreme in Heaven, on earth, and in Tartarus; but the Hellenes emphasized her destructive powers at the expense of her creative ones . . . Lion, dog, and horse (were) her heads . . . the dog being the Dog-star Sirius': Robert Graves, *The Greek Myths*, 31.7. Hesiod says (*Theogony* 416): 'In starry heaven she has her place, and the immortal gods greatly respect her'.

up from the earth of the magically sown soldiers in the *Argonautica* must partially refer to the Egyptian soldiers buried in 'the cemetery of Circe' who were meant to rise from the dead under the auspices of the Egyptian god of resurrection, Horus, whose symbol was the falcon, or 'circe'. (Excavations could unearth the Colchian necropolis some day.)

Circe lived on the island of Aea, which has the same name as the city which Jason visited in Colchis and from where Medea came. In Greek mythology, Circe is the daughter of Helios and Perse and the sister of King Aeetes, the king of Colchis. She is therefore Medea's aunt (Medea eloped with Jason). As for the 'island' of Aea, I believe it was a holm, or river-island, in the Phasis River near the city Aea.

Circe's father Helios is the sun, who rose every morning from his magnificent palace near Colchis where he slept and stabled his horses overnight. And likewise the father of the Egyptian Horus was the sun, and Horus himself represents the rising sun. The Greek word χίρχη (*kirke* latinized as *circe*) revealingly means 'an unknown bird', if we consult (as we shall do from now on) Liddell and Scott's definitive Greek lexicon. In the form χίρχος (*kirkos*) the meaning is 'a kind of hawk or falcon', 'a kind of wolf', 'a circle' (which in Latin became *circus*) or 'ring', and 'an unknown stone'. Κιρχαία (*kirkaia*) means 'an uncertain plant'. Of these only the proper noun Κίρχη (*Kirke*) has the specific meaning of Circe the Enchantress, although the same word in general is 'an unknown bird'. How appropriate a reaction for the Greeks to the falcon of Horus – a bird-symbol unknown to them. But in trying to be more precise they make χίρχος (*kirkos*) 'a kind of hawk or falcon', as that is obviously what it is from its appearance, though its especial symbolic value makes the Greeks doubt precisely what the Egyptians intended. It looked like a kind of hawk or falcon but the Greeks weren't prepared to insist on exactly what species – because it was an Egyptian, not a Greek, idea.

On a point such as this we must 'take advice' as from a lawyer. It is not sufficient merely to cite Liddell and Scott's lexicon. For this subject we turn to D'Arcy Thompson's definitive source-book *A Glossary of Greek Birds*.[8] Under the entry there for *kirkos* we read: 'A poetic and mystical name for a Hawk: the sacred Hawk of Apollo; in the main an astronomical, perhaps solar, emblem. . . . In Homer, the bird of Apollo . . . *Od.* xv. 525. . . . The bird is not identifiable as a separate species, and is so recognized by Scaliger and others. Neither the brief note as to its size in a corrupt passage of the ninth book of the History of Animals, nor the mystical references to its alleged hostilities and attributes in Aristotle, Aelian, and Phile, are sufficient to prove that the name indicated at any time a certain particular species. The word is poetical . . . The chief allusions to χίρχος are obviously mystical, though the underlying symbolism . . . is not decipherable.'

Under another entry, for *Hierax*, Thompson gives some further interesting information. The word *hierax* is a generic term for all hawks. It too seems to partake of overtones of Horus, as Thompson specifically notes when he refers to the 'Worship of Hawks in Egypt', citing Herodotus and Aelian, and says: 'In the Rig-Veda the sun is frequently compared to a hawk, hovering in the air. . . . Their heart is eaten, to obtain prophetic powers, Porph. *De Abst.* ii. 48.[9] . . . The Hawk entered in Egypt into innumerable hieroglyphics . . .

(as) Horus and Hat-Hor, the latter being the οἶκος Ὧρου of Plutarch. According to Chaeremon, fr. 8 ψυχή-ἥλιος-θεός = ἱέραξ. On the sanctity of hawks in Egypt, and the solar symbolism associated with them there, see also . . .' etc., referring to Porphyry, Plutarch, Eusebius and Clement of Alexandria. The scholarly reader who wishes to pursue all this must go to Thompson directly.

Kirkos also means 'an unknown stone'. Here again we come upon the stone motif which we encounter with Deukalion (the Greek Noah) and elsewhere. The stones of Deukalion spring up as men – men born from the earth just as the dead of the Colchian cemetery are meant to be born again from the earth.

A further connection of Circe with the Sirius complex lies in the fact[10] that the island of Circe was the place where Orion met his death. Orion as a constellation was identified (as Sah) with Osiris, the husband of Isis, who was identified, of course, with Sirius.

The stone motif in its recurring forms seems to have had a particular connection with the Minyae, as I discovered from that invaluable duffle-bag of information, the ancient Greek author Pausanius, whose *Guide to Greece* is a real 'experience'. The Minyan city was traditionally that of Orchomenos in Boeotia, and it will be recalled that all the Argonauts were Minyae and descended from Minyas, King of Orchomenos.

All my references to Pausanius will be to Peter Levi's excellent translation published in two volumes by Penguin in 1971 with extensive notes and comments by that learned Jesuit translator, who has travelled over most of the terrain described by Pausanius and attempts a running commentary on the present state of the ruins and sights (and sites).

In Book IX, 34, 5, we read: 'Over from Mount Laphystion is Orchomenos, as famous and glorious as any city in Greece.' Levi's footnotes tell us: 'No one knows which mountain this was: probably the one above Hagios Georgios and the modern Laphystion' and: '(Orchomenos is) at the north-west corner of the old Kopaic Lake.'

At Orchomenos 'there are graves of Minyas and of Hesiod' (30, 3). At Mount Laphystion near by was (34, 4) 'the sacred enclosure of Laphystian Zeus . . . The statue is stone. They say Athamas was about to slaughter Phrixos and Helle here when Zeus sent the children a ram with a golden fleece and they ran away on the ram.'

Now note what Pausanius says (38, 1) about the Minyae of Orchomenos: 'Orchomenos has a sanctuary of Dionysos, but the most ancient one is consecrated to the Graces. They pay particular worship to rocks, saying they fell out of heaven for Eteokles: finely-made statues were dedicated in my time but even these were in stone.' Levi adds: 'The ruins of these sanctuaries are on the site of the old monastery (now itself in ruins).' Now, I believe this singular observation on the Minyae's preoccupation with stones ties in with all the recurring stone motifs in our material. And now we shall see a further recurrence which ties back in another way (38, 4): 'The Orchomenians had a legend about Aktaion. *An apparition with rocks in its hand* was devastating the countryside: when Delphi was consulted the god ordered them to find anything that was left of Aktaion and cover it with earth, and then make a bronze image of the ghost and rivet it with iron to a rock. I have seen this

Figure 14

GREEK THEBES EQUIDISTANT FROM
EGYPTIAN THEBES AND AEA

riveted statue; once a year they burn offerings to Aktaion as a divine hero'
[the italics are mine].

The public furore in 1973 over the painting by Titian, *The Death of Actaeon*,
will have reminded British art lovers of the background to the myth which
the famous painting portrays. Actaeon happened to see the goddess Artemis
(known to the Romans by her Latin name of Diana) of the silver bow bathing
naked. Artemis then hunted him down, with fifty hounds, transformed him into
a stag, and killed him with her bow (not only are hounds connected with the
Dog Star, but the bow is a familiar symbol connected also with Sirius, which
was so often known in ancient times also as the Bow Star).* Not only were the
hounds of Hades who chased Actaeon fifty in number, but Robert Graves tells
us 'Actaeon was, it seems, a sacred king of the pre-Hellenic stag cult, torn to
pieces at the end of his reign of fifty months, namely half a Great Year . . .'[11]
Note the application of the number 'fifty' here to a period of time. The orbit of
Sirius B around Sirius A is fifty years; the reign of a sacred stag-king was fifty
months. We know how often in ancient traditions the numerical quantity of time
periods remains stable while their quality (as individual durations) varies. The
classic examples are in the Bible, where the seven days of creation refer to seven
aeons, and the 'years' of life of the Hebrew patriarchs such as Methusaleh
are not correctly interpreted as solar *years* but as lunar *months* or 'lunar years'
a month long (since by late times the area of the Near East which had by then
produced the people known as Hebrews had succumbed to a lunar calendrical
craze – literally 'moonstruck' – and everything was a lunar rather than a solar
period of time to those people in that area).

Note further the reference to a 'Great Year' of twice fifty months, consisting
of two reigns. This would be one hundred months. And it should not surprise
us to learn now that the name of the Greek goddess Hecate literally means in
Greek 'one hundred'.†

Perhaps something of the true meaning of the myths is now becoming
evident. The ancient peoples were not concealing information from us out of
spite. Their purpose in disguising their secrets was to see that those secrets
could survive. In fact, so successful were the ancient Egyptians in accomplishing
their purpose, that the Greeks often preserve earlier Egyptian secrets in total
ignorance of their true meaning, retaining only through an innate conservatism
certain peculiar archaic details which we now find to be so important.
Not only are the stories mythical and symbolical in that they are not meant
to be taken at face value, but they even involve 'characters' and 'events'
which have a strictly numerical significance. But this should have been quite
obvious to the reader since we began to study the Anunnaki. It is, admittedly,
difficult for those of us who have been brought up in our strictly literal
civilization, where there is no such thing as a hidden meaning and everything

---

* This scene is portrayed in Plate 17, which shows an ancient Greek vase painting from
approximately 470 B.C. of Artemis and the hounds slaying Actaeon.

† The Dogon tribe often describe the 50-year orbital period of Sirius B by saying: 'The
period of the orbit is counted double, that is, one hundred years, because . . . (of) the principle
of twin-ness' (see Chapter 1). Here we have the same custom in operation among the Greeks, of
'twinning' their sacred durations for $50 \times 2 = 100$. Hecate ('one hundred') unites them.

is on the surface, to think in such a way as to understand the ancient myths. It was, after all, only a century ago that supposedly intelligent people were maintaining that the Earth was created in 4004 B.C., on the basis of what the Bible was reputed to have said! And it is only half a century ago that the courts of Tennessee in the famous Scopes trial decided that the theory of evolution was not only unholy but illegal and could not be taught in the schools. We mistakenly assume that because we have superlative technology and science we must also be extremely civilized and come from a subtle background of sophisticated thinkers. But this is all a base illusion.

In fact, we are on a low rung of the ladder of evolutionary intelligence, and in many ways (such as ethics and aspirations to excellence) we have gone backward since those early mutants in our paltry intellectual history on this planet, Confucius, Socrates, the Buddha, and the others of whom every reader may substitute his own favourites.

But this book is not meant to be a sermon on the evils of a vacuous civilization. We are meant to be examining the names of some of the principal characters of the *Argonautica*, and it is best that we pretend to ourselves that we are rational creatures and supremely moral, and turn back to the subject again.

The name Jason means 'appeaser', which is in accordance with his vacillating character (see Rieu's introduction to his Penguin translation of the *Argonautica* for some caustic comments on Jason.)[12] 'Medea' means 'cunning'. 'Aeetes' means 'mighty' or 'eagle', and he was Medea's father, the King of Colchis from whom Jason stole the fleece.

Now we have seen that Actaeon was associated with Minyan Orchomenos, with a rock-throwing ghost (echoes of Deukalion), with fifty hounds of Hades, and with a reign of fifty months. The connections go even further. From Pausanius (34, 4) we learn that on Mount Laphystion is the place described thus: 'Higher up (from the spot where the ram with the golden fleece leapt into the air and took off) is Fire-eyed Hercules where the Boeotians say Hercules came up with the dog of Hades.' Now, this 'dog of Hades' is Cerberus, who originally had fifty heads! (Later the simplification of three heads, as for Hecate who was also of Hades, was adopted for Cerberus, when fifty must have seemed to make no sense and was probably too difficult to paint on vases. But of course three is significant too. The Egyptians portrayed three goddesses in the Sothis-boat: Sothis, Anukis, and Satis.)

Graves informs us[13] that, 'Cerberus was, at first, fifty-headed, like the spectral pack that destroyed Actaeon (see 22.1); but afterwards three-headed, like his mistress Hecate (see 134.1).' (The three-headed Hecate is the three Sothis-goddesses blended in one and is an underworld counterpart, just as with the Sumerian 'Anunnaki of the underworld'.)

What of the fleece itself? There are obvious connections of the golden fleece and Colchis with the common golden-yellow dye which comes from saffron (*crocus sativus*). The crocus with its saffron is even today confused with 'meadow saffron' (*colchicum*) which takes its name, obviously, from Colchis, which was its chief area of production. The colchicum plant which somewhat resembles the crocus in its flowering stage was terribly important to the ancient world. It was the only known medicine against the disease of gout (and indeed still is). It is known to have been used to treat gout in ancient Egypt and all over the ancient Mediterranean. As Colchis was the place to find colchicum that may explain why the Egyptians first settled there!

It is probable that the crocus and ordinary saffron was present in Colchis in abundance, along with the false or meadow saffron, colchicum, and that the two became as confused with each other in ancient times as they are today. Indeed, it is only modern botany which proclaims a difference between the two to the extent that we no longer confuse them officially. As real saffron produced a much valued dye, it is not surprising that a golden fleece dyed golden yellow by saffron dye would be said to exist in Colchis! And indeed, Medea's famous herbal knowledge was well suited to Colchis, which produced the only cure for one of antiquity's most dreaded diseases, a disease which causes terrific pain and discomfort and could only be relieved by the magic herb from the mysterious distant land of Colchis. I.Burkill[14] gives interesting information on the early history of saffron. He says that sun-worshippers speaking an Aryan language spread to India from Turkey and made the saffron crocus an object of veneration and found ways of using its colour.[15] This information, given by Täckholm and Drar,[16] offers a great deal of support to my contention.

Richard Allen[17] discusses Aries (the ram) and says that 'Miss Clerke says that the (Egyptian stellar ram's) stars were called the Fleece.' He adds that the god Zeus-Amen (Ammon)-Jupiter 'assumed the Ram's form when all the inhabitants of Olympus fled into Egypt from the giants led by Typhon'. And in this discussion of Aries, Allen mentions 'some of its titles at a different date being applied to Capella of Auriga'. This is the sort of process we shall encounter again and again – titles and descriptions of stars being applied to neighbouring or similar stars as the original traditions become confused. It is particularly evident in the application of the description of 'heavy' or 'weight' to different stars associated somehow with Sirius, as the original object to which this description was meant to apply, Sirius B, was not visible and so tradition, being conservative, kept the description and applied it to other stars related to Sirius which could actually be seen. As with numerical traditions like that of 'fifty', when the true significance was forgotten, the symbol or concept was merely given a new, impromptu explanation.

Aries was definitely identified with the golden fleece. Allen gives much information regarding this:

It always was Aries with the Romans; but Ovid called it *phrixea ovis*; and Columella *pecus athamantidos helles*, *phrixus*, and *portitor phrixi*; others *phrixeum pecus* and *phrixi vector*, Phrixus being the hero-son of Athamas, who fled on the back of this Ram with his sister Helle to Colchis. . . . On reaching his journey's end, Phrixus sacrificed the creature and hung its fleece in the Grove of Ares, where it was turned to gold and became the object of the Argonauts' quest. From this came others of Aries' titles: *ovis aurea* and *auratus*, *chrysomallus*, and the Low Latin *Chrysovellus*.

As the fleece was a solar symbol, it is just as well that we look at the concept of Horus once again. Horus in Egyptian is Ḥeru. And from Wallis Budge we learn that Ḥeru is 'the ancient name of the Sun-god'.[18] The word *ḥeru* also has the meaning of 'face'.[19] But let us consider the following: Ḥeru (Horus) and his hawk/falcon presided over the Colchian cemetery and gave the name to Circe (which means 'hawk/falcon') who was Medea's aunt. The Greek sun-god Helios was said to stable his horses at Colchis and have a magnificent palace there, from which he arose every morning. Also Colchis was the place of residence of the solar golden fleece.

Now, we recall that in Egyptian the letter 'l' and the letter 'r' are entirely interchangeable and have the same hieroglyph. Consequently, Ḥeru could just as reliably be Ḥelu. If one takes Ḥelu and puts a Greek ending on it one gets Helios! And the same word means the sun-god in both the Egyptian religion (early) and the Greek religion (early). In both lands the name was eventually superseded, in Greece by Apollo, for instance. So here we have a further connection between the Greek tradition as centring round Colchis and the Egyptian tradition as settled there, only this time the evidence is linguistic.

It seems that the curious Greek word *hero* comes also from *ḥeru*, though a word similar to *hero* exists in Sanskrit, the language of ancient India after 1200 B.C. The word in Sanskrit which has the meaning of 'hero' is the related *Vīra*. It is used in the precise sense of 'hero (as opposed to a god)' in the early *Rig-veda* and is thus attested at the time of the first migrations of Aryans into India. There is no question that the two words are cognates of each other. However, I propose for them (and we shall see more examples of this later in the book) a common derivation: from the Egyptian *ḥeru*.

The word *ḥeru* is given a meaning by Wallis Budge[20] almost identical with that of *hero* and *vīra* and is described as follows: 'applied to the king as the representative of the sun-god on earth'. This is a precise meaning applying to a human being on earth who is neither god nor daemon, but *hero*. Liddell and Scott make clear that the word was not used solely for those warriors who were prominent in battle, but was used to describe the minstrel Demodocus, the herald Mulius, and even (in the *Odyssey*, 7, 44) 'the unwarlike Phaeacian people are so called'. In Homer 'the heroes were exalted above the race of common men', but particularly in Pindar the poet, we find the word used to describe a race 'between gods and men', in precisely the sense that we should expect the word *ḥeru* to survive in another language. This Egyptian application of the word to their Pharaohs survived almost without change in Greek and Sanskrit and later in Latin and the later Indo-European languages.

It is interesting to note in the account of the word Helios as given by Liddell and Scott, Homer used the term in reference to 'the rising and setting, light and darkness, morning and evening'. In Egypt the precise application of Horus as sun-god was in his activity as rising and setting. He was the child who was born afresh each morning (and to the Greeks Helios was born afresh every morning at Colchis). Homer has thus used the *ḥeru*-derived Helios in precisely the manner which we might have expected of an Egyptian, rather than a Greek, poet.

In Liddell and Scott we find the listing immediately after Helios of Helio-Serapis, which is 'an Egyptian divinity'. I leave the reader to draw his own conclusions regarding this clear use of the word Helio to preface a description of Serapis. Serapis was the Greek form of Ȧsȧr-Hep, Hep being what is known in Greek as Apis the Bull. Ȧsȧr is, of course, Osiris. In Egyptian it was quite common for there to be references to 'Horus-Osiris' combining Ḥeru and Ȧsȧr. Here in Greek we find this, if we accept my thesis of the derivation of Helio from *ḥelu* or *ḥeru*.

The reader is by now presumably immune to shock at the endless 'surprises' which arise in the course of this enquiry. Hence he will no doubt be prepared to learn that if we shorten the 'e' (from eta to epsilon) in Greek, we have the *heru*-derived word (which has dropped the aspirate, probably in connection with the shortening of the vowel) *erion*, which means – 'woollen fleece'!

There is a possibility that Herakles ('the glory of Hera'), the original captain of the *Argo* according to Graves, and his protectress the goddess Hera (wife to Zeus and Queen of the gods) are derived from *heru* and they are known to be related to the word Seirios which gave us Sirius and the Sanskrit *svar*, *suryas*, etc. In sanskrit *Sūra* means 'hero', indicating that these words may relate also. Liddell and Scott believe this complex of words to be separate from the Helios-complex, but their opinion is only an opinion. *Sūrana* means 'fiery', just as Seirios can in the sense of 'scorching' (due to the supposed 'scorching' of the Dog Star, etc.)

Back to our fleece. We find that the Greek word for a woollen fleece is related to the Egyptian word for Horus, the Greek word for sun, etc., etc. So much for the puzzling nature of that now moot question: Why a fleece? Back to sacred puns again, which besiege us endlessly.

Let us not forget the Sumerians. Let us look again at that list of the fifty names of Marduk. One of them is the name Nebiru. It is commonly taken to be the name of the planet Jupiter, but there is confusion there, and the word is discussed in *Hamlet's Mill* and many other places as one of the infuriating Sumerian words which we would like to understand. Where did it come from? What does it mean? Why is it one of the fifty names?

Immediately after this forty-ninth name, Marduk is called 'Lord of the Lands' (its Akkadian form, which has no significance for us, is Bēl Mātāti; I do not know the Sumerian form, which might be of interest to us). Then, after this supposed fiftieth name comes another name, namely Ea (Enki). Then Marduk is described as being of fifty names. It seems not to make perfect sense, since he has just been given fifty-one names. One way in which to make it sensible is to treat 'Lord of the Lands' (which is given in English in Speiser and Heidel, unlike all the other names) as a synonym of Nebiru. If we do this, then Ea is the fiftieth name and everything is all right.

Now, let us look at the Egyptian language once again. We find that the word *Neb* is extremely common and is used in many combinations and means 'Lord'. Without further ado, let me make clear that I believe the Sumerian Nebiru to be derived from the Egyptian Neb-Ḥeru. If we treat Ḥeru in its older Egyptian sense as the sun, then the descriptions of Nebiru in the Babylonian *Enuma elish* could read as a perfect description of Neb-Ḥeru – 'the Lord the sun': 'Nebiru shall hold the crossings of heaven and earth. . . . He who the midst of the Sea restlessly crosses,/Let "Crossing" be his name, who controls its midst,' etc., though overlaid with this, as with the traditional Horus, is a strictly stellar element which is behind the more obvious solar element. However, I do not wish unduly to confuse the issue by peeling off too many layers at once. Suffice it to recall the previously mentioned associations of Horus with the Sirius system and note that there is a Ḥeru-ami-Sept-t 'Horus of Sothis' and Ḥeru-Sept 'Horus the Dog Star' and then to note, again in association with Nebiru which is supposed to have been Jupiter, that there is in

Egyptian a Heru-sba-res 'Horus, star of the south, i.e. Jupiter', and Heru-up-Shet, 'the planet Jupiter'; also in the *Enuma elish* Nebiru is clearly described as 'a star'. Horus also exists as Heru-ami-u which is 'a hawk-headed crocodile with a tail terminating in a dog's head'. The dog is related to Sirius. Heru-ur-shefit is a jackal form of Horus, *heru* is also the name of a sceptre and of a jackal-*headed* standard in the other world. A form of Horus using the common word Neb is Heru-Neb-urr-t, meaning 'Horus as possessor of the supreme crown'. Another of several is Heru-Neb-pāt, meaning 'Horus, lord of men'. Heru-Neb-taui is 'Horus, Lord of the Two Lands'. Recall our synonym for Nebiru– 'Lord of the Lands'!

We are getting deeper and deeper into the legend of the golden fleece, of origins of Greek and Middle Eastern ideas in Egypt, along with key words and names, etc. All these centre round the curious Sirius complex. What more will we uncover? Perhaps we need a break from all these Egyptian words. There are many other aspects of our subject, and it leads us ever closer to the solution of our mystery – which is the origin of the subject.

Notes

1. *Toward the Image of Tammuz and Other Essays*, Harvard, 1970.
2. Kramer, S. N. *History Begins at Sumer*, Doubleday Anchor Book, New York, 1959, pp. 91–4.
3. *Antiquity of the Jews*, Book I, Chapter 2.
4. *Herodotus*, trans. A. de Selincourt, Book 2, 103.
5. In Pritchard, *Ancient Near Eastern Texts*, p. 8.
6. 'The Rise of Mycenaean Civilization', *Cambridge Ancient History*.
7. Graves, Robert. *The Greek Myths*, 2 vols., Penguin Books, London, 1969, 170.5.
8. Thompson, D'Arcy Wentworth. *A Glossary of Greek Birds*, Oxford, 1896.
9. Porphyry, *On Abstinence from Animal Food*, for those who are not familiar with the traditional abbreviations. Porphyry was an early Neoplatonist, a student of Plotinus, who transcribed the *Enneads*. Thomas Taylor translated much of what survives of Porphyry's own writings, including *On Abstinence*, in *Select Works of Porphyry*, London, 1823.
10. Graves, op. cit., 170.6.
11. Ibid., 22.1.
12. Robert Graves takes the view that Jason means 'healer'.
13. Graves, op. cit., 31.3.
14. The reference is to I. Burkill (1935) but I have not been able to trace the publication concerned and have gone to immense pains over it. Burkill was a noted botanist. A botanical publication of his for 1936 is not the correct reference. See Note 15 for source.
15. Täckholm and Drar, 'Flora of Egypt', Vol. III, *Bulletin of the Faculty of Science*, No. 30, Cairo University Faculty of Science, Cairo University Press, 1954.
16. See Note 15.
17. *Star Names*, op. cit. See entry under Aries.
18. Wallis Budge, *Hieroglyphic Vocabulary to the Theban Recension of the Book of the Dead*, London, 1911. See entry for Her, p. 273.
19. Ibid., p. 271.
20. Ibid., p. 273, entry for Her.

SUMMARY

The Sumerian god An had a daughter, Bau (representing the sound of a dog barking, as does the ancient Egyptian word for 'dog', *auau*), who was a dog-headed goddess. The Egyptian god Anubis (Anpu) was a dog-headed god.

The Sumerian Bau, as a daughter of An, is a sister of the fifty great gods (Anunnaki) who are also children of An. Since Bau may be a goddess of the Dog Star Sirius, the fact that she is the sister of 'the fifty' is significant, as Sirius B has an orbital period of fifty years.

The golden fleece was situated at Colchis in the Black Sea, where Jason and his Argonauts went to seek it. Colchis was an ancient Egyptian colony before 1200 B.C.

Herodotus emphasizes that the Egyptians originated the practice of circumcision, which survived also among the Colchians, whom he visited (the Hebrews acquired circumcision from the Egyptians while in bondage). It is noteworthy that the Dogon ceremony of the Sigui, which is connected with the Dogon Sirius-mysteries, centres largely round rites of circumcision.

Prominent in the story of the *Argo* is the female character Circe (whose name means 'falcon' or 'hawk'). Horus, son of Isis and Osiris, was symbolized by a falcon or hawk. Circe presided over the Colchian cemetery (which was originally Egyptian, Colchis having been an Egyptian colony). Horus, who presided over the cemetery of Memphis in Egypt, would have presided also over the one at Colchis while Egyptian influence was still directly exercised. Circe is obviously a Greek derivation of Horus.

The word *kirke* (Circe) in Greek, which we customarily write 'Circe' due to our habit of changing Greek k's into Latin c's, specifically means 'a kind of hawk or falcon' or 'an unknown bird' – just the sort of confusion we should expect among the Greeks with regard to a concept derived from Egyptian culture and imperfectly understood.

Actaeon, representing a sacred stag-king, was hunted down by fifty hounds (the dog motif joined to fifty) and killed with a silver bow (Sirius has also traditionally been known as 'the Bow Star', and in Egypt the goddess Sirius holds a bow).

The sacred king, such as Actaeon represented, had a 'sacred reign' of fifty months. It is arguable that 'fifty months' is a shorthand version of 'fifty years', but we now see undeniable ancient traditions connecting Sirius with fifty intervals of time (whether months or years) comprising 'a reign'. And of course the orbital period of Sirius B is fifty years comprising 'an orbit', which in mythological parlance could quite easily be considered 'a reign'.

As is explained in Chapter Six, the fifty-month period later became applied to the Olympic Games when they were established. It defined the interval of time separating them – approximating four solar years. In fact, the Olympic Games were actually separated by alternating intervals of 49 months, then 50 months, then 49 months, etc. This suggests even further an attempt more closely to approximate the $49\frac{1}{2}$ years of Sirius B's orbit in 'month-code'. For by doubling up in this way, using the nearest two whole numbers in alternation, the exact correspondence was obtained, for 49 plus 50 gives the same as $49\frac{1}{2}$ plus $49\frac{1}{2}$. Robert Graves has offered the only previous theory to explain the 'fifty months' in ancient Greece, but his lunar theory does not explain the alternation between 49 and 50, or other mysterious aspects. It is probable that the true explanation based on the Sirius mystery was later overlaid by a lunar tradition which was offered as an 'explanation' to non-initiates, despite its obvious flaws.

It was customary in ancient times also to group together two sacred reigns of fifty months each to form a 'Great Year' of one hundred months. (In practice, as with the Olympic Games, 99 months were actually used, but in theory one used the round figure of 100 months conceived of as 'two reigns'.) The name of the Greek goddess Hekate (Hecate) literally means 'one hundred'. She was involved with the *Argo* tale and specifically identified by Robert Graves with Isis, and in other ways linked to Sirius as an 'underworld version'.

The fifty hounds of hell who pursued Actaeon have a counterpart in Cerberus, the hound of hell who had fifty heads in the earlier tradition. These fifty heads were later discarded in the tradition, like Gilgamesh's original fifty companions, and Cerberus was said to have three heads. But originally he had fifty, as Hesiod describes him. This is thus yet another dog-motif connected with fifty (Sirius being the Dog Star), and linked to Sirius in various ways, such as through the goddess Hekate as an underworld version of Sirius. (The fifty Sumerian Anunnaki also had their counterparts in the underworld. Fifty in the underworld as 'death-counterparts' or shadows to fifty in heaven makes one hundred – the very meaning of Hekate.)

The only known cure for gout (a serious ancient Egyptian complaint) is a substance taken from the plant colchicum, named after Colchis where it grew. This may explain a colony at Colchis. Colchicum is also called 'meadow saffron' and resembles true saffron (which also grows along the Black Sea coasts), which gives a golden dye, perhaps explaining the 'golden' fleece. A golden fleece is a solar symbol. Horus was a solar god. The letters 'l' and 'r' are interchangeable phonetic liquids. The Egyptian form of Horus, Ḥeru, can become Ḥelu and give us the Greek solar god's name Helios. Helios was supposed to stable his horses at Colchis. The Greek word for 'woollen fleece' is *erion*, a word similar to Ḥeru with a dropped aspirate ('h').

CHAPTER FIVE

The Oracle Centres

A consideration of the ancient oracle centres will now be useful in our quest. These centres in the Middle East seem at a casual glance to be dotted around apparently at random. However, there is actually a pattern in their distribution which we will find bears some relation to our subject, and which indicates a highly advanced science of geography and related disciplines in the ancient world. Examination of the oracle centres will be seen to have a connection with the ship *Argo* and will help us to fill in some of the missing background to the entire system of the ancient religious mysteries. The oracle centres were the main places where religion was practised in the ancient world. It makes sense that their occurrence would not be the product of pure chance, and certainly not of convenience. What place could be more out of the way than Dodona in Greece? It was geographically outside the sphere of the civilized world of the Greeks – somewhat more north and more west than any Greek could call comfortable. Why was such an important and senior place of worship in the wilds? Indeed, for that matter, why did Noah's ark land on a mountain nobody ever visits and which is far more remote than even Dodona? The ark and *Argo* and their connections with the Sirius mystery will now be seen to have an intimate connection with the entire geographical structure of the practice of religion in the ancient Mediterranean world. It is important that we explore these extraordinary ramifications fully.

Now we are about to consider a most difficult and complex web of ancient practice which it seems to be possible for us to decipher. Let us approach it in a simpler way than that by which I was originally led to it. Let us look at the ship *Argo* as if it were spread over the surface of the globe by projection. This may seem a curious idea, but the reader must bear with me. After all, the boat is celestial, so why not a projection on the earth's surface from above? Most prominent in the constellation is the star Canopus which was called 'the Rudder', *pedalion*, by Aratos, Eudoxus, and Hipparchos (the leading Greek astronomical figures before Ptolemy), as we are informed by Allen.[1]

There was a place named Canopus on the northern coast of Egypt, which was quite a famous city to the Greeks, and Allen describes it thus: 'Ancient Canopus is now in ruins, but its site is occupied by the village of Al Bekūr, or Aboukir, famous from Lord Nelson's Battle of the Nile, 1 August 1798, and from Napoleon's victory over the Turks a year afterwards; and it is interesting to remember that it was here, from the terraced walls of the Serapeum, the temple of Serapis, that Ptolemy made his observations.' In his book *Hellenistic*

Figure 15. The above geodetic pattern (left) seems to match a stellar pattern of Argo (right)

Civilization, W. W. Tarn comments on Canopus after Alexander the Great had founded Alexandria near it, that from Alexandria 'the gardens of the wealthy extended to Canopus, Alexandria's playground'. To the Greeks, Canopus was the most famous Egyptian city on the northern coast before the foundation of Alexandria. In earlier times the fame of Canopus was held by a city called Behdet, which was a pre-dynastic capital of Egypt before the unification of Egypt and the transferring of the capital to Memphis further south. So, just as Canopus became superseded by Alexandria, Canopus had itself superseded the extremely ancient Behdet which existed before 3200 B.C. as the most important city on the Egyptian coast. In our discussion which follows we must realize that in the times just preceding and during the classical period in Greece the fame that had once attached to Behdet had shifted to Canopus, along with many traditions which were in actuality native to Behdet, which was by then a neglected place which no Greek knew.*

Richard Allen says further of the city of Canopus: 'Our name for it is that of the chief pilot of the fleet of Menelaos, who, on his return from the destruction of Troy, 1183 B.C., touched at Egypt, where, twelve miles to the north-eastward from Alexandria, Canopus died and was honoured, according to Scylax, by a monument raised by his grateful master, giving his name to the city and to this splendid star, which at that time rose about $7\frac{1}{2}°$ above that horizon.' Sir Norman Lockyer in *The Dawn of Astronomy* describes ancient Egyptian temples oriented to the rising of the star Canopus.[2]

Note in the above story of the pilot Canopus that the names of the city and the star are specifically said to have the same origin and that it is from a famous pilot of a fleet, the man at the helm who steers the rudder in the lead ship. Once again, in another way, the star (and the place) are identified with the rudder, which was the other name for the same star.

Allen brings forward another interesting aspect of the star's name, which will be something familiar to us:

> The foregoing derivation of the word Canopus is an early and popular one; but another, perhaps as old, and more probable, being on the authority of Aristides, is from the Coptic, or Egyptian, *Kahi Nub*, Golden Earth. Ideler, coinciding in this, claimed these words as also the source of other titles for Canopus, the Arabic *Wazn*, Weight, and *Ḥadar*, Ground; and of the occasional later Ponderosus and Terrestris. Although I find no reason assigned for the appropriateness of these names, it is easy to infer that they may come from the magnitude of the star and its nearness to the horizon; this last certainly made it the Περίγειος [*Perigeios* – 'near the earth'] of Eratosthenes.

Notice how the irrepressible *Al Wazn*, 'Weight', and its Latin form *Ponderosus*, keep springing up whenever there seems to be a connection with Sirius.

---

* Behdet is on the same latitude as Hebron in the present-day Israeli-occupied west bank of Jordan. In Chapter Four of *The White Goddess*, Robert Graves tells of '. . . the Philistines, who captured the shrine of Hebron in southern Judaea from the Edomite clan of Caleb; but the Calebites ("Dog-men"), allies of the Israelite tribe of Judah, recovered it about two hundred years later. . .'. 'The Dog-men' are probably connected with Sirius the Dog Star and Hebron is the eastern counterpart of Behdet.

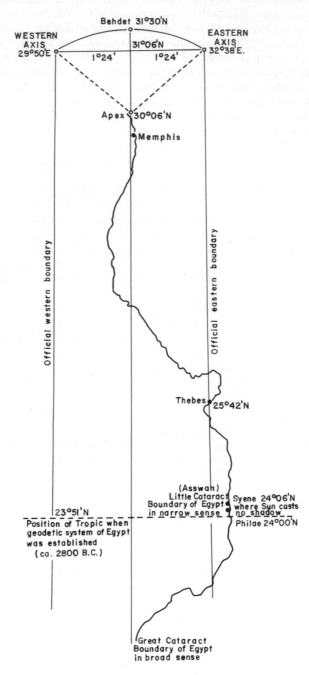

Figure 16. Plan of ancient Egyptian geodetic schema based on Behdet

Allen mentions that 'The Hindus called (Canopus) Agastya, one of their Rishis, or inspired sages, and helmsman of their Argha . . .' which is in striking agreement with the Mediterranean concepts.

Further in line with our previous discoveries it will be interesting to note what Allen says of another of the stars of Argo, the star η (*eta*): '(Jensen) claims it as one of the (Babylonian) temple stars associated with Ea, or Ia [Ea was his Akkadian name, Enki was his Sumerian name; Eridu was his geodetic city, which was the southernmost of all the Sumerian cities. A whole book could easily be written on this subject; a good start for the interested reader would be *Hamlet's Mill* and also the relevant section in *Expedition Tortoise* – see Bibliography], of Eridhu, the Lord of the Waves, otherwise known as Oannes, the mysterious human fish and greatest god of the kingdom.'

Here again we have our amphibious creature Oannes, identified now with the god Enki, who in Sumerian myth did indeed reside at the bottom of the Abzu, or Abyss, in fresh (not salt) water. It was, in fact, the god Enki who assisted man before the flood came by warning the proto-Noah of the Sumerian deluge story to build his ark. He thus fulfilled the function of the special presiding deity of the Hebrews, the Jehovah of the Old Testament. How many Jews know that their god was originally amphibious?

This early Noah or proto-Noah, whom the god Enki warned, was called either Ziusudra or Utnapishtim, depending on which period of pre-Biblical literature one consults. In the early deluge stories, the proto-Noah in his ark sends forth birds to seek dry land just as does Noah in his ark and rather as Jason sends forth birds to find the way through the clashing rocks. H. W. Parke in his book *The Oracles of Zeus*, specifically associates the birds sent forth by Jason with Dodona. Both Dodona and Delphi claimed the 'Greek Noah' Deukalion as having landed his ark on the mountain tops at their locations. Noah himself landed his ark on Mount Ararat, which his bird found for him. We shall see in a little while the importance of these birds and the locations espied by them. But recall now the connections between Dodona and Mount Ararat implied by a common tale of their having both been found by a 'Noah' in an ark who sent forth a bird who found the mountain. It is true that one tale is purely Greek and the other tale purely Hebrew. Naturally, there cannot be any real connection between Dodona and Mount Ararat. After all, they are probably purely arbitrary locations. It is all myth and fable, isn't it? The Jews and the Greeks were never in contact. There could have been no liaison between them. It is all separate hermetically sealed cultures with vague fairy-tales and nonsense. Isn't it? Can anyone challenge such a view? Of course not.

So it is interesting that Dodona and Mount Ararat are on the same parallel and have the same latitude.

Furthermore, Mount Ararat has a centre associated with it which served much the same function to the Caucasians as Dodona did to the Greeks. It is called Metsamor. Here is a description of it by Professor David Lang and Dr Charles Burney:[3]

Archaeological research during the past half century has materially altered our concept of the history of literature, science, and learning in Transcaucasia. A key site here is the village of Metsamor, a few miles to the west of

Echmiadzin, and within sight of Mount Ararat and Alagöz. Close to the village is a massive rocky hummock, perhaps half a mile in circumference, with outcrops of craggy stone. The hummock is riddled with caves, underground storage vaults, and prehistoric dwellings, and is now seen to have been a major scientific, astronomical and industrial centre, operating in the fields of metallurgy, astrology and primitive magic from a period hardly less than five thousand years ago.

The Metsamor 'observatory' is covered with mysterious, cabbalistic signs. Indeed, hieroglyphic writing in Armenia goes back to very early times, perhaps to the New Stone Age. All over Armenia, we find pictograms or petroglyphs, carved or scratched on rocks, caves and cliff faces, and showing simplified human and animal figures. There is little doubt that these served as means of communication, as well as of ritual and artistic self-expression.

They also describe Metsamor's wide-ranging contacts with the outside world:[4]

Sumerian achievements as pioneers in copper and bronze metallurgy must not be underestimated. . . . The early Transcaucasian cultural zone, though geographically within the Near East, was divided only by the high but narrow Caucasus from the northern steppes; and, once there, nothing could prevent the traders reaching the central European copper-working centres. Thus Georgia, with its neighbouring regions, was perhaps open as much to influences from Europe as to those from the Near East. Transcaucasia may have been not so much an original centre as a region into which metal-working arrived from two different directions, and where, though present in earlier periods in a modest way, it took root and from the late third millennium B.C. began to develop along distinctive lines, no longer owing its forms to external inspiration. . . . Metsamor gives a hint that, just as earlier in Europe, once foreign merchants had arrived seeking sources of metals, bringing their copper and later their bronze products with them, and explaining, by choice or otherwise, their techniques to the local population, it was no time before a local industry began to arise. If present evidence indeed points to Armenia as the oldest centre of metallurgy in Transcaucasia, it points also to a Near Eastern inspiration.

It is extraordinary that if you place a compass point on Thebes in Egypt you can draw an arc through both Dodona and Metsamor.

We now return to Allen and his further remarks[5] about Oannes: 'Berōssōs described Oannes as the teacher of early man in all knowledge; and in mythology he was even the creator of man . . . and some have regarded him as the prototype of Noah.'

Allen also describes the star Canopus in this way: 'And, as the constellation (of Argo) was associated on the Nile with the great god Osiris, so its great star became the Star of Osiris. . . .' He gives a further application of the title 'heavy': 'The *Alfonsine Tables* had (for Canopus) Suhel Ponderosus ("Among the Persians Suhail is a synonym for wisdom . . ." and there was also, therefore, a "Suhel Sirius"), that appeared in a contemporary chronicle as Sihil Ponderosa, a translation of Al Suhail al Wazn.' Allen then gives several tales indicating that this designation was once applied to another star 'formerly located near Orion's stars' and 'had to flee south', being an apparent admission that Canopus is being called by another star's title. Canopus is south of Sirius (which is 'near Orion's stars'), and so obviously the description of the invisible Sirius B 'fled south' to a likely visible star, Canopus.

Now to return to our projection of the *Argo* on the earth's surface. We put the stern of the ship and its rudder at the obvious place – Canopus. (But really slightly altered eastwards to the original city Behdet.)

Now we must consider Dodona. We are told that oak from Dodona was placed 'in the middle of the keel' of *Argo* by Athena. It obviously ran the whole length of the ship. It is also referred to as being in the *prow*. Allen says of this:

> Mythology insisted that (the *Argo*) was built by Glaucus, or by Argos, for Jason, leader of the fifty Argonauts, whose number equalled that of the oars of the ship, aided by Pallas Athene, who herself set in the prow a piece from the speaking oak of Dodona; the Argo being 'thus endowed with the power of warning and guiding the chieftains who form its crew'. She carried the famous expedition from Iolchis in Thessaly to Aea in Colchis, in search of the golden fleece, and when the voyage was over Athene placed the boat in the sky.

In measuring with the *Argo's* projection one does so from the site of Behdet, which is a bit east of Canopus on the northern Mediterranean coast of Egypt, but it was common classical Greek practice to think of Canopus in place of the forgotten Behdet, as for instance with 'the Canopic Hercules' who went to Delphi and is mentioned by Pausanius as predecessor to the Greek Hercules from Tiryns who was of much later date. (It is important that the original Hercules was admitted by the Greeks to have been an Egyptian.) In fact, the Delphic oracle itself compares the Greek Hercules most unfavourably with the original Egyptian one – and remember it is said that in the earliest versions of the story it was Hercules, not Jason, who led the Argonauts. Also, it is well accepted today among scholars that Hercules was in many ways a survival of Gilgamesh, with particular motifs and deeds being identical in both heroes.

Well, if we project the *Argo* on the earth with its rudder at Canopus (really Behdet) we put the other end at Dodona because the oak in the prow came from there. Canopus-Behdet is named after the rudder, and Dodona produced the prow. Therefore we are not merely fantasizing when we project the image of the *Argo* in such a way that the rudder is at the rudder on earth and the prow is at the earthly source of the prow.

If we then keep the rudder at the same spot and swing the boat over a map so that the prow which touched Dodona points towards Metsamor, we discover that the angle made is exactly a right-angle of 90°.

Now we get into geodetics, a fearsome subject. The fact is that geodetics involves a bit of bother. It concerns latitudes and longitudes, and most people would run a mile upon hearing those mentioned (sailors and pilots of aircraft excepted). In fact no one is more likely to flee with terror from the subject than an archaeologist. There is almost nothing an archaeologist likes less than being reminded how little he may know about the Earth as a body in space

PROJECTION FROM BEHDET

Figure 17

and about astronomy. The average archaeologist is almost bound to be ignorant of even the most elementary astronomical facts. There are many caustic comments on this state of affairs to be found in *The Dawn of Astronomy*, written by the distinguished Victorian astronomer and friend of Sir Wallis Budge, Sir Norman Lockyer,[6] and more recently some severe remarks have been made also by Santillana and von Dechend in *Hamlet's Mill*.

But we must come now to some extremely interesting further discoveries. Egypt is 7° long – in latitude – from Behdet to the Great Cataract. I have reasons for believing that the ancient Egyptians thought of distances of 7° as an octave, by analogy with music. Most readers will know that an octave contains eight notes on a scale over a space of seven intervals (five tones and two semitones actually, but let us think only of the seven intervals).

Just as this book was about to go to press, confirmation appeared in the newspapers that the ancient Mediterranean peoples did indeed know the principles of our musical octave. In the London *Times*[7] an article appeared describing the work of Dr Richard L. Crocker, Professor of Music History, and Dr Anne D. Kilmer, Professor of Assyriology and Dean of Humanities, both at the University of California, Berkeley. The article quoted Dr Crocker as saying: 'We always knew there was music in the earlier Assyro-Babylonian civilization. But until this, we did not know that it had the same heptatonic diatonic scale that is characteristic of contemporary Western music and Greek music of the first millennium B.C.' After fifteen years of research, Crocker and Kilmer have demonstrated that some clay tablets from Ugarit on the coast of present-day Syria, dating from about 1800 B.C., bore a musical text based on our familiar octave. Dr Kilmer summed it up by saying: 'It is the oldest "sheet music" known to exist.' The two professors have even played the tune on a reconstruction of an ancient lyre in public, after an interval of only 3,700 years.[8]

I believe that the Egyptians laid out a 'geodetic octave' commencing at 1° north of Behdet (to emphasize its separateness from Egypt) and culminating at Dodona. For Dodona is precisely 8° north of Behdet in latitude! And the related oracle centre of Delphi is exactly 7° in latitude north of Behdet! (These last two facts were discovered by Livio Stecchini, as will be explained somewhat later.)

I have arrived at this sequence for a geodetic oracle octave (see Fig. 25 below):

8. Dodona
7. Delphi (with its famous *omphalos*, a stone navel)
6. Delos, the famous shrine of Apollo, once an oracle centre (also with an omphalos)
5. Kythera (Cythera), a site on the north-east coast (see later); or Thera
4. Omphalos (Thenae) near Knossos on Crete (on the Plain of Omphaleion)
3. Undiscovered site on Southern or South-western coast of Cyprus? (Paphos?) (Cape Gata?)
2. Lake Triton (or Tritonis) in Libya
1. El Marj (Barce or Barca)

The ones which I have identified are spaced apart by one degree of latitude from each other in sequence and are integral degrees of latitude from Behdet, which we shall see was the geodetic centre of the ancient world (akin to Greenwich in the modern world) and was also a pre-dynastic capital of Egypt.

What justification have I for speaking of a link between the oracle centres and the musical octave? I have several reasons, and it would be just as well for me to give some slight indications here to make the reader who is justifiably puzzled at this point a little less so.

Graves[9] informs us of some interesting facts about Apollo, who was official patron god of Delphi and Delos (two of the centres on our list): 'In Classical times, music, poetry, philosophy, astronomy, mathematics, medicine, and science all came under Apollo's control. As the enemy of barbarism, he stood for moderation in all things, and *the seven strings of his lute* were connected with the seven vowels of the later Greek alphabet, *given mystical significance*, and used for therapeutic music. Finally, because of his identification with the Child Horus, a solar concept, he was worshipped as the sun, whose Corinthian cult had been taken over by solar Zeus. . . .' (The italics are mine.) Note also the reference to Horus, whose falcon would have presided over the Colchian dead in their hope of resurrection. In fact, one meaning of *kirkos* (Circe – 'falcon'), which I did not elaborate on earlier, is 'ring'. I wish to comment in passing that not only was the ring traditionally a solar symbol (as was the golden fleece, and as was the falcon), but the Cyclopes who were one-eyed were really one-ring-eyed. Cyclopes means 'ring-eyed', in fact. Graves says:[10] 'One-eyed Polyphemus . . . can be traced back to the Caucasus. . . . Whatever the meaning of the Caucasian tale may have been, A. B. Cook in his *Zeus* (pp. 302–23) shows that the Cyclops's eye was a Greek solar emblem.'

The following remarks by Graves then tend to dissociate Cyclops from Cyclopes, but perhaps this should not be done, in the light of all these new insights. After all, the older Cyclopes were three, wild, and ring-eyed, and sons again of Gaia the Earth goddess just as were the three fifty-headed monsters (there is to be much discussion of this later). They would, according to my 'system', be solar too, and 'ring', 'falcon', 'earth-born of Gaia' and solar seem always to go together in the schema. Gaia, indeed, preceded the solar Apollo as presiding deity at Delphi. Not surprising, as Deukalion's ark landed on Mount Parnassus above Delphi (according to Delphic propaganda) and his 'mother' was Gaia, whose 'bones' he threw behind him to people the desolated Earth once again.

It is not only Deukalion's ark that is connected with Delphi. There are connections also with the *Argo*, as we learn from Godfrey Higgins:[11] 'In the religious ceremonies at Delphi a boat of immense size was carried about in processions; it was shaped like a lunar crescent, pointed alike at each end: it was called an Omphalos or Umbilicus, or the ship *Argo*. Of this ship *Argo* I shall have very much to say hereafter. My reader will please to recollect that the os minxae or Δελφνς (Delphys) is called by the name of the ship *Argo*.'

Other matters which Higgins connects with Delphi are the sacred syllable *om* of the Indo-Europeans which he says 'is not far from the *divina vox* of the Greek. Hesychius, also Suidas in voce, interprets the word *omph* to be θεῖα χληδων (*theia chlēdōn*), the sacred voice, the holy sound – and hence arose the ὀμφαλός (*omphalos*), or place of *Omphe*.' He relates all this with sacred music and the traditional sacred name of God which consists of the seven vowels spoken in sequence to form one word, which is the *'not-to-be-spoken* word'. He says: 'As a pious Jew will not utter the word Ieue, so a pious Hindu will not utter the word Om.'

Higgins says φη, *phē*, is the verb root in Greek of *phaō* 'to speak or pronounce' and *phēmi*, 'to say'. (I might add that φηγός, *phēgos*, is the word for oak, as at Dodona, and φήμη, *phēmē*, literally means 'oracle'.) Hence *Omphē* means 'the speaking of Om'. (At the *phēmē* Dodona the *phēgos* literally practised *omphē* because the oak spoke there.)

Delphi was said to be the *omphalos*, 'navel', of the world. But it was in fact only one of many.[12] The reader will have noticed that there is an Omphalos near Knossos in Crete which is one of the octave sequence of oracle centres laid out in geodetic integral degrees of latitude from Behdet, pre-dynastic capital of Egypt. A photograph of the omphalos stone of Delos may be seen in Plate 12 as well. The seven vowels, the seven strings of Apollo's lyre, the seven notes of the octave (the eighth being a repetition one octave higher of the first, as most people will know), the eight oracle centres in the 'northern octave' of oracles, the seven degrees of latitude marking the official length of ancient Egypt itself, the mystic and unspeakable name of God consisting of the seven vowels run together in one breath – all these are part of a coherent complex of elements forming a system.

Before going much further, I should justify my tentative selection of a site on the island of Kythera (Cythera), which is off the southern coast of the Greek Peloponnese, as possibly being associated with the fifth in my series of geodetically sited oracle centres. I found the necessary information while reading Professor Cyrus H. Gordon's remarkable book, *The Common Background of Greek and Hebrew Civilizations*.[13] At the end of Chapter II, Gordon tells us the following:

> Sometimes cultic centres attracted people from remote areas. Probably the most common cause for such magnetism was an efficacious priesthood, that earned a reputation for helping people in need of practical advice, psychological guidance or medical aid. Cythera began to attract foreigners as early as the Pyramid Age. A stone cup, with the name of a Fifth Dynasty [the chronology of Richard A. Parker gives the dates 2501–2342 B.C. for the Fifth Dynasty] solar temple [of Pharaoh Userkaf at Abusir] (sp-r^e) inscribed in Egyptian hieroglyphs, has been found on Cythera. Early in the second quarter of the second millennium, a Bablyonian inscription of Naram-Sin, King of Eshnunna, was dedicated on Cythera 'for the life' of that Mesopotamian monarch. [This is one of the reasons for believing that both texts were sent to Cythera in antiquity. Modern deception is unlikely because the Naram-Sin text was found on Cythera in 1849 before the decipherment of cuneiform.] The interesting thing is that both of these texts found on Cythera are religious in character. Herodotus (1:105) relates that the Phoenicians erected a temple on Cythera to the goddess of the heavens. Finally in classical times, Cythera was a great centre of the cult of Aphrodite. The ancient temples were built in the vicinity of Palaiopolis around the middle of the eastern shore. I visited the site in 1958 and found it extensive and promising for excavation. . . . Egyptians, Babylonians and Phoenicians came to worship the great goddess there. [At that time the

great goddess, Gaia, was also in charge of Delphi, before the usurpation by Apollo.] Ancient cultic installations, carved out of the living rock, can still be seen on a high place at the north end, near the shore. A well, cleared some years ago, had, at its bottom, ancient statuary . . . [there are] ancient stone walls. . . . The whole area is covered with ceramics that show the site was occupied in Middle Minoan III (c. 1700–1570), Late Minoan I–III (c. 1570–1100) [Note: 'Late Minoan III (c. 1400–1100) is the Mycenaean Age'] and subsequently in classical times (5th–4th centuries B.C.).

The problem posed by ancient Cythera has not yet been answered. The island is rather remote from Egypt and Asia for men to have sailed there, for religious purposes alone. And yet it is hard to discover any more practical reason. Cythera is not remarkable for its natural resources. . . . Meanwhile we must reckon with Cythera as a site where all the evidence so far points to its importance as a religious centre with international attraction. . . . Such shrines have remained well known throughout the ages. In classical antiquity, the oracle at Delphi was sought within a wide radius. Today Lourdes attracts from every continent people in need of help that they have not succeeded in finding nearer home.

Cythera thus became a centre for Egyptians and Semites and still other people, from Abusir along the Nile to Eshnunna beyond the Euphrates. Such visitors brought their influence to bear upon the Aegean, and on returning home, carried some Aegean culture with them. . . . It is gratifying that Cythera is now being excavated by Professor George Huxley for the University of Pennsylvania Museum.

So much for Cythera; an alternative possible site is on the island of Thera. Or the two may be linked. Some justification for my guess that site number three would be in the south of Cyprus comes from the famous references to 'Aphrodite Kytherean, even as far as Cyprus', in the ancient literature. Also, Herodotus (Book I, 105) refers to the temple of Aphrodite Urania at Ascalon in Syria and says: '[it is] the most ancient, I am told, of all the temples of this goddess. The one in Cyprus the Cyprians themselves admit was derived from it, and the one in Cythera was built by the Phoenicians, who belong to this part of Syria.' In the latter (unquoted) part of his last footnote given above, Gordon mentions that 'Phoenicians' is Herodotean language inclusive of the Minoans.

In passing, I might mention that a little island opposite Cythera is called Anti-Cythera and there a famous shipwreck was recovered from which came the miniature mechanical computer dated from the first century B.C. (concerning which Professor Derek Price of Yale University has written a good deal, including a 'cover story' for the *Scientific American*). This little computer is one of many survivals of ancient times which demonstrate conclusively that the conventional attitudes today to ancient technology are inadequate, and seriously underestimate the early peoples.

Now as for the site of Delos, I will give information here from H. W. Parke's authoritative book *Greek Oracles*[14] which will indicate its importance as an oracle centre in my postulated 'northern octave' of geodetic centres:

The other point which Dodona could urge against Delphi in its favour was that it was the oracle of Zeus himself. Apollo was at most the son of Zeus, inserted somewhat awkwardly into the Greek pantheon. On the face of it his prophecies could not be as significant as the utterances of the father of gods and men. Delphi replied with an elaborate piece of theological propaganda. While not attempting to detract from the supreme position of Zeus, it was argued that Apollo was his chosen prophet. This doctrine appears first in the Homeric *Hymn to Apollo*, but not in the sections connected with Delphi. It is in the Delian hymn where the infant god bursts from his swaddling clothes and cries: 'May the harp and the bending bow be my delight, and I shall prophesy to men the unerring will of Zeus.' In the rest of the same poem there are other references to Delos as an oracle-centre, a function which had lapsed in the classical period. But this part of the Homeric *Hymn* with its description of the Delian festival evidently dates back to an early stage of the archaic period – probably about 700 B.C.

The concept of Apollo as the prophet of Zeus may, then, have started in Delos, but it was certainly taken over and largely developed by Delphi.

Also '. . . Delos, though later mainly famous as (Apollo's) birthplace, evidently once had been a centre of divination.'[15]

My contention that the oracle centres of Dodona, Delphi, Delos, Cythera, Knossos, and Cyprus are linked as a series – apart from the obvious facts that they are all separated from each other by a degree of latitude and are integral degrees of latitude from Behdet in Egypt and have demonstrable connections with Egypt in tradition or archaeology – is further cemented by another passage in H. W. Parke's book:[16]

At Delphi, namely the site of the classical shrine of Athena Pronaia on the east of Castalia . . . as excavation has shown, there was not a settlement, but a cult centre going back to Mycenaean times. . . . It is interesting archaeologically that a number of important finds from the earlier archaic periods show clear affinities or actual derivation from Crete. For, as we have mentioned, the Homeric *Hymn to Apollo* ends by describing how, 'Phoebus Apollo then took it in mind whom he would bring of men as his worshippers who would serve him in rocky Pytho. Then while pondering he was aware of a swift ship on the wine-dark sea, and in it were good men and many – Cretans from Minoan Knossos who offer sacrifices to the lord Apollo and announce the oracles of Phoebus Apollo of the golden sword whatever he speaks in prophecy from the laurel-tree . . .' . . . Some scholars have seen in the evident archaeological links between early archaic Delphi and Crete a basis of fact behind this facade of legend, and it is possible that the cult of Apollo was introduced by sea from Crete. . . .

In the Homeric *Hymn* quoted we find it specifically stated that Minoan Cretans (contemporaneous with ancient Egypt, of course, and who traded with the Egyptians) from Knossos took Apollo to Delphi, the site of an omphalos. And these Knossians are stated to respect oracles. And near Knossos is a site called Omphalos which is one degree of latitude south of the site of Kythera, which is one degree south of Delos, which is one degree south of Delphi.

Parke gives further information.[17] He mentions the connections well

known to have existed *between Delos and Dodona* through what are known as
'the Hyperborean gifts', which were sent to Delos by way of Dodona from the
mysterious northern Hyperboreans, whose land has never been located with any
certainty at all, but which is thought by many to have been Britain. In Book II
of Diodorus Siculus one finds a description of the Hyperboreans observing
celestial objects through what sounds to me and some other scholars distinctly
like a telescope. The description should be consulted by the interested reader.

Figure 18. Detail of mural from Pompeii reproduced by W. H. Roscher. The omphalos
is identical to the one at Delos (see Plate 12, top right). Here the friendly omphalos-
serpent is being harassed by a python

Parke tells us: 'In the Cyclades Delos had once had an Apolline oracle
of importance. . . . One can suppose that this institution existed . . . at the
end of the eighth century, and may have dwindled away in the seventh
century. . . . By the time when Pisistratus and Polycrates in the latter half of
the sixth century revived the sanctity of Delos, the oracle appears to have
already ceased and was not restored.'[18]

It is a daunting prospect to try to set forth at proper length all the complex
tangle of information concerning the 'northern octave' and its many links with
the Sirius tradition. It is impossible for me to do justice in this book to the
subject of the astronomical knowledge of the ancients.[19]

From *Hamlet's Mill* we have a passage which is now relevant. The reader
will have to accept on trust that the seven notes of the octave and the seven
planets of ancient times were thought of in connection with one another. We
cannot here take on the debate concerning early Pythagoreanism versus Neo-
Pythagoreanism and the genesis of different concepts of 'harmony of the spheres'.
Here is the passage: 'And Aristotle says (*Rhet.* 2.24, 1401a15) that, wishing to
circumscribe a "dog", one was permitted to use "Dog star" (Sirius) or Pan,
because Pindar states him to be the "shape-shifting dog of the Great Goddess
[Gaia]" . . . The amazing significance of Sirius as leader of the planets, as the
eighth planet, so to speak, and of Pan, the dance-master (*choreutēs*) as well as
the real *kosmokrator*, ruling over the "three worlds", would take a whole volume.'[20]

Now this reference to Sirius as 'the eighth planet, so to speak' is an extremely
interesting clue. (In fact, there is some evidence to suggest that the ancients
knew of the existence of the eighth planet Uranus because the Egyptians could
just have managed to observe it in the way suggested by Peter Tompkins in
Secrets of the Great Pyramid.[21] And I believe both that this was probably the case
and that Uranus was sometimes compared to Sirius B because they were both
'invisible'. Also, Sirius B orbits Sirius A as a planet orbits a sun, as I have
mentioned before, for its orbital period is less than that of our own planets

Uranus, Neptune, and Pluto. The fact that Sirius B, a star, moves faster than Uranus, a planet, is an additional reason for the two to be thought of as similar. Sirius B was additionally compared in some obscure way to the innermost tiny planet Mercury, the nature of whose orbit was symbolized by the human intestines – see Figure 13 for this – and Uranus was the 'octave' expression of Mercury.)

Consider this 'eighth planet' theme in relation to the oracle centres. Dodona is the eighth oracle centre of the 'northern octave'. In music, the eighth note closes the octave by repeating the first note an octave higher. The 'eighth planet' would therefore repeat the first planet which was Hermes (in Latin, Mercury). Now it was Hermes (Mercury) who supplied the golden ram to Phrixus so that he could make his getaway to Colchis. And it was the oak of Dodona which was fitted into the prow of the *Argo* which returned the golden fleece. During the interval of the fleece's stay in Colchis the fleece rested 'in the grove of Ares (Mars)'. The important points to note are that the fleece went to Colchis under the auspices of the first planet, rested there under the auspices of (the planet?) Mars, and returned under the auspices of Sirius the 'eighth planet' with the oak of the eighth oracle centre in the *Argo*'s prow. And we have already seen how *Argo*, if swung through a 90° angle, touches its prow first at Dodona and then points directly at Metsamor near Mount Ararat. But if an extended *Argo* has its prow touch Dodona and its rudder at Egyptian Thebes, the *Argo* may be swung to Ararat/Metsamor and touches its prow there too.

Parke says: 'On Asia Minor Didyma near Miletus is the only oracle-centre for whose activity we have some evidence in the sixth century.'[22] Miletus seems to be on the same parallel as Delos, just as Sardis is on the same parallel as Delphi.[23] And we have seen that Mount Ararat (having its associated centre at Metsamor) is on the same parallel as Dodona. There may be a 'north-eastern octave' to correspond to the 'northern octave'. But we shall see later that geodetic points exist over great stretches of territory, marked out from Behdet, the ancient Greenwich. (For instance, an arc swung through Aca in Colchis would pass through Mecca as well, if the compass point were on Behdet. A line from Egyptian Thebes to Dodona intersects the vicinity of Omphalos and Knossos on Crete. The lines connecting Thebes, Dodona, and Metsamor, form an equilateral triangle. A line from Behdet to Dodona intersects Thera. Also, a straight line passes through the three points Behdet, Mecca, Dodona. As for Mecca, I doubt that many Moslem scholars will be at all surprised to learn of these aspects of their holy centre. They know very well that the centre has geodetic aspects and the central shrine of the Kaaba dates from prehistoric times; they say it was established by the prophet Abraham.)

Associations of Delphi with the Sirius tradition are not limited to the Canopic Egyptian Hercules's visit, the carrying of an *Argo* in procession, and the desire to claim the ark of Deukalion instead of Dodona's claiming it (the centres then being rivals for power and attention, as I have said).

Other Sirius-tradition elements present in connection with Delphi are concerned with the *Argo* and the Minyae. It was an oracle from Delphi which stated the golden fleece would have to be brought back to Iolchus from Colchis. It was a series of insisten toracles from Delphi that were ultimately responsible for our knowing the Sirius tradition from the Dogon today, as we will see near

Figure 19

the end of the book. For Delphi determined the later fate of the Minyae, and it is their tradition which survives today in the former French Sudan. The explanation of this will be left to somewhat later.

Now, as to the omphalos stone and also Behdet. For these subjects we must turn to an amazing book published in 1971 *The Secrets of the Great Pyramid* by Peter Tompkins (with a scholarly appendix by Livio Stecchini). Tompkins tells us:[24]

> The prime meridian of Egypt was made to split the country longitudinally precisely in half, running from Behdet on the Mediterranean, right through an island in the Nile just northeast of the Great Pyramid, all the way to where it crossed the Nile again at the Second Cataract. . . . Cities and temples, says Stecchini, were deliberately built at distances in round figures and simple fractions from the tropic or the prime meridian. The predynastic capital of Egypt was set near the mouth of the Nile at Behdet, right on the prime meridian, at 31° 30'. . . . Memphis, the first capital of united Egypt, was again laid out on the prime meridian and at 29° 51', precisely 6° north of the tropic. . . . As each of these geodetic centres was a political as well as a geographical 'navel' of the world, an omphalos, or stone navel, was placed there to represent the northern hemisphere from equator to pole, marked out with meridians and parallels, showing the direction and distance of other such navels. In Thebes the stone omphalos was placed in the main room of the temple of Amon, where the meridian and parallel actually cross. . . . For the ancient Egyptians to have laid out an absolutely straight meridian of 30° of latitude from the Mediterranean to the equator, over 2,000 miles, and drawn two more, equidistant, east and west, as boundaries of the country [see illustrations in the book], must have required an enormous amount of personnel and careful astronomical sightings. Even more sophisticated was their method of establishing longitude, as reconstructed by Stecchini.
>
> With the aid of an elementary system of telegraphy, consisting of a series of beacons, the Egyptians, says Stecchini, were able to note what star was at its zenith at a certain moment, and flash the data, via a string of flares, to other observers, so many degrees to east and west. . . . Because of the advanced geodetic and geographic science of the Egyptians, Egypt became the geodetic centre of the known world. Other countries located their shrines and capital cities in terms of the Egyptian meridian 'zero', including such capitals as Nimrod, Sardis, Susa, Persepolis, and, apparently, even the ancient Chinese capital of An-Yang.
>
> All of these localities, says Stecchini, were set and oriented on the basis of the most exact sightings. The same applies to the centres of worship of the Jews, the Greeks, and the Arabs.
>
> According to Hebrew historians the original Jewish centre of worship was not Jerusalem, but Mount Gerizim, a strictly geodetic point 4° east of the main axis of Egypt. It was only moved to Jerusalem after 980 B.C.
>
> The two great oracular centres of Greece – Delphi and Dodona – were also geodetic markers according to Stecchini. Delphi is 7° and Dodona 8° north of Behdet, the northernmost part of Egypt, on the prime meridian of Egypt.

This is obviously where I got the original idea for my 'northern octave', from this brilliant observation of Stecchini's.

Readers who have pondered the strange story of Pharaoh Tutankhamen – whose previous name had been Tutankhaten – and his father-in-law, Akhenaten

Figure 20. This representation of the sacred basket found at Khorsabad is important evidence connecting Oannes with the omphalos stone tradition. The basket, which was invariably carried by Oannes, is seen here with the two doves with heads turned away – motif of the omphalos. The basket-work is also seen to resemble the mesh which usually covers the omphalos

and mother-in-law Nefertiti – might do well to note that a geodetic-religious dispute lay behind Akhenaten's desire to build a new geodetic capital city, which he did, but outraged the priests in the process. Why were the boundary stones of this city later ferociously mutilated? Because the Pharaoh had tried to establish a variation on the geodetic system of Egypt (for some very sound reasons, of course), and those marker stones represented it quite literally!

In Plate 12 the reader may see for himself the surviving omphalos stones of Delphi and of Delos[25] – both of which are spread with 'nets' representing a latitudinal and longitudinal geodetic mesh.[26] It is this mesh which is probably carried at all times by Oannes (see Plates 6, 7, 8 and 9) as a 'basket'. For the 'warp and woof' of the sacred basket of Oannes/Dagon – surviving as the *lyknos* basket of Greek Demeter (who succeeded the Philistine fish-tailed Dagon as agricultural deity, keeping Dagon's 'basket') – represent perfectly the warp and woof of latitude and longitude. The Dogon have traditions of the religious and mythological importance of 'warp and woof' in weaving, and of sacred baskets 'which are not baskets', all of which may be found described in many places in *Le Renard pâle*.

In Plate 12 the reader may see the omphalos stone found by Reisner in the great temple of Amon at Thebes in Egypt. This stone was placed in the main room of the temple where the meridian and parallel actually cross.[27] In Figure 23 is a reproduction of a figure from an Egyptian papyrus of omphalos stones with two doves perched on top. These two doves are the standard glyph meaning 'to lay out parallels and meridians'.[28] They are the 'two doves' who flew to Dodona from Thebes according to the account of Herodotus.[29] Of course, the two doves are in fact carrier-pigeons. To keep in touch over such enormous distances, and to maintain prompt communication between oracle-centres which was essential to the successful operation of a coherent 'world-wide' religious network spread over thousand of miles, the only available means were carrier-pigeons. I am informed that carrier-pigeons could fly from Thebes to Dodona in about a day. To travel such a distance oneself by sea and land would take months. Daily communication between the Egyptian religious centre of Thebes and all its oracle 'colonies' would have been transacted by the very carrier-pigeons whom we see plainly depicted on omphalos stones by both Greek (see Plate 12) and Egyptian (see additionally Figure 24) representations and documented clearly by Herodotus. Also, I should imagine such instantaneous 'news coverage' would surreptitiously find its way into the oracular pronouncements at the various centres and exercise a considerable political influence. For after all, there was hardly a king or potentate anywhere in the ancient world who would disregard an oracular order 'from the gods'. Probably the political forces were totally ignorant of the 'hot news line' ticking away secretly in the local oracle centre's temple complex.

I realize that acknowledgement of all these facts is bound to evoke howls and cries of anguish from any of those archaeologists to whom a drastic revision of their ideas is more painful than would be an amputation of all their limbs without an anaesthetic. Such are the hazards which go with the addictive and opiate pleasures of submersion in a body of orthodox theory.

As the philosopher David Hume pointed out concerning the revolutionary discovery of the circulation of the blood by William Harvey: 'It is remarked that no physician in Europe who had reached forty years of age ever, to the end of his life, adopted Harvey's doctrine of the circulation of the blood; and that his practice in London diminished extremely from the reproach drawn upon him by that great and signal discovery. So slow is the progress of truth in every science, even when not opposed by factions or superstitious prejudices!'[30]

It should be strongly emphasized that Dodona and Metsamor/Ararat are equidistant from Egyptian Thebes. The Greek ark landed at Dodona and the Hebrew ark landed at Ararat. The process of 'landing an ark', therefore, consists of starting at Thebes and going north to either of the two places which are 8 degrees of latitude northwards and which are joined to each other by a distance equal to their distances from Thebes. That may sound complicated. The fact is that an equilateral triangle is formed by the lines joining Thebes with Dodona and Ararat. These facts cannot possibly be an accident. There cannot be supposedly separate Greek and Hebrew traditions giving the landing points of the ark in their respective regions of the world, which then both turn out by chance to be equidistant from Thebes and the same distance from each other, as well as on the same latitude. Since Mount Tomaros at Dodona and Mount Ararat are both 'landing sites' for an ark, this must mean that the tip of the prow of the ark literally does touch either of them when projected on the globe from Thebes. This may be seen clearly drawn by a cartographer in Figure 19.

Also founded from Thebes by flying doves, according to Herodotus,[31] was the Oracle of Ammon in Libya, known to be at the Oasis of Siwa. In Figure 15 we may even see a comparison of the line patterns made by joining Thebes, Dodona, and Siwa with each other, with the line patterns formed by joining certain stars in the constellation of Argo together. The pattern is seen to be identical. The site of Siwa may have been chosen simply to display this. In both instances we have the helm of the *Argo* as the starting point: in the celestial pattern we start from the star Canopus, identified with the *Argo's* helm; and in the geodetic pattern we start with Thebes, which is the site for the global *Argo's* helm when projected either to Dodona or Ararat. But there is another means of projecting the Argo, using Behdet, to convey other meanings – bearing in mind always the interconnecting relationships of the sites, with Behdet equidistant from both Siwa and Thebes, and also on the northernmost point of Egypt and (see Figure 16) on the prime meridian dividing Egypt as demonstrated by Livio Stecchini.[32]

When the helm of the *Argo* is placed at Behdet (near the geographical Canopus) rather than at Thebes, with the prow touching Mount Ararat, if we swing the prow across to Dodona through an arc of exactly 90° (a right angle), we find that the prow is then too long and must be shortened. In fact, for this extraordinary point, documentary evidence actually exists in a Babylonian text. In Chapter Three we cited the passage in another context, and I will here return to it. It is from the brief Sumerian epic poem 'Gilgamesh and Agga', of extreme antiquity, the surviving tablets preserving it dating from the first half of the second millennium B.C. This Sumerian poem contains, within the framework of what seems to be a local political diatribe, a certain bizarre core of material which no scholar has ever satisfactorily interpreted.[33] (The political aspect of the poem has, in my opinion, been overemphasized due to Jacobsen and Kramer's understandable excitement at finding in the poem actual evidence of the existence 4,000 years ago of a bicameral parliament, which Kramer wrote up as one of the world's 'firsts' in his excellent book, *History Begins at Sumer*.[34])

Babylonian Zodiac (?)

Figure 21. The design carved on to the Babylonian omphalos. Rawlinson suggested that the design was of a zodiac. He thought it obvious that the figures were of constellations. It would seem definitely to be a star-map, but it is not necessarily true that the intention is to represent the sky accurately. Attempts to interpret such complex maps (the Egyptian zodiac of Denderah being a notorious example) usually fall short, so I will not here tempt the fates

The poem mentions (line 104) a 'fleeing bird' which I believe may be a reference to the carrier-pigeon network which we have just discussed. But the most important elements in the poem seem to me to be two apparently contradictory statements:

(1) 'The prow of the *magurru*-boat was not cut down' (line 80)
(2) 'The prow of the *magurru*-boat was cut down.' (line 98)

In Chapter Three I discussed why the *magurru*-boat and the *magan*-boat of another poem were in fact that boat which was later known as the *Argo*.

I believe that statement (1) refers to the *Argo* as projected from Behdet to Ararat, and that statement (2) refers to the projection of the *Argo* from Behdet to Dodona. The latter requires the cutting down or shortening of the prow lest the *Argo* extend beyond Dodona.

As long as the prow was not cut down in 'Gilgamesh and Agga', we find that 'The multitude did not cover itself with dust' in mourning. For the projection was still extended over the north-west of Mesopotamia, the Sumerian homeland being at least in the general vicinity. The Behdet–Ararat line actually intersects the famous oracle centre of Hierapolis[35] which I propose as the fifth eastern oracle centre at 36° 30'.

Figure 22. A Babylonian omphalos stone (from Rawlinson). A flattened view of its entire conical design is seen in the accompanying illustration

The poem says also, as long as the prow is not cut down, that 'The people of all the foreign lands were not overwhelmed'. In other words, the projection did not fall over foreigners such as those living in Greece. It did not literally 'overwhelm' people of foreign lands, meaning overshadow or pass over them.

However, when the prow was shortened, the projection of *Argo* left Mesopotamia altogether, and then 'The multitude covered itself with dust' and the people of foreign lands were overwhelmed. It is at this point that Gilgamesh says to Agga, 'O Agga, the fleeing bird thou hast filled with grain' (in other words, fed the carrier-pigeon in preparation for his flight to another and different oracle centre – namely, Dodona rather than Metsamor). The entire poem is based round a repeated refrain which Kramer calls 'a riddle',[36] and which concerns the digging and completing of wells, of 'the small bowls of the land', and wishes 'to complete the fastening ropes'. At this point only a Sumerian scholar can tell us whether there are any other shades of meaning or alternative readings which might make the passage clearer, following the clue that 'the fastening ropes' may refer to the rope-like mesh which we see, for instance, on the omphali of Delphi and Delos. Can 'the small bowls of the land' be either geodetic points or their markers, the omphalos stones themselves, which are like small bowls? Could 'small bowls' be an accepted expression for omphali in Sumerian parlance? Answers to these questions are entirely beyond the competence of any but a dozen or so scholars. Even experts in the Akkadian language cannot help us here, with non-Semitic Sumerian. And even answers from one of the experts might be wrong through human error. Sighing, therefore, at the difficulty of our subject-matter, let us look again at Egypt.

Stecchini says:[37] 'Because Egyptologists have ignored the issue of geodetic points and of the linear units, the figure of the revolutionary Pharaoh Akhenaten has turned out to be the most mysterious and controversial in the long history of the Egyptian monarchy.' He then makes some extremely critical remarks about Cyril Aldred and others and continues:

Because they have resisted accepting the solidly documented facts, established scholars have devoted their energies to debating theories such as that Akhenaten was impotent, was a practising homosexual, or a woman masquerading as a man; there are historians who profess to be informed about the intimate relations between him and his wife, the beautiful Nefertiti. Since the picture of Akhenaten has remained indefinite and blurred, scholars have used it to project their own emotions. Those who do not like Akhenaten present him as a psychopath and dispute about the clinical definition of his illness. . . . If instead of trying to imagine what were the hieroglyphic notes of the psychoanalyst of the royal family, we consider the documented facts, the most important action in the revolutionary reign of Akhenaten proves to be the establishment of a new capital for Egypt, the city of Akhet-Aten, 'Resting-point of Aten'. The miles-long remains of the buildings of this city have been found and excavated in the locality known today as Tell el-Amarna. During the reign of Akhenaten a substantial percentage of the national resources was dedicated to the construction of this city.

Scholars of the last century, who had not yet adopted the psychologizing fashion, at least recognized the political meaning of the shift in the location of the capital of Egypt. Akhenaten intended to cut at the root of the power of the priests of the Temple of Amon in Thebes, who through their control of the national oracle, identified with the god of this temple, had usurped the royal functions. But what these scholars did not know is that the Temple of Amon was the geodetic centre of Egypt, the 'navel' of Egypt, being located where the eastern axis (32° 38' east) crosses the Nile, at the parallel which is at 2/7 of the distance from the equator to the pole (25° 42' 51" north), and that the god Amon was identified with the hemispheric stone which marked this point.

The new city which was intended to replace Thebes as the capital and geodetic centre of Egypt was planted in a position which seems undesirable in terms of what we would consider the function of a capital city. Some scholars have interpreted this fact as further evidence of the mental derangement of its founder. . . . The new capital for the god Aten, who was raised to the status of the one true god, was set at latitude 27° 45' north, at the middle point between the northernmost point Behdet and the southern limit of Egypt at latitude 24° 00' north. . . . Akhenaten wanted to prove that Thebes could not properly claim to be the geodetic centre of Egypt and that he had chosen the geodetic centre conforming to an absolutely rigorous interpretation of *maet*, the cosmic order of which the dimensions of Egypt were an embodiment. In order to follow absolutely exact standards of measurement, he reverted to the pre-dynastic geodetic system which counted in geographic cubits starting from Behdet. . . . In terms of the system based on the pre-dynastic capital of Behdet, there could be no question that Akhet-Aten is the 'true and just' navel of Egypt.

This conclusion implies that one should re-evaluate the entire historical role of Akhenaten, taking as the starting-point what he himself considered the initial step in his program to establish true and just conformity with *maet*. There is a possibility that his revolutionary reforms, which extended from religion to art and family relations, were understood as a general return to pre-dynastic ideas and practices.

Note the fact that Thebes had established itself as the 'navel' of Egypt but not on the basis of the 'Behdet system' which Akhenaten apparently tried to revive. It shows how ancient the 'northern octave' must be if it was based on the 'Behdet system' whereas Thebes was not. The clear involvement of Thebes in the 'northern octave' system is not exclusive but is complementary to that of Behdet. In Herodotus, Book Two (54) we find this significant tale:

At Dodona . . . the priestesses who deliver the oracles have a . . . story: two black doves, they say, flew away from Thebes in Egypt, and one of them alighted at Dodona, the other in Libya. The former, perched on an oak, and speaking with a human voice, told them that there, on that very spot, there should be an oracle of Zeus. Those who heard her understood the words to be a command from heaven, and at once obeyed. Similarly the dove which flew to Libya told the Libyans to found the oracle of Amon – which is also an oracle of Zeus. The people who gave me this information were the three priestesses at Dodona – Promeneia the eldest, Timarete the next, and Nicandra the youngest – and their account is confirmed by the other Dodonaeans who have any connection with the temple.

It is really interesting to see how chummy Herodotus was with the priestesses of Dodona, for Plutarch centuries later was to be similarly chummy with the priestess Clea of Delphi, as we have seen already. Obviously these priestesses were really good informants for aspiring historians. Just how vividly accurate the Dodonaean story really is, will in a moment become even more clear. But as for the question of Thebes versus Behdet, tied in as it is with the Akhenaten question, I beg to bow out of that controversy. Put me down as having 'no opinion'.

We must note Stecchini's remarks about Delphi as follows:[38]

The god of Delphi, Apollo, whose name means 'the stone', was identified with an object, the *omphalos*, 'navel', which has been found. It consisted of an ovoidal stone. . . . The *omphalos* of Delphi was similar to the object which represented the god Amon in Thebes, the 'navel' of Egypt. In 1966 I presented to the annual meeting of the Archaeological Institute of America a paper in which I maintained that historical accounts, myths, and legends, and some monuments of Delphi, indicate that the oracle was established there by the Pharaohs of the Ethiopian Dynasty. This is the reason why the Greeks portrayed Delphos, the eponymous hero of Delphi, as a Negro.

Stecchini also explains his theory that the oracles originally functioned through the operations of computing devices:

An object which resembles a roulette wheel, and actually is its historical antecedent, was centred on top of the *omphalos*. The spinning of a ball gave the answers; each of the 36 spokes of the wheel corresponded to a letter symbol.

In studying ancient computing devices, I have discovered that they were used also to obtain oracular answers. This is the origin of many of the oracular instruments we still use today, such as cards and ouija boards. . . . The roulette wheel of Delphi originally was a special kind of abacus for calculating in terms of angles.

The following information from Stecchini is also both surprising and informative with regard to the story of the *Argo*, Colchis, etc.:[39]

Very revealing is that a base line was marked along parallel 45° 12′ north on the north side of the Black Sea. This base line started from the mouth of the Danube, cut across the Crimea, and ended at the foot of the Caucasus. Beginning from this base, Russia was surveyed for a length of 10 degrees, along with the three meridians which formed the three axes of Egypt, up to latitude 55° 12′ north. The river Dnieper was understood to be a symmetric counterpart of the Nile, running between the same meridians. Key positions along the course of the Dnieper were identified with corresponding key positions along the course of the Nile, up to the point of transferring Egyptian place names to Russia. The information about the existence of this geodetic system is provided by the description of a map of Russia which is based on it. The description of the map indicates that it was used at the end of the sixth century B.C., but the map may be older; in any case there are other sources of information about the base line which indicate that it was marked in very early times.

In Tompkins and Stecchini's marvellous book[40] there are some first-rate photographs and drawings of stone omphalos navels which are extremely helpful in trying to understand all these matters. It makes all the difference to see the fantastic nature of these objects, representative as they are of a highly developed ancient science which until recently was completely unknown. These are reproduced here in Figures 23 and 24 and Plate 12.

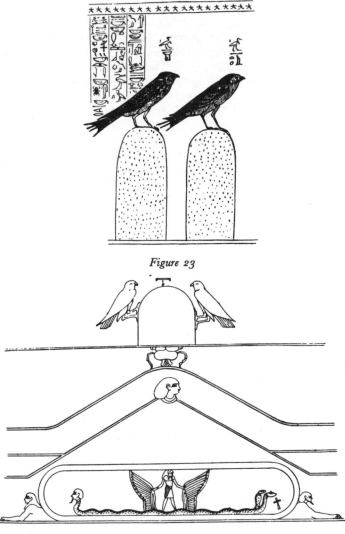

Figure 23

Figure 24

PLATES SECTION

1. A family portrait: the first photograph ever taken (1970) of Sirius B, which is the tiny dot to the lower right of the large star, Sirius (small multiple images of Sirius itself are seen here extending off to left and right). (See Notes to the Plates.) *Dr Irving Lindenblad, U.S. Naval Observatory*

Manda D'Orosongo

Innekouzou

Ongnonlou

Yébéné

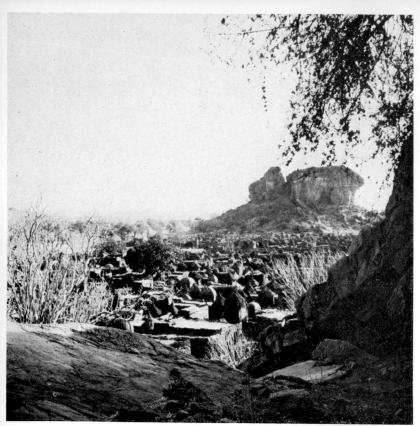

3. Two Dogon villages in Mali. Above: the village of Songho. Below: the cliff and village of Banani. *A. Costa*

4. Above: a Dogon priest's house. A libation has been offered to the gods and has dripped down the front of the house. Below: Dogon tribal dancers in religious procession to the village of Komakan. *A. Costa*

5. The Egyptian goddess Isis, showing the small fishtail in her headdress

6. The Babylonian semi-daemon Oannes, a fishtailed amphibious being from the heavens who, according to the Babylonians, founded civilization on earth. *From Nimrud*

7, 8 and 9. Further representations of the amphibious heavenly being, Oannes. Two are from Assyrian cylinder-seals and one shows the remains of a giant statue of Oannes found at Kouyunjik. *Staatliche Museen zu Berlin, Pierpont Morgan Library, Layard (1853)*

9

10. The towering mass of Mount Ararat in Turkey, where the Biblical ark landed. *Sonia Halliday*

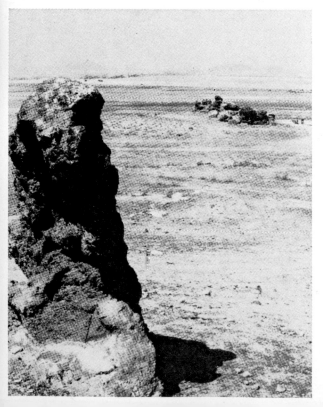

11. The nearby site of Metsamor, a major religious cult centre and astronomical observatory which has never been satisfactorily studied (all relevant publications are in the Russian Language). *Mrs Charles Burney*

I: Delphi (*Scala*)

II: Delos

III: Miletus (*Sharing*). Palm motif with Delos on same latitude

IV: Babylonian (*Michael Holford*)

Geodetic omphalos found by Reisner in the great temple of Amon.

V: Egyptian

VI: Egyptian

13. The magnificent site of Delphi in Greece, with ruins of the oracle shrine, the Temple of Apollo. *Alinari*

14. Bas reliefs and coins showing evidence of oracle centres and use of omphalos ('navel') stones. Two coins, bottom right, from Delphi show the famous 'E' suspended in the centre of the entrance to Delphi's Temple of Apollo (Ref. Appendix IV). See Notes to the Plates. *Bodleian and British Museum*

15. Jason, Medea, and the teeth of the dragon, from an ancient vase painting. See Notes to the Plates. *Mansell*

16. Jason and Medea with a living fleece being transmuted alchemically into gold (*Michael Holford*). See Notes to the Plates

17. Above: Actaeon hunted down by Artemis (Diana) and the fifty hounds of hell (*Deutsche Fotothek Dresden*). Below: Artemis stands by as the infant Apollo, held by their mother Leto, lets fly an arrow at the Python (*Mansell*). For both, see Notes to the Plates

18. Above: an ancient representation of the construction of the ship *Argo*. On the left the goddess Athena bestows the oak timber of Dodona. Argus is hard at work on the prow, which will contain the oak beam. An oak tree graces the scene, with a branch pointedly missing (*Alinari*). Below: an ancient Babylonian cylinder seal which may show the sowing of the serpent's/dragon's teeth (*Oriental Institute, University of Chicago*). See Notes to the Plates

19. Cadmus slays the serpent/dragon, which represents Sirius. He is in the position of Orion, standing on Lepus, the hare, in the sky. See Notes to the Plates

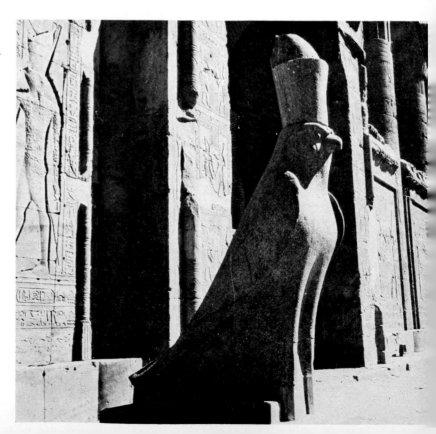

20. A statue of the divine hawk of Horus, outside a temple at Edfu in Egypt. See Notes to the Plates. *Michael Holford*

21. Front and side
    views of a bust
    identified as that
    of the Greek
    philosopher Proclus,
    for whom see
    Appendix I; see
    also Notes to the
    Plates. *Athens
    Museum*

Notes to the Plates

Plate 1: The scientific achievement represented by this extraordinary photograph is considerable. Until 1970, no photographic record of the small white dwarf star Sirius B existed, despite attempts over several decades to obtain one. With much ingenuity, Dr Irving W. Lindenblad of the U.S. Naval Observatory in Washington, D.C., finally devised a technique which made this photograph possible. Lindenblad (1970; see Bibliography) says: '. . . simultaneous observation of Sirius A and B by conventional photography has always presented a problem due to the small separation and large magnitude difference between the components, and because of various emulsion effects.' Since Sirius A is enormously brighter than Sirius B, it is easily understood that it washes out the smaller star which orbits it. How, then, to photograph the smaller star at all?

Dr Paul Murdin of the Royal Greenwich Observatory has provided some explanatory notes on Lindenblad's photograph and given his permission for me to quote them here: 'The six spikes on Sirius A are caused by the hexagon used on the front of the telescope. The point of making the photo in this way is that Sirius A is about 100 times as bright as Sirius B so that its light tends to spread out over Sirius B rendering it invisible. By using a hexagonal lens (actually a 26-inch circular lens with a hexagonal mask) in his telescope, Lindenblad was able to compress the star image in certain directions; he chose the orientation of the hexagon so that Sirius B's image fell in one of the compressed zones and was thus able to be seen . . . The wire grating referred to by Lindenblad makes the small images of Sirius A on either side of the bright one (there are small images of B too, but they are too small to be visible). The point of this is that the bright image of Sirius A (the "zero order" image) is so big that Lindenblad couldn't measure the position of Sirius B with respect to A. He made first and second order images, measured B with respect to them and was able to *calculate* where B was with respect to the zero order image of A.'

These calculations enabled Lindenblad to angle his hexagonal aperture so that Sirius B would 'hit' a depressed area of Sirius's light – a dip where the light was teased inwards, and Sirius B could peek through. But it could only peek through if Lindenblad had first found it! The reader can by this point appreciate how clever Lindenblad had to be in order to achieve any results at all. However, these were not all of his problems. There was a serious emulsion contraction effect for the photograph, with such close images. Lindenblad (1970) says: 'The important correction to the separation of the components of Sirius due to emulsion contraction, or the Ross (1924) effect, depended, in van Albada's method, upon measurements of second-order [images] . . . However, this procedure could not be employed in the present work because the dispersion affecting the second-order images generally rendered them unmeasurable. Consequently, another technique for determining the emulsion contraction was devised.'

This is a perfect example of technological feats taking place constantly behind the scenes in order to produce results which the public then take for granted, with no appreciation of the difficulties involved. This photograph could have been reproduced with no comment or explanation, but the story behind it is part of the saga of the attempt to unravel the mysteries of Sirius. So loth has Sirius been to give up her secrets that she has denied us even this photograph until 1970. All the more reason to wonder at the Dogon, who, oblivious of our scientific labours, have always drawn pictures of Sirius in the sand, with its companion – nothing to it!

Plate 12: Top left: The beautiful omphalos stone found at Delphi in Greece, covered in the mesh thought to symbolize the latitudinal and longitudinal grid on the Earth. (For an exhaustive treatment of that theory, see *Secrets of the Great Pyramid* by Tompkins and Stecchini, particularly Appendix by Stecchini.)

Top right: The superb omphalos stone discovered at Delos, which incorporates the Delian palm design. (Reproduced in W. H. Roscher, *Neue Omphalosstudien*, Leipzig, 1915.)

Middle left: Relief discovered at Miletus in Asia Minor. The figure of Apollo is resting on an omphalos stone (and an actual omphalos stone has also been discovered at Miletus) covered in mesh, while a second, smaller omphalos stone with a serpent is seen in foreground. The palm is prominent here again. Miletus is on the same parallel as Delos, and the palm is the 'tree-code' for that latitude in the oracle octaves schema. Delos is the western centre and Miletus is the eastern centre at 37°30′. The nearby site of Branchidae (also known as Didyma) to the south seems to have adopted the oracular functions presumably associated with Miletus itself originally. This relief appears as Figure 101 (the last in the volume), page 411, of *Das Delphinion in Milet* by Georg Kawerau and Albert Rehm, Berlin, 1914. Roscher also reproduced it. Kawerau and Rehm say with relation to it (page 410): 'We have already noted here in later periods the distinctive likeness of Pythian Apollo which is universally known, and there is nothing extraordinary in finding this cult image of the Delphinion, the omphalos-and-serpent. . . .'

Middle right: Two Babylonian altars to the god Anu which bear what appear to be omphali.

Bottom left: An Egyptian omphalos stone found in the temple of Amon at Napata in Nubia. (See *Journal of Egyptian Archaeology*, Vol. III, Part IV, 1916, page 255.) This drawing is reproduced by W. H. Roscher in *Der Omphalosgedanke*, Leipzig, 1918, as Figure 6. Roscher says of the stone: 'On the 21st of April, 1917, I received a letter from Professor Gunther Roeder, now Director of the Pelizaeus Museum in Hildesheim saying that Reisner (Harvard University) had, in excavations for the Boston Museum at Gebel Barka (Napata) in the Sudan, found a stone in a temple of the Nubian-Merotic kings which was the omphalos of the Amon-oracle of Napata. . . .'

Bottom right: Another Egyptian omphalos marker reproduced from Tompkins and Stecchini (see Bibliography).

Plate 14: Top left: Votive relief of fifth century B.C. from Sparta; Apollo and Artemis, between them an omphalos flanked by two doves with their heads turned away in the customary manner for these scenes. (From Plate VII, No. 4, of W. H. Roscher, *Omphalos*, Leipzig, 1913.)

Centre top: Votive relief from Aigina, showing omphalos with two doves, their heads turned away. (From Plate VIII, No. 3, of W. H. Roscher, *Omphalos*, Leipzig, 1913.)

Top right coin: Coin from Delphi showing Apollo sitting on the omphalos stone and leaning on his lyre. He holds a laurel branch, which is the 'tree-code' for Delphi. Note the clear differentiation of trees in this compared with the earlier Delos and Miletus examples of Plate 12; at Delphi the laurel is appropriately shown, whereas Delos and Miletus display the palm. This coin is from Imhoof-Blumer's *A Numismatic Commentary on Pausanius*.

Two bottom left-hand coins: Two further examples of omphali on ancient coins, with serpents and geodetic mesh visible; both in British Museum. One is from Delphi and the other from Pergamum.

Two bottom right-hand coins: Two coins from Delphi showing the entrance to the Temple of Apollo in ancient times. The letter 'E' hangs suspended in the entrance way; it is the second vowel, and Delphi is the second oracle centre in descending order (the ancient octave was taken as descending rather than as ascending – the ignorance of which fact has led many modern experts astray when trying to unravel the complexities of Pythagorean harmonic theory). These two coins may be found reproduced also in Imhoof-Blumer (above). The second of these coins is to be found in the Copenhagen Museum, while the first was in Dr Imhoof-Blumer's private collection in the last century, and its fate today is unknown to this author.

Plate 15: Painting from ancient vase in the Etruscan Museum, Rome. Jason apparently being vomited forth by the serpent/dragon, rests on the serpent's teeth. 'Serpent's tooth' is euphemism for Sirius (see Chapter Seven). Looking on is a female figure in serpent-headed robes, holding an oracular dove; she may be Medea or a goddess. In the background the golden fleece is seen suspended in the grove guarded by the serpent. Note that the breastplate of the female figure, on which is a fanged Gorgon's face, is composed of scales identical to those of the serpent/dragon. On her helmet is the Greek sphinx (a mythological being associated with Greek Thebes). Though the elements can here be identified in this way, the story implied by them cannot so easily be unravelled. The author has not been able to learn the mythological incidents referred to in this curious vase.

Plate 16: The ram is in the crucible, its fleece presumably being transmuted into gold in what we would call an alchemical sense. Was there such a thing as alchemy at this time in history? Alchemy is generally thought of as a mediaeval discipline. But perhaps the attempt to transmute base materials into gold is an ageless concept, and in antiquity it could have been less concerned with chemistry and more with symbolism, as I suspect is the intention here. (No mediaeval alchemist ever put a ram in the dish for this purpose!)

Plate 17: Above: The goddess Artemis sets the hounds of hell upon Actaeon and slays him. She holds the bow of Sirius the Bow Star. The hounds are the hounds of Sirius the Dog Star. She is herself, in this guise, a Greek version of Sirius the goddess. But the tradition has become confused and fragmented by the Greeks, broken down into elements which are used to construct other myths. Artemis is not generally a representation of Sirius, but of the moon. The bow and the dogs are here merely left-over trappings from an earlier forgotten symbolic system. (From a red-figured vase in the Berlin Museum *c.* 470 B.C.)

Below: The infant god Apollo, four days after his birth, shoots an arrow at the serpent Python from his mother's arms. However, this scene is not Delphi but Delos, for the palm trees are the 'tree-code' of Delos. This Attic vase painting provides important confirmation that the story, which was supposed to have occurred at Delphi, was also linked with Delos. If Python was not only at Delphi but at Delos as well, then Python is a concept rather than a creature. This is all further evidence for the geodetic oracle-octave which includes both Delphi and Delos, which are one degree of latitude apart. Delos had ceased to have any function as an oracle centre by about 600 B.C., which helps one appreciate the antiquity of the system, since Delos had no oracular functions at all by the time of classical Greece, when Socrates was gadding about the agora in Athens.

Plate 18: Below: This is one of the most interesting cylinder seals to survive from the Babylonian culture. It is reproduced in Henri Frankfort, *Cylinder Seals*, Plate XX; and in *Sumerian Mythology*, Plate XII, by Samuel Noah Kramer, where Kramer says of it: '. . . two gods are guiding a plow, which is perhaps drawn by a lion and a wormlike dragon.' Frankfort says of it: 'Two gods plowing; one holding a plow, the other driving span (consisting of snakelike dragon and lion) with left hand, which either holds or is shaped like a scorpion; bird, eight-pointed star, and crescent in field.' It is Plate 62 in Frankfort's later book *Stratified Cylinder Seals*. It is Akkadian style, Late Agade period in date.

This cylinder seal is such an important item of evidence that it requires extended comment. The lion is the earth-lion well known as the earth goddess's symbol from the ancient Near East. (See, for instance, *The Syrian Goddess* by Strong and Garstang.) But note that directly beneath the symbol of a star, ploughing is taking place, and leading right down to the plough blade is the strange form of a serpentlike dragon. It looks almost as if the mouth of the serpent/dragon is being ploughed into the ground. And this, I suspect, is exactly what is intended. For what seems to be represented is the act of ploughing and sowing the serpent's teeth, which we know to be a hieroglyphic pun in Egyptian for 'the goddess Sirius'; we also know that the growing up from the ground of the 'serpent's teeth' is another pun for the rising over the horizon of the star for which 'serpent's tooth' is the other meaning, i.e., Sirius. Its once-yearly rising was the basis of the Egyptian calendar.

If we assume this to be the case, the figure whose hand has become a scorpion can be explained. Obviously, the constellation Scorpio is intended, which is approximately a third of the sky 'round' from Sirius. From the ancient Greek astronomical writer Aratus, we know that when Scorpio rises, it chases Sirius and Orion away below the horizon. He describes it as follows (*Phaenomena* 634–80):

'The winding River (the constellation Eridanus near Orion) will straightaway sink in fair flowing ocean at the coming of Scorpio, whose rising puts to flight even the mighty Orion . . . Wherefore, too, men say that at the rising of the Scorpion in the East Orion flees at the Western verge . . . what time all the rays of the mighty Dog (Sirius is in this constellation) are sinking and all of Orion setting, yea, all the Hare (the constellations Lepus), which the Dog pursues in an unending race.'

The disappearance below the western horizon, then, of the 'serpent's tooth' (Sirius) which is going into the ground (to 'grow up' from it again in 70 days' time at its heliacal rising) seems to be indicated here, for the figure representing the sky has had his left hand (the east) become Scorpio, while his right hand (the west) is swallowing the 'serpent's tooth'. Over this proceeding of the setting of Sirius presides, as would be expected, the earth-lion itself, which pulls the plough that makes the furrows (three of which are visible) into which will be swallowed that fast-disappearing star just above the plough-blade. The crescent may be taken as an indication of the waning of the light of the star, almost to vanishing point – not surprising, as the moon is a 'front man' for Sirius in many myths. (Kramer thought, because of the ploughing, that this scene involved 'gods of vegetation'.)

Plate 19: An extremely important representation in the Louvre. Cadmus of Thebes (Greek Thebes, that is) is seen slaying the serpent/dragon. Its teeth are almost more prominent than it is. Cadmus seems to represent the constellation Orion, for beneath his feet figures prominently a hare which appears to be meant as the constellation Lepus. As if to emphasize the stellar symbolism, on either side of Lepus are what appear to be stars. The serpent itself, to the left and slightly lower than Cadmus, would therefore correspond with the position in the sky of Sirius. (The reader should be advised that in Figure 12 of this book is a star map of this area of the sky which will help him visualize the constellations, though the conventional figures of a man, a hare, etc., are not drawn in.) Since we know that Cadmus and Jason were the two heroes who sowed the serpent's teeth, and this serpent has prominent rows of teeth (notably not fangs, the emphasis instead being upon the rows), and the serpent is placed in the position of the star Sirius in this pictorial star-map, we have evidence (if we accept the star-map interpretation) that the Greeks must have been conscious of the Egyptian pun whereby 'serpent's tooth' in hieroglyphics is a synonym for 'the Goddess Sirius'. The doves and the shrine with serpents are both elements of the oracle centres associated with the Sirius tradition in Greece.

Plate 20: The great hawk of Horus which stands before the temple of Edfu in Egypt. Similar statues would have stood at the Egyptian cemetery of Colchis and given rise to the Greek traditions of Circe ('hawk') through the spread of legends about the Argonauts and their search for the Golden Fleece at Colchis, which Herodotus tells us was an Egyptian colony.

Plate 21: The identification is found in the classical *Encyclopaedia* of Pauly-Wissowa under 'Proclus'. The bust is in the Athens Museum, and may be found reproduced (though unidentified) in Gerhart Rodenwaldt *Griechische Porträts*. Rodenwaldt also reproduces photographs of front and side view of a bust later identified as being that of the earlier neo-platonist philosopher Iamblichus.

Figure 25. The latitudinal bands – such as those that criss-cross the omphalos stones (see Plate 12) – graphically demonstrate the oracle octaves descending from Dodona to Behdet and from Mount Ararat to Hebron

It is also interesting to note, by way of relation with the ark of Noah, the ark of Ziusudra (or Utnapishtim), the ark of Deukalion, and the *Argo* – all of whom sent forth birds over the water (like those birds from Thebes as well) – that the standard Egyptian hieroglyph for the act of laying out of parallels and meridians is, as we have seen, two pigeons facing each other. Stecchini says: 'In the religion of the Old Kingdom (of Egypt), Sokar is an important god of orientation and of cemeteries. The god and the geodetic point were represented by the stone object which the Greeks called *omphalos*, 'navel'; it is a hemisphere (the northern hemisphere) resting on a cylinder (the foundations of the cosmos). Usually on top of Sokar, as on top of any *omphalos*, there are portrayed two birds facing each other; in ancient iconography these two birds, usually doves, are a standard symbol for the stretching of meridians and parallels.'

Hence we see even further Egyptian connections with the Greek and Near Eastern tales in which the birds are let fly and the ship finds the oracle centre's mountain.

Associated with oracle centres was probably also a 'tree-code'. Dodona had its oak. Delphi was associated with laurel. And we learn from the *Elegies* of the sixth century B.C. poet Theognis (5–8) and from the Homeric *Hymns* that the oracle centre of Apollo at Delos was specifically associated with the palm tree. Any site in the Lebanon, of course, such as Mt. Lebanon and its possibly related centre of Sidon, would be associated with the famous cedars, known to us also from the *Epic of Gilgamesh* as intimately connected with Gilgamesh's exploits at 'Cedar Mountain' in the Lebanon. In putting together a schema of trees we are faced with considerable problems, but this is at least a beginning. A great deal of information on 'tree alphabets' is to be found in Robert Graves's books *The Greek Myths*[41] and even more so in his *The White Goddess*.[42] The willow was associated with the Colchian cemetery and with the island of Aeaea of Circe, but particularly it is connected with the island of Crete in tradition. But this subject will have to be tackled at some other time, lest I blow this book up into a puffball of miscellaneous odds and ends. We do know from Robert Graves that the oracle centre of Hebron – which is on the same latitude as Behdet and seems to be its eastern counterpart, was connected with the tree *sant*, or wild acacia, 'the sort with golden flowers and sharp thorns. . . . It is . . . the oracular Burning Bush in which Jehovah appeared to Moses.' Graves adds: 'The acacia is still a sacred tree in Arabia Deserta and anyone who even breaks off a twig is expected to die within the year.'[43]

Its symbolism for the Sirius Mystery is an act of pure genius, and is graphically elucidated by Theophrastus:[44] 'There are two kinds, the white and the black; the white is weak and easily decays, the black is stronger and less liable to decay . . .' A perfect symbol of the two stars, the 'black' Sirius B being 'strong' for its size compared with the white Sirius A. Also of the willow (fourth centres), Theophrastus tells us:[45] 'There is that which is called the black willow . . . and that which is called the white . . . The black kind has boughs which are fairer and more serviceable . . . There is a (dwarf) form . . .'

CHART OF THE ORACLE OCTAVES

WESTERN CENTRE	EASTERN CENTRE	TREE-CODE	'PLANET'-CODE	DIVINE BIRTHS
8. Dodona (Mt. Tomaros)	Metsamor (Mt. Ararat)	oak (phegus)	Saturn?	Mankind born from stones ('bones of Earth') at Dodona
7. Delphi (Mt. Parnassus)	Sardis (Mt. Sipylus)	laurel	Sun?	(Mankind born from stones at Delphi according to rival tradition)
6. Delos (Mt. Cynthus)	Miletus (Didyma, also known as Branchidae, its associated oracle centre) Mt. Latmus	palm	Moon (Artemis was born first, not Apollo)	Artemis (Diana) and Apollo born on Delos
5. a. Somewhere on north-east coast of Cythera? b. Rhodes? c. Thera on Island of Thera? (If so, destroyed by the volcano)	Hierapolis (Bambyce)	?	Mars?	?
4. Omphalos (Thenae) near Knossos on Crete	Mt. Kasion (near Latakia) seat of Zeus Kasios; coins survive showing an omphalos there (A.B.Cook, II, 982)	willow (according to Pliny, a willow grew out of the Cretan cave where Zeus was born)	Jupiter	Zeus (Jupiter) was born on Crete
3. Somewhere on south coast of Cyprus? (associated with Paphos? Akrotiri?) Cape Gata?	near Tripoli? Palmyra?	cypress (the word cypress is derived from Cyprus)	Venus	Aphrodite (Venus) born at Cyprus
2. Lake Tritonis (also known as Lake Triton) in Libya/Tunisia	Sidon (Mt. Lebanon)	cedar	Mercury? (seb in Egyptian means both 'cedar' and 'the planet Mercury')	Athena (Pallas) born at Lake Tritonis
1. El Marj (Barce) Libya	Babylon	?	?	?
0. Behdet	Hebron	wild acacia	Earth?	—

Note: At one degree of latitude north of Dodona and Ararat is the mystery centre of the Cabeiroi on the island of Samothrace.

Notes

1. *Star Names*, op. cit., p. 67.
2. Lockyer, Sir Norman. *The Dawn of Astronomy*, London, 1894. (Reprinted in the 1960s by M.I.T. Press in U.S.A., introduction by Prof. de Santillana.)
3. *The Peoples of the Hills, Ancient Ararat and Caucasus*, London, 1971, p. 226.
4. Op. cit., p. 73.
5. Allen, *Star Names*, op. cit., p. 73.
6. See Note 2.
7. 7 March 1974.
8. A week later, on 14 March, a letter appeared in *The Times* from Brian Galpin claiming that his father, Canon F. W. Galpin, had previously established the certain antiquity of the heptatonic diatonic scale in his book *Music of the Sumerians, Babylonians, and Assyrians*, Cambridge University Press, 1937. A month after this, on 15 April 1974, a letter appeared in *The Times* from Dr Crocker and Dr Kilmer themselves, in California, which was long and not particularly clear. It seemed to be trying to acknowledge Professor Gurney of Oxford for some assistance and condemning Canon Galpin for reaching his conclusions on a different basis from themselves. Crocker and Kilmer obviously aimed at clearing up some mis-understandings, but only succeeded in muddying the waters (at least the letter befuddled me).
9. *The Greek Myths*, 21, 10.
10. Ibid., 170.3.
11. Higgins, Godfrey. *The Anacalypsis*, New York, 1927, Vol. I, Book III, Chapter 2, Section 4.
12. According to the Dogon: 'Sirius is the navel of the world.' See *Le Renard pâle*, pp. 324–5.
13. Op. cit.
14. Parke, H. W. *Greek Oracles*, Hutchinson (paperback), London, 1967, p. 38.
15. Ibid., p. 32.
16. Ibid., pp. 33–4.
17. Ibid., pp. 94–5.
18. Ibid., p. 94.
19. I refer the reader who suffers from a desperate urge to purge his ignorance to that magnificent work by Sir Norman Lockyer, *The Dawn of Astronomy*. His book should be required reading in all schools, even though it becomes quite technical in places (which the non-technical reader is well advised to skim over quickly). This book was published in 1894 in London by Cassell, but at the instigation of Professor Santillana, has been brought out again by M.I.T. Press in America in the 1960s (see Note 2).

    Of course another excellent, perhaps essential, book on the subject is Santillana and von Dechend's *Hamlet's Mill* (see ch. 3, n. 11). Though it is a long book, the authors admit it amounts only to a preliminary essay, and it is a good deal more confusing to read than it should be. In fact, the authors have frankly let their material overwhelm them; but they were coping with material on a far grander scale than Lockyer, and it was like trying to hold back a tidal wave. They have opened up an entirely new field for modern scholars and they may wear the badge of the pioneer and perhaps the pioneer's smile as well.
20. *Hamlet's Mill*, op. cit., p. 286.
21. Tompkins, Peter. *Secrets of the Great Pyramid*, Harper and Row, New York, London, 1971. Appendix by Livio Stecchini.
22. Parke, op. cit., p. 95.
23. Livio Stecchini mentions: '. . . a number of Greek accounts which associate Delphi with Sardis, the capital of the kingdom of Lydia in Asia Minor, which is on the same parallel (38° 28′ north)', p. 349 (Stecchini's Appendix) in Tompkins, op. cit. I believe that the mountain associated with this geodetic centre is Mount Sipylus, north-east of Smyrna (now Izmir). See Pausanius III, xxii.4 and p. 13 of Garstang, John, *The Syrian Goddess*, London, 1913. Mt. Sipylus boasts an extremely ancient gigantic carving from the living rock of the Great Goddess whose main centre came to be Hierapolis, another oracle centre in the series. The Great Goddess as Gaia (to the Greeks) was the original patroness of Delphi before the usurpation by Apollo. ('. . . the earth-goddess was the original female deity . . . in Late Mycenaean times . . . there may have been an oracle as part of the cult. . . . the arrival of Apollo as a god of divination was originally a hostile intrusion . . .' p. 36, Parke, op. cit.) I believe that Malatia (Malatya), further inland than Sardis on the same parallel, may be

connected somehow with Delphi and Sardis as well (obviously more with Sardis than Delphi). For this, see Garstang, pp. 14–15.

24. See Notes 20 and 22.
25. See also Appendix IV.
26. It is such a mesh to which the Dogon presumably refer when they speak of 'the basket which is not a basket'. See *A Sudanese Sirius System* by Griaule and Dieterlen in this book.
27. Tompkins, op. cit., p. 182.
28. Ibid., p. 298.
29. Herodotus. *The Histories*, Penguin paperback, London, 1971, p. 124. (Textual reference: Book II, 54–9.)
30. Hume, David. *The History of England*, Porter and Coates, Philadelphia, undated (nineteenth century), 5 vols. p. 57, Vol. V (end of Chapter 62). See also John Aubrey, *Brief Lives*, entry for William Harvey; Hume got much of this from Aubrey. (Hume is not always to be trusted; he does misrepresent General Monk's motives shamelessly despite Aubrey's explicit account. Perhaps the reader uninterested in seventeenth-century English history will forgive this aside.)
31. See Note 28. The famous oracle of Ammon in Libya, visited by Alexander the Great following his conquest of Egypt (if a fruit falling on one's head is a conquest), was at the Oasis of Siwa, where some ruins are still preserved. Also see maps in this book.
32. Tompkins, op. cit., p. 181.
33. Pritchard, op. cit., p. 44 ff. (Scholarly references, including Jacobsen, on p. 45.)
34. Kramer, S. N. *History Begins at Sumer* (originally entitled *From the Tablets of Sumer*, 1956, before revision), Doubleday Anchor Book (paperback), New York, 1959.
35. Garstang, op. cit. (see Note 22). Garstang's book contains a translation of Lucian's *De Dea Syria* concerning the Great Goddess at Hierapolis.
36. See Note 32.
37. Tompkins, op. cit., p. 336.
38. Ibid., p. 349.
39. Ibid., p. 346.
40. See Note 20.
41. Op. cit.
42. Graves, Robert. *The White Goddess, A Historical Grammar of Poetic Myth*, Vintage paperback, New York, undated (originally copyright 1948 by Graves).
43. Ibid. See pages listed under *acacia* in index. (I leave this to the reader because my edition of this book is undated and will probably not match the reader's in pagination.)
44. Theophrastus, *Enquiry into Plants*, Book IV, ii, 8., trans. by A. F. Hort, Loeb Classical Library, William Heinemann Ltd., London, and Harvard University Press, U.S.A., 2 vols. (This ref. vol. I, p. 299). Theophrastus was the 'father of botany', and succeeded his friend Aristotle as Head of the Peripatetic School at the Lyceum in Athens. He lived 370–c. 285 B.C., and at the peak of his teaching career actually had 2000 students.
45. Ibid., Book III, xiii, 7. (Vol. I, p. 249).

SUMMARY

The other Arabian star named 'Weight' was in the constellation Argo. But we see the *Argo* was associated with Sirius, as well as was the first star named 'Weight' which was in the Great Dog constellation and a visible companion of Sirius.

If an *Argo* is projected on the globe with its rudder near the ancient Egyptian city Canopus on the coast of the Mediterranean (the star Canopus forms the rudder of the *Argo* in the sky) and with its prow at Dodona (from where the oak came which was placed in the *Argo's* prow), if we hold the stern firmly on Canopus but swing the ship eastwards at the top, so that the prow points towards Mount Ararat, where Noah's ark was supposed to have landed, we find that the arc thus described is a right-angle of 90°.

Instead of Canopus we must really use the neighbouring site of the now entirely vanished city of Behdet, which was the capital of pre-dynastic Egypt prior to the foundation of Memphis.

Dodona is exactly 8° of latitude north of Behdet. Delphi is exactly 7° north of Behdet. Delos (another important early oracle centre, vanished by classical Greek times) is exactly 6° north of Behdet. Behdet was the Greenwich of the ancient world prior to 3200 B.C. and was used as a geodetic headquarters.

Associated with near-by Mount Ararat as a mystery-centre was the now little-known site of Metsamor. Mt Ararat is 8° north of Behdet and on the same parallel as Dodona.

A site on Kythera is known to have connections with early dynastic Egypt as a religious centre and is about 5° north of Behdet. The island of Thera may, however, have been an oracle centre. It was destroyed by a famous volcanic eruption in Minoan times.

All these sites were revealed as a pattern now termed a 'geodetic octave' by the projection on the globe of the *Argo*, which is connected with Sirius. Sirius was not only the element of the most sacred traditions of the Dogon and the ancient Egyptians, but apparently of the entire civilized and cosmopolitan Mediterranean world prior at least to 3000 B.C. and probably well before 3200 B.C.

The amphibious creature Oannes, who brought civilization to the Sumerians, is sometimes equated with the god Enki (Ea) who ruled the star Canopus of the *Argo*. Enki is a god who sleeps at the bottom of a watery abyss, reminiscent of Oannes who retired to the sea at night. Enki is also the god responsible for the ark in those early tales of the Sumerians and Babylonians from which the Biblical ark and deluge story was derived.

The 'Greek ark' was claimed to have landed at both Dodona and Delphi. An 'ark' was carried in procession at Delphi.

At Delphi and at Delos are surviving omphalos ('navel') stones. Omphalos near Knossos in Crete is 4° north of Behdet. We know from the Homeric *Hymn to Apollo* that Minoans (before 1200 B.C.) 'from Knossos took Apollo to Delphi'.

The Egyptian Pharaoh Akhenaten's reform was really at least partially a geodetic one, explaining the move of his capital city. He may have wished to return to the 'pure' system of pre-dynastic times.

Herodotus tells us that Dodona (according to its priestesses, whom he knew) was founded from Egypt – specifically Egyptian Thebes. Thebes is equidistant from both Dodona, where the Greek ark landed, and Mount Ararat, where the Hebrew ark landed. The three points, when joined, form an equilateral triangle on the globe. Also according to Herodotus, the Oasis of Siwa, with its oracle of Ammon, was founded from Thebes. This oasis centre and Thebes are both equidistant from Behdet. Geodetic surveys of immense accuracy were thus practised in ancient Egypt with a knowledge of the Earth as a spherical body in space and projections upon it envisaged as part of the institutions embodying Sirius lore for posterity.

CHAPTER SIX

Origins of the Dogon

We shall now return to Hercules and the number fifty. A connection between them arises in Pausanius, Book IX (27, 5), when Pausanius is discussing a city in Boeotia, which is the region where Orchomenos is. The city is called Thespiai 'below Mount Helikon', as he says. He continues:

> They have a sanctuary of Herakles [Hercules] where a virgin priestess serves until she dies. They say this is because Herakles slept with all the fifty daughters of Thestios in the same night, except for one. She alone refused to mate with him. Thinking she was insulting him he sentenced her to be his virgin priestess all her life. I have also heard another legend about it: that Herakles went through all Thestios's virgin daughters on the same night and they all bore him male children, but the youngest and the eldest bore him twins. But I am quite unable to believe that other story, that Herakles could behave so arrogantly to the daughter of a friend. Besides, even when he was on earth he used to punish arrogant outrages, particularly if they were against religion: so he would hardly have founded his own temple and set it up with a priestess like a god. But in fact this sanctuary seemed to me older than the days of Herakles son of Amphitryon, and to belong to the Idaian Daktylos called Herakles, whose sanctuaries I also discovered at Erythrai in Ionia and at Tyre. Actually even the Boiotians knew the name, since they say themselves that the sanctuary of Mykalessian Demeter has Idaian Herakles as patron.

Levi adds in a footnote that the sanctuary at Tyre is mentioned by Herodotus (2, 45), and gives other references as well.[1]

To return to the amorous labour of Hercules: I hope it will be noted that Pausanius had here elucidated a Middle-Eastern connection for this tale with the important city of Tyre, the site of which is off the coast of present-day Lebanon. Here, at least, we have a bit of evidence from ancient times bearing direct witness to the connections between these endless curious traditions in Greece about the fifty and their Middle-Eastern counterparts, or at least Middle-Eastern locale.

It would now be worth while for us to see what Robert Graves has to say about this tale. Graves calls Thestios by the name of Thespius and spends some time pondering the meaning.[2] He says it means 'divinely sounding', but wishes he could find another meaning. I am inclined to be happy with 'divinely sounding' because of what I believe to be the heavy emphasis on music, sound and harmony among the ancients. The Greeks were reputed, for instance, to have considered music the highest art; and the Pythagoreans made harmony and number into an actual religion. We have already come across the use of the octave as a relevant theme in our considerations and we have seen the possible connection of *omphalos* and *om* – the latter being the Indo-Aryan sacred syllable chanted for its 'divinely sounding' qualities and surviving in Christianity and Islam as 'Amen'. Since if we were to look for a Greek word to describe the sacred syllable *om* we could choose the appropriate name meaning 'divinely sounding', it seems that this meaning is by no means unsatisfactory.

Graves tells us the following:[3]

> King Thespius had fifty daughters by his wife Megamede [mega-*medea?*] daughter of Arneus, as gay as any in Thespiae. Fearing that they might make unsuitable matches, he determined that every one of them should have a child by Heracles [Hercules], who was now engaged all day in hunting the lion; for Heracles lodged at Thespiae for fifty nights running. [Notice fifty applied here as a succession of *days*: days, months, years. They can become blurred as long as *fifty* remains.] 'You may have my eldest daughter Procris as your bedfellow,' Thespius told him hospitably. But each night another of his daughters visited Heracles, until he had lain with every one. Some say, however, that he enjoyed them all in a single night.

It is interesting to note that the name Procris of the eldest daughter means 'chosen first'. *Prokrossoi*, which is a closely related form of the same stem means, 'ranged at regular intervals like steps'. Now, what could be a more obvious name for the eldest daughter than one with such overtones and signification if it were clearly intended, as it obviously was, to emphasize that the daughters were not meant to be thought of as individuals but as successive expressions of fifty successive periods of time – in this case, twenty-four-hour periods, or days? But the intention obviously was to highlight the sequence of fifty time periods, personified as 'daughters' enjoyed by our ubiquitous Hercules who is connected in so many ways with the Sirius complex.

Graves adds:[4] 'Thespius's fifty daughters – like the fifty Danaids, Pallantids, and Nereids, or the fifty maidens with whom the Celtic god Bran (Phoroneus) lay in a single night – must have been a college of priestesses serving the Moon-goddess, to whom the lion-pelted sacred king had access once a year during their erotic orgies around the stone phallus called Eros ('erotic desire'). Their number corresponded with the lunations which fell between one Olympic Festival and the next.'

Here is Graves's irrepressible moon-goddess – and here are her lunations! She carries them about with her wherever she goes. But unfortunately, Graves's brave attempt to find a lunar rationale for the fifty is not sufficient. The Olympic Games were, as they are now, held every four years, and the Olympiads or four-year periods were understood to have commenced in 776 B.C., which is an extremely recent date compared with the extreme antiquity of 'the fifty' in all its myriad occurrences. For instance, there were no Olympiads in Homer's day when 'the tale of the *Argo* was on everybody's lips', and the fifty Minyae were on their way into literary immortality in what was to become the Western world. Much more likely that a period of fifty lunations was modelled after a long-established tradition – the esoteric fifty-*year* period. Thus the fifty-month and fifty-day sequences were probably derived in emulation.

I assume that the cycle of fifty lunations which Graves mentions here is identical to his fifty-month period of the reign of a sacred king, which is supposed to be 'half of a Great Year of a hundred months'. Can it be that fifty, as half of one hundred, is meant to represent by its reduplication the two-to-one ratio as a means of signifying the concept of the musical octave with its two-to-one ratio?*

And can this be why the *Argo* is supposed to be 'whole in the sky' (Aratos) and yet the constellation also supposed to represent only the latter half of a ship? Can this apparent double-talk be yet another way of signifying the two-to-one ratio?

It also seems significant that each fifty-month period is carefully specified to constitute 'one reign', even though it is only half of 'the Great Year'. Can 'one reign' be analogous to 'one orbit' and the 'Great Year' of two orbits be contrived to communicate the two-to-one harmonic ratio of the octave?

Another occurrence of fifty and a hundred together is with the three monsters born to Uranus the sky and Gaia the earth. Their names were Cottus, Briareus, and Gyges. ' "From their shoulders sprang a hundred invincible arms and above these powerful limbs rose fifty heads attached to their backs." For this reason they were called the Hecatoncheires or the Centimanes,' as we are reliably told.[5]

These monsters resemble the monster Cerberus, the hound of Hades who originally had fifty heads, but later became simplified and had only three heads – presumably for the same reason that these monsters are three in number, and also the reason that Hecate (whose pet Cerberus was, and who was a form of Isis-Sirius and whose name literally means 'one hundred') had three heads or forms, and that the boat of Sirius in ancient Egypt had three goddesses together in it. In other words, probably the same reason that the Dogon insist that there are three stars in the Sirius system. (Despite the fact that the astronomical evidence has recently gone against the existence of a third star, the case is by no means closed. If there is a third star, it does not produce the perturbation which had been claimed for it before the seven years' observations recently concluded by astronomer Irving Lindenblad.[6])

We will recall that originally Hercules is supposed to have led the expedition of the *Argo*. In the version of Apollonius Rhodios he accompanies the expedition. Well, in Graves we may read of another traditional exploit of Hercules in the Black Sea.[7] He went 'in search of Hippolyte's girdle in the Black Sea' and 'the girdle belonged to a daughter of Briareus ("strong"), one of the Hundred-handed Ones . . . ,' who was of course a fifty-headed one as well. And note his name: Strong! The word βϱιαϱός (*briaros*) means 'strong', and another form is βϱιαϱότης (*briarotēs*) which means 'strength, might', and a related form βϱίθος (*brithos*) means 'weight', and βϱιθοσύνη (*brithosynē*) means 'weight, heaviness'. Where have we encountered this idea before?

We should note that Hippolyte means simply 'letting horses loose'. And it

---

* The frequency of a note is doubled when it is raised an octave – hence a ratio of 2 to 1. This may be demonstrated visually on a single string and does not require the modern measurements of frequency.

was from Colchis that the horses of the sun were let loose every morning, for it was there that they were stabled, according to Greek tradition. There is also a really peculiar use of the word *hippopedē*, which has the normal mundane meaning of 'a horse fetter', in a cosmic sense. It appears from Liddell and Scott that this word was used by the astronomer Eudoxus (the one who went to Egypt and who was mentioned earlier) as the word for the curve described by a planet. We know this from Simplicius on Aristotle's *De Caelo* and Proclus on Euclid.* Two sources are better than one. There is probably more to this than we can ever discover, for the necessary texts are lost.

If we examine the name Gyges, who was one of the other three monsters which included Briareus, we find its meaning has the same origins as *gygantelos*, which in English became 'gigantic', but the meaning of this word was not by any means simply 'giant'. Graves gives Gyges the meaning of 'earth-born', another concept we have come to expect in connection with our Sirius-complex of myths. Just as the stones Deukalion and his wife Pyrrha threw over their shoulders had been torn from their mother earth, Gaia, and were her bones turning into men to repopulate the earth after the flood and the voyage of the Greek ark, and just as Jason and also Cadmus sowed the teeth and they sprang up as 'earth-born men', so we find that Gyges is also 'earth-born'.

And just as Gilgamesh sought *strength* from the earth when 'his teeth shook' in the earth, so we discover that *gygas* means 'mighty' or 'strong', and is also used in Hesiod to refer to 'the sons of Gaia (Earth)', which is as specific as we could wish, for it gives an undeniable and conscious connection between 'the children of Gaia' of Deukalion, 'the offspring of Gaia' of the Colchian teeth, and 'the sons of Gaia' who were a race of giants, and Gyges, whose mother was Gaia.

And we are not to forget that Gyges, like Briareus, can mean 'strength' and 'might', though with the particular shade of meaning added that it is strength and might drawn from the earth, which could be one way of describing a super-dense body of degenerate matter. After all, super-dense matter is 'strong earth'. We must also remember that Gyges has fifty heads.

As for the name Cottus, the third of the three monsters, Graves tells us that it is not Greek. Graves says (3, 1): 'Cottus was the eponymous [name-giving] ancestor of the Cottians who worshipped the orgiastic Cotytto, and spread her worship from Thrace throughout North-western Europe. These tribes are described as "hundred-handed", perhaps because their priestesses were organized in colleges of fifty, like the Danaids and Nereids; perhaps because the men were organized in war-bands of one hundred, like the early Romans.'

The Cottians might possibly derive their name from an Egyptian word.

Perhaps it was 𓂝, 𓈖 *qeṭi*, which means 'oarsmen' and has been applied to 'divine oarsmen'. With a different determinative and when not applied to a man, the word means 'orbit', 'revolution', 'to go around'. And the word in Egyptian was also applied to a group of specific people in a specific region. The *Qeṭu* were the natives of *Qeṭi*, which Wallis Budge says was 'The Circle', that is,

---

* Simplicius and Proclus are despised by the orthodox mentalities because they were *neoplatonists*. See Appendix One.[8]

'the North Syrian coast about the Gulf of Issus and the deserts between the Euphrates and the Mediterranean'.

There was also an Egyptian precedent for applying the same name to a god. Qeti is 'a god of the abyss', and a reduplicated version of the name which repeats the 't' as Cotytto does is Qeṭqeṭ, who is significantly one of the thirty-six decans. In addition, Qeṭshu refers specifically to 'the "nude" or Syrian goddess',* which seems clearly to be an orgiastic element, for Graves says that Cotytto was an orgiastic goddess. It seems fairly clear, then, that Cottus is of Egyptian origin and originally applies to the orbit of Sirius B, and in the Egyptian era the particular term came to be associated with a people of Syria who moved to Thrace, and even in Egyptian times the name had all its applications to a foreign people, a foreign orgiastic goddess, and Sirius-related concepts including both oarsmen and an orbit, two ideas which I have frequently connected before. Here in Egyptian we find an orbit called by a name which applies equally well to divine oarsmen. And the word survives in the fifty-headed Cottus! Fifty oarsmen, fifty years in the orbit, fifty heads to the Sirius-monster. How simple, how elegant.

I am indebted to my friend Michael Scott, who once rowed at Oxford, for the fine suggestion that there could hardly be a better analogy of any symbol with its intended meaning of 'a specific interval both of space and time' than the oar-stroke. Rowing is a precisely paced discipline when practised in earnest, as it would certainly have been in ancient times when it was one of the two principal means of navigation at sea, and the only reliable one if the winds failed, as they so often did. It also represents a self-reliance which illustrates the self-impelled motion of a body in space which is orbiting (or what seems to be self-impelled).

I should point out here that the earliest name for the figure known to us as Hercules was, according to Robert Graves in *The Greek Myths* (132. h.), none other than Briareus. And we also have learned that the earliest form of Jason was Hercules (whose earliest form was Briareus). We thus find that Briareus, with his fifty heads, was the earliest captain of the fifty-oared *Argo*. Briareus, whose name means 'weight'. And whose brother's name means both 'oarsman' and 'orbit'.

Apart from the three monsters each with fifty heads, Gaia also gave birth to Garamas, who was not only earth-born, but who 'rose from the plain' like the earth-born men of Colchis. Graves says:[9] 'The Libyans, however, claim that Garamas was born before the Hundred-handed Ones and that, when he rose from the plain, he offered Mother Earth (Gaia) a sacrifice of the sweet acorn.' The acorn of the oak – the oaks being representative of Dodona, of the piece of the *Argo*'s prow, and of the Colchian grove!

It is in the footnote of Graves[10] that we learn something of really immense significance to us: 'Garamas is the eponymous ancestor of the Libyan Garamantians who occupied the Oasis of Djado [sic], south of the Fezzan, and were conquered by the Roman General Balbus in 19 B.C. They are said to have been

---

* The great goddess of Hierapolis (one of the oracle centres) must be intended by this 'Syrian goddess'. See note 34 to Chapter Five, reference to Lucian's *De Dea Syria*, and Garstang; also see Bibliography.

of Cushite–Berber stock, and in the second century A.D. were subdued by the matrilineal Lemta Berbers. Later they fused with the Negro aboriginals on the south bank of the Upper Niger, and adopted their language. They survive today in a single village under the name of Koromantse.'

I need hardly point out to the alert reader that the southern bank of the Upper Niger is the home of the Dogon! What should be investigated on the spot is the relations which subsist between this sad shaggy remnant of the Garamantians and the surrounding Dogon and other tribes. Also, the villagers of Koromantse might be discovered to possess the Sirius lore themselves.

On the most detailed French map of this area there is a village called Korienze only sixty miles from Bandiagara and in the heart of Dogon country. It is on the south bank of the Upper Niger and is presumably the place Graves means.

In line with this important discovery I should point out that Herodotus says in Book Two (103 and 106): 'It is undoubtedly a fact that the Colchians are of Egyptian descent . . . the Colchians, the Egyptians, and the Ethiopians are the only races which from ancient times have practised circumcision. The Phoenicians and the Syrians of Palestine themselves admit that they adopted the practice from Egypt, and the Syrians who live near the rivers Thermodon and Parthenius, as well as their neighbours the Macronians, say that they learnt it only a short time ago from the Colchians. No other nations use circumcision, and all these are without doubt following the Egyptian lead.'

Circumcision is fundamental to Dogon culture and forms the central part of the ritual of the Sigui which the Dogon hold every sixty years – and though I have pointed all this out earlier, it does no harm to repeat it.

We shall recall if we read the *Argonautica* that the Argonauts were blown off course to Libya, where they were stranded for some time. In his book *Herodotean Inquiries*,[11] Seth Benardete speaks of the Garamantes to whom he gives an alternative name, the Gamphasantes. They are described in Herodotus, Book Four (after 178) as inhabitants of 'Further inland to the southward, in the part of Libya where wild beasts are found'. At 179 Herodotus connects Jason and the Argonauts' visit to Libya with the eventual foundation in Libya 'of a hundred Grecian cities'. Benardete's comments in his book connect the *Argo*'s visit to Libya and the Libyan city of Cyrene:

> Herodotus first indicates how closely Libya, Egypt, Scythia, and Greece are joined. The ancestors of Cyrene's founders were descendants of Jason's companions, who sailed to Colchis, originally an Egyptian colony on the eastern shore of the Black Sea; and the third generation from these Argonauts were expelled from Lemmos by the very same Pelasgians who later abducted Athenian women from Brauron, where a cult of Artemis-Iphigeneia was practised, just as among the Taurians in the Crimea; and Jason is said to have been carried off course to Libya. Cyrene is the melting-pot of Egyptian, Libyan, and Scythian things. Its founding suggests the Scythian account of their origins. They said that golden objects fell from heaven, which flashed fire when the two older brothers of Kolaxais approached them, but Kolaxais himself was able to take them home. To these celestial ποιήματα [sic: poiēmata] there here correspond the oracular

verses of Delphi which, in both the Theban and Cyrenaic versions, prompted the sending of a colony to Libya.

Robert Graves got his information[12] on the Garamantians going to the Upper Niger by way of Libya from a series of books by Eva Meyrowitz, an anthropologist who spent many years studying the Akan tribe of Ghana, directly south of the Dogon.[13] Graves paraphrases her books: 'The Akan people result from an ancient southward emigration of Libyo-Berbers – cousins to the pre-Hellenic population of Greece – from the Sahara desert oases (see 3, 3) and their intermarriage at Timbuctoo with Niger River Negroes.' Timbuctoo – or Timbuktu – is the nearest big city to the Dogon. Graves continues: 'In the eleventh century A.D. they moved still further south to what is now Ghana.' I might point out that the path of migration from Timbuctu to Ghana goes straight through the country of the Dogon, whose territory is directly south of Timbuctu. So it is quite clear by now that peoples intimately connected with the Sirius tradition came from Greece to Libya and thence south to the Libyan oases of the Sahara, thence further south-west past the Sahara to Timbuctu and the region of the Dogon, where they mingled with Negroes of the Dogon region and took their local language for themselves, eventually becoming indistinguishable from the local African population in appearance and speech, but retaining their old traditions as their most secret doctrines. The migration route is shown in Figure 27.[14]

There is something incredible in the survival of the Argonauts in the obscure reaches of the French Sudan! In fact, these people, which I assume must include the Dogon as well as their immediate southern neighbours (and the Dogon sell onions to Ghana as part of their livelihood), seem to be direct descendants of Lemnian Greeks who claimed to be the grandsons of the actual Argonauts! It almost seems too amazing to be true, that we should have begun this book by considering a strange African tribe, then considered similar Sirius traditions in the Mediterranean stemming from ancient Egypt, and then be led back again to the African tribe whom we discover to be directly descended from the Mediterranean peoples privy to the Sirius complex!

Later, I shall mention a bit more about the Pelasgians, who lived in Arcadia and, so Herodotus informs us, were not conquered by the Dorian invaders of Greece in pre-classical times. They have been among the main continuers of the Sirius tradition as, apparently, have the people they displaced by force. But I mention them now to give more relevant information for this Libyan connection. Graves says:[15] 'According to the Pelasgians, the goddess Athene was born beside Lake Tritonis in Libya', and: 'Plato identified Athene, patroness of Athens, with the Libyan goddess Neith . . . Neith had a temple at Sais (in Egypt), where Solon was treated well merely because he was an Athenian . . . Herodotus writes (IV, 189): "Athene's garments and aegis were borrowed by the Greeks from the Libyan women . . ." . . . Ethiopian girls still wear this costume . . . Herodotus adds here that the loud cries of triumph, *olulu, ololu,* uttered in honour of Athene above (*Iliad,* vi. 297–301) were of Libyan origin. *Tritone* means "the third queen".' Again the reference to the three goddesses. And recall that in Libya was the shrine of Ammon equivalent to the Dodona oracle of Zeus, where the other of the two birds flew from Egyptian Thebes.

DISTRIBUTION OF LIBYAN TRIBES
ACCORDING TO HERODOTUS

Figure 26

Figure 27. Migration route of the Dogon

And Athene, the daughter of Zeus, is equivalently the daughter of Ammon, who is identified with Zeus.

Athene was also known as Pallas Athene, for reasons given in Graves. He adds that 'the third Pallas' was father of 'the fifty Pallantids, Theseus's enemies (see 97.g and 99.a), who seem to have been originally fighting priestesses of Athene'. Once again the fifty.

Graves gives some interesting information:[16] 'Pottery finds suggest a Libyan immigration into Crete as early as 4000 B.C.; and a large number of goddess-worshipping Libyan refugees from the Western Delta seem to have arrived there when Upper and Lower Egypt were forcibly united under the First Dynasty about the year 3000 B.C. The First Minoan Age began soon afterwards, and Cretan culture spread to Thrace and Early Helladic Greece.'

While again on the subject of the fifty, I want to note more information concerning Cerberus, the fifty-headed hound of Hades. Graves says:[17] 'Echidne bore a dreadful brood to Typhon: namely, Cerberus . . .', etc. Recall that Typhon was identified with Python[18] in the Homeric *Hymn to Apollo* and elsewhere; Python was the particular monster, slain by Apollo according to legend, whose rotting corpse lay directly under the oracle of Delphi.

Graves continues:[19] 'Cerberus, associated by the Dorians with the dog-headed Egyptian god Anubis who conducted souls to the Underworld, seems to have originally been the Death-goddess Hecate, or Hecabe; she was portrayed as a bitch because dogs eat corpse flesh and howl at the moon. . . . Orthrus, who fathered [various creatures] on Echidne was Sirius, the Dog-star, which inaugurated the Athenian New Year. He had two heads, like Janus, because the reformed year at Athens had two seasons, not three.' The three heads of Hecate, of Cerberus in his simplified form, etc., possibly all represent the old, original year which had three seasons and originated in Egypt with the three seasons of their (1) inundation, (2) sowing, (3) harvesting, which were traditional there. But it seems unlikely. For why would the three goddesses sail in their Sirius boat in Egyptian representations which have absolutely nothing to do with a calendar? In short, the three goddesses and the three-headedness always to do with Sirius are not calendrical at all. But by the extremely late times of Athens, calendrical explanations may have become fashionable for what could not otherwise be explained.

In the above passages I hope the reader will note the specific information that connects Anubis (which much earlier I identified on altogether separate grounds with the orbit of Sirius B) with the Greek version of Anubis, Cerberus, with his fifty heads. In the Egyptian tradition I hadn't found any specific connection between Anubis and fifty. It is true that we have found the Egyptian word *qeṭi* means both 'oarsman' and 'orbit', and as there were always fifty oarsmen in the Sirius-related boats, both in Greek and Sumerian saga, we were on our way to an identification on solid grounds. But here at last a specific connection has come to light, and would seem to be a splendid confirmation of my identification! And furthermore, we see that the dog Orthrus who was the brother of Cerberus, was specifically identified with Sirius. We thus have found in the Mediterranean world all the elements of the description of the Sirius system which were possessed by the Dogon. And we have also traced the Mediterranean Sirius lore to the Dogon by way of Libya, then the Saharan oases, then Timbuktu, and finally the south bank of the Upper Niger and the Dogon region. Thus, through thousands of miles and thousands of years, we have discovered the source of that strange tradition still intact among a tribe deep in 'darkest Africa'. But there is more to be learnt. We must examine the Mediterranean tradition more closely, and particularly its oldest Egyptian origins in the shadowy pre-dynastic world of Behdet (which seems not to have been excavated and has presumably been lost in the mud of the Nile delta).

The father of Orthrus the Sirius-dog and his brother Cerberus the fifty-headed dog was the monster Typhon whom we mentioned a moment ago. And it is worth while for us to see what Liddell and Scott's *Greek Lexicon* has to say about the meaning of the name Typhon and also related forms of this word.

One meaning of Τῠφῶν (*Typhon*), curiously enough, is 'a kind of comet' – in other words, a moving star! Another form is either Typhoeus or Typhos and specifically refers to the youngest son of Gaia, who was mother also of the three fifty-headed monsters and of Garamas. *Typhos* means 'smoke, vapour', and also 'conceit, vanity (because it clouds or darkens a man's intellect)'. *Typhlos* means 'blind' and specifically 'in the sense of misty, darkened'. The verb *Typhloō* means 'to blind, make blind' or 'to blind, baffle'. It also means 'to wrap in smoke'.

Since Typhon is specifically said to be the father of Sirius (Orthrus) and one of its unexplained definitions is a description of a moving star, and its son has fifty heads, I take all the references to obscurity and invisibility to mean that Typhon represents Sirius B which is the dark companion of Sirius and is invisible to us. In other words, we are *typhlos* (blind) to Typhon because it seems as if it were obscured or *typhloo*'d by *typhos* (vapour, smoke), and we are baffled, blind (*typhlos*) in the sense of the subject being darkened (*typhloō*).

A possible origin of the word Typhon may be the Egyptian word *tephit* or *teph-t*, both of which have the meaning of 'cave, cavern, hole in the ground'. This Egyptian word describes perfectly the chasm at Delphi in which Python was supposed to lie rotting, his corpse giving off the fumes out of the earth. And, as we have seen, Python was equated with Typhon in early times.

If we take the Egyptian word *tep* we discover that it means 'mouth' and in the form *tep ra* it means 'mouth of the god' literally, but in fact the real meaning of this is 'divine oracle'. *Tep* is an unaspirated *teph*. Hence the *tep* of Delphi has a *tephit*, or cavernous abyss beneath it. Later I shall consider the Egyptian word *tep* in its further ramifications. But for the moment it is sufficient to see that Typhon almost certainly originates from the Egyptian word describing a cavern or hole in the earth, as the Egyptians founded the *tep* or oracle at Delphi and naturally used their own word to describe the cavern. As Delphi passed into Greek culture and the Egyptians became forgotten in all but vague legends such as the famous visit of the Canopic Herakles to Delphi, etc., the original word to describe Delphi's cavern would have been retained through the natural conservative inclinations of religious organizations who retain antique words and language for notoriously long periods of time, forgetting their origins. Hence a Greek who had no knowledge of Egyptian culture or that it had ever penetrated to his homeland in earlier days would nevertheless call the cavern at Delphi which produced the sulphurous fumes the den of Typhon after its original Egyptian designation of *tephit*. It has been noted by people other than myself and with greater knowledge that the Sumerian word for cavern, *abzu*, survived in Greek as *abyssos*, leading to our English 'abyss'.

The fumes arising from the Delphic cavern obviously gave rise to the usage of forms of the word for 'obscuring with smoke, dark', etc. And the fact that the personified Typhon became closely associated with Sirius was obviously due to the fact that this word which had entered Greek usage and been extended to considerations of 'darkness, obscurity', was useful in the traditional Sirius lore as adopted in Greece. The other meanings for the word then developed from there, except for the obvious popular usages, such as applying the word to a description of 'vanity' because vanity clouds a man's intellect – a really superb extension of the meaning for use in poetic and common expression.

It is probably considerations such as the Typhonic in the sense of Sirius B's association with darkness and obscurity, and hence with cavernous blackness, that some of the Sirius-related divinities were reputed to live in the dark underworld in later times. The prototype of these is quite specifically Anubis, the embalmer of mummies. Anubis was not originally meant to be a death god *per se* and his association with mummies and the underworld has been previously explained. Egyptian mummies were, as I have said, embalmed over a period of seventy days, to correspond with the number of days each year when the star Sirius was 'in the Duat, or Underworld', and was not visible in the night sky. Hence the seventy-day 'death' of Sirius each year was the fundamental and earliest underworld aspect of the Sirius lore. Of course, Anubis, as the expression of the orbit of Sirius B, was invisible all the time, and not only for seventy days a year. Hence the permanent Typhonic darkness could be even further extended in later lore and a heightened sense of the importance of the underworld aspects could arise. This concept of invisibility and darkness must have become more and more important as time went on and the grasp of the nature of the mysteries became weakened by successive generations of initiates who were further and further from the original sources of information, though the Dogon even down to our time have maintained the information in a remarkably pure state. So there developed the underworld nature of the fifty-headed Cerberus-Anubis in Greek times. With the earlier Egyptians, as always with them, the underworld concept had been on more than one level. To the public the underworld aspect seemed to be entirely explicable by the disappearance of Sirius for seventy days – a fact which anyone could notice – and its reappearance following that period at dawn on the occasion of the star's heliacal rising. But the priests knew that the dark companion of Sirius was never visible.

It would be worth while now to look a little more closely at the dog Orthrus, who was Sirius. Orthrus is the dog of the herdsman Eurytion. Graves interestingly compares this Eurytion with the Sumerian Enkidu, the companion of Gilgamesh who was hairy and wild and came from the steppes and was imbued with incredible strength:[20] 'Eurytion is the "interloper", a stock character . . . The earliest mythical example of the interloper is the same Enkidu: he interrupted Gilgamesh's sacred marriage with the Goddess of Erech [Uruk], and challenged him to battle.' It is particularly interesting to find the Greek companion of Sirius compared by Graves to the Sumerian Enkidu, whom I also have identified with the companion of Sirius. For 'companion of Sirius' is precisely what Eurytion is; if Orthrus is Sirius and Eurytion the herdsman accompanies him, then Eurytion is the 'companion of Sirius'. And Enkidu is the strong hairy wild man who endured a trial of strength against Gilgamesh and became his companion after their wrestling match. Both Eurytion and Enkidu are hairy and rustic characters, and they seem to be related also to the god Pan, whose hairy and rustic nature classes him with them.

The motif of 'interloper' and 'interrupting' and of challenging to a test of strength has to do with the fact that the bright star Sirius is challenged by its strong companion star. Graves adds: 'Another interloper is Agenor' and Agenor means 'very manly'. He interrupted the wedding of Perseus with Andromeda. Perseus was the son of Danae, great-granddaughter of Danaos, who had fifty daughters. As we learn in Graves,[21] Danae herself had connections with an ark. Her father 'locked her and the infant Perseus in a wooden ark, which he cast into the sea'. Later companions of Perseus in his exploits were 'a party of Cyclopes'.[22] This is yet another familiar ingredient.

Perseus fell in love with Andromeda, the daughter of Cassiopeia. Graves says:[23] 'Cassiopeia had boasted that both she and her daughter were more beautiful than the Nereids, who complained of this insult', etc. And, of course, the number of the Nereids, it should surprise no one, was fifty. Of them, Graves says:[24] 'The fifty Nereids seem to have been a college of Moon-priestesses'. Graves explains the recurring fifty in relation to moon lore. It is a brave but unconvincing solution, but how many scholars have even tried to find a solution?

It is interesting in the light of our knowledge of Danaus having fifty daughters to read the opening of Pindar's tenth Nemean Ode[25] which is written largely about the city of Argos (a name related to Argo just as was the name Argus of the *Argo*'s builder and as was the word 'ark'):

The city of Danaos
And his fifty daughters on shining thrones,
Sing of it, Graces,
Of Argos, home of Hera, fit for the gods.

Perseus and Danae also have a connection with Argos. And as for the Graces here mentioned, their worship was first instituted at Orchomenos. The Graces are often associated with Hermes and called 'the Graces of Hermes' and this occurs especially in a work such as *The Lives of the Philosophers*[26] by the historian Eunapius, whose *Universal History* was unfortunately lost. In the work just referred to, Eunapius tells us something extremely interesting about the area of Behdet and Canopus in Egypt. In speaking of Antoninus, the son of the remarkable and brilliant woman Sosipatra, Eunapius tells us: 'He crossed to Alexandria, and then so greatly admired and preferred the mouth of the Nile at Canobus, that he wholly dedicated and applied himself to the worship of the gods there, and to their secret rites.'[27] And also: 'Antoninus was worthy of his parents, for he settled at the Canobic mouth of the Nile and devoted himself wholly to the religious rites of that place'[28] This is interesting, that there were rites peculiar to Canopus to which one could exclusively devote oneself. A little later,[29] Eunapius mentions that the Christians destroyed the temples in the vicinity and demolished the Serapeum at Alexandria, and set-

tled their black-robed monks on the spot of Canopus in order to supplant pagan-
ism there. Hence, we see that that particular place had a unique importance.
Surely it should be excavated. The pagan mysteries of the place, eventually
destroyed by the Christians, probably continued the Behdet tradition and were
related to our Sirius question.

But back now to the quotations from Pindar given above. What is so
especially significant about this passage of Pindar's is the expression 'and his
fifty daughters on shining thrones'. It will be remembered that the throne

$\int$ is the hieroglyph for Ast or Isis identified with Sirius, that the fifty
Anunnaki of Sumer were on thrones, etc. All through the earlier traditions
there has been a great deal of emphasis on the throne in connection with the
Sirius material, and here in the late Pindar we find the same. By describing him
as 'late' I do so on our Sirius time-scale, for of course he was at the very earliest
portion of the Greek classical age.

There are further connections between the Sirius system and Argos and
Danaos. Connections with the Minyan Libyans are many. The father of Danaos
was himself 'the son of Libya by Poseidon'.[30] Danaos was also 'sent to rule
Libya'.[31] However, the connection with Egypt is also strong. Danaos's twin
brother was called Aegyptos, of whom we read:[32] 'Aegyptus was given Arabia
as his kingdom; but also subdued the country of the Melampodes [the 'black-
footed people' – the Egyptians], and named it Egypt after himself. Fifty sons
were born to him of various mothers: Libyans, Arabians, Phoenicians, and the
like.' So we see Danaos's twin brother had fifty sons. And Danaos had fifty
daughters. This demolishes Graves's argument that they must refer to a college
of fifty moon-priestesses, and emphasizes the connection with the fifty male
companions of Gilgamesh, fifty male Argonauts, fifty male Anunnaki, etc.
Notice the two related but also quite definitely separate groups of fifty here.
Together they add up to a hundred – a *hecate* – and have the same grandparents,
but they are basically two separate fifties. Not only do they have separate parents
and especially separate fathers, but they are separately distinguished by sex.

Danaos learns that his brother wishes to marry his fifty sons to Danaos's
fifty daughters with the aim of their killing the fifty daughters after marrying
them. So Danaos and his daughters all take flight to Rhodes* and then to Greece
where they land and Danaos announces that he is divinely chosen to become the
King of Argos. Note that he chooses Argos. This and his connection with fifty
are especially important later when I give the derivation of the words *Argo*,
Argos, etc. And it is particularly interesting that when Danaos flees his brother
he does so in a ship which he built with Athena's assistance – exactly the case
with the Argonauts, who built the *Argo* with Athena's assistance.

The way in which Danaos became King of Argos was that a wolf came down
from the hills and killed the lead bull and the Argives accepted the omen.
'Danaus, convinced that the wolf had been Apollo in disguise, dedicated the
famous shrine to wolfish Apollo at Argos, and became so powerful a ruler that
all the Pelasgians of Greece called themselves Danaans. He also built the citadel

---

* This may be an indication that Rhodes, at latitude 36° 30', does indeed belong in the
sequence of oracle centres as was only tentatively suggested in the chart at the end of Chapter
Five.

of Argos, and his daughters brought the Mysteries of Demeter, called Thesmo-phoria, from Egypt and taught these to the Pelasgian women. But, since the Dorian invasion, the Thesmophoria are no longer performed in the Peloponnese, except by the Arcadians.'[33]

It is well known that the Pelasgians survived in Greece only in remote Arcadia after the Dorian invasion. This is why some of the older traditions continued in that strange region after they had ceased to exist elsewhere in Greece. Arcadia was in a sense the Wales of Greece. The Pelasgians considered themselves 'earth-born', as I shall discuss in a moment. Note that there is a specific reference to Egyptian mysteries being transplanted in Greece among the Pelasgians. When Danaos fled from Egypt to Argos, he is specifically said to have brought Egyptian mysteries, the Thesmophoria. Presumably the Sirius-complex was thus transplanted. (One should read Herodotus II, 165-70.) The element of the wolf, sometimes substituted for the dog in the Sirius tradi-tion of the Dog Star, is important. It is an obvious European substitute for the non-existent jackal of Anubis. With no jackal in Europe, the wolf was the candi-date. Wolfish Apollo is jackalish. It was from this changing of the jackal into the wolf through adaptation to the European clime that those peculiar wolf traditions arose in wild Arcadia which developed in pre-classical times into the werewolf concepts. Human blood-sucking vampires, the use of garlic for protection against them, and lycanthropy of werewolves all luxuriated in the wilds of Arcady among the Pelasgian survivors in pre-classical Greece after the Dorian invasion. The phenomenon is rather like the plethora of fairy-tales and 'Celtic twilight' to be found in Ireland, with the multitude of fantastic stories and creatures. What is a werewolf? It is a man's body with a wolf's head. That is exactly what Anubis became when transferred to Greece; instead of a man's body with a jackal's head, he was a man with a wolf's head because there was no jackal in Greece. And the temples of Wolfish (or Lycian) Apollo, were not altogether rare in Greece. Aristotle's famous school at Athens, the Lyceum, was in the grounds of the Lycian Apollo's temple just outside the Athens Gate of Diochares. The name 'Lyceum' comes from the Lycian Apollo, which is the Wolfish Apollo.

It is extremely interesting, incidentally, to read in Pausanius (Book II, 38, 4) that near Argos 'are the Landings, where they say Danaos and his sons first landed in the Argolid'. Here we read that Danaos had sons, not daughters. This is a strong indication that what was really meant to be significant about Danaos's progeny was not their sex but their number of fifty. And from Pindar we see that they were on fifty thrones. The fact that Aegyptus of Egypt had fifty sons as well and that Danaos's daughters (or sons) taught the Egyptian mysteries to the Greeks all indicates that what transpired was a transplanting from Egypt to Greece of the all-important tradition to be common to both countries from then on – the fifty as linked with the Dog Star Sirius and as celes-tial thrones. In other words, the mystery of the orbit of Sirius B around Sirius A in its fifty celestial steps.

According to Graves,[34] the serpent's teeth sown by Jason were 'a few left over from Cadmus's sowing at Thebes'. Graves says of the latter:[35] 'A small tribe, speaking a Semitic language, seems to have moved up from the Syrian plains to Cadmeia in Caria – Cadmus is a Semitic word meaning "eastern" –

whence they crossed over to Boeotia towards the end of the second millennium, seized Thebes, and became masters of the country. The myth of the Sown Men . . .' But before continuing his explanation I shall quote his description of the events. In Plate 15 is an ancient Greek vase painting of Cadmus standing above a hare, just as Orion 'stands' on Lepus, the Hare, in the night sky.

Graves tells us:[36]

> Cadmus sailed with Telephassa to Rhodes [where Danaos also stopped in his flight to Argos], where he dedicated a brazen cauldron to Athene of Lindus, and built Poseidon's temple, leaving a hereditary priesthood behind to care for it. [Like Danaos, Cadmus instituted religious rites where he went.] They next touched at Thera [the place from which the Minyae later left their settlements there to go to Libya], and built a similar temple, finally reaching the land of the Thracian Edonians, who received them hospitably. Here Telephassa [who was Cadmus's mother and whose name means 'far shiner'; her husband and Cadmus's father was 'Agenor, Libya's son by Poseidon and twin to Belus (who) left Egypt to settle in the Land of Canaan, where he married Telephassa, otherwise called Argiope ("bright-face"), who bore him Cadmus', etc. And notice the name Argiope, related as it is to what we will discuss in a moment as the *Argo*-complex of words and the related meaning of *argent*, silver, taken here as the shade of meaning from this large *Argo*-complex.] died suddenly and, after her funeral, Cadmus and his companions proceeded on foot to the Delphic Oracle. When he asked where Europe (his lost sister) might be found, the Pythoness (of Delphi) advised him to give up his search and, instead, follow a cow and build a city wherever she should sink down for weariness. . . . at last (the cow) sank down where the city of Thebes now stands, and here (Cadmus) erected an image of Athene, calling it by her Phoenician name of Onga. Cadmus, warning his companions that the cow must be sacrificed to Athene without delay, sent them to fetch lustral water from the Spring of Ares [Mars], now called the Castalian Spring, but did not know that it was guarded by a great serpent. This serpent killed most of Cadmus's men, and he took vengeance by crushing its head with a rock. No sooner had he offered to Athene the sacrifice than she appeared, praising him for what he had done, and ordering him to sow the serpent's teeth in the soil. When he obeyed her, armed Sparti, or Sown Men, at once sprang up, clashing their weapons together. Cadmus tossed a stone among them [just as Jason later did] and they began to brawl, each accusing the other of having thrown it, and fought so fiercely that, at last, only five survived; Echion, Udaeus, Chthonius, Hyperenor, and Pelorus, who unanimously offered Cadmus their services. But Ares demanded vengeance for the death of the serpent, and Cadmus was sentenced by a divine court to become his bondsman for a Great Year.

Note here that the serpent's teeth motif is again linked with the concept of fifty. For the Great Year is a hundred months long and consists of two separate cycles of fifty months, as I have mentioned before. It is just as well for us that Hyginus and Apollodorus have preserved this interesting bit of information which Graves has passed on from them. The 'Spring of Ares' resembles 'the grove of Ares' where the golden fleece was hung, and both were guarded by serpents. And in both the story of the *Argo* and this story the hero throws a stone in the midst of the sown men – the stone motif again, a thrown stone being central to the Deukalion story and to the Orchomenos ghost, etc. And it was a stone with which Cadmus crushed the serpent's head as well.

The cow in the Cadmus story is also reminiscent of the Egyptian sacred cow Hathor, who was identified with Isis. *Hathor* is the form we use for the original Egyptian *He-t-Ḥer*, which means 'the House of Horus'. (Horus is, of course, our form for the Egyptian *Heru*, or *Ḥer*.)

It is interesting that the cow Hathor – 'House of Horus' – is identified with Isis, who, as Sothis, is the star Sirius and who is also the Mother of Horus. Hathor seems to be meant to represent the actual Sirius system, the 'house' or area in the celestial regions. And significantly the sister of Isis, Nephthys, whom I have earlier identified with Sirius B, the dark star of the system, is our form for the original Egyptian *Neb-t-He-t*, which means 'Lady of the House'. The reader will recall a previous discussion of the word *Neb* meaning 'Lord'. *Neb-t* is merely the female form of the word, and means 'Lady'. And presumably the house of which Nephthys is the Lady is the House of Horus. In other words, the lady is just as much a resident of the area of Sirius as is Sirius herself. Just because she is the dark sister does not mean that she is not quite as much at home in the House of Horus as Isis.

So much for the cow who led Cadmus to the serpent's teeth. It will all make even more sense as we go along. Wait till we find out what 'serpent's teeth' really means.

Now to resume Graves's commentary on all these Cadmean adventures at Thebes:[37] 'The myth of the Sown Men and Cadmus's bondage to Ares suggests that the invading Cadmeans secured their hold on Boeotia by successfully intervening in a civil war among the Pelasgian tribes who claimed to be autochthonous ['sprung from the earth']; and that they accepted the local rule of an eight-year [one hundred months according to Graves's lunar theories, but it really comes to only ninety-six] reign for the sacred king. Cadmus killed the serpent in the same sense as Apollo killed the Python at Delphi (see 21.12). The names of the Sown Men – Echion ("viper"); Udaeus ("of the earth")'...

At this point I shall interrupt him once again.[38] Let us look at this strange name Udaeus. We should note that the similar word ὀδάξ (*odax*) means 'by biting with the teeth' and comes from the verb root *ΔAK* (*dak*) and its infinitive *dakein* which means 'to bite – of dogs'! Perhaps this is a clue as to the importance of *teeth*, since in Greek there was this word 'to bite' which specifically referred to the biting of dogs and it may be that this aspect of dogs was incorporated at a pre-Hellenic early date into the lore of the Dog Star by one of those many puns which proliferated in all the high civilizations of the Mediterranean. We must, in order to understand the ancient inclinations to punning, rid ourselves of our modern prejudice against puns as a form of humour. Puns in the ancient world had no direct humorous intent. In a milieu where codes and allegories were sorely needed, puns provided the 'handles' to new ways of cloaking truths by use of synonyms. If it was a game, it was a sacred game, a *ludens*. For Thebes was the site of the Castalian Spring, as just mentioned a moment ago, and was intimately part of the milieu of the *ludi* of the ancient world.

Figure 28. Hieroglyphics for tooth and thorn

Also, where *circe* meant 'rings', so does *daktylios* – which specifically means 'anything ring-shaped'. Thus we see another meaning in common in our complex of interweaving terms connected with Sirius traditions. A possible further example of this is in the hieroglyphics of Egypt. Wallis Budge informs us in *Egyptian Language*, in his list of hieroglyphs,[39] that the sign for 'thorn' (which is the tooth of a plant) is almost identical with the sign for Sothis-Sirius. The same sign tilted 45° represents *ăṭeb*, the land on one side of the Nile, and if placed one on top of another, forming a pair, means 'all Egypt'. The very same sign is incorporated in the sign for *ārt* meaning 'jawbone with teeth'. Remember Gilgamesh with his jaw to the earth 'and his teeth shook'. Certainly this all seems to mean something. In fact, the same single sign which means 'the land on one side of the Nile' and looks like a tilted tooth, also has the general meaning of 'earth', which latter concept is so important in all the later Greek Sirius-traditions. It may well be that all these puns on the determinative hieroglyphic sign for Sirius came, in the usual way with the pun-loving Egyptian priests, to form a complicated body of Sirius doctrine involving teeth, Earth-born, ring-shaped, falcon or hawk (Circe), etc., etc. It should therefore not surprise us in the least to learn that the ancient Egyptian word for 'tooth', *ăbeḥ*, has exactly the same hieroglyph as the word for Earth. Hence the origin, almost without question, of the connection between teeth and the Earth! For in ancient Egypt they were written by the identical sign, which were tilted forms of the same sign used to represent Sirius!

Notes

1. Peter Levi's translation of Pausanias, op. cit.
2. Graves, *The Greek Myths*, op. cit., 120.1.
3. Ibid.
4. Ibid., 120.1.
5. Larousse *Encyclopaedia of Mythology*, Paul Hamlyn, London, 1965, pp. 90–1.
6. Lindenblad, op. cit. (see Notes to Chapter One). See also further discussion in Chapter Eight.
7. *Greek Myths*, 131.g. and 131.2.
8. Proclus on Euclid's *Elements*, op. cit.: two translations, one by Thomas Taylor (1792) and one by Glenn Morrow (1960s). A translation by Thomas Taylor of much of Simplicius's commentary on Aristotle's *De Caelo* (*On the Heavens*) may be found in *The Works of Aristotle*, London, 1806–12, 9 vols., all trans. by Thomas Taylor and 'printed for the translator'. However, only fifty copies were printed and not a single volume of this work is to be found either in the British Museum Library or in the Bodleian Library at Oxford. The publication was financed originally by William and George Meredith, patrons of learning at the beginning of the nineteenth century. Patrons of this kind of learning seem thin on the ground these days, since the Bollingen Foundation in New York has ceased its benefactions; Geoffrey Watkins, the London publisher and bookseller who would occasionally reprint Thomas Taylor's work in small editions, has now retired and his successors have abandoned his policies to concentrate on ecology. The above 9 vol. work contains the only English translations ever done of the majority of the Neoplatonic commentaries on Aristotle. And yet, not only are these translations unavailable in print, but they are even not available for consultation in the world's most respected libraries, so that one may not even *see* them. (These libraries really should make some effort to obtain photostats or microfilms of the books.) A friend of mine owns a few volumes of this set and an acquaintance had a chance to buy some of the volumes at a Sotheby's auction but said they reached a terrible price which he thought beyond his range.
9. *Greek Myths*, 3.c.

10. Ibid., 3.3.
11. Benardete, Seth. *Herodotean Inquiries*, The Hague, 1969, p. 126.
12. See the end of his Introduction to *Greek Myths*, op. cit.
13. The four books by Eva Meyrowitz are now out of print. In the fourth book of the series (see Note 14) the author describes the series: 'This is the fourth volume of the series of which the first, *The Sacred State of the Akan* [1951], gives a picture of the old Akan civilization. The second, *Akan Traditions of Origin* [1952], deals with the early history of the people who now call themselves Akan. The third, *The Akan of Ghana, their Ancient Beliefs* [1958, originally entitled *The Akan Cosmological Drama*], showed the development of their religion. The fourth, here presented, attempts to show that Akan religion, which includes the cult of the divine king and the main features of their social organization, is largely derived from Ancient Egypt.' Eva Meyrowitz is an anthropologist from Cape Town who worked in the Gold Coast (now Ghana) from 1936–45 studying the peoples of that country. The third volume mentioned above (1958) contains a final chapter which is entitled 'Analogies to Akan Beliefs and Customs in Libyan North Africa'. As for the Akan peoples, they speak languages of the Twi branch of the Kwa sub-family of the Western Sudanic linguistic stock and inhabit the eastern part of Ivory Coast, the southern half of Ghana, and parts of Togo. The majority are in Ghana, where they settled in successive waves between the 11th and 18th centuries. All of Meyrowitz's books above, and the fourth mentioned in Note 14, were published by Faber in London.
14. *The Divine Kingship in Ghana and Ancient Egypt* (originally entitled *The Akan of Ghana, the Akan Divine Kingship and Its Prototype in Ancient Egypt*), Faber, London, 1960. Went out of print in February 1963. The map is adapted from one in this book.
15. *Greek Myths*, op. cit., 8.
16. Ibid., 8.2.
17. Ibid., 34.
18. Ibid., 21.2.
19. Ibid., 34.1. and 34.3.
20. Ibid., 143.5.
21. Ibid., 73.c.
22. Ibid., 73.p.
23. Ibid., 73.j.
24. Ibid., 33.3.
25. *The Odes of Pindar*, trans. by C. M. Bowra, Penguin paperback, 1969, p. 176.
26. Eunapius, *Lives of the Philosophers and Sophists*, trans. by W. C. Wright, in Vol. No. 134 of Loeb Library Series (*Philostratus and Eunapius*), Heinemann, London; Harvard University Press, U.S.A., 1961.
27. Ibid., p. 419 (text, 471).
28. Ibid., p. 417 (text, 470).
29. Ibid., pp. 421–5 (text 472): 'Next, into the sacred places they imported monks, as they called them, who were men in appearance but led the lives of swine, and openly did and allowed countless unspeakable crimes. But this they accounted piety, to show contempt for things divine. For in those days every man who wore a black robe and consented to behave in unseemly fashion in public possessed the power of a tyrant, to such a pitch of virtue had the human race advanced! All this however I have described in my *Universal History*. They settled these monks at Canobus also, and thus fettered the human race to the worship of slaves . . .' Among the unspeakable crimes being referred to was the destruction by Bishop Theodosius of the Great Library of Alexandria because it contained 'heathen literature'. Hence, the loss of the hundreds of thousands of books from the ancient world, which everyone laments so often, took place at the hands of a fanatical Christian bishop attempting to wipe out all trace of history before Christ, and not as the result of an accidental fire from the time of Mark Anthony, as the story is usually told.
30. Graves, *Greek Myths*, op. cit., 60.a.
31. Ibid., 60.b.
32. Ibid., 60.b.
33. Ibid., 60.f.
34. Ibid., 152.e.
35. Ibid., 58.5.

36. Ibid., 58.e–g.
37. Ibid., 58.e–g.
38. I will complete the quotation from Graves here: '. . . Chthonius ("of the soil"); Hyperenor ("man who comes up") and Pelorus ("serpent") – are characteristic of oracular heroes. But "Pelorus" suggests that all Pelasgians, not merely the Thebans, claimed to be born in this way; their common feast is the Peloria (see 1.2.)'. The remaining three names are thus seen to be quite as one would expect.
39. Wallis Budge, E. A. *Egyptian Language*, Routledge, Kegan Paul Ltd., London, 1951, pp. 43–94.

SUMMARY

In Greek mythology there were fifty daughters of King Thestios (or Thespius) with whom Hercules (in Greek, Herakles), who is said to have been the predecessor of Jason as leader of the *Argo* and who is demonstrably derived in part from Gilgamesh, had sexual intercourse on fifty successive nights. Again, the number fifty is seen as related to intervals of time – in this instance days instead of months – and again in connection with the complex of myths concerning Sirius.

The monsters Cottus, Briareus, and Gyges of Greek mythology each had fifty heads. Briareus was the original name of the figure later called Hercules, and as Hercules was the original Jason, it is seen that the original commander of the fifty-oared *Argo* was a fifty-headed gentleman. The name Briareus is derived from words meaning 'strength' and 'weight'. Gyges also means 'strength'. As for the name Cottus, Robert Graves says that it is not Greek. In fact, it seems to be derived ultimately from Egyptian *qeṭi* meaning 'oarsmen' (not surprising, since Briareus was the original commander of the fifty oarsmen), and also 'orbit'. The fact that in Egyptian the words for 'oarsman' and 'orbit' are the same may explain why fifty oarsmen are symbolic of a fifty-year orbit. Oar-strokes are ideal constant intervals of time combined with constant intervals of space (distance traversed) and thus perfect symbols of intervals of an orbit. In Greek the Egyptian word meaning both 'orbit' and 'oarsmen' seems to survive as the name of a fifty-headed monster. The conclusion: an orbit of fifty intervals (years) concerned somehow with Sirius and with something called 'Weight' (already known to be assigned by the Arabs to a visible companion of Sirius) – obviously, the fifty-year orbit of Sirius B is being referred to.

Garamas, a brother of the three above-named monsters, is a name also adopted by the Garamantian people. These Garamantians were Libyan residents who migrated from there by way of Algeria to the banks of the Niger River in Mali where they intermarried with local Negroes.

The *Argo* was reported to have stopped in Libya for some time, which resulted in the foundation in Libya of 'a hundred Grecian cities'. The Libyans from whom the Garamantians came are reputed to be 'descended from the Argonauts' through migrant Lemnian Greeks who settled in Libya. These same Garamantians over hundreds – indeed, thousands – of years in their migration to Mali obviously brought to that region as the most secret and holy of all their sacred traditions the sacred Sirius tradition now propounded by the Dogon, who are presumably their descendants. (The Dogon themselves insist that they were definitely not originally native to their present homeland in Mali.)

The Libyan version of the Greek goddess Athena had 'fifty Pallantids' as priestesses, with evident association at an early time with the Garamantians.

The dog Orthrus, brother of the god Cerberus who had fifty heads, was specifically identified by the Greeks with the star Sirius. Robert Graves equates Anubis, Cerberus, and Hecate with each other. This brings together Anubis-the-orbit with Cerberus the fifty-headed dog, and Hecate meaning 'one hundred', as well as Orthrus who is Sirius the Dog Star.

The father of Orthrus was Typhon, one meaning of which is 'a kind of comet' or a 'moving star'. Another meaning is 'blind' or 'darkened'; that is, we see it could refer to a moving but invisible star. And his son Orthrus is clearly identified with Sirius, and had a brother with fifty heads.

Orthrus (Sirius) was the dog of the herdsman Eurytion whom Robert Graves compares with Enkidu, the companion of Gilgamesh. It is possible the name Orthrus may be derived from the Egyptian *urţ* meaning 'the setting of a star'. We see this same word used in reference in Chapter Seven to the Sirius complex.

The *Argo* carried the fifty daughters of Danaos, who was 'sent to rule Libya' and had a twin brother Aegyptos, king of Egypt (which got its name from him), who had fifty sons. Sometimes Danaos is said to have fifty sons instead of fifty daughters. It was obviously their number which mattered, not their sex.

'The old man of the sea', named Nereus to the Greeks, had fifty daughters called the Nereids (who are enumerated by Hesiod in his *Theogony*, 241). An 'old man of the sea' is reminiscent of Oannes and Enki – of amphibious wise men generally.

The Greek poet Pindar (fifth century B.C.) describes the fifty Danaids as 'on shining thrones', reminiscent of the fifty Anunnaki on their shining thrones, of Isis on her shining throne. (The throne is the hieroglyph of Isis who is identified with Sirius.) Danaos is also associated with the wolf- or dog-motif, and that motif refers to the Dog Star, Sirius.

CHAPTER SEVEN

The Rising of 'Serpent's Tooth'

It would now do to elaborate further on the points so recently made. It should be noted that in Egyptian the hieroglyph *tchet* of a serpent means both 'serpent' and 'body'. The cobra hieroglyph *ārā* means both 'serpent' and 'goddess'. Elsewhere we encounter *ārā* frequently having the common general meaning of 'goddess'. The frequent incorporation of the serpent into late Sirius-lore among the Greeks probably stems from a pun or corruption of the Egyptian determinative form for 'goddess' in reference to the goddess Sothis-Isis (Sirius). In fact, if an Egyptian were to write 'the Goddess Sirius' in hieroglyphs, the result would be:

$$\triangle\,\text{Ᾰ}$$

which can also (by pun) be read quite literally as: 'serpent's tooth'! In addition to this Egyptian pun, there is a Greek pun connected with the story of Jason sowing the teeth. In Greek the word which describes the growing of a tooth from the gum is *anatolē*; a variant is *anatellō*. These words would describe the growing from the ground of the teeth, and 'to make to rise up' or 'to give birth to' is their basic meaning. However, these words are also used to describe the risings of stars and constellations. Hence, if one wanted to say that the star Sirius was rising at the horizon, one could pun and say: 'The tooth is growing up from the ground as from a gum, that is, the ground is giving birth to a tooth.' Hence all the many 'earth-born' creatures linked to the stars, and especially Sirius. As a matter of fact, in translating the now lost early *Argo* tales from Greek into English it is problematical whether instead of saying 'the teeth in the ground gave birth to . . .', etc., one should really have considered the equally literal translation 'Sirius, namely "the tooth", rose over the horizon.' In short, when does a pun cease to be a pun and merely consist of a mistranslation based on ignorance of the true subject-matter?

It may be that some of the puns taken over from Egyptian into Greek might have involved the same misunderstandings that ours could do with regard to translating the Greek into English. There may thus be a double layer of obfuscation between English readers and the true subject-matter. Those experts in Greek mythology who may feel safe in discussing 'earth-born' mythological creatures as being sprung from the earth in a direct sense, mud and grime no doubt still caking their hides as they pop up into the air, may be better advised to take into consideration that these creatures were not meant really to be described as coming out of holes in the ground so much as rising over the horizon, due to the fact that they are stars and constellations. And if they are such cosmic figures their peculiar shapes and characteristics become immediately less bizarre and, instead, more meaningful.

We know that Colchis was the place where Helios stabled his horses and rose each morning, according to Greek mythological tradition. Since Colchis was thus the archetypal eastern rising point to the Greeks, being at the far eastern end of the Black Sea and being 'as far east as you can get' to a Greek, it actually represented 'the East'. Thus it makes sense that Jason should have sowed the serpent's teeth there. For the growing of the teeth from the ground at that precise point was symbolic language for: 'The star (goddess) Sirius, known in code as "serpent's tooth", is rising heliacally on the eastern horizon which is symbolically represented by Colchis.' And since the sun follows immediately upon the star at its heliacal rising, all the more reason that 'Serpent's Tooth' should spring up at the place where the Sun, Helios, spends the night and then rises.

The reason why the only other example of serpent's teeth being sown took place at Greek Thebes, when Cadmus sowed them there, is that Egyptian Thebes and Aea at Colchis are equidistant from Greek Thebes (see Figure 14). Hence, a probable reason for the name of Thebes being used in Greece. Greek Thebes is in a sense a 'code' for Colchis, since an action performed there may be understood as taking place within the symbolic framework of the Thebes – Colchis–Thebes triangle (Figure 14). To go to Thebes in Greece was symbolically to step on to the Colchis axis. To sow the teeth at Greek Thebes was to perform the Colchian action on Greek soil because of the knowledge of their geodetic interrelation. This kind of thinking is based on a theory of correspondences such as the Dogon exhibit in all their most minute daily acts.[1] In my opinion, a mind is healthy which can perform symbolic acts within mental frameworks which are not immediately obvious. A mind is diseased when it no longer comprehends this kind of linkage and refuses to acknowledge any basis for such symbolic thinking. The twentieth century specializes in producing diseased minds of the type I refer to – minds which uniquely combine ignorance with arrogance. The twentieth century's hard core hyper-rationalist would deride a theory of correspondences in daily life and ritual as 'primitive superstition'. However, the rationalist's comment is not one upon symbolic thinking but merely one upon himself, acting as a label to define him as one of the walking dead.

Greek Thebes Phthiotides – quite distinct from the main Greek Thebes – almost adjoins Iolchus in Thessaly, a few miles away, from which port Jason and the *Argo* sailed to Colchis. The voyage of the *Argo* may be seen as a symbolic journey. For to travel from Greek Thebes – either the proper one or a nominal substitute – to Colchis was equivalent to travelling from Greek Thebes to Egyptian Thebes: the distance was the same. Greek Thebes, where 'serpent's teeth' were sown, is equidistant from Colchis, where 'serpent's teeth' were sown, and Egyptian Thebes, where 'Serpent's Tooth' was worshipped. And a ship travelling on one of the lines in effect travels on both. The voyage of the *Argo*, a later form of the *magan*-boat, or 'Egypt-boat', was both to Colchis and to the equidistant Egyptian centre of Thebes, where the prime omphalos was placed in the temple of Ammon.

The name of Danaos who fled Egypt with his fifty daughters (or sons) and went to Argos seems to be derived from $Δανάη$ (Danaē) which is 'the mythological name for *Dry Earth*', according to Liddell and Scott, 'whose union with the fructifying air is expressed in the fable of Zeus and Danae'. And Danae, as we have seen, is associated with the Sirius complex and was also set adrift in an ark. It may or may not be relevant that the Egyptian hieroglyph for wind or air, with which Danae is supposed to have united, is a boat's sail.

The word 'ark' itself is an interesting one worth investigating. We already know that the related word *Argo* was the ship of fifty oars which we believe symbolized Sirius B in its fifty-year orbit. Could this word 'ark' also have a tie-in with the other characteristic of Sirius B, namely its strength? In this we are not disappointed. The Greek verb $ἀρκέω$ (arkeo) has the meaning, according to Liddell and Scott's lexicon, of 'to be strong enough'!

The word Argus has even applied to a dog. It was the name of the old hunting hound of Odysseus (Ulysses) who recognized his master Odysseus when he finally returned from his voyages, and died as it greeted him. No one else had recognized Odysseus after twenty years' absence except for the faithful old dog, who upon greeting his long lost master, expired on the spot.

Argus has also been used by the Greeks as their name for the hundred-eyed monster set by Hera to watch over Io. And it was Io the cow who led Cadmus from Delphi to Thebes where he sowed the serpent's teeth.

If the words ark, *Argo*, Argus, etc., could be construed as having an actual linguistic derivation from the ancient Egyptian (which would have had to precede by some time the Aryan invasion of India *circa* 1500 B.C., as the word exists in Sanskrit, as we shall see shortly), then it might ultimately be from $ārq$ and $ārqi$ which are

These related words have various curious meanings in Egyptian and can be written many ways other than the simplest given above. *Arq* means 'to complete, to finish', in the sense of a cycle. It also means 'the last' or 'the end of anything'. For instance, $ārq$ $renpet$ means 'the festival of the last day of the year'. *Arqit* means 'the conclusion of a matter'. All these meanings are reminiscent of the meaning of 'Argus' in Homer – to represent the dog who witnesses Odysseus's return and immediately dies, having seen his master's face once again after so many years. The great cycle was completed – Odysseus was home. And immediately Argus dies. Here in the earliest Greek literature we see 'Argus' used as a synonym for the Egyptian $ārq$.

The Egyptian $ārqi$ is even more significant. Note the final determinative (picture not used as a letter) sign $\odot$ which is a circle with a dot in the middle. The meaning of this word is 'the end of a period, the last day of the month'. This term, then, has calendrical usage. It can be applied as well to any culmination of a period. Hera's monster Argus has a hundred eyes, and there are a hundred months (comprising two sets of fifty) to a Great Year. Here 'Argus' is a poetic synonym in early Greek tradition for $ārqi$, 'the end of a period' – its culmination, its total when completed.

Our suspicion that there is a distinct reference to an orbital period of

Figure 29. Io watched by Argus, with Hermes. From 1st-century B.C. Italian temple of Isis, preserved on wall of inner sanctum

Sirius B is hinted at by the additional meaning of $\bar{a}rq$ – 'girdle', representing as it does something around a centre. $\bar{A}rq$ has the further verbal meaning of 'to bind around', implying specifically a revolution. The Latin *arcere* means 'to enclose' and our present-day word 'arc' carries on the circular motion idea.

Not surprisingly, an $\bar{a}rqu$ is 'an educated man, a wise man, an expert, an adept'. It is not difficult to realize that anyone privy to the mysteries of $\bar{a}rq$ would have to be an adept, an initiate and wise man. Hence this meaning for someone who knows about $\bar{a}rq$, an $\bar{a}rqu$.

In Wallis Budge we find[2] a description (taken from Mau) of an Egyptian-influenced Italian temple of the first century B.C. which contained 'seven large paintings representing Egyptian landscapes, and Io watched by Argus, and Io received by Isis in Egypt. [A drawing of the painting of Io watched by Argus is reproduced in Figure 29. It is in Roman style, of course, and artistically quite mediocre.] In this room the Mysteries of Isis were probably acted. – 'So we have specific archaeological evidence that Argus of the hundred eyes was pictured on the wall of the inner sanctum of an Isis temple, and Isis was, as we know, identified with Sirius. Also pictured there was Io, whom I earlier compared to the Egyptian Hathor who was identified with the Sirius system, and it was of course this same Io who led Cadmus to the Greek Thebes (there being an Egyptian Thebes as well, as the reader well recalls).

What were these mysteries of Isis? Well, they seem to have been related to the Thesmophoria Mysteries which the daughters of Danaos were said to have brought from Egypt to Argos. For in Liddell and Scott we find that the name Thesmophoros ('law giving') was a name given to Isis. The name was most commonly applied to Demeter, a Greek goddess, but was also the name of Isis in Greece. In short, Isis was represented as Demeter in connection with these mysteries, but in the Italian temple referred to above was obviously represented as herself. The 'fifty' and 'hundred', connected as we have seen with Danaos, are found again here in the ruins of this Italian temple, where hundred-eyed Argus is portrayed in the inner sanctum of the Isis temple. The name Thesmophoros should not distract us too much. It comes from Thesis, with a meaning including our *thesis* of today – and *thesmos* means 'that which is laid down or established, or instituted'. And *thesmōdeō* is a verb meaning 'to deliver oracular precepts', once again a meaning which should not surprise us.*

In Wallis Budge we read[3] from an Egyptian text of 'the star Septet (Sothis, the Dog Star), whose seats are pure', which is a specific reference to there being *seats* around Sirius – and, of course, there are fifty seats as we know, which led to the fifty thrones of the Anunnaki, the fifty oarsmen of the *Argo*, etc.

In Wallis Budge we also read[4] excerpts of Egyptian texts speaking of holy emanations proceeding from Sirius and Orion which 'vivify gods, men, cattle, and creeping things . . . both gods and men', and are a pouring out of the seed of the soul. Of course, the Dogon maintain the same thing in almost precisely the same terms. To them the seed which energizes the world pours forth from the Sirius system.

In Wallis Budge we find also a particularly interesting bit of further

* Plutarch in 'Isis and Osiris' (378 D) informs us: 'Among the Greeks also many things are done which are similar to the Egyptian ceremonies in the shrines of Isis, and they do them at about the same time. At Athens the women fast at the Thesmophoria sitting upon the ground.'[5]

information.[6] There we learn that the deceased spirit of a man 'goes to Nephthys' and the celestial boat. We have much earlier identified the dark Nephthys with Sirius B. It is therefore interesting to learn that as soon as the deceased visits Nephthys and his 'double' (*ka*) is recorded in heaven, he immediately 'revolves like the sun' – which I think is a pretty specific astronomical description. As he *revolves* he 'leads on the Ṭuat (underworld or heaven)', which is a curious turn of phrase implying a round dance or at least motion which is purposeful, 'and is pure of life in the horizon like Saḥu (Orion) and Sept (Sirius, the Dog-star)'. I hope it will be noticed that the phrase here reads '*in* the horizon' – and much earlier I said I believed the term 'the horizon' applied specifically to the orbit of Sirius B. Here we have the deceased revolving like a sun in a purposeful way in 'the horizon'. I don't think the Egyptians could possibly have been more specific and clear than this. Wallis Budge comments: 'The mention of Orion and Sothis is interesting, for it shows that at one time the Egyptians believed that these stars were the homes of departed souls.'

Having learned this (a belief held as well by the Dogon, as we know), let us return to our word *ārq* which I believe to be the origin of *ark* and *Argo* and *Argus* in Greek, all of which I claim are related to Sirius. Perhaps the reader will not be too amazed if by now I inform him that *ārq ḥeḥ* is a 'necropolis' and *ārq-ḥeḥtt* is 'the Other World' – which we have just this moment learned was located by the early Egyptians at the star Sirius! (Also remember that the guardian of the necropolis in Greek was a *circe* in the *Argo* story.)

Ārq has the further meaning of 'a measure', possibly because spirits are normally measured in *Ārq-ḥeḥtt*.

And for final touches of mystery, I will add that *ārq* can mean 'to wriggle (of a serpent)' – from 'binding around' – and *ārq ur* is the word for that mystery of mysteries, the Sphinx!

The same word means also 'silver', and Wallis Budge claims that the Greek ἄργυρος (*argyros*) is derived from it, which gave us our heraldic term *argent* and the country's name Argentina. Since this term in Greek is derived from *ārq ur* (*ur* means 'chief' or 'Great'), in the opinion of an eminent expert, I believe there is no objection then to my suggestion that the other Greek words came from *ārq* and its forms.* But, as I said, this derivation is one which entered Indo-European from Egypt before the Aryan invasion of India, for in Sanskrit *ārksha* means 'stellar, belonging to or regulated by the stars or constellations', and *ārksha-varsha* is 'a stellar year or revolution of a constellation'. This is very similar to the meaning in Egyptian of 'the end of a period', and a calendrical application to the end of a month. In Sanskrit again *ārka* means 'belonging or relating to the sun'. *Arkam* means 'as far as the sun, even to the sun inclusively'. *Ārki* has become a name for Saturn, thought at that time to be the most distant planet. *Arc* means 'to shine, be brilliant', and can mean 'to cause to shine'. *Ārkin* means 'radiant with light'. *Arka* means 'a ray' and is also a religious ceremony. An *arka-kara* is a 'sunbeam'. *Arkaja* means 'sun-born, coming from the sun', and it and *arkanandana* can be applied to the planet Saturn. *Arkaparṇa*

---

* In discussion with Professor O. R. Gurney of Oxford, who was sceptical of Egyptian origins of Indo-European words, I found that he considered Wallis Budge's suggestion possible on two bases: (1) The word is a technical one, (2) my explanation of the Colchian connection as providing a geographical forum for such linguistic influence.

, is the name of a snake demon. *Arka-putra* is also Saturn. Forms of the word relate also to various specific astronomical events and the Arka ceremony and the arka plant which has 'a grain of fruit' of some importance, reminding one of all the grains of the Dogon (which one learns about by reading more about the Dogon than I have given in this book), particularly the grain Digitaria which gave its name to Sirius B among the Dogon – in their own language, of course!

Arcā means 'worship, adoration'. *Arjuna*, besides being the famous Hindu mythical personage, means 'white, clear' and 'made of silver' – this latter being clearly a form of *ārq ur*, the Egyptian variant form of *ārq* meaning 'silver', which I mentioned a moment ago and which, according to Wallis Budge, has the cognate in Greek which was just mentioned, *argyros* meaning 'silver'.

And as Argo is a constellation in the sky, it should not be a surprise to us to find that in India the Sanskrit *Arjuna* refers to a specific Vedic constellation. The actual name of the constellation is *Phalgunī*. *Phala* means 'grain' or 'seed'. The *Phal-grantha* is a work describing the effects of celestial phenomena on the destiny of men.

There is also a connection of the Sanskrit with an expression involving a thigh; in Greek, *Arktos* became a name for our constellation Ursa Major, which was known to the Egyptians as 'the thigh'.

If the reader can bear some other words, I propose to consider a few which are important in other ways. I beg to refer again to the work of Wallis Budge, which is becoming rather familiar to us now,[7] since I have cited it so frequently in recent pages. The reader must realize that we are nearing the end of the matter and summon his last reserves of patience for the final trudge across hieroglyphic soil, craggy though it may be.

In Wallis Budge, then,[8] we find a passage from one of the Pyramid Texts where Osiris is described in his role of husband of Sothis (Sirius) and implored: 'Be not wroth in thy name of Tchenteru'. This plaintive plea must be examined. What on earth is so terrible about this 'Tchenteru'? Well, to begin an explanation, the word *tchentch* means 'wrath, anger'. So that is obviously the meaning of the word. But we have to continue to pursue this.

Shortly afterwards in the same Pyramid Text we read of the birth of Horus, the son of Osiris, by Sothis: 'Horus-Sept [Horus-Sirius] cometh forth from thee in the form of "Horus, dweller in Sept [Sirius]". Thou makest him to have a spirit in his name of "Spirit, dweller in Tchenteru".'

Well! Here we have an interesting new light on this Tchenteru which seemed so important for no reason which was immediately apparent. It is something to do with Sirius. What, then? Obviously the close association of the place Tchenteru and the Sirius system led me to investigate the word and its related forms.

I found that *tchentha* means 'throne'. I found that *tchenḫ-t* means 'beam (of a ship)' – second significant meaning. And I discovered a third. Namely, that *tchens* means 'weight, heavy'! This was just too much to be coincidence. We first have the Sirius system described as being the place Tchenteru and then discover that that word in related forms means three strictly Sirius-related things: 'throne', 'beam of a ship', and 'weight, heavy'. Tchenteru is 'the place of weight or heaviness' and is identified by the Egyptians with the

Sirius system! I also discovered that Tchenti is a two-headed god (later this name became one of the seventy-five names of Ra and lost its original import-ance). Now, a two-headed god with each head representing one orbit and having fifty eyes, gives us a hundred-eyed god, and the hundred-eyed monster of the Greeks was Argus.

Wallis Budge says another form of *tchens*, 'weight', is *tens*, which also means 'weight, heavy'. And the very next word in the giant dictionary is *teng* which means 'dwarf'! We thus see an apparent variation of the same word meaning 'heavy' and 'dwarf', and this word is specifically applied to the Sirius system.

But just in case there are any sceptics left (and there always are), a look at the Egyptian word *shenit* will be helpful. This word means 'the divine court of Osiris'. The same word *shenit* means 'circle, circuit', and *shent* means 'a circuiting, a going round, revolution'. *Shenu* means 'circuit, circle, periphery, circumference, orbit, revolution', and there is a specific expression written:

$$\Omega \quad \Omega$$

which Wallis Budge gives, and which means 'the two circuits' – and twice fifty is a hundred, giving us the Great Year. *Shen ur* means 'the Great Circle' or 'the circuit of the Great Circle' or 'the islands of Shen-ur', which last is interesting in that it indicates that this place of the Great Circle is not only 'the divine court of Osiris', who is the husband of Sothis (Sirius), but is also a place with islands (stars or planets) where one can presumably live. It does seem that the Egyptians had quite as clear a conception of the Sirius system as the Dogon have.

The verb *shenu* means 'to go round, to encircle', but the verb *shen* means 'to hover over', and presumably the great orbit is above us in the sky, hovering over us in space.

The Egyptian word *khemut* means 'hot parching winds, the khamāsin, or khamsin, i.e. winds of the "fifty" hot days'. This is rather interesting.* In late times 'the dog days' about the time of the rising of Sirius and called 'dog days' from 'the Dog Star' were supposed to be hot and scorching. There are many references to this in writers like Pliny and Virgil. Here is an earlier tradition of hot days incorporating the Sirian number *fifty*. This same word *khemut* has familiar meanings in its related forms. *Khemiu-urtu* means 'the stars that rest not'. *Khemiu-hepu* means 'a class of stars'. *Khemiu-hemu* also means 'a class of stars'. In short, *khemiu* means 'stars'. So *khem* (though apparently not used on its own in surviving texts) really means 'star', as well as referring to fifty days. *Khem* also has the meanings 'shrine, holy of holies, sanctuary', and 'little, small', also 'he whose name is unknown, i.e. God', also 'god of procreation and generative power', also 'to be hot', and 'unknown'. All these meanings are relevant to the Sirius mysteries. The Sirius system was held to be the source of generative and procreative power as we have already seen, Sirius B was of course 'unknown', and was 'little, small', and was a star that rests not (that is, it is always orbiting, which is not at all usual for a star). And what is a star that rests not unless it be Sirius B? For only the planets, which were well known and differentiated by the ancient Egyptians, 'rested not' with the remarkable

* Arabic *khamsin*, 'fifty' and Hebrew *khamshin*, 'fifty', are obviously derived from this Egyptian source.

exception of Sirius B. Comets and meteors apart, and they too were well classed to themselves.

There is a Hymn to Osiris preserved on a stele in the Bibliothèque Nationale, Paris, which dates from the XVIIIth Dynasty around 1500 B.C., and which we find in Wallis Budge. We find *khem* used in this interesting hymn in the following passage:[9]

àukhemu	–	seku		kher àst	ḥrà-f
The stars which never diminish				are under the throne	of his face,

àst	–	f		pu		àukhemu-urṭu
his thrones				are		the stars which never rest.

This passage is extremely interesting because of the recurrent theme of 'thrones' (which word as a proper noun in the singular is the name of Isis) as applied to the celestial region of Osiris – which, as we know, is the Sirius system. Of course, in the superficial view this passage may seem merely to describe some vague kind of reference to a great god who is in the sky somewhere or other, and has a heavenly throne and has a lot of stars twinkling here and there around him for added glamour. But a close inspection of the way things are said here won't let that kind of interpretation stand up. Apart from the fact that the Egyptians were incredibly precise in what they said: what is said in the texts is what is said in the texts. One cannot just gloss over inconvenient precise statements which seem unintelligible and tempt one to brush them aside in order to 'get on with it'. In the above passage describing the *khem* or stars, we find them associated with – indeed identified with – thrones, which are quite separate from the throne of Osiris himself. Now, this is precisely equivalent to the description of the throne of Anu and the thrones of the Anunnaki which surround it, as we meet in Sumer. And here too the context is both celestial and related to Sirius. And here too the thrones are 'stars which never rest' – which could be a description of the movement of Sirius B, with the familiar meaning of each year's 'step' in the orbit equated with a 'throne'. All that is lacking here is their number of fifty.

The same word, *khemut*, however, refers to fifty days; and to Sirius! We therefore have the one remaining ingredient!

There is another Egyptian word which can shed some light on our subject. A possible explanation of serpent's teeth and their springing up as soldiers may result from a pun on the Egyptian word *meni*. This word means both 'soldier' and 'to plough, to till the earth, to cultivate'. A combination of the two meanings yields the strange idea of soldiers resulting from ploughing. And in the Jason story, Jason has to yoke the bulls and plough the field – only after which can he sow the serpent's teeth. Anyone who has read the *Argonautica* will know this. Jason didn't just walk into some field, throw some serpent's teeth about like birdseed, stand back and presto! He had to plough the field. He had to practise *meni* in order to produce *meni*.

Now we must turn our attention to the mysterious Egyptian word *tchām*. A general meaning of *tchām* is 'sceptre', possibly because the meaning of *tchām en Anpu* is the name of 'the magical sceptre of Ánpu (Anubis)'.

Tchāmti are 'bowmen' and Sirius is the Bow Star, as we know. Now, the really intriguing meaning of *tchām* is 'a kind of precious metal'. There are various expressions in the literature such as 'the finest *tchām*', 'real *tchām*', and '*tchām* from the hill-top'. The impression one gets is that this *tchām* is a pretty special commodity. Presumably Anubis's sceptre, which is the *tchām* sceptre, is made of this *tchām* material. A sceptre is an object which exercises rule and force. The fact that there is '*tchām* from the hill-top' could either have a mundane meaning to the effect that the stuff is a metal mined in the hills or more likely is connected with Anubis, not only through his sceptre, but through the hilltop as the residence of the god in the ziggurat sense such as one finds in Sumer. For Anubis was known as 'Anubis of the hill'.

In Wallis Budge we find more information from Pyramid Texts about *tchām*.[10] The references are entirely stellar. There is a description of the deceased Pharaoh, in this case Pepi I. Pepi's father is Tem 'the great god of An (Heliopolis) and the first living Man-god; the creator of heaven and earth'. In Sumer too the great god of An was the creator of heaven and earth, but there was not, as far as we know, a city named after him as was the Egyptian city of An which came to be known to the Greeks as Heliopolis.

Of Pepi we read in the text that 'the appearance of this god in heaven, which is like unto the appearance of Tem in heaven'. This is all gross flattery – typical for the texts mourning the dead Pharaohs. Every Pharaoh looks like the great god of An and every other great god and does every conceivable celestial thing. The Pharaoh is dead, long live the Pharaoh!

Now various gods, including the Governor of the Land of the Bow and Sept (Sirius) 'under his trees', carry a ladder for Pepi. Pepi then 'appeareth on the two thighs of Isis, Pepi reposeth on the two thighs of Nephthys'. Tem puts Pepi at the head of all the gods, and 'Pepi setteth out in his boat', with Horus. He then stands 'among the imperishable stars, which stand up on their *tchām* sceptres, and support themselves on their staves'. This seems to make clear that the metal *tchām* is also a specifically stellar material which supports the stars!*

Then we read:[11] 'This Pepi liveth life more than your sceptres *āu*.' The word *au au* means 'dog, jackal', and I suspect a connection with 'dog star' and Anubis who is jackal/dog. Also the *āu-t en āthen* is the *āu-t* of the sun, or 'the course of the sun'. But, to resume:

> O ye gods of the Sky, ye imperishable ones, who sail over the Land of Tehenu [the Teḥentiu are 'the sparkling gods, the stellar luminaries' from *teḥen* which means 'to sparkle, to scintillate'] in your boats, and direct them with your sceptres, this Pepi directeth his boat with you by means of the *uas* sceptre [Uasàr is a variant form of Asàr, the name of Osiris, and *uas-t* is 'a kind of animal, dog (?)'[12]] and the *tchām* sceptre, and he is fourth with you. [indicating that he joins a group of three stars!] O ye gods of

---

* The Greeks had a tradition of 'the strongest metal' and called it *adamant*. Kronos used it to castrate Ouranos (Uranus); mythically it was the strongest metal.

heaven, ye imperishable ones, who sail over the Land of Taḥennu, who transport yourselves by means of your sceptres, this Pepi transporteth himself with you by means of the *uas* and *tchām*, and he is the fourth with you. . . . This Pepi is the *ānes* matter which cometh forth from Nephthys. . . . Pepi is a star . . . Pepi is Sept, under his *sebt* trees . . . The star Septet (Sothis) graspeth the hand of Pepi. Pepi plougheth the earth . . . Osiris [Pepi is addressed by the name], thou art the double of all the gods. [Uas is also the Egyptian name of Thebes.]

Here we see the dead Pharaoh Pepi's celestial after-death experiences described. He goes to the stellar regions and joins three stars, becoming 'the fourth'. He uses three sceptres for power, the *āu* (similar to a word for dog/ jackal), the *uas* (also the name of Thebes, similar to another word for dog, and related to a variant form of the name of Osiris), and the *tchām* (a mysterious metal and the sceptre of the dog/jackal-headed god Anubis). The star Sirius is specifically described as taking his hand. Pepi himself is transformed into a star, as clearly stated: 'Pepi is a star.' He becomes a star and his hand is taken by the star Sirius, which can only mean that he becomes a star in the Sirius system, and he 'becomes fourth with them'. He then is identified in turn with the three other stars of the Sirius system, which are Isis-Sothis, Nephthys, and Osiris. The first emits '*anes* matter', the second is the female Nephthys, which may be identical with the 'female Sorgho' or Sirius C of the Dogon (though sometimes Nephthys refers to Sirius B in other contexts), and the third is called 'the double of all the gods' – being the circling companion and the archetypal 'double' of many figures from Isis to Gilgamesh. This is quite obviously Sirius B.

And there is *tchām*, the mysterious, potent stellar 'metal' which is said to be the power of Anubis, whom we have earlier identified as the personification of the *orbit* of Sirius B. And *tchām* is quite similar to the word we dealt with earlier, *tchens*, meaning 'weight', and its related forms *tens* 'heavy, weight', *tensmen* 'to be heavy' and the similar word *teng* 'dwarf'. If we spoke of something described only by a series of these apparently related words, namely: *tchens tens teng tchām*, the meaning would be, quite literally, allowing for the absence of proper grammar, 'the weight (of) heavy dwarf star-metal', remembering that *tchām* is also specifically identified as the power of the god Anubis whom we have identified previously as the orbit of Sirius B, the dwarf star composed of super-heavy 'star metal'.

Concerning this star-metal it is as well to take notice that in 'Isis and Osiris' (376 B), Plutarch says of the Egyptians:[13] 'Moreover, they call the lodestone the bone of Horus, and iron the bone of Typhon, as Manetho records' (Manetho fragment 77.) Recall that 'the bones of Earth' in ancient tradition are stones. It is interesting that a heavy metal is 'the bone' of Typhon which we have earlier determined as a description of Sirius B. And magnetized iron or lode-stone is 'the bone' of Horus, the son of Isis and Osiris. This is exactly the sort of tradition one would expect.

We must recall that Anubis is our form of writing the actual Egyptian word Ånp or Ånpu. The verb *ånp* means 'to wrap around', obviously connected with Anubis's role as sacred embalmer. It is significant that Ånp heni is 'a jackal-

headed god who guarded the river of fire, a form of Anubis'. We have already
postulated that 'the river of fire' may be a way of describing the orbit of the
star Sirius B, so it is quite interesting to see that Anubis, whom we have already
identified as representing the orbit, is specifically said to be the guardian of
the same river of fire. And 'wrap around' could have an orbital meaning as
well as its obvious meaning of 'swathe'.

We recall that a special description of *tcham* given in Wallis Budge's
Dictionary[14] was '*tcham* from the hill-top'. Also we have just equated *tchām*
with Anubis. So it should not surprise us that a title of Anubis is *Tepi ṭu-f*
'he who is on his hill'. As I mentioned a moment ago, this seems to be a
ziggurat-concept such as one finds in Mesopotamia. The *tepi* complex of words
is quite interesting and bears examination.

Tepi means 'the foremost point of the bows of the ship, the hindmost part
of the stern' – extremely specific and exactly fitting my specification of what
was important about the ship *Argo*. *Tepi* also means 'the first day of a period
of time', and I maintained earlier that the tip of the prow and the tip of the
stern of *Argo* (with fifty oar-places between them) was a symbol of the orbit of
Sirius B. Also we will recall that *ārqi* means 'the last day of a period of time'.
So any period of time has a first day called *tepi* and a last day called *ārqi* in
Egyptian. And *tepi* describes the *Argo* just as *ārq* is the origin of the very word
Argo. And *Tepi* is part of a crucial descriptive title of Anubis whom I have
equated with the *Argo*. There is even a further connection between *tepi* and
the Sirius-complex. The word *tep ra* means 'the base of a triangle' and the words
septu and *septch* both mean 'triangle' – Septit is Sirius and the triangle is its
hieroglyph.

The basic meaning of *tep* is 'mouth' (hence the meaning *tep ra sebek*
' "crocodile's mouth" – a disease of the eye') and even more fundamentally
'beginning or commencement of anything'. It is interesting for the study of
concepts of geometry to note that the Egyptians thought of the base of a
triangle as its 'mouth' or beginning.

Now, the link-up which takes place between *ārqi* and *tepi* – that is, the end
of a cycle and the beginning of the next – could lead to some confusion without
much trouble. If the last day of the old cycle is the *ārqi* and the first day of the
new cycle is the *tepi*, it would be easy to begin to think of the *ārqi* as the beginning
– after all, it and the *tepi* are adjoining each other and amount to practically
the same thing. In a sense one could say that the true end of a cycle *is* the
beginning of the next. For us, New Year's Day is represented by a combination
of an old man with a sickle or scythe walking away and a baby, representing
the New Year. The two figures are together. Similarly, the *ārqi* and the *tepi*
are inescapable companions. As time passed and traditions decayed a bit, it
must have been an easy thing to think of *ārqi* as the actual beginning of a new
cycle, since it was the end of the old. And it is this which I presume happened
in Greek, for the verb ἄρχομαι *arkomai* means 'one must begin' or 'one must
make a beginning'. And it is related to *arche*, which means 'beginning, starting-
point', etc., and which survives in our *architecture* and *archetype*. So here is further
evidence that the 'ark' words in the Indo-European languages derived from
the Egyptian *arq* words.

Another link of the 'ark' words complex with the Argonaut story is found in a strange place. One of the most peculiar of all treatises to survive from ancient times is the curious *Of the Names of Rivers and Mountains and of such Things as are to be found therein*.[15] This treatise survived in the corpus of Plutarch's writings but is obviously not by him. In fact ,the treatise strikes me as basically a wild satire on a type of writing which was then common. One of the rivers discussed in this treatise is the Phasis, up which Jason sailed to Aea in Colchis. Of this river we read: 'It was formerly called Arcturus . . .'. Without elaborating on this point, I merely wish to note that the very river at Colchis once may have had a name which may be related to the 'ark' word complex. Arcturus supposedly means 'bear-ward', referring to the ward of the bear known to us as Ursa Major, the Big Dipper. Arcturus in Bootes is conceived of as its companion according to Allen, who says it had connections with Osiris and possibly Horus. This is probably another of the many confusions arising from 'companions' who are compared to each other. But as I said, I do not wish to be led astray by elaborating on the question of the name Arcturus and all that that would involve. I merely note the fact that the Phasis was once the Arcturus and leave it at that.

The name Phasis had connections with birds, such as with an expression 'the Phasian bird'. Recall the *kirke* or Circe connections with Colchis. It is interesting then to note that the *phassa* in Greek is 'the ringdove'. Forms of this word refer to doves and doves are, as we have seen previously, intimately associated with omphalos-oracle centres marked out from Behdet. And we know that Aea in Colchis, which is on the River Phasis and has such associations with the *Argo* and the oracles, is related to doves in this way and also because of the doves let fly from the arks and *Argo*. So the fact that *Phasis* and *phassa* are connected is no surprise. This river, whether named Phasis or Arcturus, seems to be aptly designated. It is also to be noted that in Greek a *phasso-phonos* or 'dove-killer' is the name of a kind of hawk. And *kirke* is likewise!

Before leaving Plutarch behind, we might note also that in 'Isis and Osiris', he tells us that a name for Osiris was *Omphis*. An interesting tie-in with the oracles, attested by Plutarch as current in Egypt in his day.

To return to *tepi*, we note that *tep ra* means not only 'the base of a triangle' but 'divine oracle', which is also quite relevant. I have postulated that the oracles are connected with the *Argo* as representative of the orbit of Sirius B, the beginning of which I designate by *tepi*, and we discover that the name in Egyptian for 'oracle' is *tep ra*.

Tepi ā became the word for 'ancestors', due to the connection of *tepi* with the *beginnings* of things. And the *tepi-āui-qerr-en-pet* were 'the ancestor-gods of the circle of the sky', which is again significant. Visitors, perhaps?

Gods of the circle in the sky seem to be referred to by Plutarch's account of the Persian religion in 'Isis and Osiris' (370 A–B). As many people know, the Persian religion prior to Islam was Zoroastrianism, which survives today as the religion of the Parsees of Bombay in India, to which city they fled from their Persian homeland when it was being conquered by the Moslem invaders. The Persians are not Semitic Arabs but are Indo-European, with a language and original religion closely related to the Aryan Indians and to Sanskrit. In fact, the earliest form of Sanskrit, which is called Vedic, is very little different from the earliest form of Persian, which is called Avestan.

Zoroaster (also known as Zarathusthra) is known to have postulated two basic divine principles: Ahura Mazda the principle of light and goodness, and Ahriman the principle of evil and darkness. These two principles are also known by the names of Oromazes and Areimanius, which are the names used for them in Plutarch's treatise. If we recall Plutarch's description, cited by us earlier, that Anubis was the circle dividing the light from the dark in Egyptian religion, it will be interesting to note that in 369 E–F he equates with this concept, by describing it in similar terms, the Persian god Mithras who mediates between the darkness and the light. Then in 370 we find this remarkable passage: '(The Persians) also tell many fabulous stories about their gods, such, for example, as the following: Oromazes, born from the purest light, and Areimanius, born from the darkness, are constantly at war with each other; and Oromazes created six gods, the first of Good Thought, the second of Truth, the third of Order, and, of the rest, one of Wisdom, one of Wealth, and one the Artificer of Pleasure in what is Honourable. But Areimanius created rivals, as it were, equal to these in number.' These twelve gods would seem to be zodiacal. But it is the following passage, immediately after this, which becomes really interesting: 'Then Oromazes enlarged himself to thrice his former size, and removed himself as far distant from the Sun as the Sun is distant from the Earth, and adorned the heavens with stars. One star he set there before all others as a guardian and watchman, the Dog-star. Twenty-four other gods he created and placed in an egg. But those created by Areimanius, who were equal in number to the others, pierced through the egg and made their way inside; hence evils are now combined with good.' A footnote to the Loeb edition adds: 'It is plain that the two sets of gods became intermingled, but whether the bad gods got in or the good gods got out is not clear from the text.'

This passage is really deserving of some attention. We find a quite specific description of all this taking place in a region meant to be distinct from our solar system. The Persians seem to have quite clearly understood the fixed stars to have been beyond the system of the sun. This, at least, is what they seem to be trying to convey – a distinction of locale. In any case, the 'light' god Oromazes and the 'dark' god Areimanius each create twenty-five gods, which gives fifty. And they are placed in an egg, which is an elliptical shape just as in an orbit. One of the twenty-five gods created by Oromazes is by a slight garbling said to be Sirius, but in any case, there were created by Oromazes the Dog Star Sirius plus twenty-four other gods which makes twenty-five and a corresponding twenty-five created by Areimanius – and they mingle in the shape of an egg. What does that sound like? And Sirius is specifically stated to be the chief one. And as Areimanius was the 'dark' god and his creations were 'dark', then his creation in opposition to Sirius would be a 'dark' Sirius, wouldn't it? And as for the fifty gods arrayed round Sirius (speaking strictly from this text one would have to say the forty-nine gods arrayed around Sirius, but I speak of garbling of the tradition because, from what we already know from other such descriptions from elsewhere, Sirius should really be the fifty-first element) they obviously represent the fifty years of the orbit of Sirius B in an egg shape around the Dog Star as its 'guardian and watchman'.

There are further examples of a wavering between forty-nine and fifty in the ancient traditions. Graves has these interesting remarks:[16] 'Chief priestesses were chosen by a foot race (the origin of the Olympic Games), run at the end of the fifty months, or of forty-nine in alternate years.' Apart from the fact that Graves here speaks of 'the fifty months' as antecedent to the Olympiads, a point which we discussed much earlier, we see the alternative use of forty-nine and fifty as a quantitative time measurement. This is rather like the shilly-shallying between forty-nine and fifty in the above Persian description. There is also this example from the Bible, in Leviticus 25, 8–13:

> You shall count seven sabbaths of years, that is seven times seven years, forty-nine years, and in the seventh month on the tenth day of the month, on the Day of Atonement, you shall send the ram's horn round. You shall send it through all your land to sound a blast, and so you shall hallow the fiftieth year and proclaim liberation in the land for all its inhabitants. You shall make this your year of jubilee. Every man of you shall return to his patrimony, every man to his family. The fiftieth year shall be your jubilee. You shall not sow, and you shall not harvest the self-sown crop, nor shall you gather in the grapes from the unpruned vines, because it is a jubilee, to be kept holy by you. You shall eat the produce direct from the land.

The above words and many which follow them, but which I will not quote (as anyone can refer to the Bible for the full account), were spoken by God to Moses on Mount Sinai, and are Jehovah's directions as to what the Israelites must do. It is even more significant that Jehovah is made to say much later in the same speech, all of which has been devoted to his talk of his fifty-year jubilee and what must be done about it by the Israelites: '. . . for it is to me that the Israelites are slaves, my slaves whom I brought out of Egypt. I am the Lord your God.' Remember that Egypt as the source of the Sirius tradition had had 'brought out' of it the Sirius mysteries and traditions by Danaos to Argos, etc. It seems the Israelites too are part of this, though there will probably not be a single rabbi unshaken by such a suggestion.

What, then, of the forty-nine versus the fifty? Perhaps for explanation we should return to Robert Aitken's book *The Binary Stars*.[17] In discussing the length of time of the orbit of Sirius B around Sirius A he says: 'Thus, Volet's orbit, computed in 1931, which differs very little from my own, published in 1918, has the revolution period 49·94, whereas Auwers gave 49·42 years' – the point being that the orbit of Sirius B takes between forty-nine and fifty years and is somewhat less than fifty.

The Aitken book also firmly informs us that the orbit is an ellipse, as are the orbits of all heavenly bodies. But of course, when speaking generally of the orbit of Sirius B one does not say 'the ellipse', one says 'the circle'. We say in common parlance: 'The planets circle round the sun,' even though we know their orbits are elliptical. And most mentions of the orbit of Sirius B in our sources are to 'the circle'. But, naturally, the Dogon draw a specific ellipse in the sand to represent the orbit of Digitaria (Sirius B). Figure 6 clearly compares the Dogon tribal diagram of the orbit of Sirius B around Sirius A with a modern astronomical diagram of the same.

We have already seen near the beginning of the book how the Dogon not only know that the orbit of Sirius B around Sirius A is an ellipse, but they also know the astounding principle of elliptical orbits whereby that body around which the orbit takes place inevitably tends to be at one of the two foci of the ellipse. For the Dogon specifically say: 'Sirius . . . is one of the centres of the orbit of a tiny star Digitaria'. Kepler first formulated this principle as a law of planetary motion – a revolutionary step forward in Western science. The Dogon also describe the orbit of the 'Star of Women' (a planet around Sirius C) as forming an ellipse with Sirius C at one of the centres.

Now, in light of the dithering over forty-nine and fifty just referred to, and the references to seven times seven equals forty-nine, seen in the light of the fact that the orbital period of Sirius B is between forty-nine and fifty years, which can be well accommodated as Graves says of the Sacred Year, 'fifty months, or of forty-nine in alternate years', thereby balancing out to a close approximation to reality by alternating the count successively as fifty years, then forty-nine years, then fifty years . . . etc., one can understand why the orbit of Sirius B around Sirius A is 'counted twice to be a hundred years', as the Dogon say and as was done in Egypt and in Greece, and which led to the double-Sacred Year of one hundred and the Greek goddess Hekate which means 'one hundred', and the hundred-handed ones of Greek mythology, etc. It was because orbits of Sirius B had to be counted in pairs in order better to approximate a whole number. And the fact that this was the case among the Dogon and the people of the Mediterranean area seems to confirm beyond all doubt that the Sirius tradition of the Dogon is a survival of the Mediterranean (namely, Egyptian) tradition brought by the ancestors of the Dogon from the Garamantes Kingdom of Libya where it had been taken by the Minyan immigrants.

It is also significant and conclusive that the Dogon specifically say: 'The period of the orbiting of Digitaria is about fifty years and corresponds with the first seven reigns of seven years each of the first seven chiefs . . .' And: 'This rule was in operation for forty-nine years for the first seven chiefs who thus nourished the star and enabled the star to periodically renew the world. But, the eighth chief having discovered the star . . .', etc., combining also the sacrifice of the sacred chief concept emphasized over and over by Graves in his many references to the Sacred Year of fifty months. This passage from Griaule's account of what the Dogon told him almost reads like a straight quotation from the Book of Leviticus in the Bible. Or from *The Greek Myths* by Graves! Can there be any further doubt that the two traditions are identical? That the Dogon brought it from the Mediterranean world into an obscure wilderness area where it has survived the ravages of time and empire amazingly intact and specific? And that the Mediterranean tradition in turn really was about Sirius and the orbit of Sirius B, the *great invisible*?

The Dogon tribe are really the last of the Argonauts, from whom they are quite literally descended – being Minyans in the middle of West Africa.

Turning to the Egyptian word *henti*, one finds that it is a name for Osiris and it also is 'a crocodile-headed god in the Tuat', which is the Egyptian underworld, and it also means simply 'crocodile gods'.

Hent is specifically 'the crocodile of Set'; *hen-t* is, interestingly, a specific locality of the underworld and means 'a district in the Taut'. But, more widely, *hen-t* is 'a mythological locality' which is not necessarily in the underworld.

It would seem that the fabulous Hen-t was a locality which had an underworld counterpart and obviously is somehow connected closely with both Osiris and crocodiles.

The name of this region, Hen-t, when taken as a common noun rather than as a name, means 'dual'. This is a strong clue as to the nature of the fabulous region. A region intimately connected with Osiris and whose name means 'dual' is reminiscent of Plutarch's description of that circle or ellipse with its dual aspect of separating the light from the darkness. Lest the reader think this far-fetched I must hasten to add a further meaning of *hen-t* which is 'border, boundary', and another which is 'the two ends of heaven' – which all appear to refer to a circle and have the *hen-t* ('dual') nature of outside and inside and the two extremes connected by a diameter. *Hen-t* also means 'end, limit', and a *henti* is a specific period of time lasting for 120 years. Remember that the Sigui of the Dogon was every sixty years and two Dogon Sigui make one Egyptian *henti*. In fact, a *hen-t henti* would be a Sigui or, perhaps, vice versa, depending upon one's grammatical preference. (The use of the word 'dual' can be rather ambivalent and be construed as either halving or doubling by the context.) And this dual time period is also rather like the two fifty-month periods which make the hundred-month period of that sacred Great Year connected with Sirius, which has a dual aspect.

Henti also has the meaning 'endless' – and the endless circling of Sirius B around Sirius A could be referred to here. Some such idea must be at work, otherwise how can the same word have the meaning of 'endless' and also of '120 years'? It must be a reference to an 'endless' cycling of perhaps the orbit of Sirius B or of the Sigui cycle's own basis. In any case, it signifies that the 120-year period was arrived at as an endlessly recurring cycle, and for that to have been the case, the 120-year period must have been quite important, which is exactly what one would anticipate. In Appendix III there is an explanation proposed for the true nature of the Sigui . . . and of the *henti* based on certain astronomical facts.

Considering that *henti* means all this and also means 'crocodile gods', etc., it is surprising to see that *henn* means 'to plough' and a *hennti* is 'a ploughman'. One immediately thinks of Jason *ploughing* the field for the dragon's (crocodile's?) teeth. It may well be that the 'serpent's teeth' motif which was a pun for 'the goddess Sirius' was extended in another layer of pun to 'dragon's teeth' as a reference to crocodiles.

In connection with Sirius B being the hairy, bestial Enkidu-figure, we see with interest that *hen* means 'to behave in a beast-like manner' and a *henti* is also specifically 'a beast-like person'. In addition to *henti* being a name for Osiris, who is the companion of Sirius, we find it describing 'a beast-like person' who is the archetypal companion in Sirius-related legends. And additionally, we find Hathor the cow-goddess, a form of Isis-Sirius, referred to as Hennu-Neferit. (Neferit simply means 'beautiful'.) But this word *hennu* with the double 'n' has the basic meaning of 'phallus' and has a phallic determinative hieroglyph, and therefore may not be related to the *hen* words with a single 'n'.

Hen-ta significantly means 'grain' in keeping with the Dogon concept of Sirius B being a grain. *Henu* means the hawk-god Seker and his *henu* boat. This boat (echoes of celestial *Argo*) is 'the sacred boat of Seker, the Death-god of Memphis'. This reminds us of the Circe-complex and the death-god of Colchis. It must be emphasized that the hawk and the falcon are constantly being confused with each other not only in Egyptian studies, but I have asked falconers the difference between a hawk and a falcon and they vaguely suggest a difference in colour of eyes and that the falcon tends to be smallish. A hawk supposedly has golden eyes (solar?) whereas the falcon has brown eyes. But their habits are not identical and as there are various species of both hawk and falcon, confusion reigns supreme. The hawk and falcon do not seem to have been distinguished by the ancient peoples, or at least less so than the crocus and the colchicum (or 'meadow saffron'). Of course the differences were recognized in practice, but what we must realize is that in the ancient world the Aristotelian structure of genus and species for plants and animals did not obtain, and differentiation in linguistic or semantic terms did not resolve to so fine a focus. For such precision one would employ qualifying adjectives, but a systematic modern biological terminology did not exist. Hence we found much earlier that *kirke* in Greek meant 'a hawk or falcon'. In short, they are as interchangeable at the level of terminology as the 'l' and the 'r' were interchangeable in Egyptian at the level of pronunciation and symbol. It seems the Egyptians, like the Chinese of the present day with their 'flied lice' for 'fried rice' had a paralamdism and inability to differentiate the two liquid sounds. Indeed, the 'l' could be differentiated further if our ears were so trained. It is possible to pronounce a much more lingual and less dental 'l' than we use in English. But as for the French 'r', I confess to being as unable to form my tongue to pronounce that sound as Aristotle was, for instance, unable to pronounce the Greek 'rho' – this being considered by the Greeks to be a lisp.[18]

However, I have let myself digress. The subject of hawks and falcons can, it seems, be pursued to a resolution. Seton Gordon, probably the world's expert on the golden eagle, could not tell me a conclusive differentiation between them. Nor could an experienced falconer friend. I was becoming impatient at this lack of an answer until I learned from my friend Robin Baring, who had once considered becoming an ornithologist, that an extremely subtle difference between the hawk and the falcon does actually exist. According to him, on a hawk, the fourth or fifth pinion feather is longer making a rounded wing, whereas on a falcon, the second or third wing feather is longest – making a pointed wing. I am not certain whether this is fully comprehensive to all the many species. In *A Glossary of Greek Birds*,[19] D'Arcy Thompson says that the ancient Greek poet Callimachus (who was quite a scholarly gent) claimed there were ten species of hawks, and Aristotle claimed Egyptian ones were smaller than Greek ones. It looks as if people have been trying to sort out hawks and falcons since the Creation. But if the reader is as weary of these birds as the author, let us agree to drop them and face the last few remaining Egyptian words. We have survived a waterfall; can we muster the strength to pull ourselves to shore?

Ḥensekti means 'hairy one' and also Isis and Nephthys. Nephthys could be identified with Sirius B who is the archetypal 'hairy one', but it seems more likely that Nephthys varied between being a name of Sirius B and being a name of Sirius C, the female star which was also invisible. The *henmemit* are, tantalizingly, 'men and women of a bygone age'. The meaning 'to plough' of *henn* and 'boundary' of *hen-t* are linked through 'arable land' of *henb-t* in the word *hen-b* which means 'to delimit, to measure land, to make a frontier boundary'. (This seems to connect the single 'n' words with the double 'n' words after all.) Thus, further possibilities for punning between a reference to the delimiting orbit of Sirius B and 'ploughing' in connection with the ploughing of the ground for the sowing of the serpent's teeth – serpent's teeth being a pun on the goddess Sirius, as we know. Hence a series of dizzying puns all interlocking.

Just for final measure we note that Hen-b is also a serpent god of the Tuat and Henb-Requ is a jackal-god, bringing us into liaison with the jackal/dog Anubis and Sirius B's orbit and adding as a final flourish yet another pun on serpent.

We recall that the throne and the oar were the two most common allusions to the yearly 'steps' in the fifty-year orbit of Sirius B. Also the name of the goddess Isis, which in Egyptian is Ast, means 'throne', and is represented by the hieroglyph of a throne. Significantly, then, *as-ti* using the same hieroglyph of the throne, means 'one in the place of another, successor'. This is a specific reference to the sequentiality of the thrones. And the orbit which they represent, also known as Anubis, seems to be given specific recognition by the combined form Ast Anpu, which is Isis-Anubis.

Another name for Isis as Sirius specifically is Aakhu-t. In the light of this new name it is not surprising to learn that Aakhuti is 'the god who dwelleth in the horizon'. And *aakhu-t sheta-t* means 'the secret horizon'. *Aakhuti* are 'the two spirits, i.e. Isis and Nephthys'. And the *aakhu-t* are also 'the *uraei* on the royal crown', etc., demonstrating the origin of the most central of the Pharaonic insigniae. Hence yet further demonstration of the connection of the Sirius system with 'the secret horizon' of Sirius B's orbit and its profound importance to the Egyptians.

Another form of the name of Isis, Ast, is Aas-t, which is seen as significant if we note that *aasten* means 'one of the eight ape-gods of the company of Thoth. He presided over the seven . . .' For this is a parallel to the Sirius-linked story of the Dogon, whereby the eighth chief presided over the previous seven chiefs as a means of signifying the orbital period of Sirius B commencing again with the advent of the eighth chief following the seven chiefs, each with a reign of seven years giving seven times seven or forty-nine years. This Sirius concept is here referred to in another form of the very name in Egyptian for Isis, who was identified with Sirius.

Another way of referring to Isis and to Nephthys is as Aār-ti, 'the two Uraei-goddesses, Isis and Nephthys'. There is an intimately related form of this word, Aārārut, which probably is the origin of the Sumerian goddess Aruru's name. For she was the counterpart of Isis in Sumer and was known also as Ninhursag, Nintu, Ninmah, etc. It is specifically in her name of Aruru that she creates the hairy Enkidu, companion to Gilgamesh. No doubt because Enkidu is related to Sirius B, she appears in this name in the *Epic of Gilgamesh* because this particular name is closely related to the Sirius lore, through its derivation from this Egyptian form. And the fact that Aār-ti is a common name of both Isis and Nephthys, and Nephthys is more closely connected with the companion of Sirius, the appellation Aruru is closer to Sirius B, who is also represented by

Enkidu, than another name for the goddess Sirius which was not specifically shared with Nephthys, the dark companion. This word also means '*uraei*' and we have just seen that the other word for the *uraei* is related to the horizon of Sirius B's orbit, as well as also being shared with Isis and Nephthys – obviously shared because the orbit described *by* one is described *around* the other, and as we have seen several times, the orbit was common to them both and divided their respective precincts. Therefore words connected with this orbit must be common to them both. And what more appropriate name for the Sumerians to use for the goddess in her role as creator of Enkidu, the dark companion of Gilgamesh, than a name derived from this aspect of the goddess?

Sirius the Dog Star is represented by the hieroglyph of a tooth, so it is important also to know that there is a word in Egyptian which means both 'tooth' and 'dog'. I am referring to *shaār*, 'tooth', and *sha* 'a kind of dog', *sha-t* 'female dog', *shai* 'a dog-god', and *Shaāit* which is a form of Hathor who is identified with Isis.

Also *sha-t* means 'one hundred', and is the Egyptian synonym for the Greek Hekate.

Another word for 'tooth' is *ábeḥ*, and a related form of the same word means 'jackal'. In addition *ába* means 'to make strong', and *áb-t* means 'path'. *Ápp* means 'to traverse', and *áp* means 'steps'. If I may be forgiven lack of grammar, *ápp áb-t em áp* means 'to traverse a path in steps', which is exactly what Sirius B does in its orbit. Since Anubis has been identified as the orbit of Sirius B, it is not surprising that a title of Anubis was 'the counter of hearts' with 'the counter' being the word *ápi* and *ábu* meaning 'hearts'. But if we altered that slightly to *ápi-ábt* instead of *ápi-ábu*, the meaning would be 'the counter of months', for *ábṭ* means 'month'. Another pun with a deeper meaning with reference to the 'hundred months' (or years) 'counted' by Anubis, who is the orbit, as he traverses his *áb-t em áp*, his 'path in steps'.

To go on examining the Egyptian language would be superfluous to our present intentions. So would a continued elucidation of Sumerian religious names from Egyptian. But it would be just as well to fill in a bit of information on that transition which brought our Mediterranean Sirius tradition south from Libya to the Niger River. Herodotus told us how the Garamantes of Libya had been pushed further and further westwards and southwards. Graves says they were forced down to the Fezzan in the desert regions of south Libya. We find a further account in *A History of West Africa* by J. D. Fage:[20]

Herodotus, writing about 450 B.C., speaks of the Garamantes, that is the people of the oasis of Djerma in the Fezzan (who in modern terms would be accounted Tuareg), raiding the 'Ethiopians', i.e. black-skinned peoples, across the Sahara in two-wheeled chariots each drawn by four horses. About 400 years later, another great early geographer, Strabo, says much the same of the Pharusii of the western Sahara, who may perhaps be equated with ancestors of the Sanhaja. . . . The chariots of the Garamantes and Pharusii were very light fighting vehicles, unsuitable for carrying trade goods, but it is a point of considerable interest that Herodotus's and Strabo's accounts of their activities have been confirmed and given added point by the discovery on rocks in the Sahara of some hundreds of crude drawings or engravings of two-wheeled vehicles each drawn by four horses. The most significant aspect of these drawings is that they are almost all distributed along only two routes across the Sahara, a western one from southern Morocco towards the Upper Niger, and a central one running from the Fezzan to the eastern side of the Niger bend.

In *The White Goddess*, Robert Graves says also of the Garamantes:[21]

Herodotus was right in stating on the authority of the Egyptian priests that the black dove and oracular oak cults of Zeus at Ammon in the Libyan desert and of Zeus at Dodona were coeval. Professor Flinders Petrie postulates a sacred league between Libya and the Greek mainland well back into the third millennium B.C. The Ammon oak was in the care of the tribe of Garamantes: the Greeks knew of their ancestor Garamas as 'the first of men'. The Zeus of Ammon was a sort of Hercules with a ram's head akin to ram-headed Osiris, and to Amen-Ra, the ram-headed Sun-god of Egyptian Thebes from where Herodotus says that the black doves flew to Ammon and Dodona.

In his fascinating book *Lost Worlds of Africa*,[22] James Wellard in Book Three, 'The People of the Chariots', discussed the Garamantes and related topics at some length. One of the most amazing elements in the story concerns an apparently lost civilization sitting under the sands of the Sahara which once was the centre of the Garamantian empire, and which was dispersed by the Moslem Arab invaders. Wellard describes this civilization in suitably mysterious terms:

On the track which runs across the desert from Sebha, the modern capital of the Fezzan, to the oasis of Ghat on the Algerian border, the traveller crosses an underground water system that has few parallels for ingenuity and effort in African history. . . . Seen from inside, the main tunnels are at least ten feet high and twelve feet wide and have been hacked out of the limestone rock by rough tools, with no attempt to smooth the surface of the roof and walls. . . . How many of them actually remain is still not certain, though hundreds of them are still visible. In places they run less than twenty feet apart and their average length, from the cliffs where they originate to the oases where they terminate, is three miles. If we assume from the 230 that remain visible that there may have been as many as 300 of them in this region of the desert, we have, taking into account the lateral shafts, nearly 1,000 miles of tunnels hewn out of the rock under the desert floor.

We are still not clear as to how the system worked. First, where is the entrance to these tunnels? One can spend hours trying to find their inlet, and though the solution would seem easy at first, assuming that a particular mound is followed along its entire length, the investigator finally arrives at a jumble of rocks at the base of the escarpment without being able to tell where the tunnel has disappeared to. . . . (the system possibly) presupposes an adequate and regular rainfall, in which case we have to go back as far as 3000 B.C. to find such a maritime climate in the Sahara Desert. Could the *foggaras* be that old? . . . Wells are the only water sources in the

Wadi el Ajal today, and they are adequate for the present population of some 7,000 people. If we compare this figure with the 100,000 or more graves so far found in the Wadi and dating from the time of the 'people of the water tunnels', we can get some idea of how populous this region was. . . . In addition, the construction of such an enormous hydraulic complex indicates an industrious and technologically advanced people who had reached a stage of culture superior to that of northern Europe before the Roman conquest.

We can, therefore, safely assume that (a) between 5000 and 1000 B.C. a cattle-raising and agricultural people belonging to the Negro race had occupied large areas of the Sahara Desert which they kept habitable and fertile by means of the *foggaras*; and (b) it was precisely the prosperity of these defenceless Africans that incited the white settlers along the Libyan coast to invade the Fezzan. These immigrants (originally, it seems, having come to Africa from Asia Minor) were the Garamantes, the people of the four-horse chariots – first mentioned by Herodotus, who describes them as already a very great nation in his time. They thereupon appear and disappear throughout the classical period until, around A.D. 700, they vanish altogether as the last of their kings was led away to captivity by the Arab invaders of the Fezzan. Their Saharan empire had lasted over a thousand years.

Yet we know almost next to nothing about the Garamantes, and the reason is obvious: with the fall of the Roman Empire, Africa became a 'lost' continent, so much so that no European traveller reached even as far south as the Fezzan until the beginning of the nineteenth century.

I should add that it was the Emperor Justinian who destroyed North African civilization, before the Moslems came.

Wellard also says that in the Garamantian territory are myriads of tombs, pyramids, fortresses, and abandoned cities lying untouched by any archaeologist's spade. For instance, he visited 'the fortress city of Sharaba which lies out there in the desert gradually sinking beneath the sand. In the first place, perhaps not more than a few score European travellers have visited the site in any case, as it lies off the caravan routes in one of the more inaccessible pockets of the Mourzouk Sand Sea. . . . In point of fact, archaeological research in the country of the Fezzan has only just begun. . . .'

After the Arab conquest of the Garamantian empire, the survivors fled south-west and 'fused with the Negro aboriginals on the south bank of the Upper Niger, and adopted their language', as Graves tells us in *The Greek Myths*,[23] and as he learned from the books of the anthropologist Eva Meyrowitz.[24]

So that is some more light on how the Dogon and related Negro tribes of the Upper Niger came to possess their amazing information. It is a tale of thousands of years, and the drama was enacted across thousands of miles, which only seems suitable considering the nature of the message they were to carry into a much different world – the global village of twentieth-century culture. According to the Dogon, 'the shaper of the world' visited the earth and returned to the Sirius system, having given men culture. Now that our race has set foot on another heavenly body and we are looking outward to our solar system, we are prepared to give serious consideration to any neighbours who might be within a few light years of us and have solar systems of their own which they inhabit and where they pursue their lives with the same desire to know, to learn, to understand, and above all to build a genuine ethical civilization, that motivates the best of us. For if they are not so motivated it is doubtful that they will have survived their own technologies. In love one can live, but without love there is no world that will not poison itself. One must assume that any creatures living at Sirius will have come to terms with a wholesome and vital ethic. If Sirius is indeed the home of a 'shaper of the world', then it may encourage us, too, to become shapers of worlds.

Notes

1. Griaule and Dieterlen, *Le Renard pâle*, op. cit., p. 44: 'The establishment of categories, of classifications, of correspondences, constitutes an armature comparable to the framework of a construction, to the articulated bone structure of a body. What imparts life to them – gives them their own physiology – is, for the Dogon, their relationship with God and with the order in the world he created, that is to say, with the way the universe was organized and functions today.

  'It is the myth that lights up the whole. Structures appear progressively in time and are superimposed, each one with its own special meaning, also with its own interrelations which are narrowly connected. That is what lends meaning to the succession of categories and stages of classification, which give evidence of the relationships established between man and what is not of man in the universe.'

  For a more complete account of how the armature of symbolic interrelationships extends even to the smallest daily action or object for the Dogon, one should read the entire section 'The Thought of the Dogon', pp. 40–50, in *Le Renard pâle*. This section expresses quite well the mentality required to function within a society grounded in reality at all levels. The one drawback to such patterns of thought is that they can ossify if over-elaborated as a baroque maze, and stultify free inquiry, as happened in the Middle Ages in Europe when the Church had the answer to anything, and anyone who disagreed could go fetch his rope and stake, make a bonfire, and commit himself to his divinity. There are dangers to anything; no system of thinking is perfect. Only the constant unremitting exercise of a free will and attention can regulate that most ill-regulated of organisms, the human personality, and keep it on course. 'Systems' all are panaceas, whether of thought or society, and all equally useless to the nonvigilant individual. The doctrine of the mean expressed in all sound philosophies is the doctrine of exercise of the attention at all times; the high-wire performer is the archetype of the successful man. (*Successful* not in terms of bank accounts, must I add?)

2. Wallis Budge, Sir E. A., *Osiris and the Egyptian Resurrection*, 2 vols., London, 1911, Vol. II, pp. 294–5.
3. Ibid., Vol. I, p. 156.
4. Ibid., Vol. I, pp. 389–90.
5. Plutarch, op. cit. This essay in vol. discussed in my Appendix IV.
6. Ibid., Vol. I, pp. 106–7.
7. *Osiris*, op. cit., Vol. I, p. 93.
8. Ibid.
9. *Gods of the Egyptians*, op. cit., Vol. II, p. 164.
10. *Osiris*, op. cit., Vol. II, p. 311.
11. Ibid., Vol. II, p. 341.
12. See Wallis Budge, Sir E. A., *An Egyptian Hieroglyphic Dictionary*, London, 1920.
13. See Note 6.
14. See Note 12.
15. In Vol. V of Goodwin's trans. (ed.) of Plutarch's *Morals*, 1874, op. cit.
16. *Greek Myths*, op. cit., 60.3.
17. *The Binary Stars*, p. 238.

18. What is so odd about the Chinese inability to distinguish the two liquids is that they have both of them more or less in their own languages. For the 'l' is quite common and a sound rather close to an 'r' is used in words which we commonly transcribe by a 'j', such as in the word *jen*, which is pronounced almost like 'run' in English and is the Confucian term for virtue.
19. Op. cit., p. 65 under *hierax*.
20. Fage, J. D. *A History of West Africa*, Cambridge University Press, 1969, pp. 14–16.
21. Op. cit., p. 182 (Chapter Ten under 'D for Duir').
22. Wellard, James. *Lost Worlds of Africa*, Hutchinson, London, 1967; also reprinted by The Travel Book Club, London, 1967.
23. Op. cit., 3.3.
24. See Notes 13 and 14 to previous chapter.

SUMMARY

In ancient Egyptian, the hieroglyph and word for 'goddess' also means 'serpent'. The hieroglyph for Sirius also means 'tooth'. Hence 'serpent's tooth' is a pun on 'the goddess Sirius'. In the *Argo* story, Jason sowed the 'serpent's teeth', an idea which must originally have stemmed from this Egyptian pun. The Greek word for 'the rising of a star' also refers to 'the growing of teeth from the gum'. Therefore when the serpent's teeth were sown in the ground, they grew up from it as from a gum – that is, the star Sirius ('serpent's tooth') rose over the horizon.

Thus we see the mythological code language of sacred puns in operation. Behind the myths lay concealed meanings which are decipherable by returning to the hieroglyphics and finding synonyms which form puns.

We find explanations of the words Argo, Ark, Argos, etc., by looking for Egyptian origins. These words derive from the Egyptian word *arq*. But related words in Greek give clues as well: Argus was a dog connected with a cycle. Another Argus had one hundred eyes and watched over Io, who is connected with the Sirius traditions and Isis. The Egyptian word *arqi* refers to an end of a cycle, represented in the *Odyssey* by Argus. The Egyptian word *arq* refers to a circular concept and is the origin of the Latin *arcere* and of our arc.

A temple of Isis found in southern Italy has in its inner sanctum a painting of hundred-eyed Argus (portrayed, however, with a normal face and eyes). The mysteries of Isis were celebrated in this inner sanctum. Also the fifty daughters of Danaos traditionally brought from Egypt to Greece (and hence southern Italy) the mysteries of the Thesmophoria which according to Plutarch were Isis mysteries. So we see Isis connected intimately at the most secret and sacred levels with 'fifty' and 'one hundred' (Hekate) – and Isis was identified with Sirius.

The earliest Egyptians believed Sirius was the home of departed souls, which the Dogon also believe. The Egyptians said that when a deceased spirit 'went to Nephthys' he revolved 'in the horizon' and 'revolves like the sun'. This is a pretty specific description of the dark Nephthys as a 'sun' revolving around Sirius.

The Egyptians also maintained that emanations from the region of Sirius vivified creatures on Earth. This, too, is believed by the Dogon.

Since the Egyptians believed Sirius was the other world of departed souls, it is interesting that they called 'the other world *arq-hehtt*, using the familiar word *arq* again.

In Egyptian the region of Sirius is described by a word meaning also 'throne' and 'weight' and similar to a word meaning 'dwarf'.

The Egyptian word meaning 'fifty' (from which are derived the Arabic and Hebrew words meaning 'fifty') referred to the fifty hot 'Dog Days' of Sirius and also to 'a star that rests not' – obviously a moving star, namely Sirius B with its fifty-year orbit.

Sirius in Egypt is 'the Bow Star'. The Egyptian word for 'bowman' refers also to a heavy star metal connected with Anubis (which we have previously suggested refers to the orbit of Sirius B, which is, after all, made of 'heavy star metal'). The word for heavy star metal is similar to the words for 'dwarf' and 'weight'.

The Egyptian word for 'the beginning of a cycle' (which would join up with *arq* meaning 'the end of a cycle') means also 'oracle' and 'the front and hind tips of a ship' – a vindication of my oracle-*Argo*. The same word also means 'the base of a triangle' (and the word for 'triangle' is a variation of the name for Sirius, whose hieroglyph is a triangle). We also have geodetic triangles, connected with the ark, from Thebes and Behdet.

Plutarch gives an account of a Persian description of the Dog Star Sirius, which is said to be surrounded by fifty gods forming the shape of an egg (elliptical orbit) in which the 'light god' faces the 'dark god.'

In the Biblical Book of Leviticus, Moses commands the Hebrews to observe a Jubilee every fifty years, but I have never heard of their doing so. Obviously the Hebrews did not understand the fifty-year orbit of Sirius B which Moses (who was an initiate of Egypt and 'raised by Pharoah') presumably had in mind.

In Egyptian the word for 'the secret horizon' also means 'the two spirits' – namely, the light Isis and the dark Nephthys. The same word also means 'the god who dwelleth in the horizon' and 'Isis as Sirius'. The secret horizon would seem to refer to the orbit of Sirius B in which Sirius B lives.

The Egyptian word for 'dog' also means 'tooth' (the triangle hieroglyph meaning 'Sirius' and 'tooth'), and also means specifically 'dog-god' and also 'one hundred'.

Another Egyptian word meaning 'tooth' means 'to traverse a path in steps' and 'to make strong', and is used in connection with Anubis in such a way that could be 'the counter of months while traversing the path'. A synonym means 'one hundred' and 'Sirius'. We thus have: 'counting one hundred months while traversing the Sirius path'. But Anubis who does this is 'a circle'. So we have: 'counting one hundred months while traversing the circular Sirius path'. Change months to years (as Moses might have done?) and we have two fifty-year orbital periods of Sirius B.

We see that the ancient Egyptians had the same Sirius tradition which we have encountered from the Dogon tribe in Mali. We know that the Dogon are cultural, and probably also physical, descendants of Lemnian Greeks who claimed descent 'from the Argonauts', went to Libya, migrated westwards as Garamantians (who were described by Herodotus), were driven south, and after many, many centuries reached the River Niger in Mali and intermarried with local Negroes.

The Dogon preserve as their most sacred mystery tradition one which was brought from pre-dynastic Egypt by 'Danaos' to the Greeks who took it to Libya and thence eventually to Mali, and which concerns 'the Sirius mystery'. We have thus traced back to pre-dynastic Egypt well before 3000 B.C. the extraordinary knowledge of the system of the stars Sirius A, Sirius B, and possible 'Sirius C' possessed by the Dogon.

We have thus managed to rephrase, if not to answer, the Sirius question. It is no longer: 'How did the Dogon know these things?' It is now: 'How did the pre-dynastic Egyptians before 3200 B.C. or their (unknown) predecessors know these things?'

What is the answer to the Sirius question? We do not know. But knowing the right questions is essential to an eventual understanding of anything. The many investigations which should properly follow upon the asking of the Sirius question may give us more answers than we could at present imagine.

Archaeologists have a difficult task trying to explain the many similarities between Sumer and Egypt, indicating some still undiscovered common origin for the two cultures – an entirely forgotten civilization whose remains must exist somewhere.

But in considering the very origins of the elements of what we can call human civilization on this planet, we should now take fully into account the possibility that primitive

Stone Age men were handed civilization on a platter by visiting extraterrestrial beings, who left traces behind them for us to decipher. These traces concerned detailed information about the system of the star Sirius which is only intelligible to a society as technologically advanced as ours today. Today was the time when we were meant to discover these coded facts, I feel sure. Today is the time we should prepare ourselves to face the inevitable reality that extraterrestrial civilizations exist, and are in all probability far more advanced in culture than we ourselves – not to mention in technology which could enable them to travel between the stars!

It may be difficult for us to avoid seriously entertaining that most disturbing and also exciting of notions: that intelligent beings from elsewhere in the galaxy have already visited Earth, already know of our existence, may possibly be monitoring us at this moment with a robot probe somewhere in our solar system, and may have the intention of returning in person some day to see how the civilization they established is really getting on.

PART THREE

Beyond the Mystery

CHAPTER EIGHT

A Fable

Once there was a little girl sitting by the seashore. Her mother had told her to go and play. She watched the waves and thought: 'If only something marvellous would happen to me today!' The sun was shining very hot upon the strand and the girl became drowsy. The sound of the quiet surf was like a lullaby. She began to doze.

Suddenly she awoke. The air was alive with a new coolness, a haze had lifted, everything was startlingly clear to the sight. Far out, she glimpsed a flash in the sea, then another flash, a glint of something in the sun. There it was again – something coming towards the shore and making its way through the waves. It must be a porpoise. The girl was terribly excited. Something was happening to make her day memorable. Now she would not have to sit by the seashore and be bored.

Now that the porpoise was getting nearer, it alarmed the girl. Could it be about to crash against the sand, as she had heard giant whales did from time to time in despair? Was it a dolphin actually intent on self-destruction? The girl ran hurriedly towards the spot which seemed to be the dolphin's objective. She saw its tail fin, quite close, appear for a moment. Some seaweed it seemed to be trailing with it showed through the water. It was a bright, almost shiny, porpoise . . . it was now near the sand . . . what would it do? She could see it now, through the water. It stopped. It seemed to be grovelling in the sand. Its tail splashed up, then down. It remained stationary.

The poor dolphin had crashed into the sand. Full of pity, the girl began to wade out towards it. But it moved away slightly. It wasn't stuck in the sand. It was looking up at her from under the water. What could it be trying to do? The girl went back to the shore. The fish now moved in closer again. From quite near to the fish, a woman put her head above the water. She had silver make-up on her face and eyes that went up. The little girl was worried about the fish. 'Have you got hold of the dolphin?' she asked the woman. Just beneath the woman's shoulders there was a noise like a swimming suit strap snapping against her skin. She replied to the girl with a fixed stare and a high wail which seemed to be a song. She moved towards the girl, her eyes never straying from her. Her eyes were clear blue, like the sky. It was as if there were two holes in her head and you could see the sky through them. Again her swimming suit strap snapped against her. Her eyes were like the hot sun. The girl wanted to go to sleep. The woman's eyes were like the sound of the surf. The girl sat down in the sand and tried to make herself see the woman more clearly. The woman's face appeared to be really silver.

The woman's chest showed above the water now. Her bosom was bare. Her swimming suit strap must have snapped. The woman's bosom was a beautiful silvery green and shiny in the sun. The woman seemed unable to go any farther. She stared at the girl and remained motionless, except for a slight swaying to and fro.

'Who are you?' asked the girl. 'Have you come from a boat?' The woman gave a long wail, but the expression on her face did not change. Then there was the snapping of the swimsuit again. But this time the girl saw that above the woman's bosom were two long thin slits, which had opened and snapped shut loudly as if they were muscles flexing, just under her beautiful sleek collarbones. The woman stirred as if she were resting uncomfortably on a high stool. She looked dissatisfied and, twisting her torso, she leapt forward and fell with a splash in the surf near where the girl sat. She had no legs. It was what the girl had thought was the dolphin. The woman was a mermaid. Her body stretched out long, sleek, shiny in the sun, with the surf rushing up past her and then retreating. She leaned on an elbow and raised her dolphin's tail slightly in the air, then tapped the shallow water, and did so several times in the way that the girl herself tapped her fingers on her desk at school sometimes.

The mermaid had no scales like an ordinary fish. Her skin was like that of the dolphins in the aquarium who jumped through hoops. But she was more silvery and more green. And there was a kind of hair streaming down her back like thin seaweed, which looked brown, or silver, or green, or grey, or even black. It was all those colours. And still the mermaid tapped her tail against the surf and stared at the girl. She was very much like a naked woman. She looked like the girl's mother did when she hurried to put on her dressing-gown before a bath.

Once again there was the snapping noise, only quieter. The girl saw the long thin slits in the woman's chest open and close instantly. Then the woman made a low, pleasant humming sound and looked sleepy. She leaned forward and an amazing series of clicks and pops were apparently made by her in her throat, which the girl could see constricting and moving.

The girl stood up and said to her, 'I've never seen a mermaid before. Can I tell Mummy?' The mermaid seemed to reply by smacking a fin against her skin somewhere behind her, rocking, and making a long, loud hum. She leaned forward more and looked at the girl and her eyes seemed to gloss over and go green. She opened her mouth, little pointed teeth showed in pink gums, and a long whispering sound came out which sounded like the sea at a distance. She then beckoned the girl to her with her arm, and her webbed fingers.

The girl stood in the surf and touched the mermaid. 'You're so soft,' said the girl, 'not like fish are. I mean fish are soft, but you're so smooth.' The girl liked the mermaid. She had never seen anyone so smooth and silvery and beautiful. 'I bet you can swim better than ordinary people. I'm going to run and tell Mummy you're here!' The girl began to walk away. 'You won't go away, will you? Wait here!' And she made every effort to smile and signal her intentions. The woman seemed to nod in agreement. The girl ran quickly, looking back often to see if her mermaid woman would wait for her. The mermaid made no attempt to move, but merely watched the girl.

From a distance the mother could see something lying in the surf, as her daughter tugged at her skirts excitedly. 'It's something from a wreck,' said the mother.

'No, Mummy, it's a mermaid!' said the little girl.

'Don't be silly darling, mermaids don't really exist. They're just in stories. Now what is it you've found?'

Then suddenly the thing in the surf moved. It was horrible, like a serpent. 'Oh! It's alive! It's moving! No!' and she turned and tried to push her little girl back home. 'I'm going to get Daddy. He'll know what to do. It may be a creature which is injured. Now come with me.'

But the little girl eluded her and ran towards the sea. 'No, Mummy, it's a mermaid! Come and see!'

Feeling sick in the pit of her stomach and apprehensive, the mother followed her daughter and feebly called after her. The girl quickly reached her friend from the sea, and the mother, seeing her standing beside the moving creature, cried, 'No! Get away! Get away from it!' She then ran and – it was a woman and fish, it was! It was silver. It was a mermaid! 'No, darling, no! Get away from it! It's horrible!' Her daughter came to her obediently and the mother stared in disgust and nausea at this awful slimy sea creature with a grotesque human frame grafted on to it – a monster, an abomination. She felt her stomach constrict, she gasped, she bent forward in the thought that she would be sick. 'God!' she gasped. 'Go home! Go home!' and pushed her daughter violently to make her run.

'What is it, Mummy?' asked the girl, who was now becoming terrified. 'Mummy!' she cried in alarm. Her mother was choking, eyes bulging, stumbling towards her with her flat palm outstretched to push her away towards home. 'Mummy! Mummy!' They heard a loud splash and turned just in time to see the mermaid slip away effortlessly at lightning speed into the deep water – gone instantly from sight.

'Oh God!' said the mother, as she clasped her head and fell to her knees on the sand.

'She's gone, Mummy. The mermaid's gone. But you saw her!'

The mother looked at her daughter as if the girl might at any moment herself turn into a mermaid. 'Oh darling, what was it? Tell me it isn't true!' said the mother, and put her head down into the hot, sharp sand.

A little story about a child and an adult and their different reactions to a strange, intelligent amphibian. To the child 'it could swim better' and was silvery and fascinating. To the mother it was repulsive and horrible.

In Appendix II the reader will find in English translation the surviving fragments of the lost *Babylonian History* written in Greek by a Babylonian priest named Berossus, who seems to have been an acquaintance of Aristotle and drew on his own country's temple archives (which were in cuneiform, of course) to compile the history of his country from original documents. The readership would have been the cosmopolitan inhabitants of the Hellenistic world created by the conquests of Alexander.

In his work, Berossus describes his country's tradition of the origins of its civilization. And the tale is a strange one. For a group of alien amphibious beings were credited by the Babylonians with having founded their civilization.

The main individual of the group of amphibians is called Oannes. We have had occasion to refer to him earlier. There are several illustrations of him throughout this book (Plates 6, 7, 8 and 9 and Figures 30 and 31). In somewhat later traditions than the ones Berossus drew on, Oannes became the fish-god of the Philistines known as Dagon and familiar to many readers of the Bible. By that time Oannes, as Dagon, had become an agricultural deity. In the surviving fragments of Berossus we have no reference to the Philistine tradition, and we shall probably never know whether Berossus mentioned it or not. But in the

Figure 30. Fish-tailed Oannes on gems in the British Museum. The representation on the right shows a star and eye of Osiris – an Egyptian hieroglyph on a Babylonian gem

Figure 31. Fish-tailed Oannes from Assyrian cylinder seal. He stands before an omphalos stone covered in geodetic mesh with descending octaves on either side of it. The eye-star is above, and a 'mouth of Nommo' is to lower left

Berossus fragments preserved by the historian Apollodorus, we read that 'there appeared another personage from the Erythraean sea like the former, having the same complicated form between a fish and a man, whose name was Odacon'. This seems fairly clearly to be a corrupted form of 'Dagon'. Unless 'Dagon' is a corrupted form of 'Odacon'.[1]

Apollodorus criticizes Abydenus, who was Aristotle's disciple, for not mentioning that there were other amphibious beings besides Oannes himself. He says: 'concerning these Abydenus has made no mention'. Apollodorus, therefore, seems to have given Berossus a close attention to detail which Abydenus, for his purposes, neglected. This is an extremely important point, as we shall now see. Berossus, according to the close account of Apollodorus, calls the amphibians by the collective name of 'the Annedoti'. They are described as 'semi-daemons', not as gods. For some time I thought that 'the Annedoti' must be a convenient and tradition-sanctioned name for these creatures. I was concerned to have a name for them because, as we learn in a moment, the Dogon tribe claim that amphibious creatures with fishtails founded their civilization too, and that they came from the system of the star Sirius. If there are intelligent creatures living on a planet in the Sirius system, it would seem from all the evidence that they are amphibious, resembling a kind of cross between a man and a dolphin. It is therefore necessary to come up with some name for these creatures if we are to discuss them from time to time.

With this in mind, I suddenly wondered what the word 'Annedotus', which is never translated in the Cory translations of the fragments of Berossus, could actually mean. I read once again the fragment of Berossus from the careful Apollodorus and scrutinized the translation of it, which was: '. . . in whose time appeared the Musarus Oannes the Annedotus from the Erythraean sea'. The Erythraean sea is that body of water known to the ancients which we today subdivide into the Red Sea, the Persian Gulf, and the Indian Ocean.

What was meant by the untranslated words 'Musarus' and 'Annedotus'? Strangely enough, until I purchased my own copy of Cory's *Ancient Fragments*,[2] I had never before noticed that the words 'Musarus' and 'Annedotus' were untranslated. In libraries, with a pressure of time, one tends to overlook these details. I also had overlooked this in the account of Apollodorus quoted by Carl Sagan in his *Intelligent Life in the Universe*.[3] These are all reasons why I felt that I should include as an appendix to this book the complete surviving fragments of Berossus (excluding a couple unrelated to our concerns which may be found in the third and final, 1876 posthumous edition of Cory's book). For unless all of the material is available and easy to hand, one invariably overlooks something and neglects to make the frequent and necessary comparisons which enable one gradually to read between the lines and obtain additional insights.

It so happens that the most frequently cited version of Berossus's account is usually that preserved by Alexander Polyhistor.[4] But that is where problems can begin. For Alexander Polyhistor does not use the words '*annedotus*' or '*musarus*' in his account. And the version preserved by Abydenus uses the word '*annedotus*' only as if it were a proper name: '. . . in his time a semi-daemon called Annedotus, very like to Oannes, came up a second time from the sea . . .' As for the word '*musarus*', Abydenus does not use it at all.

So I turned to the lexicon to find the meanings of these words. I assumed that Cory would have translated them into English if they had simple and obvious meanings. But to my surprise I found that their meanings were quite simple and specific. A '*musarus*' is 'an abomination', and an '*annedotus*' is a 'repulsive one'.

Now the reader may appreciate why I wrote the little fable. For the creatures credited with founding civilization in the Middle East were frankly described by the Babylonians who revered them and built huge statues of them (Plate 9) as being 'repulsive abominations'. If ever anything argued the authenticity of their account, it was this Babylonian tradition that the amphibians to whom they owed everything were disgusting, horrible, and loathsome to look upon. A more normal course for any invented tradition of the origins of civilization would have been to glorify the splendid gods or heroes who founded it. But instead we find specific descriptions of 'animals endowed with reason' (Alexander Polyhistor's account) who make their awed and thankful beneficiaries want to be sick with revulsion. And what is more, the tradition admits this freely!

The problem of revulsion is a difficult one. It seems to be partly a result of what we are taught when young. No doubt psychologists would have a great deal more to say about it. But whatever origins it may have, it seems to be almost uncontrollable once a propensity to it has developed. If someone finds snakes or spiders repulsive, it would take a great deal of persuasion to get him to change his attitude, and the chances of success are minimal at best. As humans, we tend to dislike all slimy creatures, creepy-crawling creatures, creatures which ooze or slither or wriggle. Indeed, people who have a pronounced fondness for such creatures often seem to be suffering from a pathological condition themselves. I once knew a girl who kept a pet boa-constrictor in her bedroom, next to her bed for 'company'. She fed it a live mouse every Thursday and she loved to watch it being eaten alive. She loved more than anything to hear the snake at night in the dark when it made a curious slithering fall against the side of its tank; this excited her greatly. Now, I do not wish to criticize the girl for her strange tastes but I think most readers will agree that the girl had somehow transformed the interest in a snake into something else. And that kind of substitution is the promotion of a fantasy which can probably be classed as pathological, though possibly not dangerous to anyone (except the mice).

Granted all these circumstances of human relationships to slithery creatures and the problem of revulsion in general, it does strike me as a most superb irony that a race of intelligent beings may really exist in our near neighbourhood of space who are slimy and repulsive, and yet who have founded many of the elements of our own human civilization and have a technology sufficiently advanced to enable them to travel between the stars. Indeed, when all other pleasures in life fail, the one remaining is a delight in irony. I recommend it, both to men and Annedoti.

According to Berossus as preserved by Alexander Polyhistor, the amphibians look like this:

The whole body of the animal was like that of a fish; and had under a fish's head another head, and also feet below, similar to those of a man, subjoined to the fish's tail. His voice too, and language, was articulate and human; and a representation of him is preserved even to this day. . . . When the sun set, it was the custom of this Being to plunge again into the sea, and abide all night in the deep; for he was amphibious.

Who was Berossus, and how reliable was he? It is best to quote Cory's own preface for the information:

Berossus, a Babylonian, flourished in the reign of Alexander, and lived some time at Athens: and according to many wrote his Chaldaean history in the Greek language. As a priest of Belus he possessed every advantage, which the records of the temple and the learning and traditions of the Chaldaeans could afford; and seems to have composed his work with a serious regard for truth. He has sketched his history of the earlier times from the representations on the walls of the temples. from written records and traditionary knowledge, he learned several points too well authenticated to be called into question; and correcting the one by the other has produced the strange history before us. . . . The first book of the history opens naturally enough with a description of Babylonia. . . . The second book appears to have comprehended the history of the ante-diluvian world; and in this the two first fragments ought to have been inserted.

As for two of those later writers who preserve fragments of Berossus, Abydenus the disciple of Aristotle wrote an *Assyrian History*, now lost, and Megasthenes wrote an *Indian History*, also lost. None of the four writers who have preserved Berossian fragments has had any of his own writings survive intact either. Later writers such as Eusebius, the Christian historian of the fourth century A.D., and Syncellus, the ninth-century A.D. Byzantine historian, have preserved in turn all of the fragments of Berossus which the earlier writers had quoted in their own works. For it seems that the original of Berossus was lost long before the originals of Abydenus, Apollodorus, Megasthenes, and Alexander Polyhistor. And unless some obscure Byzantine monkish library or Egyptian papyrus of Hellenistic date or Babylonian tablet produces new fragments, we may never know more about Berossus than we do now at third hand. But at least my Appendix II should be a help. For it will be the first time since 1876 that the fragments of Berossus will have been published.[5]

Let us take a look now at what the Dogon tribe have to tell us about the amphibious creatures who are credited with founding their civilization as well, and who seem to have come from Sirius. In Figures 32 and 34 are Dogon tribal drawings of what the creatures actually looked like. They are credited with having descended in an ark which, in landing, looked like Figure 35 which portrays 'the spinning or whirling of the descent of the ark'. The god of the universe, Amma (whose name I feel certain is a survival of that of the god Ammon of the Oasis of Siwa), sent the amphibians to earth. They are called the Nommos. But just as the Babylonians tended to speak of Oannes, the leader, instead of always saying 'the Annedoti' collectively, the Dogon often just speak of 'Nommo' or 'the Nommo' as an individual. The Nommos are collectively called 'the Masters of the Water' and also 'the Instructors', or 'the Monitors'. They have to live in water: 'The Nommo's seat is in the water'.[6]

The latter is much like the Babylonian tradition of their god Ea (Enki to the Sumerians), whose seat was also in the water, and who is sometimes connected with Oannes.

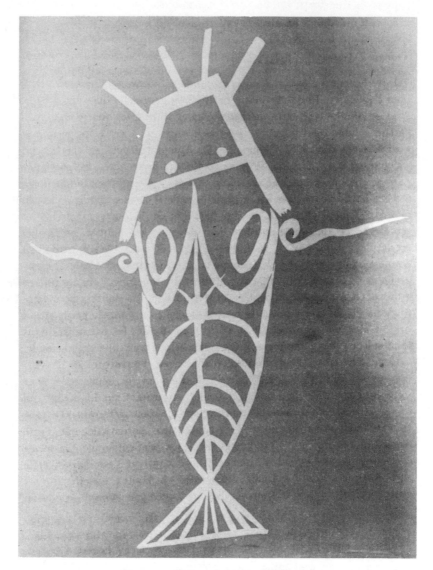

Figure 32. Dogon drawing of Nommo

The descriptions of the landing of the ark are extremely precise. The ark is said to have landed on the earth to the north-east of Dogon country,[7] which is where the Dogon claim to have come from (originally, before going to Mande) and that is, of course, the direction of Egypt and the Middle East in general.

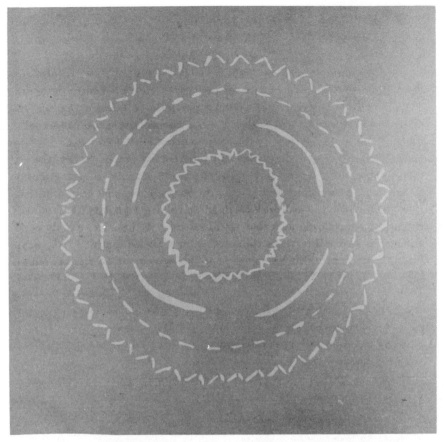

Figure 33. Descent of Nommo from the sky. Dogon drawing

The Dogon describe the sound of the landing of the ark. They say the 'word' of Nommo was cast down by him in the four directions as he descended,* and it sounded like the echoing of the four large stone blocks being struck with stones by the children, according to special rhythms, in a very small cave near Lake Debo.[8] Presumably a thunderous vibrating sound is what the Dogon are trying to convey. One can imagine standing in the cave and holding one's ears at the noise. The descent of the ark must have sounded like a jet runway at close range.

The landing of the ark is visually described:[9] 'The ark landed on the Fox's dry land and displaced a pile of dust raised by the whirlwind it caused.' For this, see Figure 33. They continue: 'The violence of the impact roughened the ground . . . it skidded on the ground.'

* The reader will recall that near the end of Chapter One I mentioned that 'the word' represents a concept like the *logos* to the Dogon, for it means 'air'. We may take this description to refer not only to noise but to a rushing wind.

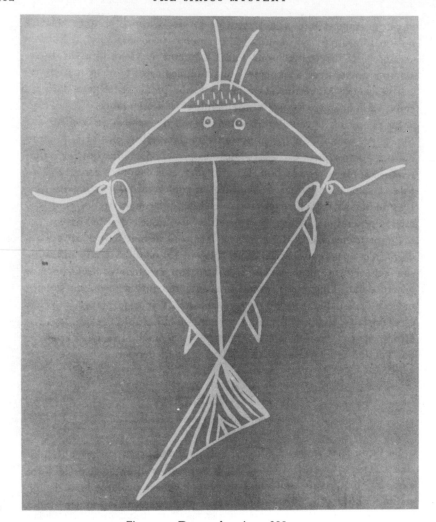

Figure 34. Dogon drawing of Nommo

It is said of Nommo, or more probably of his ark: 'He is like a flame that went out when he touched the earth'. They say: 'The Nommo was "as red as fire" . . . when he landed, he became white'.[10] And consequently a bit of folk-lore: 'The albino is the testament on Earth of the Nommo's burns as he came down; he is said to be the "trace of the burn", the scar of the Nommo.'[11]

There seems to be a use by the Dogon of 'spurting blood' to describe what we would call 'rocket exhaust'. And let us remember that, short of anti-gravity machines (which may be impossible), rocket propulsion is likely to be used by craft landing on any planet, no matter how sophisticated and non-rocket-like the interstellar main craft, or no matter how immensely advanced the civiliza-tion may be which is making a landing on a planet. For the principle of

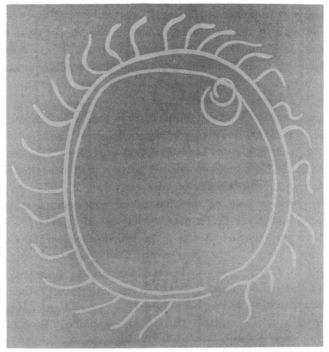

Figure 35. The whirling descent of the spaceship of Nommo. Dogon drawing

the rocket is a simple one unlikely to be dispensed with entirely in any foreseeable future technology. Actually, the Dogon seem to make a clear differentiation between the ark in which the Nommos actually landed on earth and what we may surmise was the true interstellar spaceship hovering above in the sky at a great distance, and which the Dogon seem to describe as appearing in the sky as a new star, and leaving with the Nommos at their departure from Earth. In fact, this is the sort of arrangement one would expect. An interstellar spaceship would probably look like a bright new star, possibly visible in daytime as well as by night, and the landing craft would be simple rocket-propelled craft not so different in principle from machines which we use at the present time for landing on the moon.

At this point I should make it clear that I do not believe that spaceships from extraterrestrial civilizations are flitting through the skies at this moment. I am not a 'flying saucer' enthusiast. I do not believe that spacecraft would behave in the erratic fashion in which UFOs behave. It makes no sense to me that spacecraft would fly idly around making spectacles of themselves – and ambiguous spectacles at that – for years on end. If we went to another inhabited planet, would we waste either time or resources on such apparent nonsense? What seems to be lacking in UFOs is purpose, of any kind, which could conceivably fit into a framework of extraterrestrial visitation. So I therefore do not believe that 'flying saucers' are spacecraft, although I am willing to admit I may be wrong. I have encountered nothing but flak from both sides about this –

Figure 36. Dogon drawing of *ie pelu tolo*; the ten rays, in pairs, are inside the circle, having not yet 'emerged'.

believers in flying saucers are incredulous that I am not one of them, since I have written a book on extraterrestrials and I even maintain that spaceships visited Earth in the past; those who do not entertain for one moment the notion that spaceships could ever have visited the Earth naturally assume that my book is about flying saucers. I should add, however, that I feel certain that the Earth is being monitored at this moment by a more advanced extra-terrestrial civilization, and I assume this monitoring must be by automatic computer probes left behind in this solar system at some time in the past. Although I consider most so-called UFO sightings as pure hysteria or simple error, it is possible that a small percentage of UFOs may be what the devout 'believers' in UFOs claim they are. It is unfortunate that this subject has become so burdened by the oppressive enthusiasm of people whom I can only describe by the unflattering epithet of 'the lunatic fringe'.

The Dogon may describe the interstellar spaceship hovering high above the Earth by what they call *ie pelu tolo*, 'star of the tenth moon'. The Dogon say: 'As (the ark) landed, the weight of the ark caused the "blood" to spurt to the sky'.[12] This would seem to be a rocket craft landing on earth. But this 'spurting blood' (flame?) is said to be shared with *ie pelu tolo*, and 'gave the star reality and brilliance'.[13] For three different complementary tribal drawings of *ie pelu tolo*, see Figure 37. These seem to represent the 'star' in three separate conditions, differing in the amount of 'spurting blood' being emitted by the presumed spacecraft. The Dogon also describe this 'star' specifically as having a circle of reddish rays around it, and this circle of rays is 'like a spot spreading' but remaining the same size.[14]

It is said that the Nommos will come again. There will be a 'resurrection of the Nommo'. It should thus not surprise us that 'the celestial symbol of the resurrection is the "star of the tenth moon", *ie pelu tolo* . . . This star is not easy to see. . . . The ten rays, placed in pairs, are inside the circle because the star

Figure 37. Three states of *ie pelu tolo* in the sky. Dogon drawing

has not yet "emerged"; it will be formed when the Nommo's ark descends, for it is also the resurrected Nommo's "eye" symbolically.'[15] In other words, the 'star' is not a star, and can only be seen when the Nommo returns and his ark descends to Earth.

The Nommo is 'the monitor for the universe, the "father" of mankind, guardian of its spiritual principles, dispenser of rain and master of the water generally.'[16] Not all the Nommos came to Earth. The 'one' called Nommo Die, or 'Great Nommo', remained 'in heaven with Amma, and he is his vicar'.[17] He manifests himself in the rainbow, which is called 'path of the Nommo'.[18] He is guardian of the 'spiritual principles of living creatures on Earth'.[19]

There are three other distinct kinds of Nommo, each personified as an individual. There is the Nommo Titiyayne, 'messenger (or deputy) of the Nommo Die . . . he (executes) the latter's great works.'[20] The Nommos who came to earth in the spaceship are presumably of this class. Figures 32 and 34 represent these beings in particular.

A third class of Nommos are represented by O Nommo, 'Nommo of the pond'. 'He will be sacrificed for the purification and reorganization of the

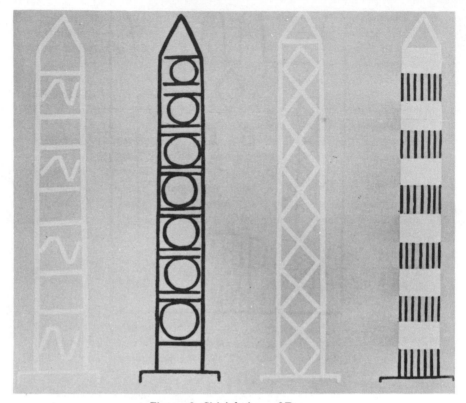

Figure 38. Sirigi designs of Dogon

universe . . . He will rise in human form and descend on Earth, in an ark, with the ancestors of men . . . then he will take on his original form, will rule from the waters and will give birth to many descendants.'[21]

The fourth Nommo is the naughty disrupter named Ogo, or Nommo Anagonno. 'As he was about to be finished (being created) he rebelled against his creator and introduced disorder into the universe. Eventually, he will become the Pale Fox (le Renard pâle) which is the image of his fall.'[22] In many ways, the Fox resembles the Egyptian deity Set.

The name Nommo comes from a Dogon word linked to the root *nōmo*, 'to make one drink'. It is said: 'The Nommo divided his body among men to feed them; that is why it is also said that as the universe "had drunk of his body" the Nommo also made men drink. He also gave all his life principles to human beings.'[23] He was crucified on a *kilena* tree which also died and was resurrected.[24]

After the ark had landed, according to the Dogon, an interesting series of events took place which make a great deal of sense if one remembers that amphibious creatures were inside. Something described both as a 'horse' and just simply as a 'quadruped' appeared which pulled the ark with ropes to a hollow.[25] 'This stage, momentarily, transformed the ark into a chariot drawn by a quadruped with ropes.'[26] The hollow then filled with water. However, an untoward incident then occurred: 'After the first rainfall, when the water had filled the pond, the water-insect . . . entered the water . . . it wanted to "bite" the Nommo's head . . . but it was unable to reach the edge of the ark.'[27]

> The bad 'water-insect' was thus unsuccessful in wishing to do harm. When the water filled the pond, the ark floated on it like a huge pirogue. . . . It is said: 'The great ark came out of the sky and came down. In the centre the Nommo was standing, he came down. Then he returned to the water.' . . . From then on he was called O Nommo, 'Nommo of the pond', – through respect men will not utter this name, but will call him instead *dì tigi*, 'master of the water'.[28]

Thus we see that the second and third categories of Nommo are really the same, but represent successive states. And as for the future:

> His twin who will descend later on with the Blacksmith, 'twin of the victim', will also be transformed in the pond. They will have many descendants and will always be present in the fresh 'male' water of the brooks, rivers, ponds and wells and also in the 'female' sea water.[29]

As for this reference to fresh water as male and sea water as female, it is similar to the ancient Babylonian and Sumerian tradition where Apsu (Abzu) was a male fresh-water deity and Tiamat a female sea-water deity. The Dogon say,[30] 'O Nommo has his seat in the waters of the earth', which could just as well be a description of Enki/Ea, whom I mentioned above.

I feel impelled to reproduce in this book as Figure 38 a Dogon drawing showing four variants of the Dogon *sirigi* mask design. Anyone can see that they look like rocket ships. Griaule and Dieterlen give[31] detailed accounts of the meanings of the lozenges, rectangles, etc. These variant designs are said specifically all to represent 'the descent and impact of the ark'.[32] The descent of the ark was like a lozenge, its impact was like a rectangle.[33] Perhaps this is why the Dogon say: 'When the ark was descending, space was four angles; when the ark was down, space had four sides.'[34] The *sirigi* design itself represents 'a "house with stories" . . . (and) indicates the ark as well as its descent.'[35] So maybe the Dogon have actually drawn a rocket ship.

The Dogon say[36] that '*po tolo* (Sirius B) and Sirius were once where the sun now is'. That seems as good a way as any to describe coming to our solar system from the Sirius system, and leaving those stars for our star, the sun. But let us now take leave of our friends the Dogon. Let us go to where Sirius and its white dwarf companion star are the suns, and where our own sun has become just another star in the sky. Let us visit the planet of the amphibians.

What are Sirius and Sirius B like as suns? We know that they revolve around a common centre, which is in fact equivalent to Sirius B revolving around Sirius A in an elliptical orbit. Sirius A, a big, bright star, has two and a half times the mass of our sun. Sirius B has ninety-five per cent of the mass of our sun, but because it is made of degenerate matter and is so tiny, this is not obvious. If Sirius B with its mass were not a white dwarf, we could easily see it from earth as a star of magnitude 2, though the problem of parallax would make it difficult to separate it from Sirius A. In any case, if Sirius B were on its own somewhere at its distance from earth, and were not a white dwarf, it would be one of the brightest stars in the sky.

In reality, Sirius A is ten thousand times brighter than Sirius B. The luminosity of Sirius A is thirty-five and a half times the luminosity of our sun. That makes it a pretty hot number. We can be certain that our planet is not too near it. The 'habitable zone' discussed in Chapter One is much farther out from Sirius than it is from our sun. As for the actual size of Sirius A, its radius is a little more than one and a half times the sun's radius. This means that Sirius will be smaller in the sky than our own sun, seen from the planet. It will be a good deal smaller, but will need to have roughly the same amount of heat, which is not too difficult, considering how terribly hot and bright it is. To us it would be a strange experience to see such a small body in the sky giving out so much heat and light. Looking directly at it would probably be as injurious as staring into an arc lamp. All the more reason to be under water, and not so tempted.

Our planet will probably be quite hot. In fact, it will probably even be covered with a vaporous layer of cloud at most or all times. It might look something like Venus from a distance, though of course Venus does not have temperatures or clouds of the sort which living creatures are likely to find agreeable. It would seem important to keep cool on this probably rather hot and steamy planet. Therefore intelligent life is likely to have evolved as amphibious and never have taken to the land. These amphibians might easily inhabit the surface of the water, of course, for they would need to breathe atmosphere and would not have gills like fish – they would probably need to be mammals of some kind in order to develop the brain sizes and other characteristics necessary for intelligence. They would probably spend a lot of time hanging about marshes and might have developed an indigenous way of life originally which involved the use of woven reeds for huts and transport, and so on. (They would long ago have got past that stage, of course.) But perhaps their first style of life, to which they may even look back with some nostalgia as 'the good old days of simplicity and a carefree existence', was something like that described by Wilfred Thesiger in his book *The Marsh Arabs*[37] in which the inhabitants of southern Iraq are pictured in the marshes of the lower Tigris and Euphrates (quite near where Oannes and his friends are said to have spent most of the time, one is tempted to note!).

If you were one of these creatures, you would be a good deal like a dolphin with arms and hands. You would, due to your amphibian nature, have a separate blowhole for breathing in adition to your mouth. You would be able to hold your breath for long periods, and when you did breathe through your blowhole, it would be a gasp and make a bit of noise. Your blowhole would open and close almost instantaneously and your breathing would tend to be infrequent but loud and quick. The blowhole might be placed in such a way that it consisted of one or of two small slits, long and thin, just beneath your clavicles (collarbones). In fact, the Dogon have a tradition that their Nommos breathed through their clavicles.[38]

You could not go about bare-skinned in any atmosphere for long. You would require moisture on your skin after a few hours at the most; when your

Figure 39. The Nommo breathes through air-holes in his clavicles that look like this Dogon drawing

skin dried you would be in absolute agony – worse than a human with sunburn. Because you would frequent the surface of the water a great deal, there would inevitably be a considerable contrast between the top half of your body and the bottom half. The tradition known to us of the mermaid expresses this state of affairs quite well. Your lower extremities would be quite fishlike, but you would have articulate limbs and fingers on your upper half and your skin would be more capable of resisting solar radiations and hence would be more like that of a land mammal. Probably cartilaginous structures would have evolved in your head to rigidify your features beyond the simple streamlined form required for a strictly undersea life, and there would be something on your upper body resembling hair – perhaps like the hair of our own walruses.

Your teeth would probably be feeble compared with those of ferocious carnivores such as sharks. You would probably have evolved from more peaceful creatures capable of feeding on small fish in considerable numbers. Your ancestors would have run in packs as the dolphins do and you would be extremely sociable because you evolved in schools (packs). Nudity is probably the natural state of your species. Overpopulation is not one of your problems because most of your planet is water and all of the water is habitable. Even on the planet Earth, it is estimated that dolphins outnumber human beings two-to-one, and the oceans are hardly overcrowded.

As one of these creatures, you might find human beings repulsive, for many reasons. Their rough hair, dry skins, bony limbs, and particularly their pungent smells might disturb you greatly. Their sweat is not continually washed away in the way that your skin is continually cleansed by the watery medium which you inhabit. And as an amphibian you have exceedingly well developed senses of smell and taste. You 'taste' smells or spoor-substances underwater at enormous distances and though your sense of smell is not quite as acute, it is competent enough. Unlike yourself, human beings tend to have areas in or near their dwellings which smell of their excrement and urine – places to which they habitually return to perform these functions. As an amphibian whose waste products dissipate in the water, you find such an idea revolting. How can human beings stand going back to those same odours day after day?

One of the most disturbing sights to you is to watch human beings walking.

When humans stand still with their legs together, they look almost normal. But then suddenly they 'split' into two and begin walking, which makes you slightly dizzy and upsets you. It makes you feel nervous with the thought of how dreadful it would be for you if you 'split' and thereby became a cripple in the water. You admire the agility of the humans on dry land. They can climb trees and cliffs, all of which is terribly impressive. They can go at a great speed on land with what they call 'running', they even have a certain capacity to jump over obstacles; they are not as swift on land as you are in water, but they do passably well. You do have difficulty in seeing them sometimes because, as you are in a watery environment, your vision is not good at long range. And the humans, being dry, do not stand out against their background as much as you could wish. When they move you can instantly detect motion without optical definition, but a stationary human who is even approximately camouflaged and blends with this background is impossible for you to differentiate with your unaided eye. You rely on your sense of smell, like a rhinoceros. But when the wind is against you, you have no hope. A human can easily elude your perception on dry land if he knows what he is doing and you do not have your goggles or technical aids with you.

You would have an extremely agile mathematical mind. Your ancestors developed from the primitive state by computing the intricate astronomical phenomena and radiations falling on your planet without benefit of direct optical observations. The brains of your species were thus engendered to conceive and solve vast intricate abstractions. Your powers of holding complicated mathematical structures suspended in your mind's eye while performing mathematical operations on them is extraordinary. You have a phenomenal conceptual and generalizing faculty. It is easy for you to conceive of invisible, and even imperceptible, forces, because your daily environment is a suggestive, allusive one. You taste and smell your ambience rather than see it. Your powers of telepathy may be extremely highly evolved – possibly a characteristic of your species from their earliest history.

The climate range of your planet is greater even than the Earth's because there are no ice caps, due to there being more radiation from the two or three stars in your multi-solar system. Your oceans are all the more extensive, therefore, for not being locked up in ice caps at the poles.

Space flight is less uncomfortable for you than for humans, as the state of weightlessness is often approximated under water (indeed, on Earth the astronauts train under water). Your blood circulation is thus better suited to the weightless condition than is the case with humans and you do not at all mind living in the gigantic water tanks orbiting your planet which constitute your many satellite space cities. It is not as difficult to simulate a watery environment in space as it is to simulate a dry land environment. Your wants are few, your existence simple. You do not eat cooked food and you do not have stoves to keep warm. Farming for you is mostly the breeding of delicious small fish, and meals are an adventure as you love a good chase and the satisfaction of catching your food. Dinner is a family sport.

The amphibians must have a name, and the Dogon name for them of 'the Monitors' may be the best to consider using. 'Monitor' is more specific than 'Instructor', and 'Masters of the Water' is too long. There is no point using the euphemism the 'Annedoti', knowing that it means the 'Repulsive Ones'. A more generic and neutral term, I suppose, would be simply the 'Sirians'. If we ever come into contact with them again, they will probably be called the 'Sirians' officially, and their civilization will be the 'Sirian civilization'. Their art will fall under the heading of 'Sirian culture' and their technology will be 'Sirian technology'. But what about their religion? There's a delicate point. It will be called the 'Sirian religion' and we will try to pretend it has nothing to do with us. But inevitably we will have to take into account that, whereas 'cultures' and 'technologies' can be localized, the greater problems of the nature of life itself and of an individual's relation to the universe – existential problems – are not localizable. There will in fact be no such ultimate thing as 'Sirian religion' except in the ethnographic sense. To speak of a 'Sirian' God will get us into deep waters. What do we mean when we speak of a 'Jewish' God or a 'Christian' God? There is no doubt that it is at the level of our deepest concerns – our religious and philosophical ones – that contact with an extraterrestrial civilization will make its deepest impact on us. And it is at this friable level of our preconceptions that we are most vulnerable. Here the foundations of our beliefs can crumble with the first shock wave. Here the entire edifice of our civilization can give way. Only by being prepared can we safeguard our own cultural integrity.

We must not dismiss speculations such as those we have just indulged ourselves in as idle, thinking that we will wait and see what turns up in a spaceship some day. If we are going to be coming into direct contact with amphibious extraterrestrials, we should try to get some thoughts together on their physical nature and requirements at the very least – if only to make them welcome. It is quite true, as Carl Sagan says: '. . . stories like the Oannes legend . . . deserve much more critical studies than have been performed heretofore.'[39] The critical studies should be institutionalized by the governments of the major powers, and made official programmes. The resources of the governments which pour into programmes to prevent their countries being overrun by military invasions, chemical warfare, nuclear blasts, should also pour into programmes to prevent our planet as a whole being overrun by a sudden extraterrestrial contact which gives little warning. No matter how much care may be taken by any superior extraterrestrial civilization in dealing with us, it is really up to us to be ready for any contact. I would even venture that we may be under observation or surveillance at this very moment, with an extraterrestrial civilization based at the Sirius system monitoring our development to see when we will *ready ourselves* for their contacting us. In other words, we may very possibly be allowed to control the forthcoming contact ourselves. One wonders what any possible amphibious extraterrestrials living at Sirius would think roughly ten years later (speed of radio transmission at speed of light – across ten light years means a ten-year lag) upon receiving news from some automatic monitoring device which picked up a radio or television programme at Earth mentioning a book just published about amphibious extraterrestrials living at Sirius. Would they think that was their cue? If what I propose in this book really is true, then am I pulling a cosmic trigger?

When this book was accepted for publication, the managing director of the publishing company asked me to his office for our first meeting. He had personally decided to accept the book and he had himself read it. On this basis his first question to me was: 'Mr Temple, do you believe it? Do you believe it *yourself*?' My answer was: 'Yes, I do. I have become convinced by my own re-search. In the beginning I was just investigating. I was sceptical. I was looking for hoaxes, thinking it couldn't be true. But then I began to discover more and more pieces which fit. And the answer is *yes, I believe it*.'

The information in this book cannot really rest with publication. I hope that many people will take an interest in exploring the ramifications of what I have here presented. This process has already begun, some months before publication. Portions or versions of this book have been read by a number of people already, nearly all of whom have made valuable comments on the material. With a subject like this which is new, fresh insights are possible from almost anyone. The least educated person might have the most profound thought on some aspect of this question. But primarily it is from the highly qualified professionals that progress should come. Astronomers in particular must deal with this material. Fortunately, they are an open-minded community, perhaps due to the open-ended nature of the universe which it is their job to study.

It may be of interest to the reader to see an example of a reaction to this book by an eminent astronomer who is internationally known in his field. Professor W. H. McCrea, F.R.S., Emeritus Professor of Astronomy at the University of Sussex and a former President of the Royal Astronomical Society, read an early draft of the book. Though a great deal of the book is changed since then, I nevertheless quote portions of his reactions in a letter to me dated 20 August 1973:

My reaction is:
A. The special interest of Egyptians and others in Sirius is well known and you have made a strong case (as I think the people you quote have done) for supposing that the Dogon interest in Sirius is connected with this.

B. In your very clever investigations of Egyptian, Sumerian, Greek . . . myths, you seem to have shown that some of these people *may* have had ideas about a dark, dense star possibly associated with Sirius. But, as I say, anything beyond that seems to me not established.

C. In spite of all this, if you will allow me to say so, I think your investi-gations are fascinating and they make an exciting book.

D. Your work does appear to bring out more strongly than ever the *impression* that, as you say, ancient cultures did not develop gradually. I do not know whether this impression is significant, but it bears investi-gation. I cannot see how it could have anything to do with space travellers. But you may think it right to argue the case. [Unfortunately none of the material in Chapter Eight of this book was known to Dr McCrea when he wrote this, for it was added in a later version of the book, as was much more.]

I may add that I realize that some of the matters about which you write may have been mysteries of religion, and so it may be hopeless to expect anything more explicit than what you describe. Also, as you say, there seems to have been a liking for puns. So it could be that the revelations by the Dogon tell us what has been left secret for 6,000 years. . . . To some extent, I am being *advocatus diaboli* so that maybe I am letting you see the sort of thing you will be up against when your work is published.

A great many of the criticisms which I have not quoted were dealt with in the complete rewrite of the book which took place after Professor McCrea and others had kindly blasted me with specific points. I was less fortunate in obtaining such comments from authorities on the ancient world.

On the whole it is the astronomical community who have shown the most interest in this matter, for it is they who are directly concerned with such a subject. And no astronomer has contributed a more detailed appraisal of the actual Dogon accounts than Dr Irving W. Lindenblad of the U.S. Naval Observatory in Washington, who in a letter to me dated 14 June 1974, made these comments:

I agree that one should think twice before disagreeing with the Dogon. From an astronomical viewpoint, however, there are difficulties with the Dogon's suggestion of a third Sirius component having a period of 32 or 50 yrs., yet having a 'greater trajectory'. Kepler's third law states that the squares of the orbital periods are proportional to the cubes of the orbital semimajor axes. Thus, a 'greater trajectory' must be accompanied by a greater period.

Among the numerous observed triple systems of stars circling a common center of gravity, it has been found that the third member *always* has a *much* greater distance and period than the other two components. Celestial mechanics illuminates this phenomenon by demonstrating that a triple system is unstable if the two secondary stars are nearly equidistant from the system's center of gravity.

If the periods of B (Digitaria) and C (*emme ya*) are similar, as stated by the Dogon, their orbits must have similar dimensions (Kepler's Law). But this constitutes an unstable system (celestial mechanics) and it would also contradict the Dogon's thesis that *emme ya* has a 'greater trajectory'.

The Dogon must have realized that the orbital radii of Digitaria and *emme ya* could not remain at right angles with one another unless the periods were the same. If he did, this would constitute an argument in favour of accepting the tradition assigning a 50 yr. period to *emme ya*, as opposed to the tradition assigning a period of 32 years.

As to the diagrams to be found in this book, Figures 6 and 7, showing the comparison between Dogon tribal and modern astronomical conceptions of the relative orbits of Sirius A and Sirius B, Lindenblad, who has been studying the Sirius system for seven years, comments on them in a letter dated 7 March 1974:

'Regarding your orbital diagrams of Sirius, my work would not affect them at all. The changes I have been dealing with involve very minute quantities which can be detected only in large telescopes and even with such instruments a great amount of observation is required.'

Dr Lindenblad had not read this book prior to going to press, although he did read the Griaule and Dieterlen account of the Dogon Sirius system and see the diagrams. As for Professor McCrea, he had discovered quite independently of my own work that the Dogon knew of the existence of an invisible companion star to Sirius. He was informed of this by a friend in Argentina who had read a French account, which mentioned Griaule and Dieterlen's work. McCrea has spent a considerable amount of time analysing the Dogon tradition, but I leave to him an exposition of his own views when the full material is available to him, which it has not been to date. (Indeed, I received a great deal of it after the book was written and therefore I had to rewrite the book to incorporate it. The new material all served to strengthen rather than weaken my thesis.)

In considering the material set forth in this book, I hope that serious scholars will bear in mind that the existence of amphibious beings with high intelligence and advanced civilization is not a previously unheard of idea. As far back as 1966, in their book *Intelligence in the Universe*, Roger MacGowan and Frederick Ordway wrote:[40]

Little can be said specifically about universal physical characteristics . . . life, especially the more intelligent forms, tends to be physically small, discrete, and highly mobile. . . . Humans, being land animals, tend to think in terms of land animals when considering intelligence, but we know that the sea contains a great variety of life. Moreover, all evidence points to the conclusion that the primordial seas were probably the site of the origin of life. Oceans provide an excellent environment for animal life and the competition between many species should encourage rapid evolution.

A liquid environment provides more buoyancy and support for animal bodies than does an atmospheric gas. For this reason the marine environment may be expected to develop many species that are larger than most land animal species. Knowing that larger bodies can support larger brains one might expect to find superior intelligence among the larger marine animals.

Considering this larger potential size, the great variety of life, the good stable environment of the oceans, and the competition among species, one is at first tempted to assume that the majority of intelligent extrasolar life would be marine. . . . Fins, ideal for ocean locomotion, are not well suited to developing tools (and thereby brains). However, a few ocean species have developed other appendages more suited to tool manipulation. The octopus is a very well known ocean creature which could conceivably develop tool manipulation capability with further evolution. Some other ocean floor creatures could develop the equivalent of human arms and hands. . . . The patently high intelligence of certain whales and dolphins raises the question as to whether tool manipulating appendages are really vital to the development of superior intelligence. And it makes it difficult to say whether some intelligent extrasolar life may be marine rather than land dwelling. . . . We conclude that the majority of intelligent biological species will not differ greatly in gross morphological characteristics when compared to humans. They can be expected to range from less than half the size of a human to several times larger, and they should be expected to have, in most case, two legs and two arms with hands and fingers. In a

few cases centaur-like animals having four legs and two arms with hands
and fingers, or elephant-like animals having four legs and one arm or a
trunk might be possible. Another possibility is some form of marine life
having fins and two short arms with large hands and webbed fingers.

As I remarked in Chapter One and now I mention again, it may well be that
Sirius C follows a figure-eight orbit around both Sirius A and Sirius B alternately. Perhaps its total orbital period is 50 years and its larger loop period is 32
years. It may orbit in a plane which is at right angles to the plane of Sirius B's
orbit. It would genuinely be a 'greater trajectory' because its figure-eight would
encompass both of the other stars, but its actual distance and time would still
obey Kepler's third law and would not exceed those of Sirius B with the same
period. Indeed, the identity of the periods of Sirius B and Sirius C might be a
synchronous phenomenon lending stability to such a complex system. The
Dogon seem to claim that the planet on which the amphibians live elliptically
orbits the star *emme ya*, Sirius C. What is required now is a great deal of calculation by a professional astronomer to consider the amount of radiation to which
a planet would be exposed following the star Sirius C in a figure-eight orbit
of the kind I have proposed. Would life be possible on such a body? The
astronomer Su-Shu Huang has written an essay 'Life Supporting Regions
in the Vicinity of Binary Systems' which appears in the book *Interstellar Communication.* [41] This essay examines the conditions under which planets supporting life can exist in systems with more than one sun. I reproduce as Figure 40

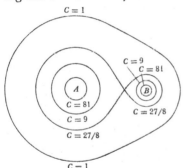

Figure 40. Dr Su-Shu Huang's diagram for possible
orbits of habitable planet in binary star system.
A and B are stars. The curves with different values
for C are suggested orbits, one of which is a figure-
eight configuration. The most recent suggestion by
an astronomer that habitable planets could exist
without difficulty in binary or multiple star systems
is that of Dr B. M. Oliver, 'Proximity of Galactic
Civilizations', in ICARUS, 25, 360–7 (1975),
noticed at time of going finally to press

his diagram showing the general orbits of planets capable of supporting life in
binary systems. Notice that one such orbit is a figure-eight exactly of the kind
I suggest for Sirius C, with its accompanying planet. However, this kind of
orbit would more probably be unstable. It is a possibility, but if it has existed
at one stage, it would probably have collapsed into some other configuration
after a short time – long before life could have evolved in the Sirius system. Dr
Paul Murdin of the Royal Greenwich Observatory summed the situation up
brilliantly when he said that a coin, when tossed, may indeed land on its edge;
but even if it does, it will soon topple over, so that the probabilities for a tossed
coin landing on its edge become meaningless in real situations. Our figure-8
orbit therefore probably cannot exist as a permanently stable feature of the
Sirius system, no matter how attractive it may be to us in theory. But my idea
of an orbit for Sirius C at right angles to the plane of Sirius B's motion (but

without the figure-8) was, I was assured by Murdin, probably the ideal solution. For the hypothetical star could penetrate the Sirius B plane of motion in a vast range of places without disrupting Sirius B's orbit, as long as the perpendicularity of the two planes of motion was retained. A 50-year or 32-year elliptical orbit for Sirius C, therefore, in a plane perpendicular to that of Sirius B's orbit is entirely possible. These multiple star motions involve such complicated celestial mechanics that the necessary computations are well beyond the competence of most professional astronomers. Only certain specialist astronomers are capable of such work. Plottings have been made of the possible orbits for third stars in certain binary systems, and at the time of going finally to press, I am seeking the views of R. S. Harrington, S.-S. Huang, and D. Lauterborn on these hypothetical problems. Harrington has demonstrated that a triple-star system is stable under conditions where the perisastron distance in outer orbit divided by the semi-major axis of inner orbit is not less than 3.5 if the orbit is direct or 2.75 if it is retrograde. Bearing this in mind, Dr Paul Murdin of the Royal Greenwich Observatory concludes: 'There seems no reason to me why there should not be a Sirius C, say another white dwarf, at a distance from Sirius A of four hundred times the radius of our Sun, with orbital plane in the plane of the sky so as not to perturb the radial velocity of Sirius A.' And he says that 'its orbit will precess in time due to B, but with a period larger than the period of B, so we may be unlucky at this time in not seeing the perturbations.' (This refers to Lindenblad's negative results.)

In closing, I wish to make a final point of considerable importance. Let us assume that what I have proposed in this book really is true. Let us grant all the premises. Say that there really is an advanced civilization based at the Sirius system. No doubt we are under routine monitoring. No doubt they know by now roughly where we stand on the ladder of evolution. They have picked up our radio signals. They know we have been to the moon. Let us assume they wish us well. Let us assume even that they contact us someday when they think we are ready for it – or after we have discovered them by examining the Sirius system as I suggest and finding evidences of their existence.

Let us assume all this. Well, if that day comes – or if it doesn't and if some other day comes, some other civilization some day is known to us at some other star – there is one thing we must not forget. We must remember that no matter how grand and glorious *they* may be, they are still mortal beings in a universe which to them is still mysterious. They cannot and never will know all the answers. We may very well have a handful of answers that they have not. We may have some quirky skills which they cannot attain. We may have some peculiar native ingenuity which they lack, even if this is not obvious for centuries. There may be something about us that is so valuable that we are not just worthless primitives beside them. Let us never accept a view of ourselves as recipients of cosmic charity. We are men, and for all our faults, we have a few things about us which are worth some attention. We have had some remarkable characters in our history and we will have more. Whatever one's views of what lies beyond death – extinction, reincarnation, heaven and hell – the genetic stream goes on. There will be more men, and there will be great ones. We can rise to challenges. We have demonstrated courage throughout our history. Any superior civilizations may have even more superior civilizations behind them of whom they are curious. Let us not forget the principles of hierarchy, let us never blind ourselves to the possibility of a door behind the door behind the door. And if we ever find ourselves oppressed, let us be certain that there are others – somewhere – who would free us. The universe is finite but unbounded. There are between ten and a hundred million intelligent civilizations in our galaxy alone, in all likelihood. And there is always one more to contact than the one we have already contacted. We can afford to shop around in a shop the size of the universe.

Notes

1. The reader may wonder if the name of the Dogon tribe is in any way connected with the names 'Dagon' and 'Odacon'. This is pure speculation but not unlikely in my opinion.
2. See Appendix II, for reference.
3. With I. S. Shklovskii. Dell, New York, 1966. See Chapter 33.
4. For instance, by Kenneth Demarest in *Consciousness and Reality*, p. 351.
5. See end of Appendix II and the Bibliography. Thomas Stanley in his *The History of the Chaldaick Philosophy*, London, 1662, p. 12, notes some additional interesting information about the family of Berossus by telling us: 'A daughter of this Berossus is mention'd by Justin Martyr, a Babylonian Sibyl, who prophesied at Cumae . . .' On p. 10 Stanley describes Berossus as the man 'who first introduced Chaldaick learning into Greece'.

6. *Le Renard pâle*, p. 462.
7. Ibid., p. 458.
8. Ibid., p. 460.
9. Ibid., p. 440.
10. Ibid., p. 441.
11. Ibid., p. 441.
12. Ibid., p. 440.
13. Ibid., p. 440.
14. Ibid., p. 440.
15. Ibid., pp. 309–10.
16. Ibid., pp. 309–10.
17. Ibid., pp. 156–60.
18. Ibid., pp. 156–60.
19. Ibid., pp. 156–60.
20. Ibid., pp. 156–60.
21. Ibid., pp. 157–60.
22. Ibid., pp. 157–60.
23. Ibid., p. 287.
24. Ibid., p. 287.
25. Ibid., p. 444.
26. Ibid., pp. 444–5.
27. Ibid., pp. 444–5.
28. Ibid., pp. 444–5.
29. Ibid., pp. 444–5.
30. Ibid., p. 506.
31. Ibid., p. 439.
32. Ibid., p. 438.
33. Ibid., pp. 437–9.
34. Ibid., p. 436.
35. Ibid., pp. 436–9.
36. Ibid., p. 474.
37. *The Marsh Arabs* by Wilfred Thesiger, Penguin Books, London, 1967; and originally Longmans Green, London, 1964.
38. *Le Renard pâle*, p. 370.
39. Sagan and Shklovskii, op. cit., p. 461. (It is not true, as he says on p. 460, the previous page, that 'the idea of planets circling suns and stars is an idea which essentially originated with Copernicus', as anyone reading Appendix One will see.)
40. MacGowan, Roger, and Ordway, Frederick. *Intelligence in the Universe*, Prentice-Hall Inc., New Jersey, U.S.A., 1966, pp. 242–4.
41. *Interstellar Communication*, ed. by A. G. W. Cameron, op. cit., p. 93. Dr. Huang is currently of the Dearborn Observatory at Northwestern University in the U.S.A.

The Moons of the Planets, the Planets around Stars, and Revolutions and Rotations of Bodies in Space – Described by the Neoplatonic Philosopher Proclus

'. . . In each of the planetary spheres there are invisible stars which revolve together with their spheres . . .' So said Proclus the Platonic successor in A.D. 438.

The non-specialist reader will never have heard of Proclus, one of the greatest intellects in the history of philosophy, who lived from A.D. 410 to 485. The only easily available English translation of this Greek philosopher's gigantic output is his *Elements of Theology*[1] (which is not relevant to what we are to consider here). But the persistent inquirer may obtain his *Commentary on Euclid*[2] and his *Commentary on the First Alcibiades of Plato*[3] in English (the former from America, the latter from Holland). And from Liechtenstein one may now obtain in English the end of the seventh book of his *Commentary on the Parmenides of Plato*.[4]

What the persistent inquirer will likely *not* be told by any compendium of information on the subject is that most of the works of Proclus were translated into English by Thomas Taylor at the turn of the eighteenth and nineteenth centuries in England and are to be found in a handful of libraries (though even the British Museum has a far from complete collection of Taylor's life's work).

Perhaps it would be as well to quote the view of Proclus held by Thomas Taylor. One should bear in mind that Taylor was the first man to translate all of Plato's works into English – a mammoth task indeed, but not as wearying as translating most of Proclus! Here, then, is what Taylor says of Proclus:

> To the lovers of the wisdom of the Greeks, any remains of the writings of Proclus will always be invaluable, as he was a man who, for the variety of his powers, the beauty of his diction, the magnificence of his conceptions, and his luminous development of the abstruse dogmas of the ancients, is unrivalled among the disciples of Plato.

There are many classical scholars who like to imply that the 'Golden Age' of Greece was the only significant era in Greek philosophy. Within this period one can conveniently place Socrates, Plato, Aristotle, Euripides, Sophocles, Aeschylus, Demosthenes, and the historians Herodotus, Thucydides, and Xenophon.

These brilliant names tend to blind one into accepting the false notion that Greece at any other period in its history was merely second rate in the intellects it produced. Many scholars are passionately dedicated to deriding any Greek intellects either before or after this 'Golden Age'. Some caustic comments have been made about this by other scholars, and there is no denying the tendency to ignore or belittle – even to suppress and deny – Greeks who preceded or followed the glorious 'Golden Greeks' who are most familiar to us. It certainly is an embarrassing fact, then, for certain classical scholars to have to face, that the Platonic Academy continued to function in Athens for over nine hundred years.

Regarding the Academy, George Sarton says in *A History of Science: Ancient Science through the Golden Age of Greece*:[5]

> At the time when (the Emperor) Justinian closed its doors, (the Academy) might have celebrated its 916th anniversary. . . . the Academy changed considerably in the course of centuries; it is only the Old Academy that may be considered as Plato's Academy, and it lasted a century and a half or less. To this one might reply that every institution is bound to change with the vicissitudes of time and that the longer it lives the more it must be expected to change. Bearing these remarks in mind, we may put it this way: the Academy of Athens, the Academy founded by Plato, lasted more than nine centuries.

Those who find chronology difficult to comprehend without analogies might wish to ponder this: the duration of the Platonic Academy (apparently on the same site) in Athens was equivalent to the duration to date on English soil of Westminster Abbey; or, the 916 years of life of the Academy as a philosophical institution was equal to the amount of time which will have elapsed from the Norman Conquest of Britain in 1066 to the year 1982. (And even after the dismemberment, the Academy continued 'in exile' in Persia, etc.) We thus see that Plato's Academy existed longer on one spot than Britain has existed since William the Conqueror.

The Platonic tradition in the broader sense, with its gnostic and heretical overtones and its myriad manifestations in later ages in such bizarre and fascinating figures as Giordano Bruno, Marsilio Ficino, John Dee, and even Sir Philip Sidney and the Earl of Leicester – not to mention the troubadours of Provence, Dante in Italy, and the massacred tens of thousands of Albigensians in France, the Knights Templar, and an infinite range of hopeless causes over two and a half millennia, is an agonizing and impossible problem for the orthodox mind, whatever its creed. For Platonism in the general sense is a creed which denies creed, an anti-institutional tradition known to those who adhere to it as the 'Great Tradition'. It resembles the Society of Friends (Quakers) in insisting on nothing by way of doctrinal dogma. It is truly free, it has no membership, no tithes, no rules which are enforced; it has no Pope, no Caliph. It terrifies those weaker mentalities which crave a structured belief-system; they always try to destroy it, but succeed only in destroying individuals and individual 'movements' within the larger tradition.

How can any 'intellectual establishment' conceivably admit that this under-current of spirituality has flowed outside the orthodox boundaries of the official religion of Christianity since the third century and the time of Origen? And how confess that Proclus, who lived seven hundred years later than Plato, had a mind as luminous in his own way as Plato's? What happens to the 'hermetically sealed Greek miracle' then? If Platonism is seen to continue as a persecuted underground movement for two thousand years and more, what conclusions must we draw about the supposed openness of orthodox Western culture? If our commonly accepted pattern of civilization is seen to be based on a lie, based on the denial of the non-orthodox, the implications are so immense that nothing short of a total intellectual upheaval could result. No person with a vested interest, whether a chair at a university or a weekly newspaper, a large corporation or a television station (or a diocesan see) would be completely isolated from the results which would follow. The results need not be destructive in the sense of a political or social revolution, but they would be more funda- mental, and hence more far-reaching in the end. It is fear of constructive change (which amounts to fear of the unknown) which is here involved. These indeed are problems. And they go some way to explain why the reader hears nothing of a great many subjects which have a direct relevance to the matter. One of the many such subjects is Proclus. No one dares to discuss what Proclus really stood for and what he represents beyond his own specific ideas. Even to raise the subject of a figure such as Proclus is to bring the skeleton from the closet and rattle it with a vengeance.

Proclus does not even rate his own entry in the *Penguin Companion to Literature*, vol. 4, which deals with classical literature. He is mentioned under an entry for Neoplatonism by D. R. Dudley:

> He was a strange combination – possible in that age – of philosopher, logician, mathematician, and mystic. Neo-Platonism gave to the intellectul of the last phase of paganism a metaphysical religion. . . . The figure of the sage gazing upwards in contemplation is often found on late imperial sarcophagi.

Notice the phrase 'possible in that age', implying as it does that no person today would even consider trying to know something about so many subjects in our age of perverse over-specialization. Proclus, we are told, 'was a strange combination'. Dudley tells us nothing of what Proclus wrote, nothing of his ideas, nothing of the immense bulk of his writings, and in his bibliography refers us only to the harmless and difficult *Elements of Theology*. We are left to conclude that Proclus was an extinct species like the dodo, interesting only because he was 'a strange combination possible in that age'. There are very few historians dealing with the fifth century A.D. We assume from what Dudley says that only they could be interested in a 'strange combination possible in that age'. Surely Proclus, of whom we are told nothing of importance, is totally unimportant. Would the *Penguin Companion* mislead its readers? Such a thing is unthinkable.

Professor A. C. Lloyd of the University of Liverpool was given the task of discussing Proclus as part of his contribution to the *Cambridge History of Later Greek and Early Mediaeval Philosophy*,[6] a compendium which did not exist before 1967 and which was reprinted with corrections in 1970. The publication of this large volume of 715 pages marked the attainment of a stage in classical scholarship where many scholars were officially agreeing that they were running out of things to do in the more usual areas and had better begin compiling guidelines for a study of the long-neglected subject of the above-mentioned book. Such lonely figures as Richard Walzer, Philip Merlan, and the late

I. P. Sheldon-Williams, long engaged in these arcane pursuits out of pure interest, were summoned to help delineate the bounds within which a new generation of students might have some new fields in which to do their Ph.D. theses and where some original work remains to be done by the professors who have now tidied up the Pre-Socratic field rather well and need new ground for some genuine problem-solving.

But to return to Professor Lloyd, who has made an interesting attempt to describe Proclus and some aspects of his thought and writings. It is important for us to know more about Proclus the man.[7] Here is part of Lloyd's account:

> Proclus was born at Constantinople in 410 or shortly afterwards. But his parents, who were patricians from Lycia in south-west Asia Minor, sent him to school in their country and then to Alexandria to study literature and rhetoric. Instead of law, which was his father's profession, philosophy attracted him, so he attended lectures on mathematics and Aristotle. The next stage was Athens.

His studies at the Platonic Academy there are then described, and it was this School of which he was to become the Head: 'It is not known when he took over the School, but he remained at its head till he died in 485. He never married and his only defects were a jealous nature and a short temper.'

His short temper seems to have extended to impatience with those who were slow to understand what he was saying or who made irritating difficulties over petty details. For instance, he begins his mammoth work *Commentary on the Timaeus of Plato* with this extraordinarily testy sentence: 'That the design of the Platonic Timaeus embraces the whole of physiology and that it pertains to the theory of the universe, discussing this from the beginning to the end, appears to me to be clearly evident to those who are not entirely illiterate.'

It is now that we begin to consider the connection which Proclus has with the larger subject of our book. We will continue with Professor Lloyd's description of Proclus:

> Proclus moved in important political circles, but like other leading Platonists he was a champion of pagan worship against imperial policy and found himself more than once in trouble. There is no doubt of his personal faith in religious practices. A vegetarian diet, prayers to the sun, the rites of a Chaldaean initiate, even the observance of Egyptian holy days were scrupulously practised. He is said to have got his practical knowledge of theurgy from a daughter of Plutarch [the Platonist, not the author of the *Lives*], and according to his own claim he could conjure up luminous phantoms of Hecate. Nor is there any doubt that he put theurgy, as liberation of the soul, above philosophy. But while his philosophy is full of abstract processions and reversions, philosophy was nothing for him if not itself a reversion, a return to the One, though achieving only an incomplete union. Its place can be seen in an almost fantastically elaborated metaphysical system: but although this system would not have been created had there not been a religion to justify, its validity does not depend and was not thought by Proclus to depend on the religion.

The connnection with the mysteries of Hecate as well as Proclus's practising Egyptian and Chaldaean mysteries immediately arouses in the alert reader the suspicion that Proclus might just possibly have known something of the Sirius mystery. Could this be the case? In a moment we will consider some amazing opinions of Proclus on the heavenly bodies which no historian of science I have encountered has ever taken into account (probably because no one ever actually reads through that gigantic tome known as the *Commentary on the Timaeus of Plato* which I mentioned a moment ago). But first let us examine any further evidence than this slim fact which might link Proclus with the general milieu of our Sirius tradition. Professor Lloyd provides further interesting remarks:

> Proclus believed that his metaphysics was the true though hidden meaning of Plato and that this like all Greek 'theology' derived from the secret doctrines of Pythagoreans and Orphics. It can be studied in two works, the *Elements of Theology* and the *Theology of Plato*, with help here and there from the commentaries on the *Parmenides*, *Timaeus*, and *Alcibiades*.

It must be emphasized that in the form of such commentaries, the Neo-platonists produced much purely original and creative philosophy. It is fashionable at the moment to ridicule their commentary format as derivative and inferior. This is a pathetic attempt to deride what cannot or will not be appreciated. An example may be seen in the description by Professor Robert Browning of Birkbeck College, University of London, in the *Penguin Companion* volume, of the commentaries of Proclus's later successor Simplicius as 'misconceived and pedestrian textbooks'. The word 'misconceived' is loaded, and immediately lets us know that Professor Browning disagrees with them in principle and therefore derides them. However, in my own reading of Simplicius's *Commentary on Epictetus*, for instance, I was amazed to find a luminous intellect behind the commentary, whose dissertations on free will are so startlingly contemporary that I immediately thought of comparing them with writings of our modern cybernetic age, such as the fascinating books by Norbert Weiner. In Chapter One Simplicius speaks of 'those who pretend that our opinions and desires, and generally speaking, all of our choices and intentions, are necessary and not at our own disposal, but come from exterior causes outside ourselves, not coming from us of our own volition.' He attacks the 'Behaviourists' of his day in clear and forceful terms which are not restricted in relevance to his own times by any means. Some of his reasoning is so acute and many of his insights are so profound, that I can see no reason why not a single word of his writings can be obtained in English from any publisher in the world.

Of the works of Proclus, it is really the *Commentary on the Timaeus of Plato* (which I shall abbreviate from here on as *In Tim.*) which is the source of Proclus's views on the cosmos and of his views of the Platonic succession of an esoteric tradition from the ancient mystery religions. Professor Lloyd, in a footnote to his passage last quoted, does not give this reference on these points, but instead refers to other works by Proclus. In his entire treatment of Proclus, Lloyd gives only slight and cursory reference to the *In Tim.* However, it is to the *In Tim.* which we must now turn. Since page references to the Greek text of Lipsiae would be useless to most readers, I give page references to Taylor's English translation, vols. I and II.

At the end of Book IV of *In Tim.*, Proclus says (II, 307): 'But it is Pythagoric to follow the Orphic genealogies. For the science concerning the Gods proceeded from the Orphic tradition through Pythagoras, to the Greeks, as Pythagoras himself says in the *Sacred Discourse*.'

The fact that he entertained this view in relation to the mystery religions is shown in his remarks about Pythagoric principles in *In Tim.*, Book V (II, 312): 'But these are the Orphic traditions. For what Orpheus delivered mystically through arcane narrations, this Pythagoras learned, being initiated by Aglaophemus in the mystic wisdom which Orpheus derived from his mother Calliope.'

He attaches this view to his discussion in *In Tim.* of celestial phenomena. Not long after the above passage he says: 'For Orpheus calls the moon celestial earth'. And in Book III he says: 'The Pythagoreans say . . . (that) the moon is ethereal earth'.

Taking these views, as he does, and claiming to be a devotee of Hecate specifically (a 'Hymn to Hecate' by Proclus survives in which he calls her 'Guardian of the Gates' – an ancient Egyptian title of Horus – and Mother of the Gods – an ancient title of Isis; see IV, 4, 6, of Grant's *Hellenistic Religions*),[8] Proclus seems to stand in the position as an initiate capable of knowing something of the Sirius mystery. I have found no references, and it would have been considered impious by him to make any direct references to such an esoteric doctrine. But I have found that many theories of his clearly seem to reflect on it and be based on its premise of an invisible star. These theories are so extraordinary that I feel an account of them should be made. And the primary importance of them to us is that in them Proclus speaks with full authority in insisting that certain invisible heavenly bodies definitely exist. These bodies are the moons of the planets and the planets of other stars. Furthermore, Proclus seems to have an incredibly enlightened view of celestial phenomena in many other ways as well.

In Book III of *In Tim.* Proclus says (I, 425) that the Moon is made of

celestial earth. Or why else does the moon, being illuminated, produce a shadow, and why does not the solar light pervade through the whole of it? . . . we shall find that fire and earth subsist also analogously in the heavens; fire indeed, defining the essence of them, but each of the other elements being consubsistent with it.

Shortly afterwards he says:

The elements being conceived in one way as unmingled, but in another as mingled, the first mixture of them produces the heavens, which contain all things according to a fiery characteristic. . . . For all things are in the heaven according to a fiery mode.

We know from other citations above that the theory of the moon being 'celestial earth' is a 'Pythagoric-Orphic' one which Proclus has adopted. The fact that he here extends the observation to the remarks of the general nature of the celestial bodies implies that those ideas come from the same source. The heavens are indeed of a 'fiery mode', for we now know scientifically that stars possess all the normal chemical elements in a fiery mode. Proclus's description of celestial bodies could be perfectly in harmony with our present-day scientific knowledge. It is true, as Proclus says, that the stars may be described with 'fire indeed, describing the essence of them, but each of the other elements being consubsistent with it'. For, though they are ablaze, stars are known to contain all elements.

Proclus makes absolutely clear that when he speaks of 'fire' in the heavens he is speaking figuratively. He says (page 280): 'Hence, the fire which is there (in the heavenly bodies) is light; and it is not proper to disturb the discussion of it, by directing our attention to the gross and dark fire of the sublunary region [the below-the-moon, or earthly region].' And to make it beyond the slightest possibility of misunderstanding, he adds (page 281) that fire in the heavens is 'fire which is not perfectly fire' but, rather, star-fire is more properly 'fire which is in energy'.

These conceptions are quite astounding in the light of modern science. In fact, modern theories of there being in space an interstellar medium which is of such a tenuous nature that it is barely perceivable to us but nevertheless quite extensive (*not* the old-fashioned 'aether'!), find an uncanny forerunner in Proclus's strange statement from Book III of *In Tim.* (I, 425):

> It is also necessary that the middle elements should be in the heavenly bodies, but that different elements should abound in different parts of the celestial regions. And in some places indeed, it is necessary that the fiery nature should widely scatter its splendour, on account of solidity, as in the starry bodies; but in others, that it should be concealed from us, as in the spheres that carry the stars.

No matter what interpretation one may put on these remarks by Proclus, the fact remains that he views the stars as congealed bodies in a celestial medium and that between them lies 'fiery matter' which is invisible to us. As for his references to the spheres, these are hardly the glassy globules familiar to us from more conventional ancient astronomy, as we shall see.

In Book IV of the *In Tim.* (II, 293), Proclus ridicules epicycles and says they are valuable as 'an excellent contrivance' by which to analyse and comprehend the true simple motions of the stars,

> just as if someone, not being able to measure a spiral motion about a cylinder, but afterwards assuming a right line moved about it, and a point in the right line measuring its motions, should find what the quantity is of the motion about the spiral in a given time. To this therefore, the attention of those is directed, who employ evolvents, epicycles, and eccentrics, through simple motions, from which they discover a various motion.

We thus see that Proclus, despite his late date, is no prisoner of the Ptolemaic theory of the universe. Ptolemy lived three hundred years before him, but Proclus was a hold-out against his epicycles, preferring the views expressed above. In fact, Proclus views the spheres in a way which is extremely surprising, for in Book IV of *In Tim.* (p. 273) he says: 'Thus also the planets are moved with an advancing motion, but not the spheres of the planets'.

This is quite a clear statement that the planets move while their 'spheres' or – dare we say it? – orbits are really the spaces in which this movement takes place. However, we need not be too cautious here. Benjamin Jowett uses the word 'orbit' in his translation of the text of Plato (38–39) on which Proclus is here commenting. There is no reason why we should refrain from doing the same.

We are thus confronted with a clear description by Proclus (less obscure than Plato's own vague account) of the planets moving in orbits which themselves are clearly conceived as trajectory spaces. And this concept is so scientifically accurate and advanced, and so contrary to the then fashionable view that the 'spheres' of the planets moved and carried the planets along with them, that we must appreciate the precocity of Proclus in putting the notion forward so clearly and persistently. Plato's text may be interpreted in the same way, but it is not customary to do so, and it is too vague by far. A typical example of the standard interpretation of the passage in Plato's own *Timaeus* is that given by Professor A. C. Crombie in vol. I of *Augustine to Galileo* (though he does on page 33 describe the *Timaeus* quite starkly as a 'Pythagorean allegory', which is presumably a daring way to put it) on page 49:

> The different spheres in which the seven 'planets', Moon, Sun, Venus, Mercury, Mars, Jupiter, and Saturn, were set, revolved with different uniform velocities such as would represent the observed movements of those bodies.

This is purely an *interpretation* of a vague text. One could just as well say that Plato maintained that the spheres did not move and the planets in them were what moved, as Proclus specifically states (and as he seems to think Plato believed).

Proclus goes out of his way to say (p. 279):

> (Plato) is evidently of opinion, that the planets become through themselves, more remote from, and nearer to the earth, and that their revolutions according to breadth, are made by their own progressions, and not through being carried by other things, such as evolvents or epicycles.

This puts Proclus in a position diametrically opposite Professor Crombie in interpreting the text of Plato. I am afraid that I, for one, must come down on the side of Proclus in such a contest. In any case, Professor Crombie has shown himself quick to alter a view if presented with fresh evidence on the matter, as he has demonstrated on an entirely different subject in correspondence with the author.

Near the very end of Book IV of *In Tim.* (pp. 293 ff.) Proclus says:

> With respect to the stars, however, those that are fixed, revolve about their own centres. . . . But the planets revolve in conjunction with the inerratic sphere, and each is moved together with its sphere to the east, and revolves by itself according to breadth and depth, and about its proper centre.

It is worth while for us to examine these remarks of his closely. First of all, the 'inerratic sphere' of the fixed stars revolves around the Earth and the planets do the same in conjunction with it. That is the simplest of the motions. But on top of that are several more motions: first, the fixed stars rotate on their axes in a spin rotation; second, the planets do the same; third, the planets do more than that: each planet 'by itself' (i.e. in separate motion from all the other stars and planets as well as separate from the 'spheres') 'revolves according to breadth and depth', which obviously refers to 'becoming by itself more remote from and nearer to the earth', as seen from the previous quote. And this depth of planetary motion, which Proclus here specifically calls 'according to breadth and depth' literally adds a new dimension to any theory of planetary motion. For whereas anyone who observes the sky over long periods can see that the planets appear to get dimmer and brighter as if they were 'becoming more remote from and nearer to the earth', the formal description of planets operating in terms of a dimension at right angles to their apparent revolutions comes very close indeed to pointing to a central point of their revolutions which is something other than the Earth. There was a tradition that Plato came to believe this, which was publicly proposed by Aristarchus of Samos and partially advocated by Plato's friend Heraclides of Pontus. We know that Proclus was aware of it: 'Let Heracleides Ponticus therefore, who was an auditor of Plato, be of this opinion; for he ascribed a circular motion to the Earth' (*In Tim.* II, 288). In short – that the Earth revolves around some other centre such as the sun. '. . . But let it be admitted that Plato established it immovable' (ibid.). Thus does Proclus admit the controversy and come down on the side of caution concerning revolution about the sun.

It is phenomenal that Proclus, with an insight which is difficult for us to comprehend, attributed to all celestial bodies a spin rotation about their axes. And since the Earth is a celestial body, it is to be wondered whether Proclus gathered the appropriate conclusion – that the Earth rotates and that is what makes the sky seem to revolve about us.

In considering this point we must realize that in the *Timaeus*, Plato mentions the rotations of the heavenly bodies on their axes (40a–b): 'And (the Creator) gave to each of (the stars) two movements: the first, a movement on the same spot after the same manner . . . the second, a forward movement . . .'

This is an obscure way of saying the stars rotate and the sky circles. (If Plato inserted someone else's treatise into his dialogue without being fully *au fait* with the material – as has been maintained – it may explain the vagueness, though Plato does no better in the *Laws* and was a feeble astronomer.) In the same passage as above, Plato also clearly describes the following: 'The earth, which is our nurse, circling around the pole which is extended through the universe', which refers to the rotation of the earth itself on its axis.

Proclus apparently adds of his own volition the other motions – for Plato seems only to mention two. Furthermore, Plato's text is too brief and foggy to make it clear exactly what he did mean. The one thing of which we can be certain is that Proclus expended untold tens of thousands of words expounding Plato's meanings in all fields beyond the extent to which Plato himself managed or desired to do. On some subjects this is not particularly gripping. But with this particular subject, every scrap of evidence is essential to unravelling the intended significance of Plato's statements.

In an essay of his entitled 'Platonic Questions' (not yet published in the Loeb Library series – as the last remaining of fourteen volumes, again we see Platonic studies enjoying the lowest priority – but published in English in

1874[9]), Plutarch provides us with essential evidence that Plato definitely abandoned his earlier geocentric ideas, despite Proclus's nervous demurral. Plutarch says in Question VIII:

> What means Timaeus [see Plato's *Timaeus*, 42D] when he says that souls are dispersed into the earth, the moon, and into other instruments of time? Does the earth move like the sun, moon, and five planets, which for their motions he calls organs or instruments of time? Or is the earth fixed to the axis of the universe; yet not so built as to remain immovable, but to turn and wheel about, as Aristarchus and Seleucus have shown since; Aristarchus only supposing it, Seleucus positively asserting it? Theophrastus writes how that Plato, when he grew old repented him that he had placed the earth in the middle of the universe, which was not its place.

(Plutarch then follows with his own opinion, which is that the earth does not move.)

Theophrastus's testimony here is unimpeachable, but was probably unknown to Proclus, by whose lifetime most of Theophrastus's works would have been lost. Theophrastus was Aristotle's successor and head of the Lyceum at Athens, and an unquestionably reliable source; and Plutarch leaves us in no doubt (see 'Against Colotes the Epicurean', 14, in *Moralia*) that he read Theophrastus's actual works attentively, making a misquotation or secondhand report impossible in this instance.

The Seleucus who is mentioned here was a mathematician and astronomer described by George Sarton[10] as follows: 'This Babylonian was a follower of Aristarchus of Samos'. Seleucus is described differently by Giorgio de Santillana, who gives him another nationality in *The Origins of Scientific Thought*, page 250: 'We know of only one [astronomer] who adopted the system [of Aristarchus] a century later, Seleucus of Seleucia, an Oriental Greek from the Persian Gulf.'

However, Plato's views on the earth's position in space are less interesting to us in themselves than as they relate to Proclus's interpretation of them, and also as they relate to modern historians of science, who tend to gloss over the possibility that Plato may have adopted a heliocentric theory of a rotating earth moving round the sun, which was obscurely expressed in the *Timaeus* and less tentatively adhered to by Plato 'when he grew old', bearing in mind that the *Timaeus* itself is no early work of Plato's.

In Plutarch's same essay, 29, we find evidence of a continuity from Plato through his student Xenocrates of the belief that the heavens contain more than one element. However, Proclus seems to transcend by far the limited theory of Plato and Xenocrates as here presented. The summary of theories of Xenocrates presumably is drawn from his lost work in six books *On Astronomy* unless from his one lost book on *Things Pythagorean*. Xenocrates was head of the Academy for twenty-five years until his death at the age of eighty-two 'from the effects of a fall over some utensil in the night', as Diogenes Laertius tells us.[11]

There is clear proof that Proclus did not himself originate the third motion at right angles to revolution which we have seen that Plato does not mention. We actually find it referred to by Plutarch in his dialogue 'Of the Face Appearing in the Orb of the Moon', 24.[12] There he says:

Nor is the moon indeed moved by one motion only, but is, as they were wont to call her, Trivia, or Three-Wayed – performing her course together according to length, breadth, and depth in the Zodiac; the first of which motions mathematicians call a direct revolution, the second volutation, or an oblique winding and wheeling in and out; and the third (I know not why) an inequality; although they see that she has no motion uniform, settled, and certain, in all her circuits and reversions.

Plutarch's expressions 'mathematicians call' and 'as they were wont to call her' make clear that he is referring to some unidentified and now lost astronomical works. Plutarch's exposition is not as clear as we could wish, and in a succeeding passage is countered by another speaker who espouses the more fashionable theory of spheres which actually themselves move while, as for the moon: 'some supposing that she herself stirs not'. It is peripherally interesting that in this retort the speaker also cites Aristarchus of Samos as being involved in a controversy over a line from Homer's *Iliad* which Plutarch gives and which is missing from our present text of Homer, a line advocated by Crates and opposed by Aristarchus, which correctly describes the sea as covering 'the most part of the earth'.

We must not stray too far from Proclus. In pursuit of him, however, I wish to mention his influence on Johannes Kepler, the sixteenth-century discoverer of the three laws of planetary motion (which are the only ones we possess even now). And in this I have another complaint to make. For not one major work of Kepler's has ever been translated into English.[13] This fact is enough to send one into despair. Who wants to plough through a lot of medieval Latin to read Kepler – and who can? But what has Kepler to do with Proclus? Well, Kepler was steeped – indeed, drenched – in Proclus. The interested reader may turn to the closing pages of *Harmonies of the World* in the Encyclopaedia Brittanica vol. 16, *Ptolemy, Copernicus, and Kepler*[14], and read for himself. He will find there remarks about Proclus, after which Kepler says: 'But also I have recently fallen upon the hymn of Proclus the Platonic philosopher, of whom there has been much mention in the preceding books, which was composed to the Sun and filled full with venerable mysteries' in the context of speculation about 'what did the ancient Pythagoreans in Aristotle mean, who used to call the centre of the world (which they referred to as the "fire" but understood by that the sun) "the watchtower of Jupiter"?'

Here we see that Kepler, the great forerunner of Newton, was delighted with the 'venerable mysteries' of Proclus. In the light of what we know now and will shortly discover further, later in this appendix, about Proclus's theories, what effect did they have on Kepler's own thinking?

Was Proclus standing behind Kepler just as Aristarchus stood behind Copernicus? When will Kepler and Proclus be fully available in English so that any intelligent person can make up his own mind without first becoming fluent in often highly technical medieval Latin? But most important of all, were the greatest advances at the commencement of modern cosmological speculation made by virtue of their generation from suppressed and unorthodox ancient sources such as Proclus and Aristarchus? Did the 'secret' side of ancient astronomy from the Pythagoreans to Proclus really engender the origins of our modern cosmologies? And the corollary of this is: If so, are the possibilities of our making certain breakthroughs being stymied by the very suppression of the sources which may have engendered the earliest breakthroughs? By cutting off the root of Kepler, can we really expect the branch to continue to flower? If the facts about Proclus's theories which are being presented in this appendix really have gone unremarked by all the leading historians of science upon whom we all usually rely to tell us at second hand all the facts which we feel we have no time to discover at first hand, then something is clearly wrong with the system. We have got to overhaul the mechanics. Otherwise we shall continue to spiral downwards and think we are rising. I am referring to means and sources of inspiration. I do not question for a moment that vast progress is made in many areas. But I do maintain most strongly that our system for deriving inspiration in theorizing about the cosmos is demented because it is incomplete, therefore unbalanced. We should by now have formulated more laws or principles of planetary motion. But it is fashionable for those who read second-hand cribs of Kepler to deride him. He was a 'nut'. We do not attempt to study his means and methods of thinking or even acknowledge the existence of many of his most important sources. And one of those sources was Proclus.

The writings of Proclus are so voluminous that I have to confess that I have not gleaned from them by any means an exhaustive survey of his views. This Appendix is merely a sampling. But of course we have not yet come to the most surprising views of all, which we must now consider:

(The planets') adumbrations are situations according to which they darken us and other things. For the body which is arranged after another body, becomes situated in the front of that which is posterior to it. And . . . they run under each other.

Also there are 'their occultations under the sun, and their evolutions into light . . .' Significantly he here turns to the subject:

For it is necessary to recur from the phenomena to the reminiscences of invisible natures. For as from these instruments and shadows, we are enabled to commence the contemplation of the celestial bodies; thus also from the latter, we recall to our recollection invisible circulations.

It is not an easy thing to know what Proclus is referring to. His sudden dropping of this large but obscure hint cannot be meant to be understood by everyone – not even those 'who are not entirely illiterate', as he testily warned us in the very first sentence of his huge tome. This particular work by Proclus is extremely difficult to read, and the Thomas Taylor translation has neither any index nor any form of table of contents by which to locate subjects, names or references in the text. The Lipsiae Greek text has an index, but there is no means of correlating it with the Taylor translation, which has no textual numbering.

Can this reference to 'invisible circulations' refer to the invisible circulations of the companion of Sirius? The answer to this question cannot be a final 'no', and the possibility must be seriously considered when we read these next opinions of Proclus from *In Tim.* Book IV (II, 281):

As Aristotle, however, inquires why the sphere of the fixed stars, being one, comprehends many stars, but in each of the planetary spheres, which are many, there is only one star, the solution of this conformably to his own opinion may be obtained from his writings. But we have already said something concerning this, and now agreeably to what has been before asserted, we say, that *each of the planets is a whole world, comprehending in itself many divine genera invisible to us. Of all these however, the visible star has the government . . . in each of the (planetary spheres) there are invisible stars, which revolve together with their spheres*; so that in each, there is both the wholeness, and a leader which is allotted an exempt transcendency. . . . *each of the spheres is a world*; theologists also teaching us these things when they say that there are Gods in each prior to daemons, some of which are under the government of other. . . . from all which it is evident that *each of the planets is truly said to be the leader of many Gods, who give completion to its peculiar circulation.*

Taylor, in a footnote, rightly calls this an 'extraordinary passage' of the treatise! Italics above are mine.

Elsewhere Proclus says (*In Tim.*, II, 260): 'There are, however, other divine animals following the circulations of the planets, the leaders of which are the seven planets.' Taylor adds to this in a footnote: 'And these, as we have before observed, are what the moderns call *satellites*'.

In another of his publications, Thomas Taylor writes, as introduction to his translation of Plato's *Timaeus* itself:[15]

(For) each of these spheres . . . as we have already explained, it follows that every planet has a number of satellites surrounding it, analogous to the choir of fixed stars; and that every sphere is full of gods, angels, and daemons, subsisting according to the properties of the spheres in which they reside. This theory indeed is the grand key to the theology of the ancients, as it shews us at one view why the same god is so often celebrated with the names of other gods; which led Macrobius formerly to think that all the gods were nothing more than the different powers of the sun; and has induced the superficial, *index-groping* moderns to frame hypotheses concerning the ancient theology, so ridiculous that they deserve to be considered in no other light than the ravings of a madman, or the undisciplined conceptions of a child. But that the reader may be convinced of this, let him attend to the following extraordinary passages from the divine commentaries of Proclus on the *Timaeus*. And in the first place, that every planet is attended with a great number of satellites, is evident from the following citation: 'There are other divine animals attending upon the circulations of the planets, the leaders of which are the seven planets; and these revolve and return in their circulations in conjunction with their leaders, just as the fixed stars are governed by the circulation of the inerratic sphere.' [p. 279] . . . And in the same place he informs us, that the revolution of these satellites is similar to that of the planets which they attend; and this, he acquaints us a little before, is according to Plato a spiral revolution. . . . (and) 'about every planet there is a number (of satellites) . . . all of them subsisting with proper circulations of their own' [p. 275].

The reader should note that Thomas Taylor describes this knowledge as 'the grand key to the theology of the ancients'. We know from a fragment of Damascius[16] the Neoplatonist that 'the Egyptian philosophers, who are resident among us, have explained their occult truth, having obtained it from certain Egyptian discourses. According to them, then, it appears to be this. The One principle of the Universe is celebrated as Unknown Darkness, and this three times pronounced as such . . .' But wherever the information came from, the fact is that Proclus and his Neoplatonic colleagues believed the ultimate secrets of religion concerned two things: the invisible 'Dark' and invisible circulations of certain heavenly bodies, some of which were non-esoteric enough even to be specified, namely the satellites of our planetary system. Proclus winds up a dissertation on the source of this knowledge from 'sacred rumour' which concerns 'invisible circulations' also on page 247 of *In Tim.*, II.

Since Proclus specifically describes here and in the passage from *In Tim.* II, 281, the orbits of the heavenly bodies as their 'circulations' (Taylor's choice of English), the 'invisible circulations' which he mentioned must be invisible orbits of heavenly bodies, and he also tells us that there are invisible heavenly bodies. So . . . what invisible orbitings of invisible heavenly bodies are so important that they can, as Proclus just told us, 'enable us to commence the contemplation of celestial bodies' and vice versa? Is that not a most curious thought? How can he possibly mean that there are invisible orbitings so important that they may be set against the visible orbitings for importance, the one complementing the other even to the very base of our abilities to contemplate the heavens?

The key to the paragraph from Proclus II, 281, is the expression in it: 'theologists teaching us these things'. For in those words Proclus firmly identifies these ideas with a theological as opposed to philosophical tradition, and hence one connected with one or more of his mystery religions. This is just the evidence we need. For it is these mystery religions which we know contained the essence of the Sirius mystery as their secret doctrine. And also, as we have seen earlier, Proclus sought to interpret Plato in terms of an esoteric tradition with which Proclus himself was connected directly, as an initiate.

So we see that Proclus believed that invisible 'stars' existed which accompanied the planets, and that each of the planets was a world. And the visible star, that is the planet, 'has the government' over the invisible satellites in each case. How very like the Sirius tradition this is! And as we know from Chapter One of this book, the Dogon also knew of the moons of at least one of the planets, so that knowledge of them seems likely to have been part and parcel of the Sirius mystery. Can we then conclude that Proclus may be one further person with knowledge of the Sirius mystery?

Proclus is more specific about his planetary moons elsewhere. In his work the *Platonic Theology*, Chapter XIV of Book VII (Vol. II, pages 140–1 of Taylor's translation), we read:

But the planets are called the Governors of the world (cosmocrators), and are allotted a total power. As the inerratic sphere too has a number of starry animals, so each of the planets is the leader of a multitude of animals, or of certain other things of this kind. . . . In each of the planetary spheres, therefore, there is a number of satellites analogous to the choir of the fixed stars, subsisting with proper circulations of their own. The revolution also of these satellites is similar to that of the planets which they follow: and this according to Plato is a spiral revolution. With respect, likewise, to these satellites, the first in order about every planet are Gods; after these daemons revolve in lucid orbicular bodies; and these are followed by partial souls such as ours.

Taylor comments in a footnote in *In Tim.* Book IV (II, 299): 'For "the natures successive" to the stars, are evidently their satellites, which have more than once been mentioned by Proclus.' On the same page a second footnote adds: 'From what is here said by Proclus, it appears that the fixed stars, as well as the planets, have satellites, and that the stars which sometimes are visible, and at other times disappear, are of this description.'

This brings us extremely close to an outright statement of the principles of the Sirius mystery – but without any names. These footnotes are to the passage immediately following the one given a moment ago where we first considered Proclus's cryptic reference to the 'invisible circularities'. It is interesting to note that the passage is in the form of a commentary on a specific passage in Plato's *Timaeus* (40-c), which is not only one of the most maddeningly obscure passages in all of Plato ('Do not expect me to explain these mysteries', bewails a baffled George Sarton, p. 451, op. cit.) but a passage which Proclus quotes including missing words not otherwise known from the official text of today!

And it is even more curious that the 'missing' words quoted by Proclus are: *kai ta toutois ephexēs* of which Taylor says: 'These words, however, are not to be found in the text of Plato, but form a remarkable addition to it'. Taylor should know, as he had previously translated all of Plato's dialogues including this.

Since Proclus was head of the Academy, he may be assumed to have had a reliable copy of Plato's text in the Academy library. If he did not have a reliable copy of Plato's text in Plato's own Academy, what *did* he have a reliable text of? Hence these words must be entertained as a possibly correct version and should probably be added to the currently accepted text by classical scholars. The meaning of the words is translated by Taylor as: 'the natures successive' – that is successive to the stars. And Taylor's comment is: 'For *the natures successive* to the stars, are evidently their satellites, which have more than once been mentioned by Proclus'.

The fact that a reference to the satellites of stars was dropped from the orthodox text of Plato should come as no real surprise to us. What scribe could fathom the meaning? In copying the manuscripts over the centuries, there creep in corruptions. A reference to satellites of stars would have been too shocking, considered too bizarre. In transmission the words must have been dropped as an incomprehensible aberration or an insertion. It was only in the Academy's own library that the original words were preserved, safe and musty, in the wrappings of some really old bookrolls with which no one tampered textually. Only in the Academy would ravages against the text of the Master be forbidden.

I do not believe it is a coincidence that our search through Proclus for material relevant to the Sirius mystery has led us to a lost fragment of text of

Plato's dialogue *Timaeus*. The fact that these words have been dropped from that dialogue – out of the entire body of Plato's work, which is otherwise so well documented from the myriad commentaries and citations over the centuries – illustrates the controversial nature of our subject as strikingly as any of the 'accidents' we have already encountered in our book. Our Sirius mystery is not letting us down. Every subject we have approached in connection with it has been suddenly transformed as in a magic mirror in a fun house. Nothing that seemed staid and settled has been able to remain in its mould. Even Plato's solid text begins to quiver like a live jelly. From out of so many ossified subjects have crept mysterious little creatures, which have done disrespectful dances on their premises, indicating that these subjects do not want to lie down and be declared dead. They are living. Inside them glow sylphs and secrets. We cannot force them to turn to stone.

It seems clear that the abandoned four words of text were probably dropped in order to avoid the enormous consequences which must follow upon their being retained: that Plato himself, though not particularly well acquainted with astronomy in an active professional sense, had apparently some links to a tradition which, by being esoteric, seemed to make no sense at all outside a secret 'mystery' context. This is true whether Plato wrote the passages himself or inserted the Pythagorean treatise which has been proposed (see later).

Plato's dialogue *Timaeus* is without doubt the most difficult and bizarre of the unquestioned Platonic writings (the *Epinomis* is more bizarre, but seems to have been written by Plato's disciple Philip of Opus). Let us examine a few remarks concerning this strange work, taken from George Sarton (op. cit.): 'There is more Oriental lore in the *Timaios* than Greek wisdom' (p. 423, note). 'The astrologic nonsense that has done so much harm in the Western world and is still poisoning weak-minded people today was derived from the *Timaios*, and Plato's astrology was itself an offshoot of the Babylonian one. In justice to Plato it must be added that his own astrology remained serene and spiritual and did not degenerate into petty fortune telling' (p. 421). 'The influence of the *Timaios* upon later times was enormous and essentially evil' (p. 423.). 'Many scholars were deceived into accepting the fantasies of that book as gospel truths. That delusion hindered the progress of science; and the *Timaios* has remained to this day a source of osbcurity and superstition' (p. 430).

Those are strong words. The *Timaeus* (the more commonly used spelling in English) obviously arouses violent reactions in some! Here we see Sarton, one of the most distinguished and respected historians of science who ever lived, raving hysterically that the 'evil' *Timaeus* is responsible for 'hindering the progress of science'. Sarton's views of Plato in general are incredibly violent and hostile, though many of his criticisms of Plato are quite valid and reasonable if it were not for the purple prose. It is certainly true that there were many faults to Plato's theories, particularly his political ones which Aristotle rightly found so repulsive, and these rouse Sarton to a fury surpassing his slurs on the poor *Timaeus*. But this is common among expert scholars. They have to restrain themselves most of the time for purposes of professional poise and 'objective treatment'. But the mask can fracture and a raw nerve protrudes.

But as for the perplexity or ire which the *Timaeus* seems alternatively to arouse in so many of those who attempt to study it, we should realize that the tradition is probably true which says that the major portion of the dialogue, which consists of a lengthy speech by the character named Timaeus on the nature of the universe, is really not written by Plato, but was inserted by him as the words of an apparently imaginary character (or a disguised one). For many ancient sources maintained that this part of the dialogue was in reality a Pythagorean treatise which Plato obtained during one of his visits to Sicily. Rather than see the treatise disappear into obscurity, Plato is said to have entered it as the contribution of a character in a dialogue, using the discussion of the other characters as a means of setting it off to proper advantage. And it is this supposed Pythagorean treatise which contains all the material of interest to us in connection with the Sirius mystery. And as for the Pythagoreans, they represented a sacred community and a mystery tradition with roots in Egypt and Babylon (of both of which countries Pythagoras himself was said to be an initiate into the mysteries).

I owe it to the reader to display the evidence that the passage in the *Timaeus* which is of such concern to us, and on which Proclus's commentary is based as it concerns the heavenly bodies, was not even written by Plato. I therefore quote from Book VIII, 85, of the *Lives of Eminent Philosophers* by Diogenes Laertius (the Loeb Library translation):

> Philolaus of Croton was a Pythagorean, and it was from him that Plato requests Dion to buy the Pythagorean treatises. . . . His doctrine is that all things are brought about by necessity and in harmonious inter-relation. He was the first to declare that the earth moves in a circle (round the central fire), though some say it was Hicetas of Syracuse.
>
> He wrote one book, and it was this work which, according to Hermippus, some writer said that Plato the philosopher, when he went to Sicily to Dionysius's court, bought from Philolaus's relatives for the sum of forty Alexandrine minas of silver [an 'equivalent value', for this was before Alexander], from which also the *Timaeus* was transcribed. Others say that Plato received it as a present for having procured from Dionysius the release of a young disciple of Philolaus who had been cast into prison.
>
> According to Demetrius in his work on *Men of the Same Name*, Philolaus was the first to publish the Pythagorean treatises, to which he gave the title *On Nature*, beginning as follows: 'Nature in the ordered universe was composed of unlimited elements, and so was the whole universe and all that is therein.'

In line with this tradition that the treatise embodied into the Platonic *Timaeus* was of Pythagorean origin – and presumably from thence derived itself from Egypt and Chaldaea (Babylonia) – we may read the following interesting remarks of Proclus from *In Tim.* Book IV (II, 273):

> The Egyptians prior to (Hipparchos and Ptolemy), employing observations, and still prior to the Egyptians, the Chaldaeans (Babylonians), being taught by the gods, prior to observations, were of a similar opinion to Plato, concerning the motion of the fixed stars. For the Oracles not once only but frequently speak of the advancing procession of the fixed stars.

Note the pointed expression 'taught by the gods, prior to observations'. This highlights the aspect of the tradition as one imparted to men 'by the gods' and then later carried on in concert with observations by the ancient Egyptians. Without my going into a minute discussion of Pythagoreanism, Orphism, and what Proclus calls 'the Oracles', I hope the reader will have gathered sufficient idea of the gist of the matter.

We see that Proclus, using a slender but nevertheless substantial basis of Plato's apparently ancient Pythagorean book *On Nature*, as it is preserved in his *Timaeus*, insisted that the planets had moons, that stars also had satellites, that there were invisible bodies in space with invisible orbits which were somehow of immense importance to us, that 'the gods' instructed the ancient peoples of the Middle East in these astronomical facts which were preserved as 'Pythagorean and Orphic' traditions in the Greek world, that epicycles and other fashionable devices to explain astronomical motions were total nonsense, that the 'spheres' did not revolve but only the planets in them, and hinted at the rotation of the Earth on its axis.

Proclus was, furthermore, a known initiate of the mystery cults of the Egyptians and Babylonians and had a particular connection with rites involving Hecate, the goddess whom we know to be a form of the star Sirius. We may, therefore, conclude that Proclus is of possible interest to us in our relentless pursuit of the Sirius mystery. For he may have known its secrets and made use of the principles of that secret tradition through the indirect means of his more general writings – by hinting broadly at 'invisible orbits' without specifying all of them, and insisting on their importance without giving any really satisfactory reasons. He seems to have been trying to get the principles across without breaking sacred vows against the revealing of the specifics of the case. As he was extremely religious, we know from his character that he would honour such vows. But as he was passionately devoted to making known the general principles of the universe, he would have done exactly what it seems he did do – tell us the story without giving the names of the characters.

A closer study of Proclus in the future would certainly be rewarding. There are certainly other relevant passages in his works which remain to be dealt with. But we have seen that we must now re-examine Plato as well, for his *Timaeus* has been shown by Proclus to be a more mysterious work than even the most exasperated scholars had ever suspected.[17] And the net of the Sirius mystery is meanwhile seen to spread ever wider through the ancient traditions and literature of all eras.

Two contemporaries of Proclus, named Macrobius and Martianus Capella, also wrote advanced astronomical theories, and both were also in the Neoplatonic tradition. They advocated the notion that the Earth went around the sun. When three people in one tradition at one time write and discuss such advanced material, then a milieu may be said to exist.[18] But, of course, the historians of science have not yet got around to noticing this inconvenient little thing. Nor have they bothered to let us know much about Johannes Scotus Eriugena (otherwise known as John the Scot or Erigena, which is a misspelling) of the ninth century A.D., who promulgated the theories of Macrobius and Martianus Capella at the court of Charles the Bald, and wrote a mammoth philosophical work titled *Periphyseon* of half a million words. The latter is now being published slowly in English by the Irish Government, who have decided that Eriugena (which means 'Irish-born') was one of their great native sons and they had better make the most of him. Alas. If only Proclus too had been born in Ireland. Perhaps this is the only way to get these things into print – or even into English. Can't someone invent some more little countries looking for famous sons, and then allocate the sons? That way we might have something of a cultural revival. The Renaissance was due to the rediscovery of the Platonic tradition by the Florentines. When will we discover it?

This Appendix was conceived, researched, and written after the manuscript of the book had already been accepted for publication. It therefore suffers from tenuous treatment and scanty attire. But perhaps a little Proclus is better than none at all. In a desert no one gainsays a drop of water.

Notes

1. *Elements of Theology*, ed. and trans. by E. R. Dodds, Oxford, 1963.
2. *Commentary on the First Book of Euclid's Elements*, trans. by Professor Glenn Morrow, Princeton University Press, 1970.
3. *Commentary on the First Alcibiades of Plato*, trans. by W. O'Neill, The Hague, 1965.
4. *Corpus Platonicum Medii Aevi* Series, ed. by R. Klibansky; Vol. III of *Plato Latinus (Parmenides, Proclus in Parmenidem)*. Includes English translation by G. E. M. Anscombe and L. Labowsky. Warburg Institute, London, 1953. Obtainable: as Kraus Reprint, Nendeln, Liechtenstein, 1973.
5. See Bibliography. Ref. page 400.
6. *The Cambridge History of Later Greek & Early Mediaeval Philosophy*, ed. by A. H. Armstrong, Cambridge, 1970.
7. There is a Life of Proclus written by his student and successor Marinus. It was translated by Thomas Taylor and appears in Volume I of *The Philosophical and Mathematical Commentaries of Proclus on the First Book of Euclid's Elements*, London, 1792. A more recent publication of it in English may be found in *The Philosophy of Proclus* by L. J. Rosan, Cosmos, New York, 1949.
8. *Hellenistic Religions* ed. by F. C. Grant, in Library of Liberal Arts series, Bobbs-Merrill, Indianapolis and New York, 1953. English translations of four hymns by Proclus are found on pp. 170–2. (In all, seven hymns and a fragment of an eighth by Proclus survive today.)
9. In vol. V of *Plutarch's Morals*, ed. by W. W. Goodwin, Boston, 1874. The translation of 'Platonic Questions' is by R. Brown and on pp. 425–49.
10. *History of Science*, see note 16, page 159.
11. See Life of Xenocrates in Diogenes Laertius, *Lives of Eminent Philosophers*, 2 vols., trans. by R. D. Hicks, Loeb Library series; Heinemann, London; Harvard University Press, U.S.A., 1966.
12. Translation included in the same volume as in note 9 above. Also in Loeb Library.
13. Three short complete works of Kepler are in English: *Kepler's Dream*, trans. with full text and notes, of *Somnium, Sive Astronomia Lunaris*, by John Lear and P. F. Kirkwood, University of California Press, Berkeley and Los Angeles, 1965. *Kepler's Conversation with Galileo's Sidereal Messenger*, trans. by Edward Rosen, no. 5 of 'Sources of Science' series, Johnson Reprint Corp., London and New York, 1965. Also there is a brief treatise by Kepler on the *Six-Cornered Snowflake*, trans. by Colin Hardie and L. L. Whyte, Oxford University Press, 1965. Two chapters (IV and V) of Kepler's *Epitome of Copernican Astronomy* and one chapter (V) of his *Harmonies of the World* are in English, trans. by C. G. Wallis in vol. 16, *Ptolemy, Copernicus, Kepler*, of the 'Great Books of the Western World' series, Encyclopaedia Britannica, Inc., Chicago, London, Toronto, 1952. A second translation of Kepler's *Dream* has appeared: *Kepler's Somnium*, trans. and commentary by Edward Rosen, University of Wisconsin Press, 1967.
14. See previous note.
15. *The Cratylus, Phaedo, Parmenides and Timaeus with notes on the Cratylus*, English trans. of Plato by Thomas Taylor with notes, London, 1793. The quotation is from p. 388, in Taylor's

Introduction to the *Timaeus*. The copy of this book which I consulted once belonged to the poet Percy Bysshe Shelley, and may be found in the Shelley collection at the Bodleian Library in Oxford.
16. Preserved and trans. in Cory, *Ancient Fragments*, 2nd ed., p. 320.
17. Marinus, in his Life of Proclus, tells us that Proclus was twenty-eight years old when he wrote *In Tim.*, which gives the date A.D. 438 at beginning of appendix.
18. I did not think it right to take space here to enter into a full discussion of the generally ignored ancient heliocentric theories of Macrobius, Martianus Capella, Julian the Emperor (Apostate), Nicholas of Cusa, and so on. As an example of this tradition (which Proclus mentioned and rejected, mistakenly thinking that Plato had done so), I quote a passage from the Fourth Oration (to Helios) of the Emperor Julian the Apostate, 146 C–D, which may be found in the Loeb Library series, which publishes the works of Julian in three vols: 'For it is evident that the planets, as they dance in a circle about (the Sun), preserve as the measure of their motion a harmony between this god and their own movements. . . . To the Greeks what I say is perhaps incomprehensible – as though one were obliged to say to them only what is known and familiar.' This indicates a distinctly esoteric tradition which was imbibed from Julian's friend and teacher the Neoplatonist Iamblichus, a predecessor of Proclus. For just before this passage, Julian had said: 'Iamblichus of Chalcis, who through his writings initiated me not only into other philosophic doctrines but these also . . . (he is) by no means inferior to (Plato) in genius . . .' I also refer the reader to 135 B of the same oration by Julian for further exposition of Julian's heliocentric ideas, all of which we may treat as fragments of lost writings of Iamblichus. I also suggest consulting Thomas Whittaker's *Macrobius*, Cambridge, 1923. On page 75 we find him summarizing Macrobius's beliefs: 'Mercury and Venus (have) orbits . . . in which they follow the sun as satellites'. Unfortunately, no works of Martianus Capella exist in English.

SUMMARY

WHAT PROCLUS KNEW

1. The Ptolemaic theory of the heavens is totally wrong.
2. The moon is made of 'earth' which is placed in a celestial situation, hence 'celestial earth'.
3. The planets themselves revolve, rather than their 'spheres'. They do so 'within their spheres (or orbits)'.
4. The stars all rotate on their own axes.
5. The planets all rotate on their own axes.
6. The planets become 'more remote from and nearer to the earth' in their revolutions.
7. The heavens contain all the four elements in varying proportions but tend to do so according to a 'fiery mode'. The 'fire' in the stars is different from earthly fire and is more properly 'energy'. (Earthly fire is a dark and debased form of true fire, or as Proclus expresses it: 'the dregs and sediment of fire'.)
8. The heliocentric theory of Heracleides Ponticus is mentioned by Proclus, but rejected by him on the grounds that Plato rejected it. (Although we know from Theophrastus that Plato did accept it when old, Proclus did not know this.)
9. The planets have invisible satellites which revolve around them.
10. Certain fixed stars have invisible satellites too.
11. These invisible orbitings are as important as the visible ones to us, and can 'enable us to commence the contemplation of celestial bodies'.
12. Each planet or star is 'a world'.
13. Proclus was initiated into the Egyptian and Babylonian mysteries and would thus have known about the Sirius mystery.

The Surviving Fragments of Berossus, in English Translation

Note : The following fragments are published here for the first time since 1876 in order to make them readily available to the reader. Regrettably, the original Greek text is not here included, but may be found in Cory, *The Ancient Fragments* (for which, see Bibliography).

These ancient fragments give accounts of the Babylonian tradition that civilization was originally founded by amphibious beings known as Oannes, Musari, or Annedoti (in Greek). This tradition is in striking agreement with the Dogon tradition of the amphibious Nommos, or 'Monitors', who came from the system of Sirius to found civilization on earth.

FRAGMENT OF BEROSSUS
FROM APOLLODORUS

Of the Chaldaean Kings

This is the history which Berossus has transmitted to us. He tells us that the first king was Alorus of Babylon, a Chaldaean; he reigned ten sari: and afterwards Alaparus, and Amelon who came from Pantibiblon: then Ammenon the Chaldaean, in whose time appeared the Musarus Oannes the Annedotus from the Erythraean sea. (But Alexander Polyhistor anticipating the event, has said that he appeared in the first year; but Appollodorus says that it was after forty sari; Abydenus, however, makes the second Annedotus appear after twenty-six sari.) Then succeeded Megalarus from the city of Pantibiblon; and he reigned eighteen sari: and after him Daonus the shepherd from Pantibiblon reigned ten sari; in his time (he says) appeared again from the Erythraean sea a fourth Annedotus, having the same form with those above, the shape of a fish blended with that of a man. Then reigned Euedoreschus from Pantibiblon, for the term of eighteen sari; in his days there appeared another personage from the Erythraean sea like the former, having the same complicated form between a fish and a man, whose name was Odacon. (All these, says Apollodorus, related particularly and circumstantially whatever Oannes had informed them of: concerning these Abydenus has made no mention.) Then reigned Amempsinus, a Chaldaean from Laranchae; and he being the eighth in order reigned ten sari. Then reigned Otiartes, a Chaldaean, from Laranchae;

and he reigned eight sari. And upon the death of Otiartes, his son Xisuthrus reigned eighteen sari: in his time happened the great deluge. So that the sum of all the kings is ten; and the term which they collectively reigned an hundred and twenty sari. – *Syncel. Chron. 39. Euseb. Chron. 5.*

FRAGMENTS OF BEROSSUS
FROM ABYDENUS

Of the Chaldaean Kings and the Deluge

So much concerning the wisdom of the Chaldaeans.

It is said that the first king of the country was Alorus, who gave out a report that he was appointed by God to be the Shepherd of the people: he reigned ten sari: now a sarus is esteemed to be three thousand six hundred years; a neros six hundred; and a sossus sixty.

After him Alaparus reigned three sari: to him succeeded Amillarus from the city of Pantibiblon, who reigned thirteen sari; in his time a semidaemon called Annedotus, very like to Oannes, came up a second time from the sea; after him Ammenon reigned twelve sari, who was of the city of Pantibiblon: then Megalarus of the same place eighteen sari: then Daos, the shepherd, governed for the space of ten sari; he was of Pantibiblon; in his time four double-shaped personages came out of the sea to land, whose names were Euedocus, Eneugamus, Eneuboulus, and Anementus: after these things was Anodaphus, in the time of Euedoreschus. There were afterwards other kings, and last of all Sisithrus: so that in the whole, the number amounted to ten kings, and the term of their reigns to an hundred and twenty sari. (And among other things not irrelative to the subject, he continues thus concerning the deluge:) After Euedoreschus some others reigned, and then Sisithrus. To him the deity Cronus foretold that on the fifteenth day of the month Desius there would be a deluge, and commanded him to deposit all the writings whatever that he had, in the city of the Sun in Sippara. Sisithrus, when he had complied with these commands, instantly sailed to Armenia, and was immediately inspired by God. During the prevalence of the waters Sisithrus sent out birds, that he might judge if the flood had subsided. But the birds passing over an unbounded sea, and not finding any place of rest, returned again to Sisithrus. This he repeated. And when upon the third trial he succeeded, for they then returned with their feet stained with mud, the gods translated him from among men. With respect to the vessel, which yet remains in Armenia, it is a custom of the inhabitants to form bracelets and amulets of its wood. – *Syncel. 38. – Euseb. Praep. Evan.* lib. 9. – *Euseb. Chron. 5.* 8.

Of the Tower of Babel

They say that the first inhabitants of the earth, glorying in their own strength and size, and despising the gods, undertook to raise a tower whose top should reach the sky, where Babylon now stands: but when it approached the heaven, the winds assisted the gods, and overturned the work upon its contrivers: and its ruins are said to be at Babylon: and the gods introduced a diversity of tongues among men who till that time had all spoken the same language: and a war arose between Cronus and Titan: but the place in which they built the tower is now called Babylon, on account of the confusion of the tongues; for confusion is by the Hebrews called Babel. – *Euseb. Praep. Evan.* lib. 9. – *Syncel. Chron.* 44. – *Euseb. Chron.* 13.

FRAGMENTS OF BEROSSUS
FROM ALEXANDER POLYHISTOR

Of the Cosmogony and Causes of the Deluge

Berossus, in his first book concerning the history of Babylonia, informs us that he lived in the time of Alexander the son of Philip. And he mentions that there were written accounts preserved at Babylon with the greatest care, comprehending a term of fifteen myriads of years. These writings contained a history of the heavens and the sea; of the birth of mankind; also of those who had sovereign rule; and of the actions achieved by them.

And in the first place he describes Babylonia as a country which lay between the Tigris and Euphrates. He mentions that it abounded with wheat, barley, ocrus, sesamum; and in the lakes were found the roots called gongae, which were good to be eaten, and were in respect to nutriment like barley. There were also palm trees and apples, and most kinds of fruits; fish too and birds; both those which are merely of flight, and those which take to the element of water. The part of Babylonia which is bordered upon Arabia, was barren, and without water; but that which lay on the other side had hills, and was fruitful. At Babylon there was (in these times) a great resort of people of various nations, who inhabited Chaldea, and lived without rule and order like the beast of the field.

In the first year there made its appearance, from a part of the Erythraean sea which bordered upon Babylonia, an animal endowed with reason, who was called Oannes. (According to the account of Apollodorus) the whole body of the animal was like that of a fish; and had under a fish's head another head, and also feet below, similar to those of a man, subjoined to the fish's tail. His voice too, and language, was articulate and human; and a representation of him is preserved even to this day.

This Being in the day-time used to converse with men; but took no food at that season; and he gave them an insight into letters and sciences, and every kind of art. He taught them to construct houses, to found temples, to compile laws, and explained to them the principles of geometrical knowledge. He made them distinguish the seeds of the earth, and shewed them how to collect fruits; in short, he instructed them in every thing which could tend to soften manners and humanize mankind. From that time, so universal were his instructions, nothing has been added material by way of improvement. When the sun set, it was the custom of this Being to plunge again into the sea, and abide all night in the deep; for he was amphibious.

After this there appeared other animals like Oannes, of which Berossus promises to give an account when he comes to the history of the kings.

Moreover Oannes wrote concerning the generation of mankind; of their different ways of life, and of their civil polity; and the following is the purport of what he said:

'There was a time in which there was nothing but darkness and an abyss of waters, wherein resided most hideous beings, which were produced of a two-fold principle. Men appeared with two wings, some with four and with two faces. They had one body but two heads; the one of a man, the other of a woman. They were likewise in their several organs both male and female. Other human figures were to be seen with the legs and horns of goats. Some had horses' feet, others had the limbs of a horse behind, but before were fashioned like men, resembling hippocentaurs. Bulls likewise bred there with the heads of men; and dogs with fourfold bodies, and the tails of fishes. Also horses with the heads of dogs: men too and other animals, with the heads and bodies of horses and the tails of fishes. In short, there were creatures with the limbs of every species of animals. Add to these fishes, reptiles, serpents, with other wonderful animals, which assumed each other's shape and countenance. Of all these were preserved delineations in the temple of Belus at Babylon.

'The person, who was supposed to have presided over them, was a woman named Omoroca; which in the Chaldaic language is Thalatth; which the Greeks express Thalassa, the sea: but according to the most true computation, it is equivalent to Selene, the moon. All things being in this situation, Belus came, and cut the woman asunder: and out of one half of her he formed the earth, and of the other half the heavens; and at the same time destroyed the animals in the abyss. All this (he says) was an allegorical description of nature. For the whole universe consisting of moisture, and animals being continually generated therein; the deity (Belus) above-mentioned cut off his own head: upon which the other gods mixed the blood, as it gushed out, with the earth; and from thence men were formed. On this account it is that they are rational, and partake of divine knowledge. This Belus, whom men call Dis, divided the darkness, and separated the Heavens from the Earth, and reduced the universe to order. But the animals so lately created, not being able to bear the prevalence of light, died. Belus upon this, seeing a vast space quite uninhabited, though by nature very fruitful, ordered one of the gods to take off his head; and when it was taken off, they were to mix the blood with the soil of the earth; and from thence to form other men and animals, which should be capable of bearing the light. Belus also formed the stars, and the sun, and the moon, together with the five planets.' (Such are the contents of the first book of Berossus.)

(In the second book was the history of the ten kings of the Chaldeans, and the periods of each reign, which consisted collectively of an hundred and twenty sari, or four hundred and thirty-two thousand years; reaching to the time of the Deluge. For Alexander, following the writings of the Chaldaeans, enumerating the kings from the ninth Ardates to Xisuthrus, who is called by them the tenth, proceeds in this manner:)

After the death of Ardates, his son Xisuthrus succeeded, and reigned eighteen sari. In his time happened the great Deluge; the history of which is given in this manner. The Deity, Cronus, appeared to him in a vision, and gave him notice that upon the fifteenth day of the month Daesius there would be a flood, by which mankind would be destroyed. He therefore enjoined him to commit to writing a history of the beginning, procedure, and final conclusion of all things, down to the present term; and to bury these accounts securely in the city of the Sun at Sippara; and to build a vessel, and to take with him into it his friends and relations; and to convey on board every thing necessary to sustain life, and to take in also all species of animals, that either fly or rove upon the earth; and trust himself to the deep. Having asked the Deity, whither he was to sail? he was answered, 'To the Gods:' upon which he offered up a prayer for the good of mankind. And he obeyed the divine admonition: and built a vessel five stadia in length, and two in breadth. Into this he put every thing which he had got ready; and last of all conveyed into it his wife, children, and friends. After the flood had been upon the earth, and was in time abated, Xisuthrus sent out some birds from the vessel; which not finding any food, nor any place to rest their feet, returned to him again. After an interval of some days, he sent them forth a second time; and they now returned with their feet tinged with mud. He made a trial a third time with these birds; but they returned to him no more; from whence he formed a judgment, that the surface of the earth was now above the waters. Having therefore made an opening in the vessel, and finding upon looking out, that the vessel was driven to the side of a mountain, he immediately quitted it, being attended by his wife, his daughter, and the pilot. Xisuthrus immediately paid his adoration to the earth: and having constructed an altar, offered sacrifices to the gods. These things being duly performed, both Xisuthrus and those who came out of the vessel with him disappeared. They, who remained in the vessel, finding that the others did not return, came out with many lamentations, and called continually on the name of Xisuthrus. Him they saw no more; but they could distinguish his voice in the air, and could hear him admonish them to pay due regard to the gods; and likewise inform them that it was upon account of his piety that he was translated to live with the gods; that his wife and daughter, with the pilot, had obtained the same honour. To this he added that he would have them make the best of their way to Babylonia, and search for the writings at Sippara, which were to be made known to all mankind: and that the place where they then were was the land of Armenia. The remainder having heard these words, offered sacrifices to the gods; and taking a circuit, journeyed towards Babylonia.

The vessel being thus stranded in Armenia, some part of it yet remains in the Corcyraean* mountains in Armenia; and the people scrape off the bitumen, with which it had been outwardly coated, and make use of it by way of an alexipharmic and amulet. In this manner they returned to Babylon; and having found the writings at Sippara, they set about building cities, and erecting temples: and Babylon was thus inhabited again. – *Syncel. Chron.* 28. – *Euseb. Chron.* 5. 8.

* Or Cordyean mountains—*Corduarum montibus*; Ea. Ar.

FRAGMENTS OF BEROSSUS

FROM JOSEPHUS, ETC.

Of Abraham

After the deluge, in the tenth genertion, was a certain man among the Chaldaeans renowned for his justice and great exploits, and for his skill in the celestial sciences. – *Euseb. Praep. Evan.* lib. 9.

Of Nabonasar

From the reign of Nabonasar only are the Chaldaeans (from whom the Greek mathematicians copy) accurately acquainted with the heavenly motions: for Nabonasar collected all the mementos of the kings prior to himself, and destroyed them, that the enumeration of the Chaldaean kings might commence with him. – *Syncel. Chron.* 207.

Of the Destruction of the Jewish Temple

He (Nabopollasar) sent his son Nabuchodonosor with a great army against Egypt, and against Judea, upon his being informed that they had revolted from him; and by that means he subdued them all, and set fire to the temple that was at Jerusalem; and removed our people entirely out of their own country, and transferred them to Babylon, and it happened that our city was desolate during the interval of seventy years, until the days of Cyrus king of Persia. (He then says, that) this Babylonian king conquered Egypt, and Syria, and Phoenicia and Arabia, and exceeded in his exploits all that had reigned before him in Babylon and Chaldaea. – *Joseph. contr. Appion.* lib. 1. c. 19.

Of Nebuchadnezzar

When Nabopollasar his (Nabuchodonosor's) father, heard that the governor, whom he had set over Egypt, and the parts of Coelesyria and Phoenicia, had revolted, he was unable to put up with his delinquencies any longer, but committed certain parts of his army to his son Nabuchodonosor, who was then but young, and sent him against the rebel; and Nabuchodonosor fought with him, and conquered him, and reduced the country again under his dominion. And it happened that his father, Nabopollasar, fell into a distemper at this time and died in the city of Babylon, after he had reigned twenty-nine years.

After a short time Nabuchodonosor, receiving the intelligence of his father's death, set the affairs of Egypt and the other countries, in order, and committed the captives he had taken from the Jews, and Phoenicians, and Syrians, and of the nations belonging to Egypt, to some of his friends, that they might conduct that part of the forces that had on heavy armour, with the rest of his baggage, to Babylonia; while he went in haste, with a few followers, across the desert to Babylon; where, when he was come, he found that affairs had been well conducted by the Chaldaeans, and that the principal person among them had preserved the kingdom for him: accordingly he now obtained possession of all his father's dominions. And he ordered the captives to be distributed in colonies in the most proper places of Babylonia: and adorned the temple of Belus, and the other temples, in a sumptuous and pious manner, out of the spoils he had taken in this war. He also rebuilt the old city, and added another to it on the outside, and so far restored Babylon, that none, who should besiege it afterwards, might have it in their power to divert the river, so as to facilitate an entrance into it: and this he did by building three walls about the inner city, and three about the outer. Some of these walls he built of burnt brick and bitumen, and some of brick only. When he had thus admirably fortified the city with walls, and had magnificently adorned the gates, he added also a new palace to those in which his forefathers had dwelt, adjoining them, but exceeding them in height, and in its great splendor. It would perhaps require too long a narration, if any one were to describe it: however, as prodigiously large and magnificent as it was, it was finished in fifteen days. In this palace he erected very high walks, supported by stone pillars; and by planting what was called a pensile paradise, and replenishing it with all sorts of trees, he rendered the prospect an exact resemblance of a mountainous country. This he did to please his queen, because she had been brought up in Media, and was fond of a mountainous situation. – *Joseph. contr. Appion.* lib. 1. c. 19. – *Syncel. Chron.* 220. – *Euseb. Praep. Evan.* lib. 9.

Of the Chaldaean Kings after Nebuchadnezzar

Nabuchodonosor, after he had begun to build the above-mentioned wall, fell sick, and departed this life, when he had reigned forty-three years; whereupon his son Evilmerodachus obtained the kingdom. He governed public affairs in an illegal and improper manner, and by means of a plot laid against him by Neriglissoorus, his sister's husband, was slain when he had reigned but two years.

Upon his death Neriglissoorus, who had conspired against him, succeeded him in the kingdom, and reigned four years.

His son Laborosoarchodus inherited the kingdom though he was but a child, and kept it nine months; but by reason of the evil practices he exhibited, a plot was laid against him by his friends, and he was tortured and killed.

After his death, the conspirators assembled, and by common consent put the crown upon the head of Nabonnedus, a man of Babylon, and one of the leaders of that insurrection. In his reign it was that the walls of the city of Babylon were curiously built with burnt brick and bitumen.

But in the seventeenth year of his reign, Cyrus came out of Persia with a great army, and having conquered all the rest of Asia, he came hastily to Babylonia. When Nabonnedus perceived he was advancing to attack him, he assembled his forces and opposed him, but was defeated, and fled with a few of his attendants, and was shut up in the city Borsippus. Whereupon Cyrus took Babylon, and gave orders that the outer walls should be demolished, because the city had proved very troublesome to him, and difficult to take. He then marched to Borsippus, to besiege Nabonnedus; but as Nabonnedus delivered himself into his hands without holding out the place, he was at first kindly treated by Cyrus, who gave him an habitation in Carmania, but sent him out of Babylonia. Accordingly Nabonnedus spent the remainder of his time in that country, and there died. – *Joseph. contr. App.* lib. 1. c. 20. – *Euseb. Praep. Evan.* lib. 10.

Of the Feast of Sacea

Berossus, in the first book of his Babylonian history, says; That in the eleventh month, called Loos, is celebrated in Babylon the feast of Sacea for five days; in which it is the custom that the masters should obey their domestics, one of whom is led round the house, clothed in a royal garment, and him they call Zoganes. – *Athenaeus,* lib. 14.

Fragment of Megasthenes
FROM ABYDENUS

Of Nebuchadnezzar

Abydenus, in his history of the Assyrians, has preserved the following fragment of Megasthenes, who says: That Nabucodrosorus, having become more powerful than Hercules, invaded Libya and Iberia, and when he had rendered them tributary, he extended his conquests over the inhabitants of the shores upon the right of the sea. It is moreover related by the Chaldaeans, that as he went up into his palace he was possessed by some god; and he cried out and said: 'Oh! Babylonians, I, Nabucodrosorus, foretell unto you a calamity which must shortly come to pass, which neither Belus my ancestor, nor his queen Beltis, have power to persuade the Fates to turn away. A Persian mule shall come, and by the assistance of your gods shall impose upon you the yoke of slavery: the author of which shall be a Mede, the foolish pride of Assyria. Before he should thus betray my subjects, Oh! that some sea or whirlpool might receive him, and his memory be blotted out for ever; or that he might be cast out to wander through some desert, where there are neither cities nor the trace of men, a solitary exile among rocks and caverns, where beasts and birds alone abide. But for me, before he shall have conceived these mischiefs in his mind, a happier end will be provided.'

When he had thus prophesied, he expired: and was succeeded by his son Evilmaluruchus, who was slain by his kinsman Neriglisares: and Neriglisares left Labassoarascus his son: and when he also had suffered death by violence, they made Nabannidochus king, being no relation to the royal family; and in his reign Cyrus took Babylon, and granted him a principality in Carmania.

And concerning the rebuilding of Babylon by Nabuchodonosor, he writes thus: It is said that from the beginning all things were water, called the sea (Thalatth?): that Belus caused this state of things to cease, and appointed to each its proper place: and he surrounded Babylon with a wall: but in process of time this wall disappeared: and Nabuchodonosor walled it in again, and it remained so with its brazen gates until the time of the Macedonian conquest.

And after other things he says: Nabuchodonosor having succeeded to the kingdom, built the walls of Babylon in a triple circuit in fifteen days; and he turned the river Armacale, a branch of the Euphrates, and the Acracanus: and above the city of Sippara he dug a receptacle for the waters, whose perimeter was forty parasangs, and whose depth was twenty cubits; and he placed gates at the entrance thereof, by opening which they irrigated the plains, and these they call Echetognomones (sluices): and he constructed dykes against the irruptions of the Erythraean sea, and built the city of Teredon against the incursions of the Arabs; and he adorned the palace with trees, calling them hanging gardens. – *Euseb. Praep. Evan.* lib. 10. – *Euseb. Chron.* 49.

Fragment of Julian the Emperor
(reigned A.D. 360–3)

From Cyril's *Contra Julianum* V, 176 (Migne), we have this fragment of Julian's lost work *Against the Christians:*

That God, however, has not cared for the Hebrews only, but rather that in His love for all nations He hath bestowed on the Hebrews nothing worth very serious attention, whereas He has given us far greater and superior gifts, consider from what will follow. The Egyptians, counting up of their own race the names of not a few sages, can also say they have had many who have followed in the steps of Hermes. I mean of the Third Hermes who used to come down to them in Egypt. The Chaldaeans also can tell of the disciples of Oannes and of Belus; and the Greeks of tens of thousands who have the Wisdom from Cheirion. For it is from him that they derived their initiation into the mysteries of nature, and their knowledge of divine things; so that indeed in comparison the Hebrews seem only to give themselves airs about their own attainments.

This translation (with some gaps supplied) may be found in G. R. S. Mead's *Thrice Greatest Hermes*, vol. III, page 199 (1964).

Fragment of Helladius

PRESERVED BY PHOTIUS
(c. A.D. 820–c. 893)

PRESERVED IN THE FORM OF A SUMMARY
(Codex 279)

(Helladius) recounts the story of a man named Oe who came out of the Red Sea having a fish-like body but the head, feet and arms of a man, and who taught astronomy and letters. Some accounts say that he came out of a great egg whence his name, and that he was actually a man, but only seemed a fish because he was clothed in 'the skin of a sea creature'.

I am indebted to Kenneth Demarest for bringing attention to this obscure fragment from the Byzantine Patriarch Photius in his essay 'The Winged Power'. I also quote a portion of his own remarks following it:

Helladius' account is extremely valuable, the more so because it is confirmed by the extant pictorial representations of this wise being (called 'the Egg-Born') who exited in a strange suit from some kind of vessel – likened to an egg – that 'fell' into the sea. Hyginus, Manilius and Xanthus all furnish other corroborating details, speaking of gods in honor of whom the fish-form is sacred, who plunged from the sky into the waters of the Euphrates. In another variant (found in the commentary in Germanicus' edition of Aratus) the power of a holy fish pushed ashore on the banks of the Euphrates near Babylon, the 'egg' out of which the 'deity' appeared. Before it landed in the waters, the egg-like vessel was of a luminous appearance. Thus the historian Sozomen tells us that the same type of deity descended into the Euphrates as 'a fiery star' from the sky. . . . Just as these visitant capsules in the water were remembered as 'eggs' from which higher men in fish-garb emerged, so the capsules, when they were in the sky were metaphorically described as great fiery birds or griffons . . . or, again, as winged figures or deific men flying in a winged ring or capsule . . . 'Space visitors' we would call them today.

APPENDIX III

Why Sixty Years?

The Sigui ceremony of the Dogon is celebrated every sixty years. What precedents for such a period of time, given religious importance, are to be found in the ancient world?

The Egyptians had such a period associated with Osiris.[1] We also find the sixty-year period reduplicated by them in a manner familiar from the reduplications of the fifty-year period of Sirius B, and also in the Dogon custom of speaking of 'uniting two Sigui': 'The *henti* period consisted of two periods, each containing sixty years.' And this period is described in a *Hymn to Osiris*:[2] '. . . most terrible is his name of "Asar" (Osiris). The duration of his existence is an eternal *henti* period in his name of "Un-Nefer".'

The *henti* period may, by pun, have had some association with the phallus, *henn*. I only suggest this because of the connection of circumcision with the Sigui ceremonies of the Dogon. It is pure speculation. *Henti* is also a title of Osiris, presumably arising from the fact that the duration of Osiris's existence is said to be 'an eternal *henti* period'.

My own predilection, when considering the period of sixty years, is to think in terms of a synchronization of the orbital periods of the two planets Jupiter and Saturn, for these come together in nearly sixty years. The orbital period of Jupiter is approximately twelve years and that of Saturn approximately thirty years. Five times twelve is sixty and two times thirty is also sixty. Sixty years is the great period which brings into synchronization the movements of the two great outer planets which can be seen by the eye. I have no doubt that this sixty-year period has been of considerable importance in ancient times, and the sharp-eyed Egyptians would have been well aware of it.

In speaking of the revolutions of Jupiter and Saturn, the Neoplatonist philosopher Olympiodorus has written:[3] 'That of Jupiter . . . is effected in twelve years. And . . . that of Saturn . . . is completed in thirty years. The stars, therefore, are not conjoined with each other in their revolutions except rarely. Thus, for instance, the sphere of Saturn and the sphere of Jupiter are conjoined with each other in their revolutions, in sixty years. For if the sphere of Jupiter comes from the same to the same in twelve years, but that of Saturn in thirty years, it is evident that when Jupiter has made five, Saturn will have made two revolutions: for twice thirty is sixty, and so likewise is twelve times five; so that their revolutions will be conjoined in sixty years. Souls, therefore, are punished for such like periods.'

These observations of Olympiodorus, from his Commentary on Plato's *Gorgias* in the form of scholia, are cited by Thomas Taylor as comment on a passage by Apuleius (best known as author of *The Golden Ass*) in one of his Platonic essays:[4] 'For in order that the measures and revolutions of times might be known, and that the convolutions of the world might be visible, the light of the sun was enkindled; and vice versa, the opacity of night was invented, in order that animals might obtain the rest which they naturally desire. Month likewise was produced, when the moon, having completed the revolution of her orb, returns to the same place from whence she departed. And the spaces of the year were terminated when the sun had passed through the four vicissitudes of the seasons, and arrived at the same sign. And the numerations of these circulations, returning into, and proceeding from, themselves, was discovered by the exercise of the reasoning power. Nevertheless, there are certain circuits of the stars, which perpetually observe a legitimate course, but which the sagacity of men can scarcely comprehend. . . . the supreme of all of them (is that of the fixed stars) . . . the second is given to Saturn, the third to Jupiter . . .'

This esoteric cycle conjoining the motions of Saturn and Jupiter would have seemed of immense importance to all ancient astronomers who had a good grasp of their subject. A cycle of sixty years is so long that no single person can live long enough to verify its recurrence a second time. The knowledge of such a cycle required a continuing tradition of observation which implies a priesthood with astronomical inclinations. The discovery and verification over more than one generation of an esoteric cycle joining the two great outer planets would appear as exciting to the ancient priests as discovering DNA has been to modern biochemists. To 'crack' the mysteries of the motions of the two outer planets is quite an achievement. No wonder, then, that the Dogon maintain that a priest who 'united two Sigui' is really rather special. Apart from the fact that no one lives 120 years very easily, and thus 'uniting two Sigui' is accepted as having celebrated two Sigui ceremonies in a lifetime, the reduplication of the cycle may be taken to signify that only by checking to see if it happens a second time can the cycle be verified. To unite two of the cycles is to achieve a *henti*, which we have just seen the Egyptians describe both as 120 years and as 'eternal'. How can 120 years be 'eternity'? This can be so when eternity is seen to consist of a cyclical construction. In other words, eternity is not a straight line to infinity but is rather an endless series of coils of the same size compressed into a great spring, known as time, and with the impetus of *happening*.

By chance, I found in an extremely obscure old book[5] from early in the nineteenth century a reference to a sixty-year period in the ancient world. The book is primarily a meandering of speculations concerning Stonehenge and British stone circles. It points out that Stonehenge has sixty stones in its outer circle. Then we read: '. . . (this) outer circle is the oriental cycle of Vrihaspati, 60'.[6] The author later adds:[7] 'The great temple of Rolrich, in Oxfordshire,[8] is surrounded with 60 upright stones; the cycle of Vrihaspati, an example not far distant from the others.' Later the author adds: 'the number 60 is the base of the famous cycle called the Saros of 3,600 years of the Chaldees or Culdees of Babylon . . .' and he mentions also that it is the decimal part of the 600-year cycle of the Neros period from the ancient Near East. But as for the 'famous Indian cycle of Vrihaspati', he seems upset that Indian brahmans explained it 'by saying that it arose from 5 revolutions of the planet Jupiter . . .'[9]

Passing beyond our quaint old source book, we may investigate this rumoured Indian cycle of Vrihaspati. We soon discover that it does indeed exist in Indian tradition, where it is more properly known as that of Brihaspati. The name Brihaspati (or Vrihaspati) is the name of the planet Jupiter in Sanskrit, and the cycle which takes its name from this planet is a 60-year cycle.

Looking further into the matter of Brihaspati, I discovered that a Brihaspati-cakra has two specific meanings: the Hinnu cycle of sixty years, and also 'a particular astrological diagram'. I have not been able to locate a design of this diagram. But the fact that such a diagram exists indicates to me even further that the coincidence of five orbits of Jupiter with two of Saturn may be intended here. For it is by means of a particular astrological diagram that one traditionally computes the relative positions of Saturn and Jupiter. I reproduce two such diagrams in Figures 41 and 42. These diagrams were prepared by Johannes Kepler, discoverer of our three laws of Planetary Motion, and whom I discussed slightly in Appendix I.[10]

In reference to these very diagrams, Santillana and von Dechend tell us in *Hamlet's Mill*,[11] 'A "mighty conjunction" thus corresponds to the revolution of one angle or corner of the trigon of Jupiter–Saturn conjunctions – built up in sixty years (more correctly: 59.6 years) – through the whole zodiac . . .' And further: '. . . (in) Greece, where we have – besides the wrestling of Kronos and Saturn at Olympia – also the *Daidalia*, held in the interval of sixty years – sixty-year cycles in India, or in the West Sudan, are not likely to be understood, if the scholars prefer to inhibit the trigon of the Saturn-Jupiter conjunction . . .' And this trigon must be diagrammatically presented.

We thus see that Santillana and von Dechend specifically identify sixty-year cycles of the West Sudan, where the Dogon live, with the Jupiter–Saturn synchronism over sixty years. This was not known to me when I assumed the same thing: the reader will appreciate that such a concurrence of opinion urged me to think this idea correct.

The Dogon associate a 60-year period with the creation of the world by Amma.[12] In the light of this, it is interesting that in the Western astrological tradition, Saturn 'gives the measures of creation' to Jupiter specifically through the interconnection of their orbits in the way which we have been describing. Santillana and von Dechend explain this quite well[13] and Johannes Kepler's works *De Stella Nova* and *De Vero Anno* are relevant to the subject.[14] See also Figures 41 and 42 for the diagrams by which Saturn gives the (temporal) measures of creation to Jupiter. There is a Great Conjunction of Jupiter and Saturn every twenty years, as the diagrams show. The Dogon seem to be aware of the 20-year subdivision of the 60-year period too. If the reader turns back to the Griaule and Dieterlen article which follows Chapter One of this book, and studies Figure ii accompanying that article, as well as the text referring to it, he will see that the Sigui 60-year computation is broken down into 20-year segments.

The act of circumcision, to the Dogon, symbolizes the orbit of Sirius B around Sirius A. It may well be, then, that such a tendency to use genital symbolism in connection with heavenly motions explains the 'castration' of Saturn by Jupiter in Greek mythology. Figure xii of the Griaule and Dieterlen article in this book records the 'mutilating domination of Sirius over the femininity

Figure 41. A detailed illustration of the motions of the Trigon of Great Conjunctions from 1583 to 1763

of Yasigui'. In *Le Renard pâle* one reads a great deal about genital mutilation, castration, circumcisions, female circumcisions, and so on. These strange conceptions of genital violence associated symbolically to heavenly movements obviously came to the Dogon along with the rest of their ancient traditions, and survive as well in the Mediterranean region indigenously. The mutilation of Saturn by Jupiter, and the various creations which sprang from the resulting blood and seed, are of the same current of tradition as all the elements of a similar kind to be found among the Dogon, and which are related to these comparative orbitings of Saturn and Jupiter, as well as other heavenly bodies. The placenta comes back into the picture too. We have seen in the main text of the book that the placenta is the symbol, for the Dogon, of a planetary system, and the system of our sun and its planets is a placenta. It is therefore interesting that the Dogon say that 60 is the count of the cosmic placenta.[15] For this specifically identifies the 60 years as a count defining our planetary system,

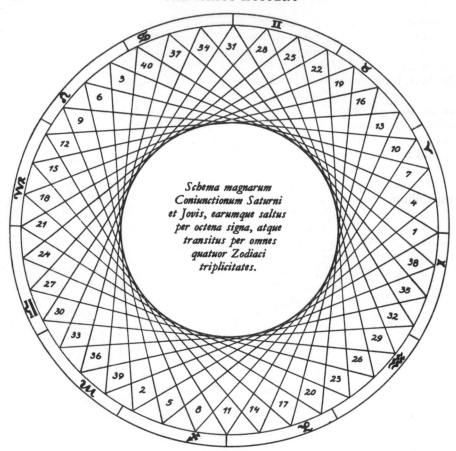

Figure 42. Scheme of the Great Conjunctions of Saturn and Jupiter, and their leap through the eighth sign and transit through all four of the triple Zodiac

and 60 years as the coordination between Saturn and Jupiter's movements can be seen as doing just that. For any system may be seen as defined by its boundaries, and as Saturn and Jupiter are recognized by the Dogon as their outermost planets for our system, their conjoinment would strictly speaking define our cosmic placenta, our solar system, for them. The Dogon even break 60 down themselves into '5 series of 12'[16] and twice thirty, which seems a fairly specific indication that our hypothesis has a sound basis. For the last point, the drawing above the door of the Dogon sanctuary of Binou[17] reinforces these ideas. This drawing is used for the computation of the Sigui. Accompanying this drawing is a drawing of the Nommo which is broken down into two major portions: his right 'leg' marks the first thirty years and his left 'leg' the second thirty years. The legs are joined to represent that only taken together do these two thirty-year periods have significance. And, as we know, Nommo did not actually have legs. He had a fish-tail extremity. The fact that each 'leg' represents a period of years is made quite clear by the information given that 'the left leg is made a little longer every year in such a way that it is the same length as the other (leg) by the time of the Sigui.' This process recalls Plutarch's remark, noted much earlier in the book, that Zeus (Jupiter) had his legs joined together. In short, Jupiter's legs were joined together because each of his 'legs' represented one of the thirty-year orbital periods of his father Saturn, and it was on his father that he stood. For Saturn upheld Jupiter's creation by providing him with the temporal measures, as Santillana and von Dechend explain.[18] And the Dogon are the people who preserve this intricate tradition most fully, which should not surprise us. They say that 60 is the 'number of the placenta', and indeed it is. Without 60 we could not define our solar system according to the traditional view of it – and this traditional view is the one resting on the capabilities of observation, which is sensible. For us to define our system today by saying it is bounded by the motions of a tiny body called Pluto doesn't mean anything to anybody. For us to ground ourselves in the weighty and ponderous motions of those two observable planets Saturn and Jupiter, and define our solar system – perhaps 'poetically' – by their motions as extremities, we would be striking a deep chord in that music of the spheres of which we have all heard fanciful tales, but of which today we know nothing. But music which cannot be heard is not necessarily lost to the inner ear. Music, after all, is not necessarily audible sound. Harmony transcends the sensibly perceptive. The observance of a celestial harmony in the ancient cultures helped keep a sane perspective. To acknowledge the deep resounding bass of the 60-year cycle was the ultimate poetic myth of the solar system, expressed in that vast mythological fabric woven around all the heavenly bodies, a whole cloth binding together both man and planets in a cosmic unity which gave man dignity and meaning in a world whose periods and cycles he had defined and celebrated in his religious festivals. Even today we do this, but have lost consciousness of it; Easter is defined by the moon. But who notices that? The cosmic bodies make their silent music but we have stopped our ears. We do not wish to be integrally related to our cosmic environment by observances of the great motions above us. All the reader need do is to take the cotton wool out of his ears and listen. He will hear silence. And the cycles and periods of that silence are the beautiful music of the cosmos. But as long as we keep our ears stopped, we will be deafened by our inner noise and will have those tortured 'modern' looks on our faces.

Notes

1. Wallis Budge. *Osiris and the Egyptian Resurrection*, op. cit., Vol. II, p. 67.
2. Ibid.
3. From his Scholia Commentary to Plato's *Gorgias*, translated by Thomas Taylor, and given by Taylor in a footnote to Apuleius's essay on the Doctrines of Plato, 'On Natural Philosophy', p. 333 in the book cited in next note.
4. Apuleius. *The Metamorphosis or Golden Ass and Philosophical Works*, trans. by Thomas Taylor, London, 1822. This book contains four of Apuleius's essays of which three are otherwise unobtainable in English translation; one is on 'The God of Socrates' and three are on the philosophy of Plato; the first of these three is relevant here; p.333-4. (The one on Socrates was also translated for Bohn's library.)

5. Higgins, Godfrey. *The Celtic Druids*, London, 1827.
6. Ibid., p. 240.
7. Ibid., p. 241.
8. The monument which Higgins calls Rolrich is now known as Rollright. It is privately owned. Anyone wishing to view it closely should contact the owner: Pauline Flick, 1 Sparke's Cottages, Graham Terrace, London S.W.1, England. The monument is Rollright Stones, at Little Rollright, Oxfordshire, England.
9. Higgins, op. cit., p. 244.
10. These figures come from Santillana and von Dechend, *Hamlet's Mill*, op. cit., and are found there opposite page 134 and opposite page 268.
11. Ibid., Appendix 23.
12. Griaule and Dieterlen, *Le Renard pâle*, op. cit., pp. 83-4.
13. See Note 11.
14. Ibid. These works of Kepler's are discussed by Santillana and von Dechend.
15. *Le Renard pâle*, p. 177.
16. Ibid., p. 185.
17. See 'A Sudanese Sirius System' in this book.
18. See Note 11.

The Meaning of the E at Delphi

Plutarch wrote a fascinating essay entitled 'The E at Delphi',[1] actually in the form of a dialogue, featuring Plutarch himself and several other speakers. It is to be remembered that Plutarch was a close personal friend of Clea, the Delphic priestess of his day, and he knew much and always sought to learn more about the nature and history of the oracles not only of Delphi but elsewhere as well. He was, however, most interested of all in Delphi itself, for he was one of the two priests of Apollo there.

The central subject of the discussion is the letter E which was a prominent inscription at the Delphic shrine. (That is, the letter E was carved in stone quite on its own at Delphi and was a subject of much curious speculation to the classical Greeks, who retained no tradition of the meaning of the ancient inscription of this single letter.) F. C. Babbitt, in his Introduction to the dialogue, says:[2]

Plutarch, in this essay on the E at Delphi, tells us that beside the well-known inscriptions at Delphi there was also a representation of the letter E, the fifth letter of the Greek alphabet. The Greek name for this letter was EI, and this diphthong, in addition to being used in Plutarch's time as the name of E (which denotes the number five), is the Greek word for 'if', and also the word for the second person singular of the verb 'to be' (thou art).

In searching for an explanation of the unexplainable it is only natural that the three meanings of EI ('five', 'if', 'thou art') should be examined to see if any hypothesis based on any one of them might possibly yield a rational explanation. . . . Plutarch puts forward seven possible explanations of the letter. . . . Attempts to explain the letter have been also made in modern times by Göttling . . . and by Schultz . . . Roscher . . . C. Robert . . . O. Lagercrantz . . . W. N. Bates, in the *American Journal of Archaeology* xxix (1925), pp. 239–46, tries to show that the E had its origin in a Minoan character E . . . later transferred to Delphi. Since the character was not understood, it, like other things at Delphi, came to be associated with Apollo. This character has been found on the old omphalos discovered in 1913 at Delphi in the temple of Apollo.

Interesting are the two coins reproduced in Imhoff-Blumer and P. Gardner, *A Numismatic Commentary on Pausanius*, plate X nos. xxii and xxiii (text p. 119), which show the E suspended between the middle columns of the temple. Learned scholars should note that the letter represented is E, not EI: therefore such explanations as are based on the true diphthong are presumably wrong.

The second explanation offered by Plutarch is in fact the correct one. This is how Plutarch suggests it:

Ammonius smiled quietly, suspecting privately that Lamprias had been indulging in a mere opinion of his own and was fabricating history and tradition regarding a matter in which he could not be held to account. Someone else among those present said that all this was similar to the nonsense which the Chaldaean visitor had uttered a short time before: that there are seven vowels in the alphabet and seven stars that have an independent and unconstrained motion; that E is the second in order of the vowels from the beginning, and the sun the second planet after the moon, and that practically all the Greeks identify Apollo with the Sun.

The facts that Delphi is the second descending centre in the geodetic octave, and that it is symbolized by the second vowel E, would seem to go well together. The seven vowels (each corresponding to one of the oracle centres) were uttered in succession as the holy 'unspeakable' name of God by Egyptian priests. Demetrius of Phalerum, the student of Aristotle's Lyceum and who founded the famous great library of Alexandria when later in life he was exiled to Egypt, tells us in his surviving treatise *On Style*: 'In Egypt the priests sing hymns to the gods by uttering the seven vowels in succession, the sound of which produces as strong a musical impression on their hearers as if flute and lyre were used.'

In Chapter XVI of *The White Goddess*, Robert Graves discusses this too, and there quotes Demetrius. Graves also refers to an eight-letter version of the sacred name. It may be that if one wants to count the base oracle centre (which in musical analogy is the octave expression of the top centre) one should have an eight-letter version. This version of the name is:

JEHUOVAŌ.
Note that E is the second letter.

We are faced with archaeological evidence that the second vowel, E, was prominently associated with the second oracle centre in descending order. (See Plate 12 of this book.) And we know from Herodotus that Dodona, the top oracle centre, was said to be founded by Egyptian priestesses from Thebes in Egypt. We also know that certain Egyptian priests sang the seven vowels (or eight vowels, including an aspirate) in succession. We have already seen that the geodetic oracle centres seem to have an octave structure. And as this book went to press a discovery became known which demonstrated the existence of the heptatonic, diatonic musical scale in the ancient Near East. We may even make a presumption that the uttering of the seven vowels in succession may possibly have corresponded to the seven notes of the octave (but we may never know that for certain). And it is most important to emphasize that, however bizarre to us, the association of a vowel with an oracle centre is not our invention or surmise. The E may not only be read about in Plutarch but seen on ancient coins and on the omphalos stone itself (for both of which see Plate 14). And this association of the second vowel with Delphi has never been explained by anyone.

So granted all the above, what follows? If each oracle centre had a vowel associated with it, then the second vowel being associated with the second centre would seem to imply a corresponding arrangement for the other centres. And if that is the case, it would seem that the entire system would be associated with and actually comprise a geodetic spelling-out, over eight degrees of latitude, of the unspeakable holy name of God, known commonly to the Hebrews as 'Jehovah'.

It is most important that anyone intrigued by this possibility should keep a wary eye for any further evidence. We should be on the lookout for representations of or associations of other vowels at the other centres. These may already be known to specialists in the field or there may be evidence of this sort languishing unclassified and unexplained in the basement of some museum. Or this sort of evidence may come to light at any time in the future. One place to begin looking would, it seems to me, be with an examination of the omphalos stone from Delos, which is to be seen in Plate 12 of this book. Does this omphalos stone have a single letter inscribed on it similarly to the Delphi omphalos stone? And what of all the other omphalos stones, such as the one from Thebes in Egypt (see Plate 12). Are any of these well enough preserved to show a puzzling single hieroglyph of a vowel? I have not carried out any investigation of this sort myself at the present time.

In closing, it would seem that the E at Delphi must fall into some coherent system of the kind I suggest, and the explanation of the enigma must be connected with Plutarch's lightly advocated second explanation – that to do with E being the second vowel. (Babbitt's exclusion of the diphthong on the basis of the ancient coins to be seen in Plate 14 of this book is therefore crucial and to my view conclusive.)

Notes

1. The dialogue 'The E at Delphi' is to be found in English in Volume V of Plutarch's *Moralia* (altogether 15 vols) published in the Loeb Classical Library series; London: William Heinemann Ltd., and U.S.A.: Harvard University Press. The volume first appeared in 1936, and the translation is by Frank Cole Babbitt. Other works of Plutarch in the same volume are 'Isis and Osiris', 'The Oracles at Delphi No Longer Given in Verse', and 'The Obsolescence of Oracles'.
2. Ibid. See Plate 14 of this book.

Why the Hittites were at Hebron in Palestine

We read in Genesis 23:7 that 'Abraham stood up and then bowed low to the Hittites, the people of that country'. The only trouble about this is that, according to our extremely sound archaeological knowledge, there should not have been any Hittites in 'that country' – namely, at Hebron in Palestine. The Hittite conquests never extended that far south. So what do we do with this riddle?

In his book *The Hittites*, Professor Oliver Gurney has an entire section (pp. 59–62) entitled 'The Hittites in Palestine'. In it he says:

> We have now to deal with the paradoxical fact that, whereas the Hittites appear in the Old Testament as a Palestinian tribe, increasing knowledge of the history of the ancient people of Hatti has led us ever farther from Palestine, until their homeland has been discovered in the heart of the Anatolian plateau. Moreover, the preceding outline of Hittite history will have shown us that before the reign of Suppiluliumas there was no Hittite state south of the Taurus; that the Syrian vassal states of the Hittite Empire were confined to the area north of Kadesh on the Orontes; and that although Hittite armies reached Damascus, they never entered Palestine itself. Of the neo-Hittite states there was none south of Hamath, and the latter did not include any part of Palestine within its territories, being separated from it by the Aramean kingdom of Damascus.

> The presence of Hittites in Palestine before the Israelite conquest thus presents a curious problem. So far from explaining it, all our accumulated knowledge of the people of Hatti [the Hittites] has only made it more perplexing.

References in the Bible include Genesis 23 (entire), Genesis 26:9–11, 34–5; 27:46 (where Rebecca says to Isaac: 'I am weary to death of Hittite women! If Jacob marries a Hittite woman like those who live here, my life will not be worth living!'), and 36:1–3. Further crucial reference to the Hittites appears in the Book of Numbers 13:29. There Moses is told by some men he had sent at the Lord's command to explore Hebron (and we are told in Numbers 13:22–3, that Hebron 'was built seven years before Zoan in Egypt' – which is a curious remark, implying a connection between Hebron and Egypt and also that there was something special at Hebron which could be described as 'built'), that at Hebron they had seen the Hittites.

We thus find clear evidence in books of the Bible for the Hittites residing in Palestine. And their settlements were specifically in the hills at Hebron.

Gurney says: 'Who, then, were these Hittites of the Palestine hills? A very ingenious answer has been put foward by E. Forrer.' The gist of this is that, considerably before 1335 B.C., some Hittites from the city of Kurustamma in the north-east of Anatolia had gone to Egypt, of which documentary evidence exists:

> However surprising it may seem, the text here quoted states explicitly that during the reign of Suppiluliumas some men from this obscure northern city entered the 'land of Egypt', a term which would include all territory under Egyptian rule. The text leaves the circumstances under which this occurred obscure, but the reference to the Weather-god of Hatti as the instigator of the move is in favour of a deliberate act of state rather than a flight of fugitives from the Hittite conquest, as suggested by Forrer. However that may be, we have here one certain instance of a group of Hittites (i.e., subjects of the King of Hatti) entering Egyptian territory, and the possibility of their having settled in the sparsely populated Palestinian hills is not to be ignored . . . (But) emigration of Anatolian Hittites to Palestine cannot have been a frequent occurrence. . . . (and) there is some hope that further excavation [of texts] among the archives of Boghazköy will bring enlightenment.

It should be pointed out that the reign of Suppiluliumas during which the above emigration took place covered the years 1380–1346 B.C. It was to him that the widow of Tutankhamen, the Egyptian Queen Ankhesenamun, third daughter of Pharaoh Akhenaten, sent a plaintive letter asking for one of his sons to become her husband. He sent a son, but the son was ambushed on the way to Egypt and killed, probably by Hor-em-heb, who seized the throne of Egypt and forced Ankhesenamun to marry him in order to legitimize his usurpation. This is a sad story but does not really concern us here. I mention it merely to bring to life the chronology of the emigration to Hebron, and also because it demonstrates the close links possible at that time between the Hittites and Egypt. Those who wish to read the letter in full and follow up this interesting tale of personal tragedy are referred to *Ancient Near Eastern Texts* (ed. Pritchard, see Bibliography), pp. 319, 395.

However, the Hittite emigration in the reign of Suppiluliumas cannot have been the original Hittite settlement at Hebron. For if Abraham met Hittites when he arrived at Hebron, then there must have been Hittites there for several hundred years before the reign of Suppiluliumas which extended 1380–1346 B.C. We learn from George Roux in his book *Ancient Iraq*, p. 242: 'Abraham and his family came from Ur in Sumer to Hebron in Canaan, probably about 1850 B.C., and there are good reasons for placing Joseph's migration to Egypt during the Hyksos period (1700–1580 B.C.).' Despite the fact that there can be a case made for Abraham's Ur being a different Ur, the main point is the date, for Abraham went to Hebron and met Hittites already there five hundred years before the emigration which Gurney mentions. Roux repeats his dating, and gives references, on page 215 of his book.

It is likely that, half a millennium after Abraham, the Hittite emigration of which we have proof during the reign of Suppiluliumas went to Egyptian territory, and quite probably to Hebron, to reinforce the Hittite community which had already been there for many centuries, but which was facing hard times. One has only to read the Amarna Letters in translation in *Ancient Near Eastern Texts* – vivid, compulsive, desperate documents – to know the anarchy into which the region of Palestine was plunged during this period. The prince of the Hebron region, Shuwardata, first fought the rapacious Apiru raiders who swarmed over the countryside and then joined them, rebelling against the Pharaoh before whom, in his correspondence, he had shortly before been 'bowing seven times and again seven times, both prone and supine'. But Egypt was weak, and Palestine degenerated into chaos. It is no wonder that during this period there was a Hittite migration to what was titular Egyptian territory. No Hittite settlement at Hebron could have felt itself entirely secure. But what was the reason for the Hittite settlement at Hebron in the first place?

In the light of our earlier elucidation of the geodetic oracle octaves, it seems clear that the presence of the Hittites at Hebron can be explained on religious grounds. For we know that Hebron was the 'base oracle' centre of the eastern geodetic oracle octave. The top centre of this same octave was Metsamor at Ararat, to the north and east of Hittite territory, and is probably the reason why the Hittites who migrated to 'Egyptian territory' during the reign of Suppiluliumas were from an obscure north-eastern city (because this was the closest Hittite region to Ararat). The area of Ararat was later to become the kingdom of Urartu, and we know that this kingdom and the Hittites were not altogether strangers, for we learn from Gurney, pages 44–5: 'The North Syrian Hittite states . . . may have felt a certain racial or cultural affinity with Urartu . . .'

Since we have documentary evidence that it was a divine command which made the Hittites of the fourteenth century B.C. go to what we assume was possibly Hebron, we can see that they were obeying an oracular injunction. This is natural if their activity was connected with the oracle centres. Indeed, they could not have gone without a divine command on such exclusively divine and non-imperial business. Gurney may be quite right in saying that the journey was a deliberate act and not a flight of fugitives. It was as deliberate as the 'doves who flew to Dodona'.

We have distinct evidence that Hebron really did have an oracle centre, apart from its being on the same latitude as Behdet. To investigate this, we turn to *The White Goddess* by Robert Graves, where in Chapter IX he discusses Hebron a great deal.

> But Caleb . . . conveyed the Holy Spirit to Hebron when, in the time of Joshua, he ousted the Anakim from the shrine of Machpelah. Machpelah, an oracular cave cut from the rock, was the sepulchre of Abraham, and Caleb went there to consult his shade . . . it is likely that neither Isaac nor Jacob nor their 'wives' were at first associated with the cave. The story of its purchase from Ephron . . . and the . . . Hittites, is told in Genesis 23. Though late and much edited, this chapter seems to record a friendly arrangement between the devotees of the goddess Sarah, the Goddess of the tribe of Isaac, and their allies the devotees of the Goddess Heth (Hathor? Tethys?) who owned the shrine: Sarah was forced out of Beer-Lahai-Roi by another tribe and came to seek an asylum at nearby Hebron (p. 162).

Graves states (p. 164) that 'Abraham' was in fact a tribe, and that this tribe also came down from Armenia (vicinity of Ararat). He says: ' "Abraham" being in this sense the far-travelled tribe that came down into Palestine from Armenia at the close of the third millennium B.C.' In fact, we must give some thought to 'the chosen people' – later known as Hebrews – being 'chosen' in the sense that they were particularly connected with tending an oracle centre or centres. Did Abraham go to Hebron for the same reasons that the Hittites did?

Graves says (p. 164):

J. N. Schofield in his *Historical Background to the Bible* notes that to this day the people of Hebron have not forgiven David for moving his capital to Jerusalem ('Holy Salem') which they refer to as 'The New Jerusalem' as though Hebron were the authentic one. There is a record in the Talmud of a heretical sect of Jews, called Melchizedekians, who frequented Hebron to worship the body (consult the spirit?) of Adam which was buried in the cave of Machpelah.

In fact, these Melchizedekians, though considered heretics, may have been adherents of a purer undistorted form of worship. And it may be that David was the great perverter of Judaism by moving Holy Salem away from Hebron. Graves continues:

For Adam, 'the red man', seems to have been the original oracular hero of Machpelah; it is likely that Caleb consulted his shade not Abraham's, unless Adam and Abraham are titles of the same hero. Elias Levita, the fifteenth-century Hebrew commentator, records the tradition that the teraphim which Rachel stole from her father Laban were mummified oracular heads and that the head of Adam was among them. If he was right, the Genesis narrative refers to a seizure of the oracular shrine of Hebron by Saul's Benjaminites from the Calebites.

Caleb was an Edomite clan; which suggests the identification of Edom with Adam: they are the same word, meaning 'red'. But if Adam was really Edom, one would expect to find a tradition that the head of Esau, the ancestor of the Edomites, was also buried at Hebron; and this is, in fact, supplied by the Talmud . . . that Esau's body was carried off for burial on Mount Seir by his sons; and that his head was buried at Hebron by Joseph.

Elsewhere (page 167) Graves says:

It is possible that though the Calebites interpreted 'Adam' as the Semitic word Edom ('red') the original hero at Hebron was the Danaan Adamos or Adamastos, 'the Unconquerable', or 'the Inexorable', a Homeric epithet of Hades, borrowed from the Death Goddess his mother.

Graves says that according to the tradition (p. 161): 'Hebron may be called the centre of the earth, from its position near the junction of two seas and the three ancient continents.' How similar this 'centre of the earth' epithet is to Delphi's, as 'the navel of the world'. All the main oracle centres were navel or *omphalos* centres of the earth. Hebron's description as such is what one would have predicted. The traditions of the creation of Adam at Hebron and of its being the site of the Garden of Eden, as Graves tells us in this chapter, make sense also when it is realized that Hebron was the base of the entire eastern geodetic octave of oracle centres. It was the eastern counterpart of Behdet itself.

Graves tells us at the beginning of Chapter Four of the later history of Hebron:

> A confederacy of mercantile tribes, called in Egypt, 'the People of the Sea' . . . invaded Syria and Canaan, among them the Philistines, who captured the shrine of Hebron in southern Judea from the Edomite clan of Caleb; but the Calebites ('Dog-men'), allies of the Israelite tribe of Judah, recovered it about the same time. These borrowings were later harmonized in the Pentateuch with a body of Semitic, Indo-European and Asianic myth which composed the religious traditions of the mixed Israelite confederacy.

In closing, we should note with a minimum of surprise, that the guardian tribe of the shrine of Hebron, the Calebites, were 'Dog-men'. Dogs are guardians, and preserve the secrets of the Dog Star Sirius, particularly as expressed in the ancient geodetic oracle octaves.

As for the Hittites, they were at Hebron – and only at that specific place in Palestine – because of its oracle centre. That is why they were 'sent by divine command', centuries later, presumably to reinforce that very place against the dangers of a turbulent time when Egyptian control under Akhenaten had collapsed.

APPENDIX VI

The Dogon Stages of Initiation

The following description of the Dogon system of graduated initiation into the mysteries of tribal religion is taken from *Le Renard pâle* (The Pale Fox) by Marcel Griaule and Germaine Dieterlen:

> The Dogon, who have classified everything, have established a layered hierarchy of their teachings they give to the initiates. Their knowledge is staggered in four degrees, that are, in the order of their importance, the *giri so*, the *benne so*, the *bolo so*, and the *so dayi*.
>
> The *giri so*, 'word at face value', is the first knowledge implying simple explanations where the mythical characters are often disguised, their adventures simplified and invented, and are not linked together. It has to do with invisible deeds, concerning the ordinary rituals and materials.
>
> The *benne so*, 'word on the side', includes 'the words in the *giri so*' and a thorough study of certain parts of the rites and representations. Their coordination only appears within the great divisions of learning which are not completely revealed.
>
> The *bolo so*, 'word from behind', completes the preceding learning, on the one hand, and on the other hand furnishes the syntheses that apply to a vaster whole. However, this stage does not yet include instruction in the truly secret parts of the tradition.
>
> The *so dayi*, 'clear word', concerns the edifice of knowledge in its ordered complexity.
>
> But initiation is not merely an accumulation of learning, nor even a philosophy, nor a way of thinking. It has an educational character, for it forms the individual, moulds him, as he assimilates the knowledge it imparts. It is more than that, because of its vital character; as it makes him understand the structure and system of the universe, it brings the initiate progressively towards a way of life which is as aware and complete as possible within his society, in the world, as he was conceived and created by God.
>
> . . . Thus, a 'fourth dimension' is introduced into the life of the Dogon, peculiar to the myth and symbol which is as necessary to their existence as food and drink, in which they move with ease and flexibility, but also with the deep sense of the immanent presence of the invisible thing they are invoking . . . at a given moment, for such and such a ceremony, they know to what sequence of the myth and to which connections (their) act belongs . . .

BIBLIOGRAPHY

Aitken, Robert G. *The Binary Stars*, Dover Publications, New York, 1964.

Allen, Richard Hinckley. *Star Names, Their Lore and Meaning* (formerly titled *Star-Names and Their Meanings*), Dover Publications, New York, 1963.

Anscombe, G. E. M., trans. See Proclus.

Apollonius of Rhodes (Apollonius Rhodius). *The Voyage of Argo* (*Argonautica*), Penguin Books, London, 1969, trans. by E. V. Rieu.

Apuleius (Lucius Apuleius of Madaura). *The Metamorphosis or Golden Ass and Philosophical Works*, trans. by Thomas Taylor, London, 1822. Contains 'The God of Socrates' and three essays on Plato.
The Works of Apuleius comprising the Metamorphoses, or Golden Ass, The God of Socrates, The Florida, and His Defence, or a Discourse on Magic, trans. apparently anonymous, Bohn's Classical Library, London, 1878.

Aratus (Aratos) of Soli. *Phaenomena*, trans. by G. R. Mair, in Vol. No. 129, *Callimachus Hymns and Epigrams, Lycophron, Aratus*, of Loeb Library series, Heinemann, London, and Harvard University Press, America, 1969.

Armstrong, A. H., ed. *The Cambridge History of Later Greek & Early Mediaeval Philosophy*, Cambridge University Press, 1970.

Asimov, Isaac. *The Universe*, Allen Lane, the Penguin Press, London, 1967.

Asimov, Isaac, and Dole, Stephen H. *Planets for Man*, Methuen, London, 1964.

Aubrey, John. *Brief Lives*, ed. by Oliver Lawson Dick, Penguin, London, 1972.

Babbitt, Frank Cole, trans. See Plutarch.

Baize, Dr P. *Le Compagnon de Sirius*, Bull. de la Société Astronomique France, 1931, 383-4.

Benardete, Seth. *Herodotean Inquiries*, Martinus Nijhoff, The Hague, 1969.

Berossus (Berossos, Berosus, etc.). *The Chaldaean History* (*The Babylonian History*), surviving fragments of which in Greek and English are in Cory's *Ancient Fragments*, for which see Cory; surviving fragments in English are published as Appendix II in this book.

Berry, Adrian. *The Next Ten Thousand Years*, Jonathan Cape, London, 1974.

Booker, Christopher. *The Neophiliacs*, Fontana/Collins, London, 1970.

Bowra, C. M., trans. See Pindar.

Bracewell, Dr R. N. 'Radio Signals from Other Planets', 'Life in the Galaxy', 'Communications from Superior Galactic Communities'; in *Interstellar Communication*; see Cameron, Dr A. G. W.

Budge, see Wallis Budge.

Burney, Charles, and Lang, David Marshall. *The Peoples of the Hills, Ancient Ararat and Caucasus*, Weidenfeld & Nicolson, London, 1971.

Burkill, I. H., reference of 1935 untraceable. See Drar.

Callimachus. *Hymns*, trans. by A. W. Mair, in *Callimachus Hymns and Epigrams, Lycophron, Aratus*, Vol. No. 129, Loeb Library series, Heinemann, London, Harvard University Press, America, 1969.

Calvin, Dr Melvin. 'Chemical Evolution', in *Interstellar Communication*; see Cameron, Dr A. G. W.

Cameron, Dr A. G. W., ed. and contrib. *Interstellar Communications*, W. A. Benjamin, New York, 1963. Contribs. to vol.: 'The History of Our Galaxy', 'The Origin of the Solar System', 'The Early Development of the Earth', 'Stellar Life Zones', 'Future Research on Interstellar Communication'.

Caton, Dr 'Delphi', 'Delos', in *Aegean Civilizations*; see Lunn, Sir Henry.

Chaldaean Oracles. See Mead, G. R. S.
Also: *The Chaldaick Oracles of Zoroaster and His Followers* (with the expositions of Pletho and Psellus) by Thomas Stanley, London, 1661.
Also: 'Chaldaean Oracles', etc., in *Collectanea* of Thomas Taylor, London, 1806.

Clarke, Arthur C. *The Coming of the Space Age* (ed.), Gollancz, London, 1967.
  Profiles of the Future, Pan Books, London, 1962.
  The Promise of Space, Hodder and Stoughton, London, 1968.
  Report on Planet Three and Other Speculations, Corgi Books, London, 1973.
  Voices from the Sky, Previews of the Coming Space Age, Gollancz, London, 1966.
Condon, Dr Edward. *Scientific Study of Unidentified Flying Objects* (with introduction by Walter
  Sullivan), Bantam Books, New York, 1968.
Copernicus, Nicolaus. 'On the Revolutions of the Heavenly Spheres' trans. by C. G. Wallis, in
  Ptolemy, Copernicus, Kepler, Vol. 16 of *Great Books of the Western World* series, pub. by Encyclo-
  paedia Britannica, Chicago, London, Toronto, 1952.
Cory, I. P. *The Ancient Fragments*, London, 1828 (first edition). See also Berossus; see Appendix
  II; see Index. Two later editions were published in London, 1832 and 1876. Each of the
  three editions differs considerably from the others in the content of the volume.
Cramp, Leonard G. *A Piece for a Jigsaw*, Somerton Publishing Company, Ltd., Newport Road,
  Cowes, Isle of Wight, England, 1967.
Crocker, Dr Richard L., and Kilmer, Dr Anne. Letter to *The Times*, London, 15 April 1974.
  Article about their discoveries in *The Times*, 7 March 1974.
Crombie, A. C. *Augustine to Galileo*, 2 vols., Penguin Books, London, 1959.

Dechend. See von Dechend.
Demarest, Kenneth. 'The Winged Power' in *Consciousness and Reality*; see Young, Arthur M.
Dieterlen, Germaine. See Griaule, Marcel.
Diogenes Laertius. *Lives of Eminent Philosophers*, trans. by R. D. Hicks, 2 vols., Vols. Nos. 184, 185,
  of Loeb Library series, Heinemann, London, and Harvard University Press, 1966.
Dittrich, E. 'Woher das Epitheton "rot" fur Sirius stammt' ('Where the Epithet "Red" for
  Sirius Originated'), *Astronomische Nachrichten*, Number 5542, 1927.
Dodds, E. R., trans. See Proclus.
Drake, Dr Frank D. *Intelligent Life in Space*, Macmillan, New York, and London, 1962.
  'How Can We Detect Radio Transmissions from Distant Planetary Systems?' and 'Project
  Ozma' in *Interstellar Communication*; see Cameron, A. G. W.
Drar and Täckholm, 'Flora of Egypt', Vol. III, *Bulletin of the Faculty of Science*, No. 30, Cairo
  University Faculty of Science, Cairo University Press, 1954. Contains reference to Burkill, I.
Dudley, D. R., ed. See *Penguin Companion to Literature*.

Emery, Dr Walter Bryan. *Archaic Egypt*, Penguin Books, London, 1972.
Encyclopaedia of Mythology; see Larousse.
Epic of Gilgamesh. trans. by Alexander Heidel, *The Gilgamesh Epic and Old Testament Parallels*,
  University of Chicago Press, 1970.
  Trans. by Kramer, S. N. (Sumerian fragments) and Speiser, E. A. (Akkadian/Babylonian
  main text) in *Ancient Near Eastern Texts* (1955); see Pritchard. Also trans. by Grayson, A. K.,
  successor to the late Dr Speiser, in *Supplement* vol. (1969); see Pritchard.
  The above are the only full-scale English translations of the *Epic of Gilgamesh* for scholarly
  use.
Epictetus. See Simplicius.
Eiselen, Frederick Carl. *Sidon: A Study in Oriental History*, Columbia University Press, New York,
  1907. The entire book is about the history and culture of the city of Sidon, one of my pro-
  posed oracle centres. It contains interesting information but came to my attention too late
  to use.
Euclid. See Proclus.
Eunapius (of Sardis). *Lives of the Philosophers and Sophists*, trans. by Wright, Wilmer Cave. In Vol.
  No. 134, *Philostratus and Eunapius*, of the Loeb Library series, Heinemann, London, Harvard
  University Press, 1961.

Fage, J. D. *A History of West Africa, An Introductory Survey*, Cambridge University Press, 1969.
Fairservis, Walter A., Jr. *The Ancient Kingdoms of the Nile*, Mentor Books, New York, 1962.
Forde, Daryll, ed. *African Worlds*, Oxford University Press, 1954. (Contains chapter on Dogon
  with *arche* mistranslated 'arch' instead of 'ark'. Written by Griaule and Dieterlen.)

Frankfort, Henri. *Ancient Egyptian Religion*, Harper Torchbooks, New York, 1961. *Cylinder Seals*, 1939. *Stratified Cylinder Seals from the Diyala Region*, Volume 72, University of Chicago Oriental Institute Publications, 1955.

Galpin, Canon Francis W. *Music of the Sumerians, Babylonians, and Assyrians*, Cambridge University Press, 1937.
    (See also *The Times*, London, 14 March, 1974, letters column for letter from Canon Galpin's son Brian Galpin on same subject.)
Gardner, P. See Imhoof-Blumer.
Garstang, John. *The Syrian Goddess* trans. by Professor Herbert A. Strong of *De Dea Syria* of Lucian with a Life of Lucian, ed. with notes and introduction by Garstang, London, 1913.
Gaster, Theodor H. *Thespis; Ritual, Myth and Drama in the Ancient Near East*, Harper & Row, New York, 1966 (Harper Torchbook).
Gilgamesh, Epic of. See *Epic of Gilgamesh*.
Goodwin, William W., trans. See Plutarch.
Gordon, Cyrus. *The Common Background of Greek and Hebrew Civilizations*, (previous title *Before the Bible*), W. W. Norton & Company, New York, 1965.
    Forgotten Scripts, Penguin Books, London, 1971.
Gow, The Rev. Dr J. 'Oracles' in *Aegean Civilizations*; see Lunn, Sir Henry.
Grant, Frederick C. *Hellenistic Religions*, Library of Liberal Arts, Bobbs-Merrill, New York, 1953. This important book is a compendium of source material in translation. It includes four hymns by Proclus, texts of oracles from Dodona, Egyptian material, etc.
Graves, Robert. *The Greek Myths*, 2 vols., Penguin Books, London, 1969–71.
    The White Goddess, Vintage Books, New York, undated. Originally published 1948.
Grayson, A. K. See *Epic of Gilgamesh*.
Greenhill, Sir George. 'Astronomy and Navigation in the Odyssey' in *Aegean Civilizations*; see Lunn, Sir Henry.
Griaule, Marcel, and Dieterlen, Germaine. *Le Renard pâle* ('*The Pale Fox*'), Tome I, Fascicule 1; Institut d'Ethnologie, Musée de l'Homme, Palais de Chaillot, Place du Trocadero, Paris 16ᵉ (75016 Paris), 1965. 544 pp.
    'Un Système Soudanais de Sirius', *Journal de la Société des Africainistes*. Tome XX, Fascicule 1, 1950, pp. 273–94. This article is published in translation in its entirety following Chapter One of this book, and accompanied with diagrams.
Gurney, O. R. *The Hittites*, Penguin Books, London, 1966.
Guthrie, W. K. C. *The Greeks and Their Gods*, Beacon Press, Boston, 1961.

Hallet, Jean-Pierre. *Pygmy Kitabu*, Random House, New York, 1973.
Hardie, Colin, trans. See Kepler.
Hawkins, Gerald. *Beyond Stonehenge*, Harper & Row, New York, 1973. Particularly interesting is the account of the rare spider drawn on the Nazca sand: pp. 143–5.
Hébert-Stevens, François; Jahan, Raoul; and Rambach, Pierre. *Expedition Tortoise*, Thames and Hudson, London, 1957.
Heidel, Alexander. See *Epic of Gilgamesh*.
    The Babylonian Genesis, University of Chicago Press, 1965.
Hermes. (*Hermetica. Hermetic Writings*, etc.) *Thrice-Greatest Hermes*, ed., trans., and comm. by G. R. S. Mead, 3 vols., John Watkins, London, 1964. Contains entire surviving *Hermetica* and fragments in English. In this work the term 'Trismegistic' is used to describe the writings.
Herodotus (Herodotos). *The Histories*, trans. by Aubrey de Sélincourt, Penguin Books, London, 1971.
Hesiod. *Theogony* and *Works and Days*, trans. by Dorothea Wender, in *Hesiod and Theognis*, Penguin Books, London, 1973.
Hicks, R. D. See Diogenes Laertius.
Higgins, Godfrey. *The Celtic Druids*, London, 1827.
    The Anacalypsis, 2 vols., Macy-Masius, New York, 1927.
Holmes, Captain David C. *The Search for Life on Other Worlds*, Bantam Books, New York, 1966.
Homer. *The Iliad* and *The Odyssey*, many editions, take your pick.
Homeric Hymns, trans. by Andrew Lang, London, 1899.

Huang, Su-Shu. 'Occurrence of Life in the Universe', 'The Problem of Life in the Universe and the Mode of Star Formation', 'Life-Supporting Regions in the Vicinity of Binary Systems', 'The Sizes of Habitable Planets', 'Problem of Transmission in Interstellar Communication', all in *Interstellar Communication*; see Cameron, A. G. W.

Hume, David. *The History of England*, 5 vols., Porter and Coates, Philadelphia, undated (nineteenth century).

Hurry, Jamieson B. *Imhotep, The Vizier and Physician of King Zoser and Afterwards the Egyptian God of Medicine*, Oxford University Press, 1926.

Hutchinson, R. W. *Prehistoric Crete*, Penguin Books, London, 1968.

Helbig, Wolfgang. *Wandgemälde der vom Vesuv Verschütteten Städte* (Wall-Paintings of the Cities Buried by the Eruption of Vesuvius), Leipzig, 1868.

Ideler, Christian Ludwig. *Untersuchungen über den Ursprung und die Bedeutung der Sternnamen*, Berlin, 1809. This is the main critical compendium of information on stellar names, consisting of a translation of the Arab Al Khazwini's *Description of the Constellations* (13th century) with Ideler's extensive additions. Ideler is the primary source in turn for Richard Hinckley Allen.

Imhooff-Blumer, Friedrich, and Gardner, P. *A Numismatic Commentary on Pausanius*, 1887.

Imhotep. See Hurry, J. B.

Jacobsen, Thorkild. *Toward the Image of Tammuz and Other Essays*, Harvard University Press, 1970.

Jahan, Raoul. See Hébert-Stevens, François.

Josephus (Flavius Josephus). *The Works of Flavius Josephus*, trans. by William Whiston, London, 1856.

Julian (Julian the Apostate, Julian the Emperor). Works in 3 vols., trans. by Wilmer Cave Wright, Vols. 13, 29, and 157 in Loeb Library series, Heinemann, London, Harvard University Press.

Jung, Carl Gustav. *Flying Saucers, A Modern Myth of Things Seen in the Skies*, Harcourt Brace, New York, 1959.

Kawerau, Georg, and Rehm, Albert. *Das Delphinion in Milet*, 1899. (Archaeological work on Miletus.)

Kepler, Johannes. *Kepler's Conversation wtih Galileo's Sidereal Messenger* trans. by Edward Rosen, No. 5 of Sources of Science Series, Johnson Reprint Corp., London and New York, 1965. *Kepler's Dream (Somnium)* trans. by John Lear and P. F. Kirkwood, University of California Press, Berkeley and Los Angeles, 1965. *Epitome of Copernican Astronomy* (Chapters 4 and 5 only) and *Harmonies of the World* (Chapter 5 only) trans. by C. G. Wallis in Vol. 16, *Ptolemy, Copernicus, Kepler*, of the 'Great Books of the Western World' series, pub. by Encyclopaedia Britannica Inc., Chicago, London, Toronto, 1952. *Six-Cornered Snowflake*, trans. by Colin Hardie and Lancelot Law Whyte, Oxford University Press, 1966.

Kepler, Johannes. *Kepler's Somnium*, trans and comm., Edward Rosen, University of Wisconsin Press, 1967.

Kerenyi, Carl. *The Gods of the Greeks*, Penguin Books, London, 1958.

Khazwini, Al. (Arab astronomical writer of 13th century). See Ideler.

Kilmer, Dr Anne. See Crocker, Dr. Richard L.

Kirkwood, P. F. See Kepler.

Klibansky, R. See Proclus.

Koestler, Arthur. *The Sleepwalkers*, Penguin Books, London, 1964.

Kramer, Samuel Noah. See Pritchard, James. *History Begins at Sumer*, Doubleday Anchor Books, New York, 1959. *Mythologies of the Ancient World*, ed. and contrib. 'Mythology of Sumer and Akkad', Doubleday Anchor Books, New York, 1961. *Sumerian Mythology*, Harper Torchbooks, New York, 1961. *The Sumerians*, University of Chicago Press, 1963.

Labowsky, L. See Proclus.

Lang, Andrew, trans. See *Homeric Hymns*.

Lang, David Marshall. See Burney, Charles.

Larousse Encyclopaedia of Mythology, Paul Hamlyn, London, 1965.

Laude, Jean. *African Art of the Dogon*, Brooklyn Museum and Viking Press, New York, 1973.

Lauterborn, Dr D. Participant in seminar held at Elsinore Castle, Denmark, and pub. as *Mass Loss and Evolution in Close Binaries*, Copenhagen University, 1970. See pp. 190–4.

Layard, Austen H. *Discoveries in the Ruins of Nineveh and Babylon* (Second Expedition), London, 1853.

Lear, John. See Kepler.

Levi, Peter, S. J., trans. See Pausanius.

Lindenblad, Dr Irving. Account: *Sky and Telescope*, June 1973, p. 354.
  'Relative Photographic Positions and Magnitude Difference of the Components of Sirius', *Astronomical Journal*, 75, No. 7 (September 1970), pp. 841–8.
  'Multiplicity of the Sirius System' *Astronomical Journal*, 78, No. 2 (March 1973), pp. 205–7.

Lockyer, Sir Norman. *The Dawn of Astronomy*, London, 1894.

Lucian, *De Dea Syria*; see Garstang.

Lunn, Sir Henry. *Aegean Civilizations*, ed., London, 1928. Contains many brief contributions by an array of scholars.

McCrea, W. H. Query in *Quarterly Journal of the Royal Astronomical Society*, 13, 506 (1972), p. 517.
  Letter to the Editor in *Journal of the British Astronomical Association*, 84, 1 (1973), p. 63.

MacGowan, Roger A. and Ordway, Frederick I., III. *Intelligence in the Universe*, Prentice-Hall Inc. New Jersey, 1966.

Macrobius. *Commentary on the Dream of Scipio*, trans. by William Harris Stahl, Columbia University Press, 1952.
  The Saturnalia, trans. by Percival Vaughan Davies, Columbia University Press, 1969.
  Macrobius, or Philosophy, Science and Letters in the Year 400, by Thomas Whittaker, Cambridge University Press, 1923.
  Macrobius and Numenius by Herman de Ley, Collection Latomus, Société d'Études Latines de Bruxelles, Brussels, 1972.

Marinus. *Life of Proclus*; see Proclus.

Marshack, Alexander. *The Roots of Civilization*, Weidenfeld and Nicolson, London, 1972.

Mathers, S. L. MacGregor. *The Kabbalah Unveiled*, Kegan Paul, London, 1926.

Matz, F. 'Minoan Civilization: Maturity and Zenith' in *Cambridge Ancient History*, Cambridge University Press, issued as fascicule, 1964.

Mau, August. *Pompeii, Its Life and Art*, trans. by F. W. Kelsey, 1899. Revised 1902.

Mead, G. R. S. See Hermes.
  The Chaldaean Oracles, Vol. VIII, *Echoes from the Gnosis* series, Theosophical Publishing Co., London and Benares, 1908.

Meissner, O. 'Über die antiken Sternfarbenschatzungen' ('Concerning the Ancient Estimates of Star Colours'), *Astronomische Nachrichten*, Number 5542, 1927, pp. 392–6.

Meyrowitz, Eva. *The Sacred State of the Akan*, Faber, London, 1951.
  Akan Traditions of Origin, Faber, London, 1952.
  The Akan of Ghana, Their Ancient Beliefs (originally entitled *The Akan Cosmological Drama*), Faber, London, 1958.
  The Divine Kingship in Ghana and Ancient Egypt (originally entitled *The Akan of Ghana, the Akan Divine Kingship and Its Prototype in Ancient Egypt*), Faber, London, 1960.

Monier-Williams, Sir Monier. *A Sanskrit–English Dictionary*, Oxford University Press, 1951. (First edition 1899.)

Morrow, Dr Glenn. See Proclus.

Moscati, Sabatino. *Ancient Semitic Civilizations*, Elek Books, London, 1957.

Müller, Max. *Lectures on the Science of Language*, Second Series, London, 1864.

Muses, Dr Charles. See Young, Arthur M.

Neugebauer, Otto. *The Exact Sciences in Antiquity*, Dover Publications, New York, 2nd edition, 1969.
  and Parker, Richard. *Egyptian Astronomical Texts*, Brown University Press, 1960–7. (Issued at intervals, completed in 1967.)

Olympiodorus (the Neoplatonist). *Scholia to Plato's Gorgias* trans. by Thomas Taylor, pub. as footnote to trans. of Apuleius's essay 'On the Natural Philosophy of Plato', p. 333 of Taylor's vol. of Apuleius (1822); see Apuleius.

Alternatively, trans. by Taylor of part of Olympiodorus's *Scholia* may be found on p. 82 of *Ocellus, Taurus, Firmicus and Select Theorems of Proclus*, trans. by Thomas Taylor, London, 1831.

O'Neill, W. See Proclus.

Ordway, Frederick I., III. See MacGowan, Roger A.

Osthoff, H. 'Zur Farbe des Sirius im Altertum' ('Concerning the Colour of Sirius in Antiquity') *Astronomische Nachrichten*, Number 5495, 1927, p. 444.

Parke, H. W. *Greek Oracles*, Hutchinson, London, 1967.

The Oracles of Zeus, Blackwell, Oxford, 1967.

Parker, Richard. See Neugebauer, Otto.

Pausanius. *Guide to Greece*, trans. by Peter Levi, S.J., 2 vols., Penguin Books, 1971. With extensive notes by Levi commenting on the state today of the sites described by Pausanius in his day. An excellent work of outstanding scholarship and dedication.

See also Imhoof-Blumer.

Penguin Companion to Literature, The, Volume 4: *Classical and Byzantine, Oriental and African*, ed. by D. R. Dudley and D. M. Lang, Penguin, London, 1969.

Philip, J. A. *Pythagoras and Early Pythagoreanism*, University of Toronto Press, 1966.

Pindar. *The Odes of Pindar* trans. by C. M. Bowra (Sir Maurice Bowra), Penguin Books, London, 1969.

Plato. *The Timaeus* trans. by B. Jowett, in *The Dialogues of Plato*, vol. 2, Random House, New York, 1937.

The Cratylus, Phaedo, Parmenides and Timaeus with Notes on the Cratylus, trans. by Thomas Taylor with notes, London, 1793. (See particularly p. 388 of Taylor's introduction to *Timaeus*.) The Bodleian Library at Oxford has two copies of this book, one of which belonged to Percy Bysshe Shelley; in the Shelley Collection.

Plato the Man and His Work by A. E. Taylor, Meridian Books, New York, 1963.

Pliny the Elder. *Natural History*, trans. by various hands, 11 vols. of Loeb Library series, Heinemann, London, Harvard University Press.

Plutarch (of Chaeronea). 'Isis and Osiris', 'The E at Delphi', 'The Oracles at Delphi No Longer Given in Verse', and 'The Obsolescence of Oracles' all trans. by Frank Cole Babbitt in vol. 5 of Plutarch's *Moralia*, Vol. No. 306 in Loeb Library series, Heinemann, London, Harvard University Press, 1962.

'On the Face Appearing within the Orb of the Moon', 'Against Colotes, the Disciple and Favorite of Epicurus', 'Platonic Questions', and pseudo-Plutarch 'Of the Names of Rivers and Mountains, and of Such Things as Are to Be Found Therein', trans. by various and all pub. in Vol. V of *Plutarch's Morals* ed. by William W. Goodwin, Little, Brown, and Co., Boston, 1874.

Porphyry (the Neoplatonist). *Select Works of Porphyry*, trans. by Thomas Taylor, London, 1823.

Pritchard, James B., ed. *Ancient Near Eastern Texts Relating to the Old Testament*, 2nd edition, Princeton University Press, 1955. The fundamental source of scholarly translations of Sumerian, Akkadian, Egyptian, Hittite, and other material, including all known portions of the *Epic of Gilgamesh*, the Babylonian creation epic, etc.

There is a supplementary volume of photographs *The Ancient Near East in Pictures*, 1969.

The Ancient Near East Supplementary Texts, Princeton University Press, 1969. A supplementary volume intended to bring the coverage up to date (to 1968), as every year new texts are either discovered or translated, with an enormous backlog due to the shortage of competent scholars to handle the material in this field. This later volume contains 274 pp., which represents less than 15 years' worth of accumulated additional material. A combined volume is available of the 1955 and 1969 volumes bound together. Presumably supplementary volumes will continue to be issued at approximate 15-year intervals. The only way to keep abreast of new material between volumes is through personal contact with some of the handful of relevant scholars, or through the scholarly journals in the field, which generally carry the new material in separate articles as it is prepared, though this procedure follows no predictable pattern.

Proclus. *Commentary on the First Alcibiades of Plato*, trans. by W. O'Neill, The Hague, 1965.
Commentary on the First Book of Euclid's Elements, trans. by Professor Glenn Morrow, Princeton University Press, 1967.
Philosophical and Mathematical Commentaries of Proclus on the First Book of Euclid's Elements, trans. by Thomas Taylor, 2 vols., London 1792. This work is bound with Marinus's *Life of Proclus*, trans. by Taylor, and other material. (Marinus was a pupil of Proclus and wrote from first hand.)
Commentary on the Parmenides of Plato, last book and *pars inedita* only, trans. by G. E. M. Anscombe and L. Labowsky, pub. in *Plato Latinus*, Vol. III, of *Corpus Platonicum Medii Aevi* series ed. by R. Klibansky, Warburg Institute, London, 1953. Obtainable as: Kraus Reprint, Nendeln, Liechtenstein, 1973.
Elements of Theology, ed. and trans. by E. R. Dodds, Oxford University Press, 1963.
Commentaries on the Parmenides of Plato and the First Alcibiades of Plato: substance of them given in notes by Thomas Taylor to his 5 vols. *The Works of Plato*, London, 1804. The same is true of the *Commentaries on the Phaedo, Gorgias, and Philebus of Plato* by the Neoplatonist Olympiodorus; see Olympiodorus.
The Six Books of Proclus . . . on the Theology of Plato, trans. by Thomas Taylor, London, 1816. 2 vols.
Commentaries of Proclus on the Timaeus of Plato, trans. by Thomas Taylor, 2 vols., London, 1820.
Lost Writings of Proclus, trans. by Thomas Taylor, London, 1825.
Two Treatises of Proclus . . . of Ten Doubts concerning Providence . . . and . . . the Nature of Evil, trans. by Thomas Taylor, London, 1833.
The Philosophy of Proclus by L. J. Rosan, Cosmos Books, New York, 1949. This book also includes an English translation of Marinus's *Life of Proclus*.
Assorted passages from other works of Proclus are to be found scattered throughout the various publications of Thomas Taylor. There have been several translations done of *Elements of Theology*. There is an Elizabethan translation of Proclus's *Sphaera*.

Ptolemy (Claudius Ptolemaeus). *The Almagest*, trans. by R. Catesby Taliaferro, pub. in *Ptolemy, Copernicus, Kepler*, Vol. 16 of *Great Books of the Western World* series, pub. by Encyclopaedia Britannica, Chicago, London, Toronto, 1952.
Tetrabiblos, trans. by J. M. Ashmand, London, undated (1920s). Another translation is available in the Loeb Library series, Heinemann, London, Harvard University Press.

Rambach, Pierre. See Hébert-Stevens, François.
Rehm, Albert. See Kawerau, Georg.
Rodenwaldt, Gerhart. *Griechische Porträts aus dem Ausgang der Antike*, Number 76 of 'Programm zum Winckelmannsfeste der Archaeologischen Gesellschaft zu Berlin', Berlin, 1919. Plate VI of this book shows both front and side views of a bust which has since been identified (Pauly-Wissowa under 'Proclus') as one of Proclus. This is reproduced in this book, its first publication as far as I know correctly identified, since Rodenwaldt does not identify it.
Rosan, L. J. See Proclus.
Roscher, W. H. *Neue Omphalos Studien*, 1915. *Die Zahl 50 in Mythus, Kultus, Epos und Taktik der Hellenen und Anderer Völker*, 1917. *Der Omphalosgedanke bei Verschiedenen Völkern*, 1918. (These three excellent books were discovered by me after my own book had gone to press – they deserve extended study.)
Rosen, Edward. See Kepler.
Roux, Georges. *Ancient Iraq*, Penguin Books, London, 1966.

Sagan, Carl, *The Cosmic Connection*, Doubleday, New York, 1973.
Sagan, Carl, and Shklovskii, I. S. *Intelligent Life in the Universe*, Delta Books, New York, 1966.
Santillana, Giorgio de. *The Origins of Scientific Thought*, London, 1961.
Santillana, Giorgio de, and von Dechend, Hertha. *Hamlet's Mill*, Macmillan, London, 1969.
Sarton, George. *A History of Science: Ancient Science through the Golden Age of Greece*, Harvard University Press, 1959.
Sarton, George. *A History of Science*, Volume 2: *Hellenistic Science and Culture in the Last Three Centuries B.C.*, Norton, New York, 1970.

Schatzman, E. 'Les naines blanches', *L'Astronomie*, 1956, pp. 364–9.

Scully, Vincent. *The Earth, The Temple, and the Gods*, Yale University Press, 1962.

See, T. J. J. 'Historical Researches Indicating a Change in the Color of Sirius, between the Epochs of Ptolemy, 138, and of Al Sufi, 980 A.D.', *Astronomische Nachrichten*, Vol. 229 (1926), pp. 245–72. Despite an appearance of erudition, this article is unreliable and contains fundamental errors of fact and translation. See maintains, for instance, that the Greek word *poikilos* means 'red', which it has never meant. *Poikilos* means 'variegated', etc., referring to the scintillation of the star. See also Dittrich, Meissner, Osthoff, and Stentzel.

Shinnie, Margaret. *Ancient African Kingdoms*, Edward Arnold, London, 1965.

Shklovskii, I. S. See Sagan, Carl.
'Is Communication Possible with Intelligent Beings on Other Planets?' in *Interstellar Communication*; see Cameron, A. G. W.

Simplicius. (Neoplatonist) *Commentary on Aristotle's Treatise 'On the Soul'*: substance given in paraphrase in notes by Thomas Taylor to his trans. of 'On the Soul' in *The Treatises of Aristotle: On the Soul* etc., London, 1808. This vol. is not in either the British Museum or the Bodleian Library, Oxford. However, a copy was owned by a friend of mine and I have used the book. Simplicius's *Commentaries on the Physics of Aristotle*, *on the Categories of Aristotle*, *on On the Heavens of Aristotle (De Caelo)* as well as Olympiodorus's *Scholia on On Meteors of Aristotle* are all given in much the same way in other like volumes of Taylor's Aristotle pub. London between 1806 and 1812, in only fifty copies! However, I have been unable to find any of these volumes anywhere.
Commentary on the Enchiridion of Epictetus, trans. by George Stanhope, pub. as *Epictetus His Morals with Simplicius His Comment*, trans. George Stanhope, London, 1694.

Smart, W. M. *Some Famous Stars*, Longmans Green, London, New York, 1950. Chapter Three concerns 'The Companion of Sirius'.

Sozomen (Salaminius Hermias Sozomen). *Ecclesiastical History*, Bohns Ecclesiastical and Theological Library, London, 18— (prior to 1878).

Speiser, E. A. See *Epic of Gilgamesh*.

Stahl, William Harris. See Macrobius.
'The Greek Heliocentric Theory and Its Abandonment', *Transactions of the American Philological Association*, lxxvi (1945), pp. 323–5.

Stanhope, George. See Simplicius.

Stanley, Thomas. *The Chaldaick Oracles*; see *Chaldean Oracles*.
The History of the Chaldaick Philosophy, London, 1662.
The History of Philosophy, 3 vols., London, 1655–6 and 1660.

Stecchini, Livio Catullo. Author of Appendix to *Secrets of the Great Pyramid* by Peter Tompkins, Harper & Row, New York, 1971.

Stentzel, A. 'Ägyptische Zeugnisse für die Farbe des Sirius im Altertum' ('Egyptian Traditions regarding the Colour of Sirius in Ancient Times') *Astronomische Nachrichten*, No. 5542 (1927), pp. 387–92.

Stirling, William. *The Canon*. Garnstone Press, London, 1974.

Stubbings, Frank H. 'The Rise of Mycenaean Civilization', 'The Expansion of Mycenaean Civilization', 'The Recession of Mycenaean Civilization' in the *Cambridge Ancient History* Cambridge University Press, issued as separate fascicules 1964 and 1965.

Strong, Professor Herbert A. See Garstang, John.

Sullivan, Walter. *We Are Not Alone*, Hodder and Stoughton, London, 1965.

Täckholm. See Drar.

Tarn, W. W. *Hellenistic Civilization*, Meridian Books, New York, 1961.

Taylor, A. E. See Plato.

Taylor, Thomas. See Proclus, see Porphyry, see Apuleius.

Temple, Robert K. G. 'Response to Appeal from W. H. McCrea Concerning Sirius', *The Observatory*, April, 1975, pp. 52–4, Royal Greenwich Observatory, England.

Theophrastus (of Eresos in Lesbos). *Enquiry into Plants*, trans. by A. F. Hort, 2 volumes, Loeb Library Series, Heinemann, London and Harvard University Press, 1916.

Thesiger, Wilfred. *The Marsh Arabs*, Penguin Books, London, 1967.

Thompson, D'Arcy Wentworth. *A Glossary of Greek Birds*, Oxford, 1896.

Tompkins, Peter. *Secrets of the Great Pyramid*, Harper & Row, New York, 1971. With Appendix by Livio Catullo Stecchini.

von Däniken, Erich. *Chariots of the Gods?* Bantam Books, New York, 1970.
von Dechend, Hertha. See Santillana, Giorgio de.

Wallis, C. G.: See Copernicus; see Kepler.
Wallis Budge, Sir E. A., trans. *The Book of the Dead*, London, 1928.
    A Hieroglyphic Vocabulary to the Theban Recension of the Book of the Dead, London, 1911.
    Egyptian Language, London, 1951.
    The Gods of the Egyptians, 2 vols., London, 1904.
    An Egyptian Hieroglyphic Dictionary, London. 1920.
    Osiris and the Egyptian Resurrection, 2 vols., London, 1911.
Wellard, James. *Lost Worlds of Africa*, Hutchinson, London, 1967.
Whittaker, Thomas. See Macrobius.
    The Neo-platonists, Cambridge University Press, 1918.
Whyte, Lancelot Law. See Kepler.

Xenocrates. *Life of Xenocrates* by Diogenes Laertius. See Diogenes Laertius.

Young, Arthur Middleton, and Muses, Dr Charles, eds. *Consciousness and Reality*, Outerbridge &
    Lazard, Inc., distributed by E. P. Dutton, New York, 1972.

Addenda:

Bibby, Geoffrey, *Looking for Dilmun*, Collins, London, 1970.
Cook, Arthur Bernard, *ZEUS: A Study in Ancient Religion,*
    Cambridge University Press, 1925.
Graves, Robert, *The Crane Bag and other Disputed Subjects*, Cassell, London, 1970.
Oliver, Dr B. M., 'Proximity of Galactic Civilizations', in *Icarus*, 25, 360–7, 1975. 'Arguments
    are presented for expecting intelligent life in certain multiple star systems . . .'
Swedenborg, Emanuel, *Arcana Coelestia: or Heavenly Mysteries*, London, 1788. Vol. III, pp. 81–3,
    86, contains possibly the earliest survey of the number 'fifty' as symbolic usage in the Old
    Testament.

INDEX

Áakhu-t, 193
Áakhu-t Sheta-t, 193
Áārārut, 193
Áar-ti, 193
Áas-t, 193
Ába, 194
Abeh, 194
Aboukir, village of, 121
Abraham, 18, 135, 253, 268-9
Áb-t, 194
Ábu, 194
Abusir, 132
Abydenus, 207, 209, 248, 249, 250, 255-6
Abydos, 62
Abzu, 125, 217
Acacia tree, 148, 149
Actaeon, see Aktaion
Aea, city of, 106, 110, 127, 135, 176, 187
Aeaea, 109, 148
Aeetes, King, 110, 114
Aegyptos, 166-7, 174
Aelian, 110
African Worlds, 2-3
Agastya, 125
Agathodaimon, 74
Agenor, 165
Agesilaus, 70
Agga, 90, 100, 140, 142-3; see also Anubis
Ahriman, 188
Ahura Mazda, 188
Aitken, R. G., 13, 189
Akan tribe, 159
Akhenaten, 138-9, 143-5, 152, 269, 272
Akhet-Aten, city of, 143
Akkadian culture, 18, 83-5, 117, 143
Akrotiri, 149
Aktaion (Actaeon), 111, 113-15, P17
Alagöz, 126
Aldred, Cyril, 143
Alexandria, 123, 165
Allen, Richard Hinckley, 65-7, 115, 121, 123, 125-7, 187
Al Wazn (weight), significance of, 65-6, 79, 93, 100, 123, 127, 151, 181; see also Ponderosus
Amarna Letters, 270
Amen-Ra, 195
Amma, 28, 33, 36-7, 209, 215, 260
Ammon, 115, 159, 176, 195, 209
Ammon, oracle of, 140, 152

Amon, temple of (Thebes), 139, 144-5, 176, P12 (notes)
Amphibians (from Sirius?), 7, 65, 80, 125, 152, 205-9, 219-21, 224-5, P6, P7, P8, P9
Amphitryon, 153
An, see Osiris
Anagonno, 216
Anatote (anatellō), 175
Ancient Fragments (Cory), 207, 248-57
Ancient Near Eastern Texts (ed. Pritchard), 269-70
Anda, 68
Andoumboulou, 36
Andromeda, 165
Ánes, 185
Ankhesenamum, Queen, 269
An-ki (heaven-earth), 102
Annedotus (i), 207-9, 221, 249
Ánp hen, 88
Ánp(u), 64, 68, 79, 100, 101, 118, 184, 185, 193
'Anpu-hursag', 88
Anti-Cythera (Anti-Kythera), 132
Antoninus, 165
Anu (God of Heaven), 67-8, 70, 79, 85, 92-7, 100, 183, P12 (notes)
Anu (in Sanskrit), 68
Anubis, 64, 68-71, 78-80, 87, 95, 99-100, 101, 118, 162, 164, 167, 173, 184-8, 193-4, 199
Anukis, 64-8, 94, 102, 114
Anunnaki, 68, 85, 89, 92, 95-100, 102, 114, 119, 183; see also under Fifty
Anupa, 67
An-Yang, city of, 137
Áp(p), 194
Apep (a monster), 97
Aphrodite, 131, 149
Aphrodite Kytherean, 132
Aphrodite Urania, 132
Ápi-(àbu), 194
Apis Bull, The, 69, 116
Apollo, 71, 110, 129-30, 132, 133, 145, 148, 152, 162, 166, 169, 266, P17; temple of, P13, P14
Apollodorus, 168, 207, 209, 248-9
Apollonius of Rhodes, 105, 155
Apsu, 217; see also Abzu
Apuleius, 259
Árā, 175

Ararat, Mt., 104, 125-6, 135, 140, 142, 147, 149, 151, 152, 270, P10
Aratos, 66, 121, 155
Aratus of Soli, 58, P18 (notes)
Arcā, 181
Arcadia, 159, 167
Arcere, 179, 198
Archaeology (ist), 129, 199
Archaic Egypt (Emery), 6
Arche (Greek word discussed), 89, 186
Arcturus, 187
Arecibo telescope, 11
Areimanius, 188
Ares, see Mars
Arete, 109
Argha, 125
Argiope, 168
Argives, 166
Argo-complex words, 168, 177, 186
Argo Constellation, 66, 125-6, 140
Argonautica (Apollonius), 105, 109-10, 114, 158, 183
Argo-(nauts), 60, 66-7, 71-2, 79-80, 85-9, 99-100, 103-6, 117, 119, 121, 127, 130, 135, 142-3, 145, 148, 151-2, 155, 158-9, 166, 169, 173-7, 180, 186-7, 190, 198-9, P18
Argos, city of, 165-7, 177, 179, 189
Argus, 177-80, 182, 198, P18
Aries, 115
Aristarchus, 238
Aristides, 123
Aristotle, 110, 134, 156, 167, 192, 205, 207, 209, 240
Ark, 89, 99, 104, 121, 125, 130, 140, 151-2, 165, 199, 209-17 passim; see also Deukalion; Noah
Ark, meaning and derivatives of, 177, 180, 186-7; in Sanskrit, 180
Arneus, 154
Árq, 186, 198
Árq and ārqi, 177, 179-81
Árq heh, 180
Árq-hehtt, 180, 198
Árqi, 177, 186, 198
Árqit, 177
Árq ur, 179-81
Arou peoples, 36
Arrows, significance of, 66; see also Bow Star
Árt, 171

Artemis, 113, 149, P17
Asàr, 184
As-Ar, see Osiris
Asar-Hapi, 69
Asàr-Hep, 116
Asaru, 97
Asarualim, 97
Asarualimnunna, 97
Asaruludu, 97
Asarluhi, 98
Asar-lutu, 97
Asar-rutu, 97
Asaru-uu, 97
Ascalon, 132
Asclepius-Imuth, 75
Assembly of the Gods, 94
Assyrian History (Abydenus), 209
Assyrians, 18
Āst, 61, 63, 94, 102, 166, 193
As-ti, 193
Astronomers' reactions (modern), 222-6
Astronomie (journal), 27
Atalanta, 105
Āṭeb, 171
Aten, 144
Athamas, 111
Athena, 71-2, 80, 127, 166, 173, P18
Athene of Lindus, 168
Athene Pronaia, 133
Athene, see Pallas Athene
Athenian New Year, 162
Au Au, 184
Āu, 184, 185
Anau, 101, 118, 184
Aubrey, John, 29
Āu-t, 184
Āu-t en äthen, 184
Auwers, 189

Babbitt, F. C., 64, 70-1, 265, 267
Babel, Tower of, 249-50
Babylon, 149
Babylonian Genesis, The (Heidel), 67, 90
Babylonian History (Berossus), 205
Babylonians, 18, 67, 85, 99, 125, 208, 209, 210; (their) omphalic stone, P12 (IV)
Bado rite, 42, 46
Baize, Dr P., 27
Balbus, 157
Bamako peoples, 18
Bambara peoples and the Sirius system, 35, 48-9
Bambyce, see Hierapolis
Banani, (Dogon) village of, P3
Bandiagara, 35, 158
Barca or Barce, see El Marj
Baring, Robin, 192
Bas reliefs, P14
Bau, 101, 118-19
Bebon, 71
Behdet, 123, 127, 129, 131, 133, 135, 140, 142, 144-5,

148, 149, 152, 163, 165-6
187, 199, 270, 272
Bēl Mātāti, 117
Belus, 168, 209, 251-4
Berossos (Berossus), 126, 205-9; translations of, 248-57; of Abraham (Josephus), 253; of Nebuchadnezzar (Josephus), 253-4; of Nebuchadnezzar (Abydenus), 255-6; of the Chaldean Kings (Apollodorus), 248-9; of the Chaldean Kings and the Deluge (Abydenus), 249; of the Chaldean Kings after Nebuchadnezzar (Josephus), 254-5; of the Cosmogony and Causes of the Deluge (Polyhistor), 250-2; of the Destruction of the Jewish Temple (Josephus), 253; of the Feast of Sacea (Josephus), 255; of Nabonasar (Josephus), 253; of the Tower of Babel (Abydenus), 249-50
Bibby, Geoffrey, 83
Bibliography, 276-82
Binary Stars, The (Aitken), 189
Binary Systems, 225
Binou, sanctuary of, 36, 262
Black rite, 74, 80, 83, 98; see also Dark mystery; Dark rite
Black Sea, 103, 106, 119, 155, 158, 176
Blood, circulation of, 29-30, 139-40, 220
Bodies in space, movements of, 228-46 passim
Bow Star, 66, 94, 113, 119, 199, P17 (notes)
Bozo peoples and the Sirius system, 35, 49, 62, 78
Bracewell, Dr R. N., 14
Bran, 154
Branchidae, 149; see also Didyma
Briareus, 106, 155-7, 173
Brick pillars, 103
Brief Lives (Aubrey), 29
Brihaspati, 260; see also Vrihaspati
Browning, Professor Robert, 232
Budge, Professor Sir E. A. Wallis, 1, 61-4, 68-70, 79, 83, 85, 97-8, 116, 156, 171 179-86
Burkill, I., 115
Burney, Dr Charles, 125
Burning Bush, The (Bible), 148

Cabeiroi (Kabeiroi), 149
Cadmus, 86-7, 156, 167-9, 176-7, 179, P19
Calebites, 123, 272
Calendars, Dogon, 27; see also Egyptian Calendar Year; Sothic calendar
Calvin, Dr Melvin, 14
Callimachus, 192

Cameron, Dr A. G. W., 14
Canis constellation, 58, 78, 151
Canis Major (Dog-star), 60, 65-6, 100, 101, 113, 134, 167, 179, 182, 184, 188, 194, 199, 272; see also Sothis
Canopus, ancient city of, 121, 123, 140, 165-6
Canopus, the star, 66, 121, 123, 125-7, 140, 151-2
Capella, Martianus, 245
Capella of Auriga, 115
Carrier-pigeons, 139, 141, 143; see also Doves
Cassiopeia, 165
Castalian Spring, 168-9
Cedar, 90, 148, 149
Centimanes, 155
Cerberus, 114, 119, 155, 162, 163, 164, 173
Chaeremon, 111
Chaldean Kings, 248-9, 254-5
Chaldeans, 248-56 passim
Chariots of the Gods (von Däniken), 4
Christ, parallels with, 32
Chronos and Cronos, 70, 101
Circe, 109-11, 115-16, 119, 148, 171, 187, 192, P20 (notes); see also Kirke
Circumcision, significance of, 40-1, 49, 105, 119, 158, 260-1
Clarke, Arthur C., 3
Clea, 70, 145, 265
Clement of Alexandria, 111
Clitoris, see Circumcision
Cnossos, see Knossos
Colchicum plant, 114-15, 120, 192
Colchis, 87, 103-10, 114-16, 119-20, 127, 135, 145, 156-7, 176, 187, 192, P20 (notes)
Commentary on the Timaeus of Plato (Proclus), see In Tim.
Common Background of Greek and Hebrew Civilizations (Gordon), 89, 131
Computer, discovery of ancient, 132
Consciousness and Reality (Young), 2
Cook, A. B., 130
Copernicus, 238
Cornwall, Peter B., 83
Cory Translations, 207, 209, 248-57
Cosimo de Medici, 73
Cottus, 155-6, 173
Cotytto, 157
Cow, significance of, 168, 177, 191; see also Hathor
Creation, The, 2, 43, 90, 113, 272
Crete, 108, 129, 133, 148, 162
Crocker, Dr Richard L., 129, 150
Crocus, 114-15, 192
Crombie, Professor A. C., 235

Cronos, *see* Chronos
Cross, significance of, 45
Cybernetics (Wiener), 72
Cyclades Delos, 134
Cyclops and Cyclopes, 130, 165
Cynopolis, 64
Cynthus, Mt., 149
Cypress tree, 149
Cyprus, 133
Cyrene, city of, 158
Cythera (Kythera), 129, 131–3, 152

Dagon, 207
Damascius, 241
Danae, 165, 177
Danaos, 66–7, 80, 165–7, 177, 179, 189, 199
Dancers (Dogon), P4
Dark mystery, 74
Dark rite, 76, 78; *see also* Black Rite; Dark mystery
Dawn of Astronomy (Lockyer), 123, 129
Death of Actaeon, The (Titian) 113
De Caelo (Aristotle), 156
Debo, Lake, 211
Degenerate matter, 12, 217
Delos, shrine of, 129–35, 143, 148, 149, 152
Delphi, oracle at, 70, 105, 111, 125, 127, 129–37, 139, 143, 145, 148, 149, 152, 159, 162–3, 168, 177; omphalos stone at, P12 (I); photograph, P13; *see also* E at Delphi, meaning of
Deluge (the Flood), 249–52
Demeter, 179
Demetrius, 244, 266
Demodocus, 116
Dendera B., 65
Denderah, 57, 141
Descent of Ishtar to the Nether World, 96
Description of the Constellations (Kazwini), 66
Deukalion, 72, 80, 88–9, 99, 111, 125, 130, 135, 148, 156, 169; *see also* Ark; Noah
Diana, 113, 149, P17
Dictionary (Budge), 186
Didyma, 135, P12 (*notes*)
Dieterlen, Germaine, *see* Griaule, Marcel and Germaine Dieterlen
Digitaria, (the Star) (Sirius B), 2–3, 11, 20–6, 33, 39, 41, 46, 101, 134–5, 181, 189–90, 217, 223, 225, 260, P1; orbit of, 39–42; *see also under* Fifty year orbit origins and features of, 42–4; position of, 44; *see also* Po
Dilmun, 83
Diodorus Siculus, 87, 105, 134
Dionysos, 111
Djado, 'Oasis of', 157

Djerma, Oasis of, 194
Dodona, sanctuary of, 72, 80, 89, 99, 105, 106, 121, 125–47 *passim*, 149, 151–2, 159, 195, 266, 270, P18
Dog, *see* Jackal
Dog Days, 58, 182, 198
Dog-headed symbols, 101–2, 118, 185–6
Dog men (Calebites), 123, 272
Dogon Tribe of Peoples, 1, 3, 5, 11–33 *passim*, 41, 78–9, 101, 105, 113, 119, 135, 155, 158–63, 173, 176, 179–81, 185, 189–93, 196–9, 206–20 *passim*, 223–5, 240, 258, 260–3; their initiation stages, 275; photograph of priest's house, P4
Dog Star, *see* Sirius A; Canis Constellation; Canis Major
Dolphins, 65, 203–4, 218–19
Doves, significance of, 139–40, 144, 148, 187, 195, 270, P14 (*notes*); *see also* Carrier-pigeons
Dragon's Teeth, 86, 99, P15, P18, P19 (*notes*); *see also* Teeth, significance of
Duat, The (Ṭuat), 56, 95, 164, 180, 190, 193
Dudley, D. R., 230
Dwarf and Dwarf Stars, 185, 198–9; *see also* G-dwarf star (our sun); White dwarf stars

Ea, 102, 117, 125, 152, 210, 217
E at Delphi, meaning of, 265–7; photograph, P14
Ebbu, 98
Ebeling, E., 93
Echidne, 162
Echion, 169
Echmiadzin, 126
Edfu, temple at, 76, P20
Edwards, I. E. S., 76
Egypt, *see* Magan
Egyptian Calendar-year, 61, 78, 99, P18 (*notes*)
Egyptian dynasties, 62, 75, 131, 183
Egyptian Hieroglyphic Dictionary (Budge), 1
Egyptian Language (Budge), 171
Egyptian Star Clocks, 84–5, 107
EI, *see* E at Delphi, meaning of
Eighth Oracle Centre, 135; *see also* Oracle centres
Eighth planet theme, 134–5
Ekur, 102
Elegies, 148
Ellipses discussed, 21–2, 68, 79, 189–91, 225
Ellu, 98
El Marj (Barce *or* Barca), 129
Emery, Professor W. B., 6, 77
Emme Sigi, 37
Emme Ya (? Sirius C), 26, 33, 44, 223, 225

Emmons, G. T., 17
Endiku, 89, 92, 164–5, 191, 193–4
Enki (Ea), 102, 117, 125, 152, 174, 210, 217
Enlil, 68, 70, 101–2
Enuma elish, 85, 94, 96–8, 117–18
Epagomenal Days, 84
Epic of Gilgamesh, 89–90, 100, 148, 193
Epsilon, *see* E at Delphi, meaning of
Epsilon Eridani, 11, 14
Erastosthenes, 123
Erech (Uruk), 164
Eridu, 125
Eridhu, 125
Erion, 117, 120
Erman, 75
Erythraean Sea, 207, 248
Eta Argus (the star), 125
Etana, 95
Eteokles, 111
Euclid (Proclus on), 156
Eudoxus, 70–1, 80, 121, 156
Euergetes I, 76
Eurytion, 164–5, 174
Eusebius, 111, 209
Euxine Sea, 103
Evil and Darkness (Zoroastrianism), 188
Exact Sciences in Antiquity, The, (Neugebauer), 83
Excision, significance of, 40, 48–9
Extra-terrestrial visitations, 4–7, 203–26 *passim*
Eye Star, significance of name, 62, 78

F.5, star type, 14
Falcon, significance of, 109–10, 115–16, 119, 130, 171, 192; *see also* Hawk
Falcon of Horus, 109–10
Female Sorgho, *see* Sorghum
Fezzan, 194–6
Ficino, Marsilio, 72–3, 229
Field of Paradise, The, 67
Fifty, significance of: Anunnaki, 85, 89, 94, 101, 105, 106, 120, 166, 174, 179; *see also* Anunnaki; argonauts, 86–7, 99, 103, 104, 106, 127, 166; colleges, 156; companions, 86, 89, 100, 106, 119, 166; daughters, 67, 80, 153–4, 165–6, 173–4, 177, 179, 198; days, 182–3; eyes, 182; gods, 188; great gods, 72, 80, 85, 89, 97, 99, 100, 119; Great Year (twice 50 months), 113, 119; *see also* Great Year; heads, 114, 119, 130, 155–7, 162–4, 173–4; heroes, 72, 80, 89, 93; hounds, 113–14, 119, P17; *khamsin* (Arabic for 50),

182 fn.; lunations, 154–5; 'mace heads, 89; maidens of the god Bran, 154; markers, 67; Minas, 89; Minyae, 154; months (period of), 189–90; months' reign, 113–14, 119, 155; moon priestesses, 166; names, 96–7, 117; Nereids, 154, 165; nights, 154, 173; oars(men), 67, 87, 127, 157, 162, 173, 177, 179; Pallantids, 154, 162; rowers, 67, 100; see also oars(men) above; seats, 179; sons, 166–7, 174, 177; thrones, 167, 179; year-Jubilee, 199; year-orbit (of Sirius), 3, 33, 44, 67, 83, 87, 113, 119, 157, 167, 173, 177, 190, 193, 198, 199, 225; years (Leviticus), 189–90

Figure-eight orbit, postulated, 225
Flat Earth theory, 14
Flood, the, 249, 250–2
Flying saucers, 213–14
Foci of the ellipse, 22, 190
Foggaras, 195–6
Foreskin, see Circumcision
Forrer, E., 269
Forty-eight gods of Good and Evil, 188–90
Forty-nine, importance of figure, 188–90
Fox, see Renard pâle, Le

Galilean Moons, 28
Gamphasantes, 158
Garamantes (-ians), 158–9, 173, 194–9
Garamas, 157, 173, 195
G-dwarf star (our sun), 13, 55–6, 58, 71, 74, 99, 217–18, 266
Gata, Cape, 129, 149
Genesis, The Book of, 268, 270
Geodetic octave, 129, 131, 132, 138, 270
Geodetics, 127–49 passim, 206, 266, 267, 270; omphalos, P12 (V)
Gerizim, Mount, 137
Ghat, Oasis of, 195
Gilgamesh, 85–93, 99–100, 106, 119, 127, 140, 142–3, 148, 156, 164–6, 171, 173, 174, 185, 193–4
Glaucus, 67, 127
Glossary of Greek Birds, A (Thompson), 110, 192
Gods of the Egyptians, The, 69
Golden Fleece, 86–7, 99, 103–5, 111, 114–15, 118–20, 135, 169, P16, P20 (notes); see also Woollen fleece
Gordon, Professor Cyrus, 89, 99, 131, 132
Gordon, Seton, 192
Graces, The, 111, 165

Graves, Robert, 106, 109, 113–14, 117, 119, 123, 130, 153–9, 162, 164–9, 173–4, 188–90, 194–6, 266, 270, 272
Gravity of Sirius, 12
Great Circle, 182
Great Dog, see Canis Major
Great Pyramid, 103, 134, 137
Great Year, 113, 119, 155, 168, 177, 182, 191
Greek Lexicon, see Liddell and Scott
Greek Myths, The (Graves), 106, 109, 148, 157, 190, 196
Greek Oracles (Parke), 72, 132; see also Parke
Greek words discussed, 110–11, 130–1, 155, 158, 163, 169, 175, 177, 179, 180, 186, 265–7
Griaule, Marcel and Germaine Dieterlen, 2–3, 5, 18, 20–21, 24, 27, 28, 31, 35–49, 70, 190, 217, 223–4, 260, 275
Gudea, 89
Guide to Greece (Pausanius), 111
Gurney, Professor O. R., 180 fn., 268–9
Gygantelos, 156
Gygas, 156
Gyges, 155–6, 173

Hadar, 123
Hamlet's Mill (Santillana and von Dechend), 66, 90, 94, 117, 125, 129, 134, 260
Hare, see Lepus (the Hare)
Harrington, R. S., 225
Harvey, William, 29, 139–40
Hathor (the sacred cow), 169, 179, 191, 194, 270
Hat-hor, 111
Hawk, significance of, 110–11, 115–16, 118–19, 171, 187, 191–2, P20; see also Falcon
Hebron, 123, 147–8, 149, 268–72
Hecate (Hekate), 109, 113–14, 119, 120, 155, 162, 173–4, 190, 232
Hecatoncheires, 155
Heidel, Alexander, 67, 90, 92, 98, 117
Hekate, see Hecate
Heliacal Rising, 56–8, 61, 95, 176
Heliopolis, 184
Helios, 110, 116, 120, 176
Helio-Serapis, 116
Hell, Hounds of, 101–18
Helladius, 256–7
Helle, 87, 103–4, 111
Hellenistic Civilization (Tarn), 121–3
Hellespont, 103
Helu, 116, 120
Hemaka plaque, 62
Henb-Requ, 193
Henb-t, 193

Henmemit, 192
Henn, 193, 298
Henn(ti), 191
Hensekti, 192
Hen-t, 190–3
Hen-ta, 191
Henti, 190, 258
Henu, 191
Hep, 116
Hephaestus, 75
Hera, 117, 165, 177
Herakles, 105, 117, 154, 163; see also Hercules
Hercules, 104, 106, 114, 127, 135, 153–5, 157, 173; see also Herakles
Hermanubis, 70
Hermes, 71, 73–7, 80, 82, 87, 99, 104, 135, 165, 178
Hermetic literature, 76
Hermetic tradition, 72–3, 103
Hero, meaning in Greek discussed, 116–17
Herodotean Inquiries (Benardete), 158
Herodotus, 87, 104, 106–10, 119, 131–2, 139, 144–5, 152, 158–9, 167, 194–6, 199, 266, P20 (notes)
Heroic Age, 109
Heru, 89, 115–20, 169
Heru-ami-Sept-t, 117
Heru-ami-u, 118
Heru-Neb-pât, 118
Heru-Neb-taui, 118
Heru-Neb-urr-t, 118
Heru-sa-Agga, 90, 100
Heru-sba-res, 118
Heru-up Shet, 118
Heru-ur-shefit, 118
Hesiod, 109, 111, 119, 156, 174
Hesychius, 130
He-t-Her, 169
Hierapolis, 142, 149, 157 fn.
Hierax, meaning of, 110
Higgins, Godfrey, 130–1
Hill, god and goddess of the, 89, 90, 100, 184, 186
Hipparchos, 121
Hippolyte's Girdle, 155
Hippopede, 156
Histories (Herodotus), 104, 107
History begins at Sumer (Kramer), 141
History of West Africa, A (Fage), 194
Hittites, 268–72
Hittites, The (Gurney), 268
Hogons, 39, 42, 46
Homer(ic), 65, 72, 105–6, 110, 133, 148, 152, 162, 177, 238
Hor, 76
Horus (the bone), 71, 80, 185
Horus (God of Resurrection), 110
Horus, origin of the word, 115–18
Horus, son of Agga, 90
Horus, son of Hermes, 76, 82

Horus, son of Isis and Osiris, 119, 181
Host of Heaven, 92–3
Hotham-Francklyn, Mary Brenda, 2
House of Horus, 169
Humbaba (Huwawa), 90
Hume, David, 139
Hurry, J. B., 75–6
Hursag, 89–90
Huwawa, 90
Huxley, Professor George, 132
Hyginus, 168
Hylas, 104
Hymn to Apollo (Homeric), 133, 152, 162
Hymn to Osiris, 183, 258
Hyperborean Gifts, 134

Ia, *see* Ea
Iamblichus, 72, P21 (*notes*)
Ideler, Dr Christian Ludwig, 65–6, 79, 123
Ie pelu tolo (Dogon 'star of the tenth moon'), 214–15
Ieue, 131
Igigi, 95
Iliad, 109, 159, 238
Imhotep, 75–7
Indian History (Megasthenes), 209
Innekouzou Dolo, Priestess, 35, 51, P2
Instructors, 209, 220
Intelligence in the Universe (MacGowan and Ordway), 224
Intelligent Life in the Universe (Sagan and Shklovskii), 13, 207
Interstellar Communication (Cameron) 225
In Tim., 231–5, 239–44
Io, 177–9
Iolchus, 127, 135, 176
Ishu (Sanskrit), discussed, 66
Isi, 66
Isis, 56, 61–4, 67, 69, 71–4, 78–83, 86, 94, 97, 101, 111, 166, 169, 174, 179, 183–4, 192–4, 198–9, P5
Isis, temple of, 57, 178, 198
Isis and Osiris (Plutarch), 64, 69–70, 179 fn., 185, 187
Isis-Sothis, 64–5, 185; *see also* Sothis
Iswara, 66

Jackal, significance of, 68–9, 79, 101, 118, 167, 184–5, 193–4; *see also* Wolf
Jacobsen, Thorkild, 101, 140–1
Janus, 162
Jason, 66–7, 79, 85–7, 99, 103, 105, 106, 109–10, 114, 119, 125, 127, 156–8, 167–8, 173, 175–6, 183, 187, 191, P15, P16, P19 (*notes*)
Jehovah, 189, 266–7

Jewish Temple, destruction of, 253
Joseph (son of Israel), 269
Josephus, 102–3, 253–5
Jowett, Benjamin, 235
Julian the Emperor, 256
Jupiter (the planet), 149, 258–63
Jupiter (Zeus), 11, 27–8, 32, 70–2, 80, 101, 115, 117–18, 133, 149, 195, 263

K.5, star type, 14
Kaaba Shrine, 135
Kahi Nub, 123
Kaleoibis, son of Apollo, 76
Kazwini, 65
Kepler, Johannes, and the laws of, 21–2, 68, 190, 223, 225, 238–9, 260
Khamsin (Khamshin) 182 fn.
Khem-, words from the root of, 182–3
Khemut, 182
Khorsabad, 138
Ki, 88–9, 102
Kilena Tree, 216
Kilmer, Dr Anne D., 129, 150
Kirke, 119, 187, 192; *see also* Circe
Kirkos, 110–11, 130
Ki-sir, double meanings of, 92
Kişru, 93
Knossos (Cnossos), 129, 131, 133, 135, 149
Kolaxais, 158
Komakon, Dogon village of, P4
Korienze, 158
Koromantse, 158
Kramer, Samuel Noah, 67, 83, 85, 87–93, 141, 143
Kythera, *see* Cythera

'l' and 'r', use of, in Egyptian, 97, 116, 120, 192
Lang, Professor David, 125
La Perouse, 17
Laphystion, Mount, 111, 114
Lapis lazuli, 101–2
Latakia, 149
Latitudes in geodetics, 129–49 *passim*
Latmus, Mt., 149
Laurel tree, 148, 149
Lauterborn, D., 13, 225
Lebanon, Mt., 148, 149
Lepus (the Hare), 60, 168, P19
Leto, P17
Levi, Peter, 111, 153
Leviticus, 189–90, 199
Lexicon, *see* Liddell and Scott
Libya, importance of visits to, 158–9, 162, 166, 173, 194–5, 199
Liddell and Scott, Lexicon of, for Greek, 65, 110, 116, 156, 163, 177, 179, 208; *see also* Greek words discussed

Lifted eye and lifted light, 101
Light and Goodness (Zoroastrianism), 188
Lindenblad, Dr Irving W., 3, 11–13, 24, 33, 155, 223, 226, P1 (*and notes*)
Little Bear, The, 58
Lloyd, Professor A. C., 230–1
Lockyer, Sir Norman, 123, 129
Lodestones, 71–2, 185
Longitudes and geodetics, 129–49 *passim*
Lost Worlds of Africa (Wellard), 195
Lussin, 109
Lyceum, 167, 237

MacGowan, Roger, 224
Machpelah, 270
Macrobius, 245
McCrea, Professor W. H., 222–4
McKay, Dr Alan, 4
Maet, interpretation of, 144
Magan and Magan-boats, 67, 79, 83, 87–90, 99–100, 106, 141
Magurru-boat, 90, 141
Manda, d'Orosongo, Priest, 35–6, 50, 51, P2
Manetho, 71, 73, 185
Marduk, 96–7, 101, 117
Mars (Ares), 28, 32, 135, 168, 169
Mars (the planet), 149
Marsh Arabs, The (Thesiger), 218
Masters of the Water, 209, 220
Matz, F., 107
Maya peoples, 84
Mead, G. R. S., 72–4
Mecca, 135
Medea, 109–110, 114–16, P15, P16
Megamede, 154
Megasthenes, 209, 255–6
Meh-urt, 97
Menelaos, 123
Menes, 1st and 3rd dynasties after, 76
Meni, 183
Mercury (planet), 90, 99, 135
Merlan, Philip, 230
Mermaids, 204–5
Mesopotamian civilization, 18, 186
Metsamor, 125–7, 135, 140, 143, 149, 152, 270, P11
Meyrowitz, Eva, 159, 196
Migration of the Dogon people, 161, 173, 199
Miletus, 135, 149; omphalos at, P12 (III)
Milky Way, The, 28–31, 48
Minianka peoples, 35
Minoan Culture, 107–8, 132, 152
Minyae, 87, 103, 105, 111, 135, 137, 166, 168, 190

Minyas, 103-4, 108, 111
Mithras, 188
Monier-Williams, 66
Monitors, 209, 220
Moon (Earth's), 149, 233, 237-8, 259
Moons of the other planets, 228-46 *passim*
Moralia (Plutarch), 64
Moses, 148, 189, 199, 268
Mousso Koroni Koudyé, 49
Mulius, 116
Murdin, Dr Paul, 13, 225-6, P1 (*notes*)
Musarus, 207-8, 248
Mycenaeans, 107-9, 132
Mysteries: of Isis, 179; of Sirius, 1-7; of Thesmophoria, *see* Thesmophoria; what is the? (of Sirius), 1-7

Nabonasar, 253
Nabopollasar, 253
Nabuchodonosor, *see* Nebuchadnezzar
Namru, 97-8
Namshub, 98
Namtillaku, 97
Naram-Sin, 131
Navel, significance of, 131, 145, 148; *see also* Omphalos
Neb, 117, 169
Neb-Heru, 117
Nebiru, 117-18
Neb-t-He-t, 169
Nebuchadnezzar, 253-4, 255-6
Nectanebo, Pharaoh, 70
Neferit, 191
Nefertiti, Queen, 139
Neith (the Goddess), 97, 159
Nemean Odes, 165
Neoplatonists, 72-3, 82, 156 fn., 230, 258; *see also* Proclus
Nephthys, 63-4, 69, 71, 78-80, 99, 169, 180, 184, 192-4, 198-9
Neptune (the planet), 83, 99, 135
Nereids, The, 165, 174
Nesi-Amsu papyrus, 97
Neugebauer, Professor Otto, 59, 61, 64-5, 83-4, 95-6
Nicandra, 145
Night, special meaning of, 83, 98
Nimrod, 137
Ninhursag, 88-9, 193
Ninmah, 88, 193
Ninsun, 86, 92-3
Nintu, 88-9, 193
Ninurta, 92, 101
Nippur, 102
Noah, 18, 88-9, 104, 121, 125, 151; *see also* Ark; Deukalion
Nommo(s), 31-3, 36, 43, 48, 206, 209-19, 262
Northern Octave theory, 132, 138, 144
Numbers, the Book of, 268

Nu Sigi, 37
Nut and Nu, 68

Oak trees, significance of, 131, 135, 148, 149, 151, 157, 195, P18
Oannes, 31, 65, 71, 80, 125-6, 139, 152, 174, 206-7, 210, 218, 221, 248, 249, 251, P6, P7, P8, P9
Octaves: geodetic, 129, 135, 144, 152, 270; musical, 129, 134, 154, 155 fn; Northern theory, *see under* Northern octave theory; oracular, chart of, 149
Odacon, 207
Odysseus (Ulysses), 177
Odyssey (Homer), 65, 72, 105, 109, 116, 198
Ogo, 31-3, 216
Ololu and Olulu, 159
Olympic Games, 119, 154, 189
Olympiodorus, 258
Om, sacred symbol of, 130-1, 154
Omph (The Sacred Voice), 130
Omphaleion, Plain of, 129, 149
Omphalos, Knossos (Cnossos), 129, 135, 187
Omphalos (the navel), 130-1, 138-9, 143, 145, 148, 152, 154, 176, 206, P12 (I-VI), P14
Omphalos stone of Delos, 131, 134, 139, P12 (II)
Omphe, 130-1
Omphis, 187
One Hundred and Twenty Years, 191, 259
Onga, 168
Ongnonlou Dolo, Priest, 35, 39, 51, P2
Oracle Centres, 121-49 *passim* location of, 129, 149; *see also* individual sites
Oracle octaves, chart of, 149
Oracle of Zeus, 159
Oracles of Zeus, The (Parke), 72, 125
Orbit relation to Great Year, 155; *see also* Great Year
Orchomenos, 104, 111, 114, 153, 165, 169
Ordway, Frederick, 224
Orientation, science of, 59
Orion and Orion's Belt, 39, 60-3, 78, 111, 127, 168, 180, P19
Oromazes, 188
Orpheus, 105
Orthrus, 162-4, 173-4
Osiris (*also known as* An *and* Às Àr), 62-4, 67-71, 74, 77, 78-85, 89, 92-4, 97, 99, 101-2, 111, 116, 126, 181-7, 190-1, 195, 258
Ouagadougou, Upper Volta, 18

Oxus River, 4
Oxyrhynchus, 64, 76
Ozma, project named, 11

Palaiopolis, 131
Pallas Athene, 127, 149, 159, 162, 168
Palm tree, 148, 149, P12 (*notes*), P14 (*notes*)
Palmyra, 149
Pan, 134, 165
Paphos, 129, 149
Parke, H. W., 72, 105, 125, 132-5
Parker, Professor Richard, 59, 61, 95, 131
Parnassus, Mt., 130, 149
Pausanius, 111, 114, 127, 153, 167
Pedalion, 121
Pelasgians, 159, 166-7, 169
Pepi I, Pharaoh, 184-5
Perigeios, 123
Perse, 110
Persepolis, 137
Perseus, 165
Petrie, Professor Flinders, 195
Phaistos Disc of Crete, 4
Pharusii, 194
Phasis River, 106, 187
Phassa, 187
Phegus (oak), *see* Oak
Pherecydes, 105
Philolaus (of Croton), 244
Phrixos (Phrixus), 87, 104, 111, 115, 135
Phile, 110
Phoebus Apollo, 133
Phoroneus, 154
Photius, 256-7
Phthiotides (Thebes Phthiotides), 176
Pillars of brick and stone, 103
Pindar, 106, 134, 165-6, 174
Pisistratus, 134
Placenta, significance of, 31-3, 48, 261; *see also* Womb
Planets: moons of, 228-46 *passim*; movements of, 258-63 *passim*
Plato, 65, 72-3, 159, 228, 231, 235-7, 240-5
Pliny, 149, 182
Plotinus, 72
Plutarch, 64, 68-73, 78-80, 95, 111, 145, 179 fn., 185, 187-8, 191, 198-9, 237-8, 262, 265-7
Pluto (the planet), 83, 99, 135, 263
Po (Dogon name for Digitaria, *q.v.*), 3, 21, 39-40, 217
Pole Star, 58
Polycrates, 134
Polyhistor, Alexander, 17, 207-9, 248, 250-2
Polyphemus, 130
Ponderosus, 123, 126; *see also* Al Wazn

Porphyry, 111
Porpoise, fairy tale of, 203; see also Mermaid
Poseidon, 166, 168
Pregnancy, significance of, 71
Price, Professor Derek, 4, 132
Proclus, 73, 228–46 passim, P21; extent of knowledge of (summarized), 247; see also Neoplatonists
Proconsul, 13
Procris, 154
Prokrossoi, 154
Promeneia, 144
Prow (of the Argonaut), significance of, 127, 135, 140–1, 143, 157, 186, P18
Prt Spdt, see Heliacal Rising
Ptah, son of, 75–6
Ptolemy III, 76
Pyramids, 103; see also Great Pyramid
Pyramid Texts, 63, 181, 184
Pyrrha, 80, 156
Pythagoras (-eans), 233, 237–8, 243–4
Python, 162–3, P17

Qeṭi, 156–7, 162, 173
Qeṭqet, 157
Qeṭshu, 157
Qeṭu, 156

Rā, 58, 67, 85, 182
Ramses II, 104, 106–7
'r' and 'l' in the Egyptian language, 97, 116, 120, 192
Re, see Rā, above
Reisner, 139, P12 (V)
Religions, Ancient, and Sirius, 55–81 passim
Renard pâle, Le (The Pale Fox), (Griaule and Dieterlen), 27, 31, 33, 216, 261, 275; see also the authors under Griaule
Revolutions of Space Bodies, 228–46 passim
Rhodes, 149
Rig-veda, 116
River of Fire, 186
Rocket systems, 211–13, 214, 217
Roscher, W. H., 134, 265, P12 (notes)
Rotations of Space Bodies, 228–46 passim
Roulette wheel, 145
Roux, George, 269
Rudder, significance of, 121, 127, 135, 151

Sacea, feast of, 255
Sacred Year, 190
Saffron, 114, 115, 120, 192
Sagala (a super-heavy metal), 24, 44
Sagan, Carl, 13–14, 16–17, 65, 207, 221
Saḥ, see Orion's Belt

Saḥu, 180
Sakkara, 76–7
Samothrace, Island of, 149
Sanskrit, derivations of Ark root words, 180
Santillana, 66, 90, 94, 117, 125, 129, 134, 260, 263
Sardis, 135, 137, 149
Sargon, 83
Sarton, George, 237, 242
Satis, 64–5, 67, 94, 114
Saturn, 27–9, 70, 149, 180–1, 258–63
Scaliger, 110
Sceptre, 184–5
Scopes trial at Tennessee, 108, 114
Scott, Michael, 157; see also Liddell and Scott
Scylax, 123
Scythia, 158
Seb, 90, 149
Sebt, 185
Secrets of the Great Pyramid (Tompkins), 134, 137, 146
Seirios, see Sirius
Seistron (Sistrum), 65
Seker, 191
Seleucus, 237
Sept, 63, 94, 180, 184–5
Septch, 186
Septet, 179, 185
Septu, 186
Serapis (-eum), 69, 71, 116, 121, 165
Serpent's tooth, see Dragon's teeth; Teeth, significance of
Sesostris, 104, 106
Set, 216
Seth, 71, 102–3
Seven, significance of figure, 113, 130, 134, 190; (ancient) planets, 134; how (lings), 276; Gods of Destiny, 94; Greek vowels, 130–1, 266; lute strings, 130; notes of the octave, 134
Seventy days, significance of, 95–6, 164
Shaät, and derivatives, 194
Sheldon-Williams, I. P., 231
Shenit, 182
Shent, 182
Shenu, 182
Shen-ur, 182
Shklovskii, I. S., 13–17
Shu (Brightness), 98
Shuba, 98
Sicily, 108
Sidon, 149, 275
Sigi Lugu, 37
Sigi tolo, 39
Sigui ceremony, 24, 36–9, 42, 45, 119, 158, 191, 258, 262
Sihil Ponderosa, 126
Simplicius, 156
Sipylus, Mt., 149
Sirens, The, 65
Sirian civilization, 221

Sirigi mask, 217
Sirius, the Star, also known as Sirius A, 3, 12, 21–2, 24, 218, 223, 225, 260, P1; as the 'eighth planet'?, 134
Sirius B, see Digitaria, the star
Sirius C (does it exist?), 12–13, 33, 185, 190, 192, 199, 223, 225, 226; see also Emme Ya
Sirius, mystery of, 1–7
Sirius system, other stars in, 44–8
Sistrum, see Seistron
Siwa, Oasis of, 140, 152, 209
Sixty years, why the period of?, 258–63; see also Sigui ceremony
Smith, Professor H. S., 77
Smu, 71
Sokar, 148
Solon, 159
Songho, Dogon village of, P3
Sorghum (the star) and Sorghum-female, 43–8, 185
Sothic calendar, 56, 95
Sothis, 55–6, 61, 64–5, 67, 71, 94, 95, 101–2, 109, 114, 169, 171, 179, 181–2, 185; see also Canis Major; Isis-Sothis
Sothis (Manetho), 73
Sown Men, 168–9
Space, Bodies in, 228–46 passim
Space-ship, -flight, 214, 220–1
Spd, Spdt, Sept, see Orion's Belt; see also Sept
Speiser, E. A., 84–5, 97, 117
Sphinx, 180
Stag-King, 113, 119
Star clocks, see Egyptian Star Clocks
Star Names, Their Lore and Meaning (Allen), 65
Stecchini, Livio, 129, 137–8, 140, 143, 145–6, P12 (notes)
Stobaeus, 73
Stonehenge, 259
Stone motif, 111, 169
Stone pillars, 103
Strabo, 194
Stubbings, F. H., 108
Sudanese Sirius System, A, (Griaule and Dieterlen), 18, 35–49; Sigui ceremony, timing of, 36–9; Digitaria, orbit of, 39–42; (origins and features of, 42–4; position of, 44); other stars in the Sirius system, 44–8; see also the authors under Griaule; Digitaria; Sigui ceremony; affecting the Bambara peoples, 48–9; affecting the Bozo peoples, 49
Suhel Ponderosus, 126
Suhel Sirius, 126
Suidas, 130
Sumer-Akkad, 67, 79
Sumerian civilization, 17–18,

67–8, 71–2, 79–80, 83, 85, 88, 117
Sumerians, The (Kramer), 89
Sun, our, 149, *sometimes referred to as* Horus, *see* G-dwarf star
Superdense matter, 12, 100
Suppiluliumas, 268–70
Sura, Suryas and Svar in Sanskrit, 117
Susa, 137
Su-Shu huang, Dr, 14, 225
Syncellus, 209

Tacitus, 87
Täckholm and Drar, 115
'Take-off point', 15
Tat (Thoth), 74–6, 193
Tau Ceti, 11, 14
Taylor, Thomas, 228, 239–42, 258
Tcham(ti), 184–6
Tchenh-t, 181
Tchens, 181–2, 185
Tchenteru, 181
Tchenti, 182
Tchet, 175
Teeth, significance of, 86, 88, 99, 156, 167–9, 171, 175–6, 183, 191, 194, 198–9, 219, P15, P18; *see also* Dragon's teeth
Tehennu, Land of, 184–5
Telephassa, 168
Tell el-Amarna, 143
Tem, 184
Temple of the Jews, destruction of, 253
Teng, 182, 185
Tennessee, Scope's trial at, 108, 114
Tens, 182, 185
Tep, 163, 186
Teph-t, 163
Tephit, 163
Tepi, 186–7
Tepi ā, 187
Tepi-aui-qerr-en-pet, 187
Tepi tu-f, 186
Tep ra, 163, 186–7
Terrestris, 123
Thebaid, 109
Thebes (Egypt), 126, 135, 139–40, 144–5, 152, 159, 167–9, 176–7, 195, 199, 266–7
Thebes (Greece), 176, 179; *see also* Pthiotides
Thenae, 129, 149
Theognis, 148
Theophrastus, 148, 237
Thera, 129, 135, 149; *see also* Cythera
Theseus, 105, 108
Thesiger, Wilfred, 218
Thesmophoria Mysteries, 179, 198

Thespiae, 153–4
Thespius, King, 153, 173
Thestios, 153
Thighs, significance of, 184
Thompson, D'Arcy, 110, 192
Thorn, sign for, 171
Thoth, *see* Tat; *see also* Hermes
Three, significance of number, 114, 119, 155, 159
Thrice Greatest Hermes (Mead), 72–3
Thrones, 183; *see also under* Fifty
Timarete, 144
Timbuctoo, 18, 159, 163
Timaeus (Plato), 235–7, 240, 242–5
Titrone, 159
Tlingit peoples, 17
Tomaros, Mt., 140, 149
Tompkins, Peter, 134, 137, 146, P12 (*notes*)
Tooth, *see* Teeth
Tree-codes, 148, 149, P12 (*notes*)
Tripoli, 149
Trismegistic literature, 71–6, 102
Triton(is), Lake, 129, 149, 159
Troy, 123
Tu, 89
Tuareg, 194
Tuat, see Duat, The
Tutankhamen, 77, 138, 269
Tutu, 97–8
Two-to-one ratio, 155
Typhlos, 163
Typhon, 71–2, 115, 162–4, 174, 185
Typhos, 163
Tyre, city of, 153

Uas, 185
Uasâr, 184
Uas-t, 184
Udaeus, 169
UFOs, 213–14
Umbilicus, *see* Omphalos; *see also* Placenta; Womb
Universal History (Eunapius), 165
Un-Nefer, 258
Unknown Bird, The, 110, 119
Ur, the cities of, 269
Uraei, 193–4
Uranus, 83, 99, 101, 134–5, 155, 184 fn.
Urartu, 270
Ursa Major, 187
Urt, 174
Uruk, *see* Erech
Utnapishtim, 89, 125, 148

van den Bos, 12
Venus (the planet), 11, 27, 32, 39, 149, 218

Vīra, 116
Virgil, 182
Virgin of the World, The, 74, 76–7, 82, 103
Volet, (astronomer), 12, 189
von Däniken, Erich, 4
von Dechend, Hertha, 66, 90, 94, 117, 125, 129, 134, 260, 263
Vrihaspati, 259–60; *see also* Brihaspati

Wadi el Ajal, 196
Wallis Budge, *see* Budge
Walzer, Richard, 230
Warps and woofs of latitude and longitude, 139
Wazn, *see* Al Wazn
Wazouba, 43
Wegner, G., 24
Weight, *see* Al Wazn
Weightlessness, 220
Wellard, James, 195, 196
White Dwarf Stars, 2, 11, 24, 217–18, 226; *see also* Dwarf; G-dwarf star
White Goddess, The (Graves), 123, 148, 195, 266, 270
Wiener, Norbert, 72
Willow tree, 148, 149
Wilson, John A., 106
Wolf, significance of, 110, 166–7, 174; *see also* Jackal
Womb, significance of, 88–9; *see also* Placenta
Woofs and warps of latitude and longitude, 139
Woollen fleece, 117, 120; *see also* Golden fleece

Yasigi tolo (the star Yasigui), 39
Yasigui, 47, 48, 49
Yébéné, Priest, 35, P2
Yougo Dogorou, 35–7, 44
Young, Arthur M., 2–3
Yourougou (a star), 39, 43, 48
Yuruga, 48
Yu Sigi, 37

Zagar (astronomer), 12
Zarathustra (Zoroaster), 75, 187–8
Zeus, *see* Jupiter (Zeus)
Zeus, oracle of, 144
Zeus (Cook), 130
Zeus-Amen, 115
Ziggurats, 103, 184
Ziusudra, 89, 125, 148
Zodiac, 73, 99, 141, 188, 238, 262
Zoroaster, *see* Zarathustra
Zoroastrianism, 187–8
Zoser, King, 75–6